Emotions in
Asian Thought

Emotions in
Asian Thought

⊠

A Dialogue in
Comparative Philosophy

Edited by
Joel Marks and Roger T. Ames

———

With a discussion by
Robert C. Solomon

STATE UNIVERSITY OF NEW YORK PRESS

Published by
State University of New York Press, Albany

For information, address the State University of New York Press,
State University Plaza, Albany, NY 12246

Marketing by Theresa Abad Swierzowski
Production by Christine Lynch

Library of Congress Cataloging-in-Publication Data

Emotions in Asian thought : a dialogue in comparative philosophy /
    edited by Joel Marks and Roger T. Ames.
        p.   cm.
    Includes bibliographical references and index.
    ISBN 0-7914-2223-2. — ISBN 0-7914-2224-0 (pbk.)
    1. Emotions (Philosophy) 2. Philosophy, Oriental. 3. Philosophy,
Comparative. I. Marks, Joel, 1949-   . II. Ames, Roger T., 1947-
B105.E45E46 1995
128'.3—dc20   94-2723
                                                                    CIP

10 9 8 7 6 5 4 3 2 1

Contents

To Linda, David, and Sean,
and to Bonnie, Jason, and Austin,
who wonder why we are
always thinking so much about feeling.

—Joel and Roger (with love)

Preface

Within the Western philosophic tradition, comparative philosophy is a relatively new and still marginal movement. This is not true elsewhere. One cannot read "Japanese" philosophy written since the Meiji Restoration (1867), for example, without constant reference to the leading representatives of German idealism. In fact, because of the strong tincture of German philosophy which colors contemporary Japanese thought, the German language itself remains the philosophical language of Japan today. In India, the comparative attitude in philosophy has gone so far that one might argue it is Western philosophy that is mainstream and indigenous traditions are only complementary. In any case, the best contemporary Indian philosophers—the late Bimal Matilal, J. N. Mohanty, Daya Krishna—have one foot planted squarely in each of the traditions. The leading minds of Chinese philosophy since Yen Fu (1853-1921) have self-consciously been Kantian or Hegelian or Whiteheadian or Marxist, using Western philosophers as a medium through which to recast traditional Chinese assumptions about ways of thinking and living.

The situation behind the general Western ignorance (in the less pernicious sense, perhaps, of "to ignore") of non-Western philosophic traditions can be captured anecdotally. A contemporary philosopher of uncommonly high regard among his peers recently did some lectures in Hong Kong. During one of these lectures at the Chinese University, the philosopher was asked by a young graduate student (to the nervous laughter of this student's teachers) if he knew anything of Chinese philosophy. With a disarming smile, he allowed that he unfortunately had not been admitted to such mysteries, but was, of course, very interested in the possibility. He is representative of Western philosophers—very good Western philosophers—who follow the custom of most good American bookstores in placing Chinese philosophy somewhere between Bantu poetry and the occult. At a minimum, Chinese philosophy has nothing to do with being a good philosopher. Winding up a rather lively and certainly entertaining session, this same philosopher thanked his audience for their many challenging questions, and congratulated them as a body somewhat removed from the center of philosophical activity on the quality of their knowledge of philosophy— actually, on the quality of their knowledge of his own work and his own exclusive tradition.

Although Western philosophy is presently experiencing a "sea change" of the greatest magnitude, with philosophers and movements from every side challenging familiar, foundational claims to methodological objectivity, there still remains a large number of philosophers who, sink or swim, are anchored firmly in the Western past and its quest for objective certainty. On the other hand, there is a growing number of increasingly influential philosophers who have abandoned "methodology" so described, and in so doing, have revalued the philosophical stock of alternative standards of evidence which derive from tradition, history, and culture. It is the latter group, representing a virtual revolution in Western thinking, who are the promise for mutual enrichment between Western and non-Western philosophical traditions.

Anticipating and always encouraging the dramatic changes that philosophy is undergoing in our historical moment, the Society for Asian and Comparative Philosophy (SACP) was formally founded in 1967 at the University of Hawai'i precisely with the objective of promoting Western literacy in non-Western traditions of philosophy and culture. The underlying assumption is that culture must be factored into the discussion of contemporary philosophical issues. SACP has contributed on several fronts. First, it organizes regular conference participation at the annual meetings of the American Philosophical Association (Eastern Division), the Association for Asian Studies, and the American Academy of Religion. Second, it has an informal affiliation with the leading journal in comparative philosophy, *Philosophy East and West*, and much of its membership participates in the work of the journal as authors, reviewers, readers, and subscribers. Third, SACP, at due intervals, sponsors major research conferences and publishes representative papers as conference volumes that have tended to shape the field and its current direction.

In recent years, it has been the policy of SACP to identify an annual philosophical theme and to sponsor panels at the several national organizations with papers that address it. These themes have generally been selected with the intention of bringing comparative philosophers into relationship with other philosophers who identify themselves by other areas of interest and research specialization. The more successful of these encounters have followed a similar pattern. For example, in 1985 a series of panels were organized on the theme "The Asian traditions as a conceptual resource for environmental philosophy," in which comparative philosophers could contribute to ongoing discussions in the area of environmental philosophy. From papers prepared on this theme, special issues of *Philosophy East and West* (37:2, April 1987) and *Environmental Ethics* (8:4, Winter 1986) were published, and subsequently a volume appeared entitled *Nature in Asian Traditions of Thought: Essays in Environmental Philosophy*, edited by J. Baird Callicott and Roger T. Ames (Albany: State University of New York Press, 1989). A similar story followed from themes on "Feminist Issues in Culture and Modernity: East & West" (*Philosophy East and West* 42:2, April 1992) and "Culture and Rationality" (*Philosophy East and West* 42:4, October 1992).

The present volume emerges from a year of panels dedicated to the theme "Emotion East and West" (*Philosophy East and West* 41:1, January 1991). In this case, however, all but three of the articles have been specially commissioned from leading scholars in both comparative philosophy and philosophy of the emotions. The article by Catherine A. Lutz has been adapted from her influential book, *Unnatural Emotions: Everyday Sentiments on a Micronesian Atoll and Their Challenge to Western Theory* (Chicago: University of Chicago Press, 1988). Padmasiri de Silva's article has been adapted from his *Twin Peaks: Compassion and Insight* (Singapore: Buddhist Research Society, 1992). The opening article by Joel Marks is a revision of his introductory article from the *Philosophy East and West* special issue; it serves to provide a background on recent Western thought on emotion, and its extensive bibliography has been updated.

Another special feature of this volume is a comprehensive afterword by Robert C. Solomon, who may be credited with having truly initiated the contemporary dialogue on emotion in the West. With his concluding statement, he now helps to inaugurate a global dialogue. His essay ranges over the issues raised by all of the other contributors to this volume and then draws lessons for his own view of emotions.

With occasional although important respite, emotion—like rhetoric, imagination, experience, and woman—has, by and large, been on the wrong side of an entrenched dualism in the history of Western philosophy. The affective aspect of human flourishing has been systematically denigrated in celebration of the more cognitive aspects of personal realization. It is with the hope that an understanding of the structure and experience of emotion in non-Western cultures will serve to enrich the way in which emotion is perceived, and will serve in some measure to rehabilitate our affective life as being of important philosophic concern, that this volume has been compiled.

—Roger T. Ames, Hong Kong

Emotions in Western Thought: Some Background for a Comparative Dialogue

Joel Marks

In recent years, emotion has become the focus of intensive theoretical work among philosophers of the West. What is striking to a comparative philosopher is the almost total lack of references to non-Western thought. This book is an attempt to redress that situation. A number of philosophers versed in non-Western traditions have been brought together to discuss emotion in comparative perspective. This introductory essay will prepare the way with some background on the contemporary debate in the West.

THE ETHICS OF EMOTION

Why philosophize about emotion? Because the central question of philosophy is, How shall one live?, and, in one way or another, any answer to that question will have to say something about emotion. So then there are *two* questions about emotion: What is the place of emotion in the good life (and the good society)? and What *is* emotion? Any answer to the former presumes an answer to the latter. No doubt much of the perplexity regarding the first question has to do with unexamined or conflicting answers to the second. But not all of it.

Emotion is a singular noun, but, of course, there are emotions. So one may object to the formulation of the first question since it suggests that all of the emotions must be treated alike in the good life.[1] Perhaps we can, and should, pick and choose: a lot of loving but little or no hating, and so on. And certainly this is a standard approach to the ethical life ("Love thy neighbor . . .").[2]

Nonetheless, the more typical terms of the debate have concerned the desirability of emotion *tout court*. The Stoic is the classic proponent in the West of a complete dispassion, but this view is so widespread as to be stereotypical of the philosopher (down to the modern-day pipe-smoking [and of course male; more on this later] don). But here we must immediately be

1

reminded of the interdependence of ethical injunction and conceptual analysis; for it is likely that the Stoic's *"pathe"* picks out only some of what we (whoever *we* are) would call "emotion,"[3] and so the universal proscription may be misleading.[4]

There are two chief objections to the dispassionate life; they trade on the ambiguity of the "good" in "the good life." For a life to be good—that is, for it to have meaning and be worth living *for the person him- or herself*—there must be feeling (or feelings); this is the first objection. What could be the value of a life that did not contain loving, to take an obvious case, or the experience of being loved? And wouldn't the absence of gratitude—*feelings* of gratitude, *strong* feelings of gratitude—and passionate curiosity and wonder and involvement and, under the appropriate conditions, even intense anger and sadness and frustration (for if one is not liable to these, perhaps one cannot really be said to care about anything) bespeak a diminished existence?

The second main objection to the dispassionate life is that a good person—that is, a *moral* person—must care. Typically what the good person cares about are other persons. But the object of care may be all sentient beings (utilitarianism), just oneself (egoism), or even not any person or persons or beings at all but only duty (Kantianism[5]). But that there must be caring of some form seems incontestable. And is not caring an emotion? And again, as above, does not caring have its other attendant emotions of anger and sadness and so forth?[6]

Meanwhile, the *appeal* of the dispassionate life is also argued to be twofold. From the standpoint of *prudence*, one is advised to consider that for every peak experience there will be a valley, whereas it is possible to avoid both and still live on a fairly high plane (pardon the pun). And, as Mill might put it, to the person who has experienced both kinds of existence, the latter is preferable (thus, this is an empirical claim). There are two kinds of reasons for this: (1) *experientially* one avoids tragedies and, because no longer riding an emotional roller coaster, ceases to be the plaything of circumstances and enjoys calm and contentment; and (2) *instrumentally* one's position is improved by an enhanced ability to reason (without distracting passions)[7] and to obey reason.[8]

From the standpoint of *morality*, the agent is more effective because of reason 2. The source of one's moral obligations and commitment will have to be found elsewhere than in emotion, of course. But this, far from fazing the antipathist, provides one of his or her main arguments. Feelings are fickle (they differ from time to time, life stage to life stage, person to person, culture to culture, era to era),[9] whereas the foundations of morality—no matter whether one is speaking of justification or motivation—must be steady.[10]

So goes the traditional ethical debate about emotion (in broad brush) in the West. It is clear, then, why reflective persons would want to understand emotion: either to cultivate it or to eradicate it (or perhaps a bit of both) for the betterment of oneself and society. More recently, this debate has moved to center stage among ethical theorists in the West because of the influence of feminist thinking.[11]

CONTEMPORARY ANALYSES OF EMOTION, PART I

What, then, is (an) emotion? The most obvious answer is "A feeling." But if this word is not merely a synonym for *emotion*, it is not clear what sense it can have that is both meaningful and true. For example, if *feeling* means *sensation*—as in tickles, pain, warmth—then it becomes doubtful that emotions are feelings; for there does not appear to be any particular sensation by which one emotional state can be distinguished from another or, for that matter, identified with itself.[12] (This is not to deny that emotions may be *accompanied* by sensations and be causes or effects of them.) Indeed, there would seem to be occasions of emotion when there is no relevant sensation at all.[13] Furthermore, sensations lack the sort of intentionality or "object-directedness" that emotions possess; for example, one is happy *to be alive* or furious *with so-and-so*, but one is only chilly or hot.[14] Finally, it seems impossible to reconcile the central place of emotions in the folk history of psychology, at the very springs of action, with a conception of them as mere dumb feelings.

The contemporary response (with historical antecedents)[15] to the apparent inadequacy of the feeling view of emotion is that emotions are (or involve) a type of cognitive state.[16] The relevant state has been variously argued to be a belief (Davis, Green, Marks, Shaffer), a judgment (Solomon), a thought (Neu), a construal (Armon-Jones, Roberts) or "seeing as" (Calhoun),[17] an evaluation (Lyons), and so forth.[18] What makes such states especially suited to the task is their intentionality; for example, one's fear *of the dog* is one's judgment that *one is about to be hurt by the dog*. Thus, emotion is not just some sensory thrill.[19]

Perhaps the most intriguing implication of the cognitive view is that emotions are subject to the same sorts of criticism and control as cognitions are. For example, if one's fear of the dog is one's belief that the dog is dangerous, then (1) one's fear may be *inappropriate* because one's belief is *false* or at least *unjustified*, and (2) one's fear may be modifiable by exposure to relevant information, such as evidence of the dog's harmlessness.[20]

The appeal of the cognitive view is strong, but there are also shortcomings. Most apparent is the fact that the relevant cognition may be present but the emotion absent. For example, one may believe that one has just been wronged and yet not be angry. One may simply not care, or one may be a practicing Christian or Buddhist. This is surely psychologically possible; therefore, it must be analytically possible; therefore, an emotion cannot be *just* a belief.[21]

One response to this objection is to qualify the cognitive view so that it is a claim about a necessary, but not a sufficient, condition of emotion; a belief is an essential *component* of an emotion, but another or others may also be required.[22] For example, one will not be angry if one believes one has been wronged *unless* one also *strongly desires* not to have been treated in that way. Given the belief *and* the strong desire, one is angry; this is one's anger, in fact.[23]

Another objection, even to a qualified cognitivism, is that a cognition is not even necessary to an emotion. For example, aren't emotions notorious for lingering even after the relevant cognitions have "died off"?[24] You have borne a grudge against your neighbor for a whole year. One day you learn incontrovertibly that your grudge has been based on a mistake (he didn't really insult you; you misheard his remark). Yet you find that your ill will toward your neighbor does not vanish. While it may retreat to dormancy, it is always there, ready to spring, even though you yourself believe it unjustified, and it must be constantly guarded lest it manifest in untoward behavior.

A reply to this objection is that, contrary to appearances, the relevant belief has *not* completely dissipated. A belief—as opposed to, say, a proposition—is not some abstract logical entity but a substantive psychological state; thus, it should not be expected to display an instantaneous reaction to relevant information. There are all sorts of psychological (not to mention physiological, if one is a physicalist or interactionist) explanations for a lingering belief; for example, one's pride may prevent one from acknowledging fully that one has been mistaken for so long, and that one has, in fact, wronged one's neighbor rather than the other way around. Furthermore, beliefs come in various degrees of strength, and so a *complete* eradication may not follow upon even a significant change of mind.[25]

Another objection to cognitivism is that *desire* can account for the intentionality of emotion as well as serve more convincingly to explain its behavioral and felt aspects.[26] Desire is just as intentional as belief; for example, just as one may believe *that it is a beautiful day*, one may also desire it.[27] This is not to say that desire *alone* constitutes emotion, but it may be the only necessary *intentional* component. This view may be called "conativism." For example, won't one be in an emotional state if one is in severe pain and strongly desires not to be? And yet one need not *cognize* one's pain in any sense other than to experience it; in other words, one need not *believe that* or *judge that* one is in pain, but only *be* in pain.

There are, however, so many more typical cases of emotion that do involve a cognition, that one is tempted to bite the bullet and assimilate even the experience of pain to a cognitive state so as to provide a uniform theory of emotion.[28] However the case of conativism may fare, though, desire would still seem to have a strong claim to be a necessary ingredient of emotion.[29]

An important point is that "desire" is here[30] being used in the sense of *strong* wanting. For it does not seem proper to assert that *every* belief/desire state is an *emotion*, although it may be an *attitude*.[31] For example, one may harbor a mild attitude of envy toward a friend, or one may positively burn with envy; the latter alone, arguably, is the case of *emotion*. This stipulation at once saves from absurdity (if not implausibility) a stoical position of complete dispassion.[32]

In any case, there are few, if any, remaining proponents of a *purely* "sensational" view of emotion. If the reader continues to resist this perhaps startling development (which is evidence either of how valuable philosophy can be or of how out of touch it can be), a little phenomenology may be recommended. For example, one day when you are in a state of unrequited yearning, attend to your sensations. Perhaps you will notice that your suffering feels localized, perhaps in your chest. Attend to the sensation in your chest. Is this a plausible candidate for the suffering that you feel? More likely it will be a barely noticeable, and certainly not *painful*, phenomenon.[33]

Then consider what it is that you desire at that moment, and consider also your belief, perhaps conviction, that it is never to be yours. Is anything more needed to account for your feeling lousy? In particular, does that sensation in your chest perform any necessary function? Might not your awareness have focused on another sensation, located elsewhere, or none at all? If so, then your *emotion* is grounded in your belief and your strong desire; whatever else accompanies it is contingent.

CONTEMPORARY ANALYSES OF EMOTION, PART II

If cognitivism is the New View of Emotion, then the last decade has seen an even Newer View rise to prominence. Its contemporary roots lie in feminism and social theory, and the basic idea is that emotions are not just things in the head but essentially involve culture. This kind of critique has been applied to the (philosophy of) mind in general,[34] but the feminist gloss is especially pertinent to emotion: Philosophical analysis (not to mention the development of preanalytic "folk psychology") occurs in a male-dominated context, which biases our conceptions in favor of the traits normally considered masculine and against those considered feminine.[35] The upshot for emotion (at least in "Western" societies), perceived as feminine, has been a general denigration, in deference to the superior "male trait" of *rationality*.[36]

Thus, emotions are dumb and troublesome. They are best kept under control or eradicated (avoided) altogether. Indeed, if emotion is essential to life, then the philosopher is advised to turn away from life itself in *his* quest for a rational existence. Hence stoicism, mysticism, the problematic of suicide for the philosopher (cf. the *Phaedo*); and hence also Kantianism, the demand for rules and strict impartiality in ethics.[37]

It might seem that this perspective clarifies the establishment of the Traditional View of emotions as feelings, for feelings (sensations) are just those dumb and troublesome states that stand opposed to and can disrupt rational thinking. And the New View of cognitivism may then seem to be the antidote to the earlier, jaundiced view, for it finds the stuff of reason (viz., beliefs) at the very heart of emotion.

But such an interpretation of the modern history of emotion theory is itself in danger of co-option by the prevailing male milieu. (One's thinking does not so easily avoid the snares laid by one's culture, if the present account is correct.) For consider that it still presumes the supremacy of reason; it is only emotion *made rational* (i.e., cognitive) that wins approval from the New View.[38] A thoroughgoing feminist theory of emotion might be expected to defend a nonrational (i.e., noncognitive) emotionality. Can't emotion be defended on its own terms? Doesn't love, for example, wear its virtue on its sleeve, without having to demonstrate some internal affinity to a faculty or realm called "Reason"?[39]

Then again, the strategy of defending a *non*rational emotionality may itself be motivated by yet another sexist holdover: the pairing of emotion and female (and of reason and male).[40] Maybe emotions—or decognized ones, anyway— *are* dumb and an annoyance, and the problem is that they have been foisted upon women.[41] Thus, women in Western society may have no more reason than men to defend emotion, or a decognized emotion, since it is no more essential to their nature than is any other socially mediated phenomenon.[42]

It is hard to see where a social-theoretic approach to issues can lead ultimately, since, if self-aware, it does not seem able to call upon any arbiter (such as Truth).[43] But without trying to settle the matter of its final legitimacy, one can certainly appreciate the heuristic value of paying attention to cultural influences on mental phenomena.[44] This means that empirical studies of an ethnographic character should play a significant role in the theory of emotion.[45]

Even so, the sort of qualified cognitivism (or qualified conativism) sketched in the preceding section—one which involves desire as well as belief—would seem likely to fare well under the jurisdiction of a socialized philosophy of mind. For what could be more socially sensitive than beliefs and desires?[46] Furthermore, insofar as one does wish to retain some notion of intrinsically male and female traits and to achieve a parity between them, one may find appealing a cognitivism that shares top billing with desire (although, again, such things as desire/female and belief/male associations would seem to be precisely what a social-theoretic feminism would be inclined to play down).

COMPARATIVE APPROACHES TO EMOTION

This book seeks to promote the comparative study of emotion in the European and Asian philosophical traditions.[47] But the study of emotion is (potentially and actually) comparative in several other respects as well. Emotion is a subject for a scientific as well as a philosophical psychology, and for several humanistic disciplines besides philosophy.

Let us begin with the sciences. The experimental literature on emotion is enormous, and includes psychological and physiological investigations.[48] It must be said, however, that philosophers do not frequently discover much of interest to them in these forays.[49] Perhaps a more comparative (i.e., philosophically or humanistically informed) orientation on the part of the psychologists would help to alleviate the situation. For example, a philosopher is not likely to take kindly to a study of "emotion" that features "euphoria" defined as feeling happy while engaged in frivolous behavior (flying a paper airplane, twirling a hula hoop).[50]

The less strictly "experimental" and the more "naturalistic" or "ecological"[51] the investigation, the more to the philosopher's liking, for under the latter conditions are emotions likely to be observed in their full richness, subtlety, and interactions. Of course, methodological hazards of a different sort arise in these settings, such as the clinical and the psychoanalytic.[52] Ultimately, there is no substitute for judgment, breadth of experience, and balance in empirical studies.

As already noted, anthropological (ethnological) investigations have been influential in the theory of emotion. These studies are usually comparative (among cultures) in their own right and have entered into higher-order comparative relations with other disciplines, including philosophy.[53] Ethological (interspecies) comparisons are also relevant.[54]

Moving ever further along the continuum from experimental to naturalistic observation, one arrives at the humanities themselves. For example, there is no richer source of "data" for reflection on emotion than literature.[55] (And, here again, the discipline is itself comparative in nature, for there is literature from all cultures.) Historical studies are also of great value,[56] having contributed in particular to the social-theoretic critique, discussed above, of the place of emotion in Western thought.

Aesthetics is forever a source of concern about emotion. The recent ascendance of cognitive theories of emotion in philosophy has made particularly acute the problem of the emotional content of, and response to, works of art.[57]

The realm of the religious is another source for emotional enlightenment.[58] And when the discussion turns to Asian philosophies, the religion/philosophy boundary observed by nontheological philosophers in the West falls away altogether.

Finally, Western philosophy itself is (potentially and evermore actually) comparative. Witness the schism and rapprochement between the Anglo-American or analytic and Continental or hermeneutic (or phenomenological or existential) contingents. This division (of labor) is reflected in the study of emotion, as elsewhere.[59]

Thus, it is against a background of comparative upon comparative endeavor (or potential thereof) that the philosophical study of emotion East *and* West should be approached.[60]

Notes

1. Indeed, even more basically, it suggests that "emotion" constitutes a category; but that has been questioned by some since the outset of the contemporary debate (e.g., in the Introduction to Rorty 1980).

2. "Some emotions and even some types of emotion are 'better' and others are 'worse', and it is only the Myth of the Passions [in which 'all of our emotions are irrational'] that could lead us to think otherwise" (Solomon 1976, 375). And cf. Aristotle (1985):

> [The bad effects of pleasure and pain] are the reason why people actually define the virtues as ways of being unaffected and undisturbed [by pleasures and pains]. They are wrong, however, because they speak [of being unaffected] without specification, not of being unaffected in the right or wrong way, at the right or wrong time, and the added specifications. (*Nicomachean Ethics* ii.3.11046)

3. Not to mention what Aristotle would call *"pathe"*; cf. Cooper (1988).

4. Shaffer (1983) offers an analysis of dispassion that leaves our desires intact.

5. Provided one is willing to subsume Kantian *will* under the psychology of motivation; cf. Blum (1980) and Hinman (1983).

6. Cf. Frank 1988; Gibbard 1990; Mackie 1982; Morris 1981; Schoeman 1987; Strawson 1962. Watson (1987) takes issue with Strawson.

7. The stoic may still indulge in *humor*, however, according to Morreall (1983).

8. If one extends the inquiry to the mystical or prayerful, then a third reason may be given: The absence of passion is likened to the emptying of a vessel, which may then be filled with the ecstatic grace of God (or whatever). (At this point another conceptual question arises: Is this ecstasy itself an emotional state?) But see Stambaugh 1983.

9. Blum (1980) provides a sustained critique of this claim. Cf. also Calhoun 1980; G. Taylor 1975.

10. Cf. Harrison 1984. Filonowicz (1989) criticizes *both* claims.

11. This discussion resumes in the third section of this Introduction, "Contemporary Analyses of Emotion, Part II." The ethical issue is often phrased in terms of *justice versus caring*, the *locus classicus* being Gilligan (1982).

12. These points have been stressed repeatedly in the recent literature; for example:

> On Monday night an occurrent state of love might result in my having palpitations (for my beloved has returned after a long absence); on Tuesday afternoon I might feel dizzy with love (because the continued presence of my beloved for the last twenty hours has over-excited me); on Wednesday morning I might feel unusually relaxed because of love (the security of the continued presence of my beloved may have caused it). And it would seem that . . . one can have palpitations because of an occurrent state of fear or guilt, or feel dizzy with anger or embarrassment, or feel unusually relaxed because of happiness or grief. (Lyons 1980, 133f.)

Leighton is a prominent holdout for a significant role for feelings in emotions.

> Grief does not have the feelings present in an orgasm. . . . It is clear that not just any feeling when combined with and caused by the relevant judgment will count as appropriate to remorse, rage, despair, grief, joy, sadness, fear, shame, delight, etc. Moreover, the feeling itself may determine the emotion present. (1984, 320)

Cf. also Perkins 1966; Stocker 1983b.

13. For instance, Othello asleep.

14. The "intentional content" of emotions can be quite complex. Consider this example from the British humorist, Gerard Hoffnung (1925-1959):

> I feel rather like the man who, when asked what organ he would like to keep, said he wanted to keep his navel. And when he was asked why, he said, "Because I have a strange habit. I eat celery in bed and it's a very convenient place to keep the salt!" ("Oxford Union Speech," 4 December 1958)

15. For example, Chrysippus the Stoic (Nussbaum 1987); and a cognitive *component* figures in many of the classic theories.

16. This brand of "cognitivism" is not to be confused with the cognitive science variety. The latter may more properly be called "computationalism" or "representationism," and is the thesis that mental activity is a matter of formal symbol manipulation; in other words, it is a theory of the mind. The cognitivism

under discussion in this essay is a (or a type of) theory of emotion; "cognitive" refers to a belieflike structure, *whatever belief turns out to be* in the theory of the mind. On the other hand, whatever belief *does* turn out to be will naturally impinge upon the plausibility of (an) emotional cognitivism; cf. Dreyfus 1979 (e.g., p. 53); Kraut 1986a (p. 648, n. 6); Rey 1980; n. 17, below.

17. There may be some question about the *cognitive* status of these notions; cf. Broad 1954; Clarke 1986; Marks 1993; n. 16, above.

18. See also Farrell 1980; Gean 1979. Gordon (1987) goes so far as to maintain that some emotions involve *knowledge*.

19. The most sustained recent defense of emotions as nonintentional feelings after all is Armon-Jones (1991). Although "cognitive" in her extended sense of involving conceptualization, Armon-Jones's notion of "construal"—central to her analysis—is "objectless."

20. Certain forms of psychotherapy are based on these ideas; cf. Brandt 1979; Ellis 1962; Greenberg, Safran, et al. 1984; Neu 1977; Shibles 1974. But the *ethical* implications are especially pertinent to the concerns of philosophy. See Pence 1979 for a cautionary note.

21. Cf. Marks 1982.

22. Solomon (1988) declares his willingness to entertain this position, if not yet to accept it.

23. Cf. Farrell 1980; Green 1979b, 1992; Marks 1982; Robinson 1983; Shaffer 1983.

24. Clarke (1986) calls this "emotional *akrasia*" (p. 673). And cf. Hursthouse 1991.

25. Another form of the belief-is-not-necessary objection is that certain emotions—love, notoriously—involve no *characteristic* beliefs (thus, this objection is analogous to the one against emotion-as-sensation); for example:

> But, though she had taken such a strong possession of me, though my fancy and my hope were so set upon her, though her influence on my boyish life and character had been all-powerful, I did not, even that romantic morning, invest her with any attributes save those she possessed. I mention this in this place, of a fixed purpose, because it is the clue by which I am to be followed into my poor labyrinth. According to my experience, the conventional notion of a

lover cannot always be true. The unqualified truth is, that when I loved Estella with the love of a man, I loved her simply because I found her irresistible. Once for all; I knew to my sorrow, often and often, if not always, that I loved her against reason, against promise, against peace, against hope, against happiness, against all discouragement that could be. Once for all; I loved her none the less because I knew it, and it had no more influence in restraining me, than if I had devoutly believed her to be human perfection. (Pip's reflections in Charles Dickens's *Great Expectations*.)

Cf. also Hamlyn 1978; Kraut 1983, 1986b; Leighton 1985; Newton-Smith 1973; Soble 1990; G. Taylor 1975-76.

26. See Donaghy 1979; Marks 1986.

27. On the other hand, a recent debate in the literature is whether desire may not itself reduce to belief; see, for example, Collins 1988; D. Lewis 1988; Price 1989.

28. Green (1992) provides the most sustained defense of a position of this sort. He argues that pain is perceptual and that perception is "belieflike."

29. The position that belief and desire are necessary *and jointly sufficient* for emotion is given its most elaborated and persuasive formulation by Green (1992). To the strategy of objection that belief and desire each have different properties from emotion (see, e.g., de Sousa 1987; Marks 1982 is subject to this kind of objection), Green replies that certain *combinations* or structures of belief and desire have distinctive properties, analogously to the relation of the properties of water to the properties of hydrogen and oxygen.

30. That is, by me, although not by Green.

31. Green (1992) argues that a belief and a desire constitute an emotion if they have their intentional content in common. Roberts (1988b, 197f.) argues that even the combination of Green's and Marks's conditions is insufficient for there to be an emotion; note, however, that Roberts construes emotions to be occurrent phenomena (1988b, 183, n. 1; cf. also Davis 1987), whereas Green and Marks take them to be dispositional (not in the sense of mere propensities but in the sense of underlying states; cf. Armstrong 1968, 85-88).

32. Cf. Marks 1988 and his comments later in this volume.

33. Cf. Budd 1989. On the other hand, there is this passage from "Falk," by Joseph Conrad:

We are in his case allowed to contemplate the foundation of all the emotions—that one joy which is to live, and the one sadness at the root of the innumerable torments. It was made plain by the way he talked. He had never suffered so. It was gnawing, it was fire; it was, like this! And after pointing below his breastbone, he made a hard wringing motion with his hands. And I assure you that, seen as I saw it with my bodily eyes, it was anything but laughable. And again, as he was presently to tell me, . . . he said that a time soon came when his heart ached (that was the expression he used).

34. See, for example, H. Putnam 1973.

35. See, for example, Scheman 1983.

36. Cf. Blum 1986; Calhoun 1989; Jaggar 1989; Lloyd 1984; Sedgwick 1990. Of course, not all male philosophers have had this kind of preference; Hume, for example, is a shining exception (cf. Baier 1991).

37. Cf. Noddings 1984.

38. Cf. Lloyd 1984:

To affirm women's equal possession of rational traits, and their right of access to the public spaces within which they are cultivated and manifested, is politically important. But it does not get to the heart of the conceptual complexities of gender difference. And in repudiating one kind of exclusion, de Beauvoir's mode of response can help reinforce another. For it seems implicitly to accept the downgrading of the excluded character traits associated with femininity, and to endorse the assumption that the only human excellences and virtues which deserve to be taken seriously are those exemplified in the range of activities and concerns that have been associated with maleness. (p. 104)

See also Jaggar 1989 (p. 156) and Noddings 1984.

39. Says Ivan to his brother Alyosha in Fyodor Dostoevsky's *The Brothers Karamazov*:

I have a longing for life, and I go on living in spite of logic. Though I may not believe in the order of the universe, yet I love the sticky little leaves as they open in spring. I love the blue sky, I love some people, whom one loves you know sometimes without knowing why. . . . It's not a matter of intellect or logic, it's loving with one's inside, with one's stomach. (Constance Garnett translation)

Furthermore, the point is not only that emotion may be of equal worth to reason but that it may succeed at *reason's own game*, viz., knowledge; for example, one may have a valid "emotional presentiment," which a strict regime of reasoning would dismiss (cf. Baier 1985, 117f.). "If emotions mirror the world as reliably as other faculties, then we should begin trusting our emotions to deliver truth in the same way we trust our perceptions or our chains of reasoning or the voice of experts" (Calhoun 1989, 198). See also Jaggar 1989; for example, "Conventionally unexpected or inappropriate emotions may precede our conscious recognition that accepted descriptions and justifications often conceal as much as reveal the prevailing state of affairs" (p. 167).

Intriguing suggestions such as these appear to have struck a raw nerve in the highly (= emotionally?) charged contemporary debate about the nature of philosophy itself; witness the following response:

> Adolf Hitler said, "Reason confuses the people, but emotion is sure." Mussolini also had much to say denouncing reason and lauding following one's emotions. Now, I don't believe that Hitler and Mussolini were closet feminists. . . . What the above references illustrate is that the advocacy of emotion over reason has nothing to do with gender. (Examples of men exalting emotion over reason can be multiplied, as can examples of women being eminently rational.) It is feminists qua feminists who condemn reason, . . . not feminists qua women. What [some feminists], Hitler and Mussolini have in common is that they are all exponents of radical political movements. . . . The leaders of political movements do not want their basic tenets questioned. . . . Rationality, the impartial examination of premises, . . . must be devalued. (Harper 1992)

40. "The affirmation of the value and importance of 'the feminine' cannot of itself be expected to shake the underlying normative structures, for, ironically, it will occur in a space already prepared for it by the intellectual tradition its seeks to reject" (Lloyd 1984, 105). See also Grimshaw 1986.

41. Cf. Jaggar 1989:

> Although there is no reason to suppose that the thoughts and actions of women are any more influenced by emotion than the thoughts and actions of men, the stereotypes of cool men and emotional women continue to flourish because they are confirmed by an uncritical daily experience. In these circumstances, where there is a differential assignment of reason and emotion, it is easy to see the ideological function of the myth of the dispassionate investigator. It functions, obviously, to bolster the epistemic authority of the currently dominant groups, composed largely of white men, and to discredit the observations and claims of the currently subordinate groups including, of course, the observations and claims of many people of color and women. The more forcefully and vehemently the latter groups express their observations and claims, the more emotional they appear and so the more easily they are discredited. The alleged epistemic authority of the dominant groups then justifies their political authority. (pp. 164f.)

42. "Emotions are not feelings that well up in some natural and untutored way from our natural selves . . . they are in fact not personal or natural at all [but] are, instead, contrivances, social constructs" (Nussbaum 1988, 226).

43. Cf. Beckett's silence (Nussbaum 1988).

44. *Normative* influence is particularly intriguing; for example:

> We understand, accept as genuine, love that remains hidden because of honor or fear or shame, but not because of greed or embarrassment. It's not that we believe those couldn't in fact be strong enough, but rather that we have standards about such things, about what sorts of feelings, in what sorts of contexts, get to count as genuine love. (Scheman 1979, 325)

Cf. also Harré 1986b; Jaggar 1989; Kraut 1986a. Leighton (1985) appears to demur: for example, "I would agree that these people *ought not* be so moved; but they are. Whether something is appropriate and whether something is present are very different matters" (p. 139).

45. See, for example, Harré 1986b; Lutz 1988; Scherer, Wallbott, and Summerfield 1986.

46. I owe this point to Harvey Green.

47. And why not also African and Native American and . . . ? Good question. Let me note that the Society for Asian and Comparative Philosophy has been taking a philosophical look at one of its own previously unexamined assumptions about the scope of "comparative." The proposal has been made to include in the Society's mission statement "a formal declaration of interest in all the philosophies of the world, North, South, East, and West" (Fitz and Burke 1993).

48. William James and the Danish physiologist C. Lange are the seminal figures here, while Schachter and Singer (1962) provide the more recent *locus classicus*. Representative samples of this kind of work are Arnold 1968, 1970; Black 1970; Glass 1967; Harris 1989; Izard 1979; Izard, Kagan, and Zajonc 1984; Levi 1975; Malatesta and Izard 1984; Panksepp et al. 1982; Plutchik and Kellerman 1980-1986; Reisenzein 1983; Reymert 1928, 1950; Simonov 1986; Strongman 1973; Vincent 1990.

49. Harré (1986a) refers to "the conceptual naivety of much psychological research" (p. 5). See also Peters 1969; Solomon 1976, 156; and the commentary of Lazarus and others in Panksepp 1982.

50. As it is in Schachter and Singer (1962, 384).

51. I adopt this word from the work of the late perception psychologist J. J. Gibson.

52. Examples of this ample literature are Ellis 1962; Gaylin 1979; Jacobson 1971; H. Lewis 1981-1983; Neu 1977; Sachs 1974. The hazards are well known; cf., for example, Weisstein 1971.

53. For example, Harkness and Kilbride 1983; Heider 1991; Heller 1979; Karim 1990; Kleinman and Good 1985; Levy and Rosaldo 1983; Lynch 1990.

54. Cf., for example, Buck 1984; Ekman 1973; Panksepp 1982; Plutchik 1980; Young 1943.

55. With the standard caveat: "Where the assessment of abstract principles and theories is concerned, . . . we must not treat the literary 'evidence' as Baconian observation data" (Nussbaum 1988, 253). G. Taylor is one of many emotion theorists who use literary examples.

56. Cf., for example, Harré 1986a; Lloyd 1984; Rorty 1982; Stocker 1983a.

57. See, for example, Belfiore 1992; Boruah 1988; Budd 1992; Carroll 1990; Daniels and Scully 1992; Davies 1986; Feagin 1988; Hanfling 1983; Kivy 1988; Levinson 1982; Morreall 1985; Neill 1993; Novitz 1980; Skulsky 1980; Speck 1988; Stecker 1984; Thompson 1989; Walton 1978; Woodruff 1988.

58. Examples are Adams 1980; Lauritzen 1988; Otto 1950; Outka 1972; Roberts 1982, 1992.

59. Examples of the latter are Barnes 1984; Buytendijk 1950; Chisholm 1982; Lemos 1989; Sartre 1962; Strasser 1977. See also part 3 of Calhoun and Solomon 1984.

60. There is yet another kind of comparative endeavor that is appropriate to the study of emotion: the integration of scholarship with *experience*. In this final section, the various approaches to emotion have been dealt with as scholarly disciplines or *literatures*. But many or all of them have their *lived* aspect as well. For example, the religious approach to emotion may require prayerful or transcendent experience in order to be fully meaningful; fictional and poetic lit-

erature take on more significance as one's experience of life lengthens and broadens; phenomenological accounts may be of interest only when one has developed the capacity to examine one's own experience in certain ways; and so forth.

And perhaps it is here relevant to borrow one of Solomon's observations from his concluding essay in this volume: "All but two of the authors [in this volume] are white North Americans." Solomon seems to view this as a strength—an admirable effort by the West to reach out to the non-West. But perhaps it is also a failing if the deepest insights into a culture normally depend on being native to the culture.

(Elsewhere in his essay, by the way, Solomon discerns a more general phenomenon at work:

> I belong to an international society for research on the emotions, and one of the perennial concerns has been . . . the almost total absence of researchers from other parts of the world. But the problem is not difficult to diagnose. The very category [of "emotion"] in question has no equivalent or much significance in other parts of the world.

I take it Solomon is here making the radical suggestion that a truly *comparative philosophy of emotion* may be an absurd undertaking, for it is something only a Westerner would seriously entertain!)

Bibliography

This list contains all of the sources referenced in the notes, and others that are relevant. Many of these sources contain extensive bibliographies of their own. Historical works (East and West) have mostly been omitted; consult Calhoun and Solomon (1984) and Gardiner, Metcalf, and Beebe-Center (1970) for the Western tradition.

Adams, Robert M. 1980. "Pure Love." *Journal of Religious Ethics* 8: 83-99.

Allen, R. T. 1991. "Governance by Emotion." *Journal of the British Society for Phenomenology* 22: 15-29.

Alston, William P. 1967. "Emotion and Feeling." In *The Encyclopedia of Philosophy*, ed. Paul Edwards, 2: 479-86. New York: Collier Macmillan.

Alt, Wayne. 1980. "There Is No Paradox of Desire in Buddhism." *Philosophy East and West* 30: 521-28.

Aristotle. 1985. *Nicomachean Ethics*, trans. Terence Irwin. Indianapolis: Hackett.

Armon-Jones, Claire. 1991. *Varieties of Affect*. New York: Harvester Wheatsheaf.

Armstrong, D. M. 1968. *A Materialist Theory of the Mind*. New York: Humanities Press.

Arnold, Magda B., ed. 1960. *Emotion and Personality*. 2 vols. New York: Columbia University Press.

———. 1968. *The Nature of Emotion*. London: Penguin.

———. 1970. *Feelings and Emotions: The Loyola Symposium*. New York: Academic Press.

Baier, Annette C. 1978. "Hume's Analysis of Pride." *Journal of Philosophy* 75: 27-40.

————. 1985. "Actions, Passions, and Reasons." In *Postures of the Mind: Essays on Mind and Morals*. Minneapolis: University of Minnesota Press.

————. 1987. "Getting in Touch with Our Own Feelings." *Topoi* 6: 89-97.

————. 1990. "What Emotions Are About." In *Action Theory and Philosophy of Mind*, ed. James E. Tomberlin. Atascadero, CA: Ridgeview.

————. 1991. *A Progress of Sentiments: Reflections on Hume's "Treatise."* Cambridge: Harvard University Press.

Baillie, Harold W. 1988. "Learning the Emotions." *New Scholasticism* 62: 221-27.

Barnes, Hazel. 1984. "Sartre on the Emotions." *Journal of the British Society for Phenomenology* 15: 3-15.

Bedford, Errol. 1956-1957. "Emotions." *Proceedings of the Aristotelian Society* 57: 281-304.

Belfiore, Elizabeth. 1992. *Tragic Pleasures: Aristotle on Plot and Emotion*. Princeton: Princeton University Press.

Ben-Ze'ev, Aaron. 1987. "The Nature of Emotions." *Philosophical Studies* 52: 393-409.

————. 1992a. "Anger and Hate." *Journal of Social Philosophy* 23: 85-110.

————. 1992b. "Emotional and Moral Evaluations." *Metaphilosophy* 23: 214-29.

————. 1993. "Envy and Pity." *International Philosophical Quarterly* 33: 3-19.

Bergmann, Frithjof. 1976. Review of Robert C. Solomon's *The Passions*. *Journal of Philosophy* 75: 200-8.

Black, Perry, ed. 1970. *Physiological Correlates of Emotion*. New York: Academic Press.

Blum, Lawrence A. 1980. *Friendship, Altruism, and Morality*. London: Routledge & Kegan Paul.

———. 1986. "Iris Murdoch and the Domain of the Moral." *Philosophical Studies* 50: 343-67.

Boruah, Bijoy H. 1988. *Fiction and Emotion: A Study in Aesthetics and the Philosophy of Mind*. Oxford: Oxford University Press.

Bovens, Luc. 1992. "Sour Grapes and Character Planning." *Journal of Philosophy* 89: 57-78.

Brandt, Richard B. 1979. *A Theory of the Good and the Right*. Oxford: Clarendon.

Broad, C. D. 1954. "Emotion and Sentiment." *Journal of Aesthetics and Art Criticism* 13: 203-14.

Brown, James Robert. 1990. Critical notice of Michael Ruse, *Taking Darwin Seriously: A Naturalistic Approach to Philosophy*. *Canadian Journal of Philosophy* 20: 129-46.

Brown, Robert. 1987. *Analyzing Love*. Cambridge: Cambridge University Press.

Buck, Ross. 1984. *The Communication of Emotion*. New York: Guilford.

Budd, Malcolm. 1989. *Wittgenstein's Philosophy of Psychology*. New York: Routledge.

———. 1992. *Music and the Emotions: The Philosophical Theories*. New York: Routledge.

Buytendijk, F. J. J. 1950. "The Phenomenological Approach to the Problem of Feelings and Emotions." In *Feelings and Emotions: The Mooseheart Symposium*, ed. M. L. Reymert, 127-41. New York: McGraw-Hill.

Calhoun, Cheshire. 1980. "The Humean Moral Sentiment: A Unique Feeling." *Southwestern Journal of Philosophy* 11: 69-78.

———. 1984. "Cognitive Emotions?" In *What Is an Emotion? Classic Readings in Philosophical Psychology*, ed. Cheshire Calhoun and Robert C. Solomon, 327-42. Oxford: Oxford University Press.

———. 1988. "Justice, Care, Gender Bias." *Journal of Philosophy* 85: 451-63.

————. 1989. "Subjectivity and Emotion." *Philosophical Forum* 20: 195-210.

————. 1992. "Changing One's Heart." *Ethics* 103: 76-96.

Calhoun, Cheshire, and Robert C. Solomon, eds. 1984. *What Is an Emotion? Classic Readings in Philosophical Psychology*. Oxford: Oxford University Press.

Callahan, Sidney. 1988. "The Role of Emotion in Ethical Decision Making." *Hastings Center Report* 18: 9-14.

Card, Claudia. 1988. "Women's Voices and Ethical Ideals: Must We Mean What We Say?" *Ethics* 99: 125-35.

Carroll, Noël. 1990. *The Philosophy of Horror, or Paradoxes of the Heart*. New York: Routledge.

Cavell, Marcia. 1989. Review of de Sousa, *The Rationality of Emotion*, and Gordon, *The Structure of Emotions*. *Journal of Philosophy* 89: 493-504.

Chisholm, Roderick M. 1982. "Correct and Incorrect Emotion." In *Brentano and Meinong Studies*. Amsterdam: Rodopi.

Cirillo, Leonard, Bernard Kaplan, and Seymour Wapner, eds. 1989. *Emotions in Ideal Human Development*. Hillsdale, NJ: Lawrence Erlbaum.

Clark, Margaret Sydnor, and Susan T. Fisk, eds. 1982. *Affect and Cognition: The Seventeenth Annual Carnegie Symposium on Cognition*. Hillsdale, NJ: Lawrence Erlbaum.

Clarke, Stanley G. 1986. "Emotions: Rationality without Cognitivism." *Dialogue* 25: 663-74.

Code, Lorraine. 1991. *What Can She Know? Feminist Theory and the Construction of Knowledge*. Ithaca, NY: Cornell University Press.

Collins, John. 1988. "Belief, Desire, and Revision." *Mind* (n.s.) 97: 333-42.

Cooper, John M. 1988. "Some Remarks on Aristotle's Moral Psychology." *Southern Journal of Philosophy* 27: 25-42.

Daniels, Charles B., and Sam Scully. 1992. "Pity, Fear, and Catharsis in Aristotle's *Poetics*." *Noûs* 26: 204-17.

Danto, Arthur C. 1988. *Mysticism and Morality*. New York: Columbia University Press.

Davidson, Donald. 1976. "Hume's Cognitive Theory of Pride." *Journal of Philosophy* 73: 744-57.

Davies, Stephen. 1986. "The Expression Theory Again." *Theoria* 52: 146-67.

Davis, Wayne A. 1982. "A Causal Theory of Enjoyment." *Mind* 91: 240-56.

————. 1987. "The Varieties of Fear." *Philosophical Studies* 51: 287-310.

————. 1988a. "A Causal Theory of Experiential Fear." *Canadian Journal of Philosophy* 18: 459-83.

————. 1988b. "Expression of Emotion." *American Philosophical Quarterly* 25: 279-91.

Davitz, Joel R. 1969. *The Language of Emotion*. New York: Academic Press.

Deigh, John, ed. 1992. *Ethics and Personality: Essays in Moral Psychology*. Chicago: University of Chicago Press.

De Sousa, Ronald. 1987. *The Rationality of Emotion*. Cambridge: MIT Press.

Deutsch, Eliot. In preparation. "The Emotions."

Donaghy, Kevin. 1979. "Emotion without Judgment." In *Understanding Human Emotions*, ed. Fred D. Miller Jr. and Thomas Attig, 36-42. Bowling Green, OH: Philosophy Documentation Center.

Dreyfus, Hubert L. 1979. *What Computers Can't Do: The Limits of Artificial Intelligence*. Rev. ed. New York: Harper & Row.

Drost, Mark. 1991. "Intentionality in Aquinas's Theory of the Emotions." *International Philosophical Quarterly* 31: 449-60.

Ekman, Paul, ed. 1973. *Darwin and Facial Expression: A Century of Research in Review*. New York: Academic Press.

————. 1982. *Emotion in the Human Face*. Cambridge: Cambridge University Press.

Ellis, Albert. 1962. *Reason and Emotion in Psychotherapy*. New York: Lyle Stuart.

Farrell, Daniel M. 1980. "Jealousy." *Philosophical Review* 89: 527-59.

Feagin, Susan L. 1988. "Imagining Emotions and Appreciating Fiction." *Canadian Journal of Philosophy* 18: 485-500.

Filonowicz, Joseph Duke. 1989. "Ethical Sentimentalism Revisited." *History of Philosophy Quarterly* 6: 189-206.

Fisher, Mark. 1977. "Reason, Emotion, and Love." *Inquiry* 20: 189-203.

Fitz, Hope, and B. David Burke. 1993. "The Boundaries of Asian-Comparative Philosophy." *SACP Forum* (The Society for Asian and Comparative Philosophy) 20 (Spring): 5.

Fonseca, Eduardo Giannetti da. 1991. *Beliefs in Action: Economic Philosophy and Social Change*. Cambridge: Cambridge University Press.

Fortenbaugh, W. W. 1975. *Aristotle on Emotion: A Contribution to Philosophical Psychology, Rhetoric, Poetics, Politics, and Ethics*. New York: Barnes & Noble.

Frank, Robert H. 1988. *Passions within Reason: The Strategic Role of the Emotions*. New York: Norton.

Gan, Barry L. 1984. *Traditions of Inquiry in the Study of Emotion and Their Limits of Explanation*. Ph.D. diss., University of Rochester.

————. 1990. "Loving One's Enemies." *In the Interest of Peace*, ed. J. Kunkel and K. H. Klein. Wakefield, NH: Longwood.

Gardiner, H. M., Ruth Metcalf, and John G. Beebe-Center. 1970. *Feeling and Emotion: A History of Theories*. [1937.] Westport, CT: Greenwood.

Gaylin, Willard. 1979. *Feelings: Our Vital Signs*. New York: Harper & Row.

Gean, William D. 1979. "Emotion, Emotional Feeling, and Passive Body Change." *Journal for the Theory of Social Behaviour* 9: 39-51.

Gibbard, Allan. 1990. *Wise Choices, Apt Feelings: A Theory of Normative Judgment*. Cambridge: Harvard University Press.

Gilligan, Carol. 1982. *In a Different Voice: Psychological Theory and Women's Development*. Cambridge: Harvard University Press.

Glass, David C., ed. 1967. *Neurophysiology and Emotion*. New York: Rockefeller University Press.

Goodman, Russell. 1990. *American Philosophy and the Romantic Tradition*. Cambridge: Cambridge University Press.

Gordon, Robert M. 1980. "Fear." *Philosophical Review* 89: 560-78.

———. 1986. "The Passivity of Emotions." *Philosophical Review* 95: 371-92.

———. 1987. *The Structure of Emotions: Investigations in Cognitive Philosophy*. Cambridge: Cambridge University Press.

Gosling, J. C. 1965. "Emotion and Object." *Philosophical Review* 74: 486-503.

Green, O. H. 1972. "Emotions and Belief." *American Philosophical Quarterly* 6: 24-40.

———. 1979a. "Obligations Regarding Passions." *Personalist* 60: 134-38.

———. 1979b. "Wittgenstein and the Possibility of a Philosophical Theory of Emotion." *Metaphilosophy* 10: 256-64.

———. 1992. *The Emotions: A Philosophical Theory*. Dordrecht: Kluwer.

Greenberg, Leslie S., Jeremy D. Safran, et al. 1984. "Integrating Affect and Cognition: A Perspective on the Process of Therapeutic Change." *Cognitive Therapy and Research* 8: 559-98.

Greenspan, Patricia S. 1980a. "A Case of Mixed Feelings: Ambivalence and the Logic of Emotion." In *Explaining Emotions*, ed. Amélie Oksenberg Rorty, 223-50. Berkeley: University of California Press.

————. 1980b. "Emotions, Reasons, and 'Self-Involvement.'" *Philosophical Studies* 38: 161-68.

————. 1981. "Emotions as Evaluations." *Pacific Philosophical Quarterly* 62: 158-69.

————. 1988. *Emotions and Reasons: An Inquiry into Emotional Justification*. New York: Routledge.

Greenwood, John D. 1987. "Emotion and Error." *Philosophy of the Social Sciences* 17: 487-99.

Grimshaw, Jean. 1986. *Philosophy and Feminist Thinking*. Minneapolis: University of Minnesota Press.

Haber, Joram Graf. 1991. *Forgiveness*. Lanham, MD: Rowman & Littlefield.

Habito, Ruben L. F. 1988. "Buddhist Philosophy as Experiential Path: A Journey through the *Sutta Nipata*." *International Philosophical Quarterly* 28: 125-39.

Hamlyn, D. W. 1978. "The Phenomena of Love and Hate." *Philosophy* 53: 5-20.

Hanfling, Oswald. 1983. "Real Life, Art, and the Grammar of Feeling." *Philosophy* 58: 237-43.

Harkness, Sara, and Philip L. Kilbride, eds. 1983. *The Socialization of Affect*. Special issue. *Ethos* 11(4).

Harper, William. 1992. Letter to the Editor. *American Philosophical Association Proceedings* 65: 61-62.

Harré, Rom. 1986a. "Accidie and Melancholy in the Psychological Context." In *The Social Construction of Emotions*, ed. Rom Harré. Oxford: Basil Blackwell.

Harré, Rom, ed. 1986b. *The Social Construction of Emotions*. New York: Blackwell.

Harris, Paul L. 1989. *Children and Emotion: The Development of Psychological Understanding*. New York: Blackwell.

Harrison, Bernard. 1984. "Moral Judgment, Action, and Emotion." *Philosophy* 59: 295-322.

Hartz, Glenn A. 1990. "Desire and Emotion in the Virtue Tradition." *Philosophia* 20: 145-65.

Haugeland, John. 1985. "Feelings." In *Artificial Intelligence: The Very Idea*, 230-38. Cambridge: MIT Press.

Heider, Karl G. 1991. *Landscapes of Emotion: Lexical Maps and Scenarios of Emotion Terms in Indonesia*. Cambridge: Cambridge University Press.

Heller, Agnes. 1979. *A Theory of Feelings*. Assen, Netherlands: Van Gorcum.

Herman, A. L. 1979. "A Solution to the Paradox of Desire in Buddhism." *Philosophy East and West* 29: 91-94.

————. 1980. "Ah, But There Is a Paradox of Desire in Buddhism." *Philosophy East and West* 30: 529-32.

Hinman, Lawrence M. 1983. "On the Purity of Our Moral Motives: A Critique of Kant's Account of the Emotions and Acting for the Sake of Duty." *Monist* 66: 251-67.

Hursthouse, Rosalind. 1984. "Plato on the Emotions." *Proceedings of the Aristotelian Society* (Suppl.) 57: 81-96.

————. 1991. "Arational Actions." *Journal of Philosophy* 88: 57-68.

Irani, K. D., and G. E. Myers, eds. 1983. *Emotions: Philosophical Studies*. New York: Haven.

Izard, Carroll E. 1982. "Comments on Emotion and Cognition: Can There Be a Working Relationship?" In *Affect and Cognition: The Seventeenth Annual Carnegie Symposium on Cognition*, ed. Margaret Sydnor Clark and Susan T. Fisk. Hillsdale, NJ: Lawrence Erlbaum.

Izard, Carroll E., ed. 1979. *Emotions in Personality and Psychopathology*. New York: Plenum.

Izard, Carroll E., Jerome Kagan, and Robert B. Zajonc, eds. 1984. *Emotions, Cognition, and Behavior*. Cambridge: Cambridge University Press.

Jacobson, Edith. 1971. "On the Psychoanalytic Theory of Affects." In *Depression: Comparative Studies of Normal, Neurotic, and Psychotic Conditions*. New York: International Universities Press.

Jacquette, Dale. 1990. "Fear and Loathing (and Other Intentional States) in Searle's Chinese Room." *Philosophical Psychology* 3: 287-304.

Jaggar, Alison M. 1989. "Love and Knowledge: Emotion in Feminist Epistemology." *Inquiry* 32: 151-76.

Karim, Wazir Jahan, ed. 1990. *Emotions of Culture: A Malay Perspective*. Oxford: Oxford University Press.

Kenny, Anthony. 1963. *Action, Emotion, and Will*. London: Routledge & Kegan Paul.

Kivy, Peter. 1988. *Osmin's Rage: Philosophical Reflections on Opera, Drama, and Text*. Princeton: Princeton University Press.

Kleinman, Arthur, and Byron Good, eds. 1985. *Culture and Depression: Studies in the Anthropology and Cross-Cultural Psychiatry of Affect and Disorder*. Berkeley: University of California Press.

Koch, Philip J. 1983. "Loneliness without Objects." *Southern Journal of Philosophy* 21: 193-210.

Kraut, Robert. 1983. "Objects of Affection." In *Emotions: Philosophical Studies*, Irani and G. E. Myers, 42-56. New York: Haven.

———. 1986a. "Feelings in Context." *Journal of Philosophy* 83: 642-52.

———. 1986b. "Love *De Re*." *Midwest Studies in Philosophy* 10: 413-30.

Lai, Whalen W. 1984. "How the Principle Rides on the Ether: Chu Hsi's Non-Buddhistic Resolution of Nature and Emotion." *Journal of Chinese Philosophy* 11: 31-66.

Lamb, Roger. 1987. "Objectless Emotions." *Philosophy and Phenomenological Research* 48: 107-17.

Lamotte, Etienne. 1974. "Passions and Impregnations of the Passions in Buddhism." In *Buddhist Studies in Honour of I. B. Horner*, ed. L. Cousins, A. Kunst, and K. R. Norman, 91-104. Dordrecht: D. Reidel.

Lauritzen, Paul. 1988. "Emotions and Religious Ethics." *Journal of Religious Ethics* 16: 307-24 .

————. 1991. "Errors of an Ill-Reasoning Reason: The Disparagement of Emotions in the Moral Life." *Journal of Value Inquiry* 25: 5-21.

Lazarus, R. S. 1984. "Thoughts on the Relations between Emotions and Cognition." In *Approaches to Emotion*, ed. Klaus R. Scherer and Paul Ekman. Hillsdale, NJ: Lawrence Erlbaum.

Leeper, R. W. 1968. "A Motivational Theory of Emotion to Replace 'Emotion as Disorganized Response.'" In *The Nature of Emotion*, ed. Magda B. Arnold, 172-88. London: Penguin.

Leighton, Stephen R. 1982. "Aristotle and the Emotions." *Phronesis* 27: 144-74.

————. 1984. "Feelings and Emotion." *Review of Metaphysics* 38: 303-20.

————. 1985. "A New View of Emotion." *American Philosophical Quarterly* 22: 133-42.

————. 1986. "Unfelt Feelings in Pain and Emotion." *Southern Journal of Philosophy* 24: 69-79.

————. 1988a. "Modern Theories of Emotion." *Journal of Speculative Philosophy* (n.s.) 2: 206-24.

————. 1988b. "On Feeling Angry and Elated." *Journal of Philosophy* 85: 253-64.

Lemos, Noah M. 1989. "Warrant, Emotion, and Value." *Philosophical Studies* 57: 175-92.

Levi, Lennart, ed. 1975. *Emotions: Their Parameters and Measurement.* New York: Raven.

Levinson, Jerrold. 1982. "Music and Negative Emotions." *Pacific Philosophical Quarterly* 63: 327-46.

Levy, Robert I., and Michelle Z. Rosaldo, eds. 1983. *Self and Emotion.* Special issue. *Ethos* 11(3).

Lewis, David. 1988. "Desire as Belief." *Mind* (n.s.) 97: 323-32.

Lewis, Helen Block. 1981-1983. *Freud and Modern Psychology.* 2 vols. New York: Plenum.

Lewis, Jan, and Peter N. Stearns, eds. In preparation. *The History of Emotions.* Series. New York: New York University Press.

Lloyd, Genevieve. 1984. *The Man of Reason: 'Male' and 'Female' in Western Philosophy.* London: Methuen.

Lutz, Catherine. 1986. "Emotion, Thought, and Estrangement: Emotion as a Cultural Category." *Cultural Anthropology* 1: 287-309.

—————. 1988. *Unnatural Emotions: Everyday Sentiments on a Micronesian Atoll and Their Challenge to Western Theory.* University of Chicago Press.

—————. 1990. *Language and the Politics of Emotion.* New York: Cambridge University Press.

Lynch, Owen, ed. 1990. *Divine Passions: The Social Construction of Emotion in India.* Berkeley: University of California Press.

Lyons, William. 1980. *Emotion.* Cambridge: Cambridge University Press.

McConnell, Terrance. 1993. *Gratitude.* Philadelphia: Temple University Press.

McCullagh, C. Behan. 1990. "The Rationality of Emotions and of Emotional Behaviour." *Australasian Journal of Philosophy* 68: 44-58.

McGill, Vivian J. 1954. *Emotions and Reason.* Springfield, IL: Charles C. Thomas.

MacIntyre, Alasdair C. 1971. "Emotion, Behavior, and Belief." In *Against the Self-Images of the Age: Essays on Ideology and Philosophy*, 230-43. New York: Schocken.

McIntyre, Jane L. 1989. "Personal Identity and the Passions." *Journal of the History of Philosophy* 27: 545-57.

Mackie, J. L. 1982. "Morality and the Retributive Emotions." *Acta Philosophica Fennica* 34: 144-57.

Malatesta, Carol Zander, and Carroll E. Izard, eds. 1984. *Emotion in Adult Development*. Beverly Hills: Sage.

Mansbridge, Jane J., ed. 1990. *Beyond Self-Interest*. Chicago: University of Chicago Press.

Marks, Joel. 1982. "A Theory of Emotion." *Philosophical Studies* 42: 227-42.

———. 1983. "The Rationality of Dispassion, or Why Richard Brandt Should Be a Buddhist." In *Emotions: Philosophical Studies*, ed. K. D. Irani and G. E. Myers, 57-71. New York: Haven.

———. 1988. "Radhakrishnan on the Buddha's Compassion: An Alternative Interpretation." Paper presented at the Radhakrishnan Centennial Conference, Miami University, Oxford, OH, 7-10 April.

———. 1993. Review of Armon-Jones, *Varieties of Affect. Mind* 102: 177-79.

Marks, Joel, ed. 1986. *The Ways of Desire: New Essays in Philosophical Psychology on the Concept of Wanting*. Chicago: Precedent.

Melden, Abraham I. 1969. "The Conceptual Dimensions of Emotions." In *Human Action*, ed. Theodore Mischel. New York: Academic Press.

Mele, Alfred R. 1989. "Akratic Feelings." *Philosophy and Phenomenological Research* 50: 277-88.

———. 1992. *Springs of Action: Understanding Intentional Behavior*. Oxford: Oxford University Press.

Mercer, Philip. 1972. *Sympathy and Ethics: With Special Reference to Hume's "Treatise."* Oxford: Clarendon.

Meyer, Max F. 1933. "That Whale among the Fishes—The Theory of Emotions." *Psychological Review* 40: 292-300.

Miller, Fred D. Jr., and Thomas Attig, eds. 1979. *Understanding Human Emotions.* Bowling Green, OH: Philosophy Documentation Center.

Mohler, James A. 1975. *Dimensions of Love, East and West.* Garden City, NY: Doubleday.

Morelli, Elizabeth A. 1986. *Anxiety: A Study of the Affectivity of Moral Consciousness.* Lanham, MD: University Press of America.

Morreall, John. 1983. "Humor and Emotion." *American Philosophical Quarterly* 20: 297-304.

————. 1985. "Enjoying Negative Emotions in Fiction." *Philosophy and Literature* 19: 95-103.

Morris, Herbert. 1981. "Reflections on Feeling Guilty." *Philosophical Studies* 40: 187-93.

————. 1987. "Nonmoral Guilt." In *Responsibility, Character, and the Emotions*, ed. Ferdinand Schoeman. Cambridge: Cambridge University Press.

Morsbach, H., and W. J. Tyler. 1986. "A Japanese Emotion: *Amae.*" In *The Social Construction of Emotions*, ed. Rom Harré, 289-307. New York: Blackwell.

Murphy, Jeffrie, and Jean Hampton. 1988. *Forgiveness and Mercy.* New York: Cambridge University Press.

Nash, Ronald Alan. 1989. "Cognitive Theories of Emotion." *Noûs* 23: 481-504.

Neill, Alex. 1993. "Fiction and the Emotions." *American Philosophical Quarterly* 30: 1-13.

Neu, Jerome. 1977. *Emotion, Thought, and Therapy.* Berkeley: University of California Press.

Newton-Smith, W. 1973. "A Conceptual Investigation of Love." In *Philosophy and Personal Relations: An Anglo-French Study*, ed. Alan Montefiore. London: Routledge & Kegan Paul.

Noddings, Nel. 1984. *Caring: A Feminine Approach to Ethics and Moral Education*. Berkeley: University of California Press.

Novitz, David. 1980. "Fiction, Imagination, and Emotion." *Journal of Aesthetics and Art Criticism* 38: 279-88.

Nussbaum, Martha. 1987. "The Stoics on the Extirpation of the Passions." *Apeiron* 20: 129-77.

———. 1988. "Narrative Emotions: Beckett's Genealogy of Love." *Ethics* 98: 225-54.

———. 1990. *Love's Knowledge: Essays on Philosophy and Literature*. Oxford: Oxford University Press.

Oakley, Justin. 1992. *Morality and the Emotions*. New York: Routledge.

Obeyesekere, Gananath. 1985. "Depression, Buddhism, and the Work of Culture in Sri Lanka." In *Culture and Depression*, ed. Arthur Kleinman and Byron Good. Berkeley: University of California Press.

Ortony, Andrew, Gerald L. Clore, and Allan Collins. 1990. *The Cognitive Structure of Emotions*. Cambridge: Cambridge University Press.

Otto, Rudolf. 1950. *The Idea of the Holy*. [1923.] Oxford: Oxford University Press.

Outka, Gene. 1972. *Agape: An Ethical Analysis*. New Haven: Yale University Press.

Panksepp, Jaak, et al. 1982. "Toward a General Psychobiological Theory of Emotions." *Behavioral and Brain Sciences* 5: 407-76.

Parkes, Graham. 1988. "The Transmutation of Emotion in Nietzsche and Zen." Paper presented at the American Philosophical Association Eastern Division Meeting, Washington, DC, 27-30 December.

Pears, David. 1975. "Causes and Objects of Some Feelings and Psychological Reactions." In *Questions in the Philosophy of Mind*, 56-79. New York: Barnes & Noble.

Pence, Terry. 1979. "Metaphysical Lunacy and Emotion." In *Understanding Human Emotions*, ed. Fred D. Miller Jr. and Thomas Attig, 51-5. Bowling Green, OH: Philosophy Documentation Center.

Perkins, Moreland. 1966. "Emotion and Feeling." *Philosophical Review* 75: 139-60.

Perrett, Roy W. 1989. "The Rationality of Asceticism." In *Rationality in Question: On Eastern and Western Views of Rationality*, ed. Shlomo Biderman and Ben-Ami Scharfstein, 57-76. Leiden: E. J. Brill.

Peters, R. S. 1969. "Motivation, Emotion, and the Conceptual Schemes of Common Sense." In *Human Action*, ed. Theodore Mischel. New York: Academic Press.

Piper, Adrian M. S. 1991. "Impartiality, Compassion, and Modal Imagination." *Ethics* 101: 726-57.

Pitcher, George. 1965. "Emotion." *Mind* 74: 326-46.

Plutchik, Robert. 1980. *Emotion: A Psychoevolutionary Synthesis*. New York: Harper & Row.

Plutchik, Robert, and Henry Kellerman, eds. 1980-1986. *Emotion: Theory, Research, and Experience*. 3 vols. New York: Academic Press.

Price, Huw. 1989. "Defending Desire-as-Belief." *Mind* (n.s.) 98: 119-27.

Putnam, Daniel. 1987. "Sympathy and Ethical Judgments: A Reconsideration." *American Philosophical Quarterly* 24: 261-66.

Putnam, Hilary. 1973. "Reductionism and the Nature of Psychology." *Cognition* 2: 131-46.

Rahula, Walpola. 1978. *What the Buddha Taught*. 2d ed. New York: Grove.

Regal, Philip J. 1990. *The Anatomy of Judgment*. Minneapolis: University of Minnesota Press.

Reisenzein, Rainer. 1983. "The Schachter Theory of Emotion: Two Decades Later." *Psychological Bulletin* 2: 239-64.

Rey, Georges. 1980. "Functionalism and the Emotions." In *Explaining Emotions*, ed. Amélie Oksenberg Rorty, 163-95. Berkeley: University of California Press.

Reymert, M. L., ed. 1928. *Feelings and Emotions: The Wittenberg Symposium*. Worcester, MA: Clark University Press.

——— . 1950. *Feelings and Emotions: The Mooseheart Symposium*. New York: McGraw-Hill.

Roberts, Robert C. 1982. *Spirituality and Human Emotion*. Grand Rapids, MI: William B. Eerdmans.

——— . 1984. "Solomon on the Control of Emotions." *Philosophy and Phenomenological Research* 44: 395-404.

——— . 1988a. "Is Amusement an Emotion?" *American Philosophical Quarterly* 25: 269-74.

——— . 1988b. "What an Emotion Is: A Sketch." *Philosophical Review* 97: 183-209.

——— . 1991. "What Is Wrong with Wicked Feelings?" *American Philosophical Quarterly* 28: 13-24.

——— . 1992. "Emotions as Access to Religious Truths." *Faith and Philosophy* 9: 83-94.

Robinson, Jenefer. 1983. "Emotion, Judgment, and Desire." *Journal of Philosophy* 80: 731-41.

Rorty, Amélie Oksenberg. 1982. "From Passions to Emotions and Sentiments." *Philosophy* 57: 159-72.

——— . 1989. *From Passions to Emotions and Sentiments*. Oxford: Oxford University Press.

——— . 1993. "From Passions to Sentiments: The Structure of Hume's *Treatise*." *History of Philosophy Quarterly* 10: 165-79.

Rorty, Amélie Oksenberg, ed. 1980. *Explaining Emotions*. Berkeley: University of California Press.

Ryle, Gilbert. 1949. *The Concept of Mind*. London: Hutchinson.

Sabini, John, and Maury Silver. 1987. "Emotions, Responsibility, and Character." In *Responsibility, Character, and the Emotions*, ed. Ferdinand Schoeman. Cambridge: Cambridge University Press.

Sachs, David. 1974. "On Freud's Doctrine of the Emotions." In *Freud: A Collection of Critical Essays*, ed. Richard Wollheim. Garden City, NY: Anchor.

Sankowski, Edward. 1977. "Responsibility of Persons for Their Emotions." *Canadian Journal of Philosophy* 7: 829-40.

Sartre, Jean-Paul. 1962. *Sketch for a Theory of the Emotions*, trans. Philip Mairet. [1939.] London: Methuen.

Schachter, Stanley, and Jerome E. Singer. 1962. "Cognitive, Social, and Physiological Determinants of Emotional State." *Psychological Review* 69: 379-99.

Scheman, Naomi. 1979. "On Sympathy." *Monist* 62: 320-30.

————. 1983. "Individualism and the Objects of Psychology." In *Discovering Reality: Feminist Perspectives on Epistemology, Metaphysics, Methodology, and Philosophy of Science*, ed. Sandra Harding and Merrill B. Hintikka. Hingham, MA: D. Reidel.

Scherer, Laus R., and Paul Ekman, eds. 1984. *Approaches to Emotion*. Hillsdale, NJ: Lawrence Erlbaum.

Scherer, Klaus R., Harald G. Wallbott, and Angela B. Summerfield, eds. 1986. *Experiencing Emotion: A Cross-Cultural Study*. Cambridge: Cambridge University Press.

Schoeman, Ferdinand, ed. 1987. *Responsibility, Character, and the Emotions: New Essays in Moral Psychology*. Cambridge: Cambridge University Press.

Scruton, Roger. 1986. *Sexual Desire: A Philosophical Investigation*. London: Weidenfeld & Nicolson.

————. 1987. "Analytical Philosophy and Emotion." *Topoi* 6: 77-81.

Sedgwick, Sally. 1990. "Can Kant's Ethics Survive the Feminist Critique?" *Pacific Philosophical Quarterly* 71: 60-79.

Shaffer, Jerome A. 1978. "Sexual Desire." *Journal of Philosophy* 75: 175-89.

————. 1983. "An Assessment of Emotion." *American Philosophical Quarterly* 20: 161-73.

Shibles, Warren A. 1974. *Emotion: The Method of Philosophical Therapy.* Whitewater, WI: Language.

Siegel, Lee. 1983. *Fires of Love, Waters of Peace: Passion and Renunciation in Indian Culture.* Honolulu: University of Hawaii Press.

Simonov, Pavel V. 1986. *The Emotional Brain: Physiology, Neuroanatomy, Psychology, and Emotion,* trans. Marie J. Hall. New York: Plenum.

Skulsky, Harold. 1980. "On Being Moved by Fiction." *Journal of Aesthetics and Art Criticism* 39: 5-14.

Sloman, Aaron, and Monica Croucher. 1981. "Why Robots Will Have Emotions." In *Proceedings of the Seventh International Joint Conference on Artificial Intelligence,* vol. 1, ed. Ann Drinan, 197-202. Los Altos, CA: William Kaufmann.

Smith, Quentin. 1986. *The Felt Meanings of the World: A Metaphysics of Feeling.* West Lafayette, IN: Purdue University Press.

Snare, Francis. 1991. *Morals, Motivation, and Convention: Hume's Influential Doctrines.* Cambridge: Cambridge University Press.

Snow, Nancy E. 1991. "Compassion." *American Philosophical Quarterly* 28: 195-205.

Soble, Alan. 1990. *The Structure of Love.* New Haven: Yale University Press.

Solomon, Robert C. 1976. *The Passions: The Myth and Nature of Human Emotion.* Garden City, NY: Anchor/Doubleday.

———. 1984. "I Can't Get It Out of My Mind (Augustine's Problem)." *Philosophy and Phenomenological Research* 44: 405-12.

———. 1988. "On Emotions as Judgments." *American Philosophical Quarterly* 25: 183-91.

———. 1990. *Passion for Justice: Emotions and the Origins of the Social Contract.* Reading, MA: Addison-Wesley.

———. 1993. "Existentialism, Emotions, and the Cultural Limits of Rationality." *Philosophy East and West* 42: 597-621.

Soupios, Michael A. 1984. "Reason and Feeling in Plato." In *New Essays on Socrates*, ed. Eugene Kelly. Lanham, MD: University Press of America.

Speck, Stanley. 1988. "Arousal Theory Reconsidered." *British Journal of Aesthetics* 28: 40-47.

Stambaugh, Joan. 1983. "The Greatest and Most Extreme Evil." *Philosophy Today* 27: 222-29.

Stecker, Robert. 1984. "Expression of Emotion in (Some of) the Arts." *Journal of Aesthetics and Art Criticism* 42: 409-18.

Stocker, Michael. 1983a. "Affectivity and Self-Concern: The Assumed Psychology in Aristotle's Ethics." *Pacific Philosophical Quarterly* 64: 211-29.

———. 1983b. "Psychic Feelings: Their Importance and Irreducibility." *Australasian Journal of Philosophy* 61: 5-26.

———. 1987. "Emotional Thoughts." *American Philosophical Quarterly* 24: 59-69.

Stoljar, Daniel. 1993. "Emotivism and Truth Conditions." *Philosophical Studies* 70: 81-101.

Strasser, Stephan. 1977. *Phenomenology of Feeling: An Essay on the Phenomena of the Heart.* Pittsburgh: Duquesne University Press.

Strawson, Peter. 1962. "Freedom and Resentment." *Proceedings of the British Academy* 48: 1-25.

Strongman, K. T. 1973. *The Psychology of Emotion.* New York: John Wiley.

Swain, Corliss G. 1992. "Passionate Objectivity." *Noûs* 26: 465-90.

Tanner, Michael. 1977. "Sentimentality." *Proceedings of the Aristotelian Society* (n.s.) 77: 127-47.

Taylor, C. C. W. 1986. "Emotions and Wants." In *The Ways of Desire*, ed. Joel Marks, 217-31. Chicago: Precedent.

Taylor, Gabriele. 1975. "Justifying the Emotions." *Mind* 84: 390-402.

————. 1975-1976. "Love." *Proceedings of the Aristotelian Society* (n.s.) 76: 147-64.

————. 1985. *Pride, Shame, and Guilt: Emotions of Self-Assessment.* Oxford: Oxford University Press.

————. 1988. "Envy and Jealousy: Emotions and Vices." *Midwest Studies in Philosophy* 13: 233-49.

Taylor, Gabriele, and Sybil Wolfram. 1971. "Virtues and Passions." *Analysis* 31: 76-83.

Thalberg, Irving. 1973. "Constituents and Causes of Emotion and Action." *Philosophical Quarterly* 23: 1-13.

————. 1977. "A Pair of Riddles about Emotion." In *Perception, Emotion, and Action.* New Haven: Yale University Press.

————. 1980. "Avoiding the Emotion-Thought Conundrum." *Philosophy* 55: 396-402.

Thompson, James M. 1989. "Painting and Knowledge: The Revelation Theory." *American Philosophical Quarterly* 26: 211-20.

Tomm, Winnie. In preparation. *Human Nature and Woman: The Relation between Reason and Emotion in Moral Development.*

Urmson, J. O. 1968. *The Emotive Theory of Ethics.* London: Hutchinson.

Vincent, Jean-Didier. 1990. *The Biology of Emotions*, trans. John Hughes. New York: Blackwell.

Walton, Kendall L. 1978. "Fearing Fictions." *Journal of Philosophy* 75: 5-27.

Warner, Richard. 1987. *Freedom, Enjoyment, and Happiness*. Ithaca, NY: Cornell University Press.

Watson, Gary. 1987. "Responsibility and the Limits of Evil: Variations on a Strawsonian Theme." In *Responsibility, Character, and the Emotions*, ed. Ferdinand Schoeman. Cambridge: Cambridge University Press.

Weisstein, Naomi. 1971. "Psychology Constructs the Female, or the Fantasy Life of the Male Psychologist (with Some Attention to the Fantasies of His Friends, the Male Biologist and the Male Anthropologist)." *Social Education* 35: 362-73.

Wierzbicka, Anna. 1986. "Human Emotions: Universal or Culture-Specific?" *American Anthropologist* 88: 584-94.

Williams, Bernard. 1971. "Morality and the Emotions." In *Morality and Moral Reasoning*, ed. John Casey. London: Methuen.

Wilson, J. R. S. 1972. *Emotion and Object*. Cambridge: Cambridge University Press.

Wood, Linda A. 1986. "Loneliness." In *The Social Construction of Emotions*, ed. Rom Harré, 184-208. New York: Blackwell.

Woodruff, Paul. 1988. "Engaging Emotion in Theater: A Brechtian Model in Theater History." *Monist* 71: 235-57.

Yasuo, Yuasa. 1987. *The Body: Toward an Eastern Mind-Body Theory*, ed. T. P. Kasulis. Albany: State University of New York Press.

Young, Paul Thomas. 1943. *Emotion in Man and Animal*. New York: John Wiley.

————. 1949. "Emotion as Disorganized Response—A Reply to Professor Leeper." *Psychological Review* 56: 184-91.

Zajonc, Robert B. 1980. "Feeling and Thinking: Preferences Need No Inferences." *American Psychologist* 35: 151-75.

Emotion in Bengali Religious Thought: Substance and Metaphor

June McDaniel

> [Emotions in India] are more likely to be objectified or substantialized, than somatized as in China, or internalized, as forces, drives, or instincts [as] in the West. . . . Contrary to Western stereotypes about India, and contrary to the Western devaluation of emotion in the face of reason, India finds emotions, like food, necessary for a reasonable life, and, like taste, cultivatable for the fullest understanding of life's meaning and purpose.
>
> —Owen Lynch, *Divine Passions*

INTRODUCTION

This paper focuses on Bengali ethnopsychology and some indigenous understandings of emotional events. The ethnological goal is not to relate or reduce the indigenous model to other theoretical perspectives but, rather, to examine how cultural and folk models interpret and express experience.

Emotion is variously viewed in both positive and negative ways in the Indian religious and philosophical traditions. In those traditions that are ascetic and emphasize mental control, emotions are distractions that need to be stilled. In those traditions emphasizing love of a deity, emotions are valuable but they must be directed and transformed.

This paper will begin by presenting a background on some early Indian traditions which understand emotion to be a distraction from clear perception and which also form a foundation for the "fluid" understanding of the world shown by later devotional traditions. It will then survey some of the major Sanskrit and Bengali terms used to express emotion. The paper will then move to a description of the Alaṅkāraśhāstra[1] and the Bengali Vaiṣhṇava and Sahajiyā devotional traditions, and comment on some differences between the Indian and Western approaches to emotion.

There is a stereotypical view in the West that Indian religion opposes emotion. This is because some of the oldest traditions in India Vedanta, Yoga and Āyurveda hold this position. However, it is important to note that these traditions are not dominant in modern India and have not been dominant for centuries. I will briefly discuss their views, however, to use them as background material.

Vedanta is the philosophy of the Vedic and Upanishadic texts. According to the *advaita* or monistic form of Vedanta, the ultimate state is a world-ground, a tranquil ocean of consciousness. It is disturbed by illusion (*māyā*), by the world of names and forms, which creates ignorance. Emotion is a part of that world of becoming, that changing universe which does not allow the person to perceive things as they really are, merged in *brahman* (infinite reality, knowledge, and bliss). The Vedantin seeks wisdom (*jñāna*) to the exclusion of emotion and renounces attachment to the illusory world. Emotion muddies the waters, disrupting awareness and distracting the sage.

A second ancient tradition is the classical yoga of Patañjali. In *sūtra* I.2 of the *Yoga Sūtras*, Patañjali gives the definition of yoga: *"Yogaś citta-vṛtti-nirodhaḥ"* (Yoga is the control or dissolution of the fluctuations of the mind).[2] The mind is understood as a field or ocean of consciousness (*citta*), which is ideally peaceful and still. However, in most human beings it is full of changes, waves, and eddies. These changes, or fluctuations, are the *vṛittis*, which disturb the clarity of the mind. Some changes are of external origin, from the physical world, and some are internal, arising from memory and impression (*saṃskāra*).

According to Patañjali's yoga, these memory impressions may become inclinations or propensities of the personality (*vāsanās*), accompanied by repeated habits of thought. The associated mental fluctuations become laden with emotion and are called *kleśhas*, impurities or afflictions. There are five *kleśhas*: ignorance, desire, hatred, fear (especially fear of death), and pride (the sense of the self as an individual entity).[3] These should be avoided: The yogi should control his emotions, withdrawing his perceptions and concerns into himself as a turtle pulls his legs inside of his shell.

The mind is often compared to a river or ocean. According to the commentary of Vyāsa on Patañjali's *Yoga Sūtras*, "The river called mind flows in two directions"[4]: toward the world of desire (*saṃsāra*) and toward the world of peace (called *kaivalya*, or isolation from the turbulence of daily life). The mind-stream, or river of consciousness (*citta-nadī*), needs to be directed and one-pointed, and one way to direct the river is to dam it through dispassion (*vairāgya*).[5]

A third source is Āyurveda, the medical tradition of India, which is based on the balance of the three humors in the body.[6] When these liquids have left their normal channels, they become imbalanced (and are then called faults, *doṣhas*), and the person becomes ill. When the flow is imbalanced, the mind can become intoxicated by these humors, and passions and mental disorganization may result.

According to Caraka, one of the most important writers in the *Āyurvedic* system, the person is born with three basic desires: the desire for life (self-preservation), the desire for wealth, and the desire for a good afterlife.[7] Other emotions (envy, grief, fear, anger, pride, hatred) are due to confusion or perversion of the understanding (*prajñaparādh*).[8] Confusion, when combined with lack of self-control and lapse of memory, causes humoral imbalance and mental and physical illness. The humors then attack the heart, and obstruct perception and sensation. This causes emotional disturbance and insanity, with their hallucination, delusion, and maladjustment to the social environment.[9] Such disturbance may also be caused by strong desires that are unfulfilled.[10] While dejection and grief aggravate disease, joy and contentment cure it.[11] Pleasure comes from organic equilibrium, and pain, from organic disequilibrium. Liquids link the system together, keep the bodily channels running smoothly, and balance the various aspects of the person.

These three traditions provide a basis for the negative view of emotion in India—a view that is different from that held by the popular culture and devotional religions of West Bengal.

THE LANGUAGE OF EMOTION

> The process of coming to understand the emotional lives of people in different cultures can be seen first and foremost as a problem of translation. . . . The interpretive task, then, is not primarily to fathom somehow "what they are feeling inside,". . . but rather to translate emotional communications from one idiom, context, language, or sociohistorical mode of understanding into another.[12]

Translation and interpretation between cultures, and between systems of thought and belief, are difficult endeavors. This section will not deal with all of the complexities of hermeneutics and cross-cultural communication, but will focus upon language and how it expresses the nature of emotion.

In the Sanskrit and Bengali languages, there is no exact term for emotion. The term used most frequently for it is *bhāva* or *anubhāva* (the physical expression of the state of *bhāva*). Sometimes the terms *rāga* or *ābeg* are used, which refer to intense emotions or passions. In the yogic literature we see the term *vedanā*, of Pali origin. It refers to a feeling, usually of a negative kind, such as pain or sorrow.

The term "*bhāva*" has many referents: The Monier-Williams *Sanskrit Dictionary* has four large columns of definitions for *bhāva*, and the *Bāngālā Bhāṣār Abhidhān* dictionary has two columns. Definitions in the *Samsad Bengali-English Dictionary* include mental state, mood, emotion, condition, love, friendship, ecstasy, rapture, passion, inner significance, essence, and existence—thus covering a wide range of phenomena.

Bhāva is an emotional complex, a form of experience, with connotations of associated perception, thought, movement, and expression. It is a way of being, a sense of identity which may be individual or shared. It is believed in many of the Bengali devotional traditions that religious ecstatics can create waves of *bhāva* (*bhāva-taraṅga*), which can spread through crowds of people, causing them all to share in the ecstatic's intense emotions.[13] The person who is *bhāvāveśh* is possessed by *bhāva*, either intensely emotional or taking on the *bhāva* (the emotion and identity) of a deity or other being. The person may be *bhāva lāgā* (affected by an emotion or idea), *bhāva prabaṇ* (emotional, sentimental, maudlin), or *bhāva bihbul* (overwhelmed with emotion or ecstasy). As terms derived from *bhāva*, *bhāvana* is thought, meditation, creation, and visualization, while *bhāvanā* is thought and contemplation but also worry and anxiety (the term is used in the Indian medical tradition for the repeated maceration, pulverization, and purification of herbal medicine—an interesting metaphor for analytic thought).

While doing fieldwork in West Bengal, in eastern India, from 1983 to 1984, I asked informants for definitions of *bhāva*. Some of these popular definitions follow:

> *Bhāva* is that aspect of mind which deals with emotion and experience; it is a result of culture and personality. It is only emotion—it does not include images, which are only fantasy. Yogis may develop stages and faculties of *bhāva*. Any experience can be called a *bhāva*, but the highest *bhāva* is *brahmabhāva*, a state of realistic expectations, a poise in which a stable equilibrium is established. (Psychiatrist)

> *Bhāva* is sentiment or emotion. It depends on the context—it may be used for poetry and art or for people—*dujon bhāva*, they are close. After fighting, children clasp fingers and say, "*Bhāva*, now we are friends." *Bhāva* is also inspired thought. (Grant administrator)

> *Bhāva* has a material and a spiritual meaning. Its material meaning is love between a man and a woman, but spiritual *bhāva* is love of God by a devotee with all his mind and heart. (Insurance salesman)

> *Bhāva* is very deep thought, deep in the heart, until one is lost within the self. The person becomes explosively pure in heart—he sees persons as other persons, such as all women as mother or sister. There are three stages of *bhāva* in the worship of *Śakti* (the Goddess)—*bhāva*, possession by *bhāva* (*bhāvāveśh*), and deep trance (*bhāva samādhi*). In *bhāva*, one becomes lost in memory and emotion. In possession by *bhāva*, one becomes lost from the material world and sees the heaven worlds. In the deepest trance of *bhāva*, one roams in the absolute (*ātman*). (Travel agent)

Bhāva is when different parts of the person come together, as when cooking Kashmiri chicken. Different spices are blended together to create a taste. In love affairs (*premer bhāva*), the parts of the soul are mixed together like spices. The soul and mind consult each other, along with the body, to decide about loving. Good worship (*pūjā*) creates good *bhāva* between the devotee and the goddess, if the person believes 100 percent. There is a relation of soul between the deity and the worshiper—they share the same actions, and adjust to each other, even if there was conflict between them at the beginning. (Store owner)

Informants show an understanding of various stages or levels of *bhāva*, usually shifting its focus (from worldly goals to divine ones) and its degree of intensity (from lesser to greater passion). All of these are understood to be forms or transformations of emotional states.

In the Bengali and Sanskrit languages, terms for emotion and thought, mind and heart, are not opposed. Indeed, most frequently the same terms are used for both. A term often heard, *mana*, means both mind and heart, as well as mood, feeling, mental state, memory, desire, attachment, interest, attention, devotion, and decision. These terms do not have a single referent in English, and must be understood through clusters of explicit and implicit meanings.[14] Verbs based on *mana* include *mana kara* (to make up one's mind, to resolve or agree); *mana kāra* (to captivate the mind or win one's heart); and *mana kholā* (to speak one's mind or open one's heart).

A term used less frequently by informants, *hridaya*, means the heart as both organ and inner seat of feeling. The heart may be melted (when a play is *hridayadravakara*, touching or evoking pathos) or broken (the heart is pierced, *hridayabhedī*), and may overflow with an outburst of emotion (*hridayochvāsa*). A person unaffected by emotion may be called unfeeling or heartless (*hridayahīn*). The heart is also understood as a space or locale, in which persons or deities may dwell. Thus, we see the heart called a canvas for painting (*hridayapaṭa*), a shrine or temple (*hridayamandir*), a seat for a loved one or deity (*hridayāsana*), or a space as broad as the sky (*hridayākāsh*). As one informant described it, his heart was an empty box that needed to be filled. In poetry, the loved one may live in the heart as in a garden; and in worship, an aspect of the god may live there enthroned, surrounded by the devotee's love like an aura of light. The poet Rāmprasād Sen spoke of the "burning ground of the heart," and had visions of the goddess Kālī dancing there.[15] In *kuṇḍalinī yoga*, the heart is a doorway to the worlds of the spirit, as the *anāhata chakra* (heart center).[16]

There are several other terms often used in discussing emotion. *Rāga*, a term more well-known in the West as a mode of Indian classical music, also means passion, ranging from love and attachment to anger and rage. It has the meaning of dye or color (especially red)—the soul is understood to be "dyed" by passion, which permeates it like a dye permeates cloth.[17] *Kāma* is desire, lust, and pleasure, while *prema* is selfless or spiritual love. *Ābeg* means tremendous force, passionate outburst, intense feeling, uneasiness, and suspense, while *anubhāva* refers to both power and physical expression of emotional states (such as tears and sighs). Yet emotion is *sūkṣmatā* (subtlety, delicacy, invisibility to the senses) as well as *komlatā* (gentleness, tenderness, softness). As *anubhuti*, it is both perception and intuition, realization and feeling.

The terms for thought, or cognition, often imply emotion. We have the word *cinta*, meaning thought, idea, and cogitation, with associated meanings of anxiety, worry, and fear. *Dhāraṇā* means idea, conception, memory, belief, impression, as well as feeling, and is associated with the term *dharaṇa*, the act of holding, catching, wearing, carrying (thought is "borne" in the mind). *Anubhāva* means knowledge, perception, and realization but also feeling, and *kalpanā* refers to thought and imagination.

We see in these terms and definitions that emotion is a powerful force which is at the same time subtle and delicate, invisible to the senses yet capable of generating physical expressions, associated with perception, intuition, and realization. There is no sharp distinction between emotion and cognition. Thought is associated with knowledge and discrimination, and the mind grasps and holds memories and ideas. Yet thought is associated with feelings, especially anxiety,[18] as well as imagination.

Bhāva in itself is a complex term with a range of meanings, from a broad understanding of experience and identity (*bhāva* as a way of being) to a specific *bhāva*, an emotion or thought that is clearly defined. Using the same term for these events shows that the range of experience—emotion, mood, identity, mental state—is understood as a continuum rather than a collection of distinct and opposed categories. Both emotion and thought are part of the wider category of *bhāva*.

THE METAPHORS OF EMOTION: FIRE AND WATER

> Swept away by rivers of love
> (swelling floods of their desire)
> Torrents dammed by their elders
> (propriety all parents require)
> Close they stand, anxious but still
> (hiding passions, restraining sights)
> Lovers drink nectars from the blossoms
> (the love that pours from lotus eyes).
>
> *Amaruśataka*[19]

Metaphorically, emotion has been linked with both fire and water in Indian religious literature. I think that a brief exploration of these metaphors would give some insight into the nature of emotion in the Bengali devotional traditions.

The metaphor of emotional heat is an old idea in India, going back to Vedic times (2000-1500 BCE). Vedic sages, or *ṛishis*, sought to control *tapas* (the universal energy of creation and destruction). *Tapas* comes from the Sanskrit root *tap*, whose most literal meaning is "to be hot" or "to create heat."[20] The heat of tapas could transform both the world and the person, and its dynamic forms include lustful heat, jealous heat, devotional heat, sorrowful heat, and the heat of hatred and anger. The sage was believed to be capable of burning animals and people with his glance if angry—the emotion would return to its original form as heat. *Tapas* is also the heat of the sacrifice and the force behind creation, linking together the divine and human worlds. In the Vedic creation hymn, the "*Nāsadīya Sukta*" (*Ṛig Veda* X.29.4), desire (*kāma*) is born out of tapas.

While the energy of *tapas* is closely linked with desire and emotion, the term also refers to an ascetic practice used to suppress emotion. Ascetics try to "burn away" their emotional lives in the heat of tapas generated by meditation, and their worldly feelings are given up into the fire of the "inner sacrifice." Thus, they accumulate tapas as transformed emotion, and this *tapas* can give power, energy, and religious experience. The practice of *tapas* enables the sage to be indifferent to desire. Even today, some practitioners walk naked and cover themselves with ash from the burning ground to show how their emotions have been burnt away.

In the later *bhakti* (devotional) traditions, passion is said to burn the hearts of devotees, causing the person to be "on fire" for the god. Some saints have stated that their bodies would burn with fever for the deity for months or years on end. Rāmakṛishṇa Paramahaṃsa, a recent Bengali Śhākta[21] saint, could not touch other people during his meditation on the deity, because his body was physically burning from passion, and he had to wear a sheet when approaching others. The Vaiṣhṇava saint Vijayakṛishṇa Goswāmin, who rebelled against a Western education to return to yogic and devotional practices, felt unbearable heat during meditation. The desire for insight showed itself as *nāmāgni* (the fire of the Name of God), which he said caused his body to burn and his limbs to separate off and later return together. Saints in meditation are said to be "heated"; Ānandamayī Mā's disciples reported that her body caused great heat wherever she sat.[22]

The physical body is understood to be subject to mental and emotional heat. The Vaiṣhṇava saint Siddha Kṛishṇadās was a visionary for whom the world of Kṛishṇa's paradise was more real than the physical world. He would often see Kṛishṇa's consort goddess Rādhā in visions, but when she refused to appear to him anymore, out of intense sorrow and force of will he set his body on fire.[23] We see a similar theme in the idea of *satī*. Many people in the West have heard of the Indian ritual in which the widow climbs on the funeral pyre of her husband, to die with him in the flames. In several early variants of the mythic story, the woman Satī was intensely angry and sorrowful over her father's poor treatment of her husband Śhiva, and she set herself on fire solely by yogic power. In this case, the visible fire was the expression of her inner emotions.[24] The chaste wife also has this power: In the Tamil story Shilappadikāram, a woman whose husband was wrongfully prosecuted caused the city to burn down.[25]

There are many folk beliefs that link emotion and heat. However, we also see the development over time of a link between emotion and liquid. The heart burns but it also melts; the person is on fire but softens. In the *Ṛig Veda*, *rasa* can be any fluid, but it is especially the fluid of life, associated with sexuality, passion, and blood.[26] The Vedantic "ocean of consciousness" uses a watery metaphor, as does the yogic "river of mind." As the tradition of *bhakti* grew up, heat became associated with the pain of separation, and water, with the joy of love in union. Remedies for the "burning sorrow" of separation included garlands, wet compresses, moist sandalwood paste, and cool breezes. The beloved "cooled the heat" of the lover, and the waves of love represented the forces that drew the lovers together. While earlier metaphors of emotion focused on heat, the focus later shifted to water and/or liquid, which came to be seen as an emotional vehicle in its own right.

THE NATURE OF EMOTION: *BHĀVA* AND *RASA*

Having thoughts of intense passion about you (Kṛishṇa), the deer-eyed woman is immersed in an ocean of passionate bliss (*rasa*), fixed in meditation.

Jayadeva, *Gīta Govinda*, VI.10

The most extensive analyses of emotion in Indian religion and philosophy have probably come from the writers of the Alaṇkāraśhāstra, the Sanskrit literary tradition which focuses on aesthetic experience, and from the Vaiṣhṇava tradition, which emphasizes religious emotion. For both traditions, aesthetic emotion is *rasa*, which is experienced by the person of taste (*rasika*) during identification with a dramatic character or situation. According to the Alaṇkāra, the spectator is totally involved in the dramatic event, and feels an emotion that is powerful, extraordinary (*alaukika*), yet impersonal and generic. It is joyful rather than pleasant or painful, and brings a sense of wonder. In some ways, it is similar to the religious goal of realization of Brahman. Viśvanātha writes that aesthetic enjoyment requires subconscious impressions (*vāsanas*) which support an emotional disposition.[27] Aesthetic emotions have a variety of effects on consciousness.[28]

The writers of the Alaṇkāra describe permanent emotions and temporary ones. They base their organization of emotions on those of Bharata in his *Nāṭyaśhāstra*: love, mirth, grief, anger, energy (zeal), fear, disgust, and wonder.[29] These permanent emotions (*sthāyibhāva*) are dominant, and cannot be suppressed by other emotions. According to Śiṅga Bhūpāla's *Rasārṇava-sudhākar*, "They are permanent emotions, which transform other emotions into themselves, even as the ocean transforms the waves into itself."[30] The transitory emotions (*vyabhichāribhāva*), according to Śaradātanaya's *Bhāvaprakāśhana*, appear and disappear within the permanent emotions as waves appear and disappear in the ocean, contributing to its excellence.[31] They are like bubbles in the ocean, or like beads or flowers of a garland, and they help, promote, and strengthen the permanent emotions they ornament. Some of the transitory emotions include shame, exhilaration, dejection, eagerness, apathy, ferocity, and anxiety.[32] In the first chapter of his *Nāṭyaśhāstra*, Bharata compared the aesthetic experience to eating—as spices add flavor (*rasa*) to the main dish, which is enjoyed by the gourmet, so the permanent emotion in drama is spiced with transitory emotions and literary ornaments, to be enjoyed by the connoisseur (*rasika*).

The sentiment of *rasa* is a transformation of the basic, more "concrete" emotion of *bhāva*. The term *rasa* means sap, juice, liquid essence, and taste, and is often translated as flavor, relish, mood, and sentiment. Emotional *rasa* can be tasted and appreciated.[33] When emotions become *rasas*, they may be viewed as art objects, and combined in aesthetic fashion. They may blend harmoniously with each other (*sandhi*), arise and disappear, or conflict with and inhibit one another. This conflict is called *rasābhāsa*, and is understood to result in a semblance or imitation of a true emotion. It is a damaged, inferior, or incomplete sort of emotion, tainted by pride or power or generated by some inappropriate source. The conflicts that may generate such a damaged emotion could include the clash between parental and erotic love or the emotions of disgust and fury combined with the attitude of loving service. They are called "compound emotions" when several transitory emotions arise in quick succession, especially when some are inhibited by others.

From this perspective, the *bhāva* is a "raw" emotion, not cooked or transformed into an aesthetic emotion. In order to transform the emotion, an internal distancing is needed from the emotion, so that the experiencer also becomes an observer, in some ways a "witness-self," as described in Vedantic philosophy.

Rasa is characterized by impersonality or generalizing (*sādhāraṇikāraṇa*), the distancing of the person from both the object and from his or her own emotions. In *bhāva*, the person experiences emotions directly; while in *rasa*, he or she empathizes and observes the emotion and situation, feeling *as if* he felt the emotion but not being involved enough to feel it directly. It is impersonal, generic, the experience of a type.[34] As De states,

> Generality is thus a state of self-identification with the imagined situation, devoid of any practical interest and, from this point of view, of any relation whatsoever with the limited self, and as it were impersonal.[35]

The feelings of the poet or actor are also excluded from the aesthetic experience. The elements of particular consciousness are expunged in order to create generalized emotion, valuing universals more than particular acts. Emotions are not undergone; instead, the aesthete is both observer and participant.

Bhāva is a personal emotion; *rasa* is an impersonal or depersonalized emotion, in which the participant is distanced as an observer. Why is a depersonalized emotion considered superior to a personal one? Because the aesthete can experience a wide range of emotions yet be protected from their painful aspects. Emotion is appreciated through a glass window, which keeps out unpleasantness. Though the glass is clear, thus allowing a union of sorts with the observed object, the window is always present, thus maintaining the dualism. This becomes important for the religious dimensions of *rasa*, where the duality between the worshipper and the god (an important concept in *bhakti* devotion) must always be maintained.

The Bengali Vaiṣṇavas also value *rasa*, but they emphasize its religious aspects. In the Vaiṣṇava understanding of emotion, *bhāva* becomes *bhakti rasa* (devotional sentiment). The religious goal is not liberation but rather love, and the devotee must go beyond dramatic emotion to become filled with religious emotion. The connoisseur (the *rasika* or *sahṛidaya*, the person with heart), who can truly appreciate the fine points of the arts, becomes the devotee (*bhakta*), tasting the forms of joy brought by the god Kṛishṇa. He or she is both observer and participant. The aesthetic experience is universal, *bhedābheda*, simultaneously individual and eternal, material and spiritual, impersonal and passionately involved.

In *bhakti* yoga, emotion becomes discipline—the emotions are generated and transformed consciously, especially in that form of practice known as *rāgānugā bhakti sādhana*.[36] There is a sort of "ladder of emotion" which one must climb to the highest emotional states, and it is described in two important texts, the *Bhaktirasāmṛitasindhu* and *Ujjvala-Nīlamaṇi* of Rūpa Gosvāmin. While the former text (*The Ocean of the Nectar of Devotional Love*) looks at the earlier stages of religious emotion and its transformation, the latter text (*The Blazing Sapphire*—a pun on the god Kṛishṇa) focuses on the more advanced states of mystical love.

The *Bhaktirasāmṛitasindhu* has the devotee begin with ritual action (*vaidhi bhakti*) and progress to ritual emotion (*rāgānugā bhakti*). Through physical action and imaginative visualization, the devotee builds a soul, a spiritual body composed of love, which can experience emotion more intensely than can the ordinary personality. The *bhāva* becomes deepened, and the heart is softened. Emotion becomes intense love (*prema*), and there is continual focus of attention on Rādhā and Kṛishṇa, the divine couple. The highest state, called the "greatest emotion" (*mahābhāva*), has the person experience all possible emotions simultaneously, including the opposite emotions of separation and union, in passionate delirium (*mādana*). As O. B. L. Kapoor states,

Mādana has the unique capacity of directly experiencing a thousand different kinds of enjoyment of union with Kṛṣṇa. . . . It presents these multifarious experiences of union simultaneously with multifarious experiences of separation (*viyoga*) involving craving (*utkaṇṭhā*) for union."[37]

The "ladder of emotion" includes *sneha* (a thickening of spiritual love, when the emotion gains a consistency and taste like clarified butter or honey); *māna* (sulking and hiding emotion); *praṇaya* (deep sharing and confidence); *rāga* (intense passion, also defined as the person being totally concentrated upon the desired object); *anurāga* (in which the beloved appears eternally new); and *mahābhāva* (the experience of emotion so intense and complex that all extremes of emotion are felt at once). In the orthodox Bengali Vaiṣṇava tradition, only Rādhā may experience the state of *mahābhāva*, though her companions and their handmaidens may share in her emotional states. Indeed, these handmaidens (*mañjaris*) are said to feel Rādhā's emotions a hundred times more intensely than she does, for they are not as personally involved (selflessness is understood to increase sensitivity to the divine).[38] The devotee may also share in these states by visualizing the mythical situations and characters in which they occur.[39]

These states of intense emotion are expressed by ecstatic bodily changes (the *sāttvika bhāvas* or *sāttvika vikāras*). There are eight of these: trembling, shedding tears, paralysis, sweating, fainting, changing skin color, faltering voice, and hair standing on end. Like the transitory emotions, these symptoms are understood to develop and intensify the permanent emotions, and they are an extreme form of emotional expression (*anubhāva*).[40] The term "*bhāva*" is also used for the five basic roles, or emotional relationships, through which the devotee may relate to the deity: through friendship, parental love, service, peace, and erotic love. Among the Bengali Vaiṣṇavas, *bhāva* is the emotional ground for subtler and more complex emotional states.

But it is among the Sahajiyās, the unorthodox, tantric branch of Vaishnavism, that we find the most literal notion of emotion as substance. Sahajiyās also value *rasa*, but their understanding of the term is different from the more traditional Bengali Vaiṣṇavas. They practice sexual yoga, literally living out the relationship of Kṛishna and Rādhā, the deity and his consort, in order to share in their emotions and experiences. Such practice involves maintaining dispassion within a setting of greatest passion, "diving deep without getting wet." By such rituals, lustful and earthly emotion is transformed into spiritual love. The process has been compared to cooking:

> To find nectar
> Stir the cauldron
> On the fire—
> And unite the act of loving

With the feeling of love.
Distill the sweetness
Of the heart
And reach the treasures.[41]

Here *rasa* is a literal fluid, which is heated, stirred, and concentrated, a fluid of pure emotion which is condensed during the practice—the sexual fluid, which can be transformed into new life or spiritual love. There is less focus on observation, and more on practice. All other emotions are secondary to those of love, which is viewed as the basic, or primordial, emotion. The emotional fire in the woman ripens the liquid *rasa* in the male; as the *Vivarta Vilāsa* states,

> Now hear about the nature of (the physical) woman. Just as milk is usually boiled with the help of fire, so the Gosvāmis have utilised the fire that is in woman (for the purpose of purifying the passion).[42]

As S. B. Dasgupta states, the Sahajiyās believed *rasa* to flow "perpetually from the eternal Vṛindāvana to earth, manifested as the stream of *rasa* flowing to and between men and women."[43] Sexuality and love linked the devotee with the heavenly Vṛindāvana, and passionate emotion showed the presence of heaven on earth. As milk is churned into butter, so the *rasa* of love for Rādhā and Kṛiṣhṇa is churned by sexuality into more intense and condensed states, becoming a pure substance of joy. As the *Premānanda-lahari* states, "If there is no *rāga* [passion], there can be no union."[44] Emotion is directed and transformed.

Thus, in these three traditions we see an evolution of ideas about emotion: It has changed from an abstract aesthetic principle to an intense style of relating with a deity to a sexual fluid which is the essence of God.

CONCLUSIONS

> *Bhāva* is like filling a pail full of tap water—when it fills up, the sound will be changed. The body is a vessel which can understand things, and whenever you feel or understand something, you have a sort of *bhāva*. But it is not called "*bhāva*" until it is overflowing. . . . When the pail flows over, the eight *sāttvikā bhāvas* emerge—the eight ways of overflowing. These are divine, supernatural events. *Bhāvas* are temporary because the body is full of pores. It is like a beautiful glass with holes in it—there is leakage. You put water in it and it comes out. The body is made in such a way, that whatever you fill it up with, it will come out. Feelings (*bhāvas*) and highest feelings (*māhābhāva*) come out through the pores of the body. But the memory is an energy that remains. (Interview, Śhākta practitioner, Calcutta)

There is a wide range of theory in Indian philosophical and religious thought on the nature of emotion. However, if we wish to generalize, there tends to be a different understanding of the nature of emotion in India than that held in the West. Emotion, like consciousness, tends to be substantial rather than conceptual, more like the early Christian notions of *ousia* (being or essence), the transformation of a common substance.

In the *bhakti* traditions of Bengal, emotion is the path to God, and is thus sacred. Rather than trying to eliminate emotion, the goal is to intensify that emotion until it becomes powerful, overwhelming, the center of the devotee's being. There is a natural tendency for that love to increase, "as the ebb tide rises into high waves at the rising of the moon." Human emotion is transformed into divine emotion: It is boiled, thickened, purified, and redirected. Emotion is a means to an end, and often it does not matter which emotion is being emphasized. Hatred of the god (*dveṣa-bhāva*) gives the same focus on the deity as loving like a parent (*vātsalya-bhāva*), and both emotions can bring the devotee to paradise.[45] Indeed, powerful enough emotion can influence the deity's will, even bring him to earth, for love can control the gods and make them slaves of their devotees.

Traditionally, the body has been compared to a vase or pot, and the soul (*jīva*) is incarnate within it. Emotion occurs within the soul but can be manifest in the body. It is inward (*antar* or *mānasa*) when not expressed and outward (*bāhya*) when shown by the physical body. As the Shākta practitioner stated in the introductory quotation, the body is like a pail that can be filled up with *bhāva*. The body as vessel of the soul is an old idea in both East and West. The practitioner later stated that the pores can be "plugged" by concentrating on love of the Goddess and chanting mantras, which maintains the intensity of the emotion.

We have looked at a wide range of beliefs about emotion in religion and folklore, and we can ask, What is the value of emotion? Let us examine some ideas from this paper.

1. Bengal tends to study emotions in ways that the West does not. The aesthetic and devotional traditions focus upon intense emotions and the disciplines which generate them. Emotion is a sea rather than a puddle or a few stray droplets, and it is studied by participant observation, by disciplined individuals who view emotion from the "inside." From the perspective of *rasa*, it is best understood in its pure and intense forms, while Western philosophy tends to focus on secular, everyday emotion rather than ecstatic or extreme emotion (though William James comes to mind as an exception). If we accept the liquid metaphor, one is more likely to understand fluid dynamics by the study of water in oceans and lakes than by studying puddles and droplets.

2. Emotion is identified by metaphors of both substance and space. It can be intensified, shared, transferred, deposited in physical locales.[46] Emotion is neither an involuntary response nor cognition and belief, but a transformation of the substance of consciousness. The Indian universe is a fluid one, a complex network of interactions between various forms of substance, according to many modern anthropologists. As Marriott states,

> Matter that is subject to such variations may well be called "fluid," and indeed
> Hindus generally refer to the world they must live in as "(that which is) mov-
> ing" (*jagat*) and as a "flowing together" (*saṃsāra*). . . . It and its inhabitants
> are generated by, and constituted of, more or less malleable substance that is
> continually moving in and out of them."

Mind and emotion are no exception to this "wholly substantial and fluid
world," and they tend to be understood through metaphors of flowing and
water. They may also be located spatially, such as in the "space of the heart," as
a throne or box or shrine. As substance, emotion is accessible to mind and
heart, and there is no absolute separation between aspects of the self. Substance gives access, for viewing emotion as intangible and invisible also makes
it inaccessible.

3. Emotion can act as an aid to concentration, helping to focus the mind
rather than acting as a distraction. Passion can direct the mind and fasten it
upon its object. In the stories of Kṛiṣhṇa and the *gopīs*, or milkmaids, who
loved him, their fascination for him is often described as meditative, and
Rādhā's passion for Kṛiṣhṇa is often compared to yogic concentration. The
love object is the focus of the mind, for there is no split between thought and
feeling. Remembrance (*smaraṇa*) involves *mana*, which is both mind and
heart, and it is directed to a single end, so that even thinking of anything else
becomes difficult. Depending on how it is used, the same emotion can distract
from concentration or be a means of mental control, and limit or increase
knowledge.

4. The "hydraulic model" of emotion is differently understood in Bengal
than in the West. Superficially, it is much like Freud's notion of the id, whose
energies overflow into the conscious mind. A good Bengali description of
bhāva using the hydraulic model was given by a woman ecstatic to describe her
own experiences:

> When something is boiled in a closed vessel, there comes a stage when the
> vapor will push up the lid and, unless force is used, the vessel cannot be kept
> covered anymore. In a similar manner, when, while being engaged in *japa*
> (chanting) or some other spiritual exercise, a wave of ecstatic emotion surges
> up from within, it becomes difficult to check it. This ecstatic emotion is called
> "*bhāva*." It emerges from deep within and expresses itself outwardly."

Her description follows Robert Solomon's rendering of the "hydraulic
metaphor," in which emotion is a force within the person, filling up and spilling
over. It is based on theories ranging from the medieval humours, animal spirits,
and bodily fluids, to the Freudian theory of the dynamic and economic forms of
psychic equilibrium within the person, where the ego holds back the repressed
libidinal forces pushing for release. He finds that, in Western philosophy, this
approach has served to limit the range and importance of the emotions, for it

relieves the person of responsibility. The emotions are inflicted by causes beyond human control or are bottled up like volcanic lava, and they render the person passive.[49] As he states,

> The key to the hydraulic model is the idea that emotions and other passions (or their determinants) exist wholly independent of consciousness, effecting (or "affecting") consciousness and often forcing us to behave in certain discernible ways.[50]

In Bengal, however, the hydraulic model has opened and expanded the concept of emotion, for it has been tied in with spirituality. The key statement might be rephrased: The emotions are normally independent of consciousness, but the person may gain access to the sources of emotion and direct them to gain certain discernible ends. Unlike Freudian psychology, the Bengali model does not understand the psyche as a closed system. People may undergo emotions but also generate, control, and share them, to gain access to the emotional sea that lies beneath the conscious mind. Different emotions may be combined, or many experienced simultaneously. Because the person has access to the source of emotion, there can be no freedom from responsibility or use of emotion as an "excuse" for unacceptable behavior.

5. Emotions can be controlled and combined to become something analogous to art objects. Rather than passions or disturbances, emotions may be aesthetic objects, which are arranged as dominant and transitory, central and peripheral, clashing and ornamental, as an artist might arrange different color relationships on a canvas. Emotions are, in a sense, colors (rāga), which define and structure experience as art. During the dramatic performance, the emotions represented by the actor are experienced by the observer, who is simultaneously a participant. As the trained observer is aware of the subtlety and interplay of emotion, he or she becomes involved in what might be called "performance art." It is a conscious awareness of his or her own shared dramatic experience, which is paradoxical because it is both close and distanced. Raw, "concrete" emotions can be transformed into aesthetic and religious ones.

6. Disciplined emotion can generate new personalities which are highly valued. The person may not be able to determine his or her secular personality, based as it is on past events, but he or she can build a soul, a spiritual body that is sculpted out of emotion. This alternative personality, or "subtle body," is composed of the emotions of love, and represents the person's ideal self.

The idea of such a self has often been dismissed as "split personality," or multiple-personality disorder, by Western observers. However, it is interesting to note that, in the West, the focus upon alternate selves has been on multiple-personality disorder generated by trauma, by abuse or events too painful for the person to bear, and, earlier on, demonic personalities that possess the person involuntarily.[51] The *DSM III* psychiatric manual's description fits the Indian case in many ways:

> A. The existence within an individual of two or more distinct personalities, each of which is dominant at a particular time. B. The personality that is dominant at any particular time determines the individual's behavior. C. Each individual personality is complex and integrated with its own unique behavior patterns and social relationships.[52]

The Western alternate personalities are considered to be pathological, a result of trauma. Emotion cannot be deliberately used and controlled to create a new personality—such generation is an involuntary and unconscious event.

From the Indian devotional perspective, developing an alternate self based on emotion is a creative act, building a spiritual body made out of overflowing love. This *siddha deha* (perfected body) or *prema deha* (body of love) becomes the true self of the person, and is believed to continue after the death of the physical body. The alternate self is generated by will rather than by pain, and emotion is utilized rather than repressed or endured. In this understanding, emotion is the foundation of identity, the substance from which it is constructed.

Thus, emotion is a means to an end in the Bengali aesthetic and devotional traditions, and that end is the good life. Emotion is not a passive response but an active eros, involving meaning, beauty, and creativity, which structures both self and world.

Notes

1. Note on transliteration: The Indian terms in this paper have been written in Sanskritized Bengali, to make them more accessible to Hindi and Sanskrit speakers. However, as the audience for this article will not be made up primarily of Indologists, I will transliterate terms as phonetically as possible (rather than follow the Sanskrit conventions). I will retain the diacriticals, however, for those who wish to research the Sanskrit and Bengali etymologies. Thus, Kṛṣṇa becomes Kṛishṇa, ṛṣi becomes ṛishi, Alaṃkāraśāstra becomes Alaṇkāraśhāstra, and so on.

2. See Arya 1986, *Yoga Sūtras* I.2.

3. Ibid., II.3. It is debated among scholars whether the sense of individuality is more a problem of ignorance (as personality and individuality are not ultimate truth) or of pride (too much focus on the illusion of individuality).

4. Ibid., I.2.

5. Ibid., I.12, Vyāsa's commentary.

6. The three humors or basic elements (*dhātus*) of Āyurveda are *vāyu*, *pitta*, and *kapha*. *Vāyu*, or *vāta*, is associated with movement, nerves, and muscles; *pitta* with enzymes, hormones, digestion, and temperature; and *kapha* with liquids and plumpness. *Kapha* also regulates the other two humors. Imbalance of humors may be endogenous (due to such factors as heredity and degeneration) or exogenous (from such causes as drugs, poison, accidents, unclean food, and animal bites).

7. Sharma and Dash 1983, *Caraka Samhita*, I.11.20.

8. Ibid., I.7.38.

9. Ibid., II.7.4.

10. Ibid., I.11.45.

11. Ibid., I.25.40.

12. Lutz 1988, 8.

13. Such waves are described in many Bengali biographies of *siddhas*, or saints. For example, the Vaiṣṇavite saint Vijayakṛiṣhṇa Gosvāmin and his devotees were described as dancing in waves of *bhāva*, which became a "sky-high typhoon." See his biography in McDaniel 1989.

14. The following terms and definitions come from the *Samsad Bengali-English Dictionary* (Dasgupta 1983).

15. In India, the dead are not buried but, rather, are burned at the *śmaśāna*, or burning ground. To compare the heart to a burning ground means that all earthly concerns have been left behind, as the corpse is left behind by the spirit, and a total devotion to the goddess has taken their place.

16. In the meditational system of *kuṇḍalinī yoga*, the person is understood to have a body composed of energy (*śhakti*), which exists invisibly within the physical body. This body is composed of seven centers (*chakras*), which are located along the spine and are foci of meditation. These centers are interpreted in different ways by different practitioners, but the heart center is usually associated with emotion, compassion, and respiration.

17. We see a similar range of meanings to the term *rāga* in the Japanese term *iro* (Chinese *se*). *Iro* means color and sensual pleasure, among other things, and includes such derivatives as *irogonomi* (sensuality, lust); *iroke* (coloring, shade, passion, romance); *irozome* (dyeing, dyed); and *irokoi* (love, sentiment). See the term *iro* in Nelson 1974.

18. There is a special kind of madness in Bengal, colloquially known as "study-*pāgal*," or study-insanity. Informants told me that too much thinking is dangerous, that it upsets the balance of the mind, and that it could result in grave mental and physical illness. I was told quite firmly that I needed more emotion and less thought in order to be healthy. This is the "folk" view, which separates thought and emotion and finds emotion to be especially important in women.

19. Siegel 1983, *Amaruśataka* 104.

20. Kaelber 1989, 3.

21. Śhāktas are worshippers of the Goddess in West Bengal, primarily the goddess Kālī in her form of Mother of the Universe.

22. Heat is often colloquially associated with negative emotion. In the Indian tradition of touching the guru's feet, the devotee is understood to get rid of his bad karma—the guru's feet absorb it like a sponge. When gurus have been touched by people with strong anger, hatred, or desire, they will often complain that their feet are burning from the passions of their devotees. Several gurus in Bengal mentioned this to me as one of the problems of the profession.

23. This story was told to me by an informant. There are many stories of Vaiṣṇava devotees who burned themselves while serving Kṛiṣhṇa and Rādhā in their paradise and who returned to their physical bodies and saw that their physical hands were burned.

24. Variants of the story of Satī are found in the *Mahābharata* and in the *Devībhāgavata, Kālikā, Matsya, Padma, Kūrma,* and *Brahmanda purāṇas,* though the most well-known version comes from Kālīdāsa's *Kumārasaṃbhava.* These variants are discussed in Sircar 1948.

25. As the story describes it: "Suddenly, with her own hands, she twisted and tore her left breast from her body. Then she walked three times round the city, repeating her curse at each gate. In her despair she threw away her lovely breast, which fell in the dirt of the street. Then before her there appeared the god of Fire, . . . and the city of Madurai . . . was immediately hidden in flames and smoke" (Adigal 1965, 131-32).

26. For a description of the role of the fluids, see the chapter titled "Sexual Fluids in Vedic and Post-Vedic India" in O'Flaherty 1982.

27. Viśvanātha Kavirāja, *Sāhityadarpaṇa,* as cited in Sinha 1961. It may be noted that Viśvanātha felt that philosophers were incapable of aesthetic enjoyment, as they are devoid of innate emotional dispositions. Dharmadatta echoes this opinion—persons devoid of emotional dispositions cannot appreciate art: They are "as good as a piece of wood, a wall, and a stone in the theatre hall" (Sinha 1961, 166).

28. According to Dhanañjaya's *Kāvyasāhityamīmāṃsā,* erotic and comic emotions cause the blooming (*vikāśa*) of consciousness; emotions of courage and wonder bring about the expansion (*vistāra*) of consciousness; horror and fear cause the agitation (*kṣobha*) of consciousness; while fury and pathos produce the obstruction (*vikṣepa*) of consciousness (Sinha 1961, 169).

29. The *Nāṭyaśhāstra* is usually dated not later than the sixth century CE, but may have elements as old as the second century BCE (Gerow 1977, 245).

Such divisions of basic emotions are also seen in Western thought—for example, in Silvano Arieti's (1970) concepts of first- (protoemotions), second-, and third-order emotions. He includes tension, fear, appetite, satisfaction, and rage as first-order emotions.

30. Cited in Sinha 1961, 175.

31. Ibid., 207.

32. *Rasa* theory also describes the causes and effects of emotion in great detail. Briefly, the dramatic emotions contain several aspects. The *vibhāva* is the stimulus or cause of emotion (such as persons and events presented); the *anubhāva* is the involuntary reaction or physical effect of emotion; and the *vyabhichāribhāva* is the associated, temporary feeling or transitory state which may accompany the permanent emotion (*sthāyibhāva*).

33. According to Bharata, the moment of gustatory *rasa* occurs when the eater rests after the meal with a smile of satisfaction, appreciating the individual tastes merging into a general mood of happiness. This is similar to the aesthete appreciating the different aspects of a drama, which merge together.

34. The *bhāvas* and *rasas* relate as follows:

Bhāva	*Rasa*
love	erotic
humor	comic
grief	tragic
anger	furious
energy	heroic
fear	fearful
disgust	terrible
astonishment	marvelous

A ninth, peaceful emotion has been added to this list by later writers, though it has been much debated (as insufficiently intense).

35. See De 1963, 21.

36. This practice involves imitation of the *anubhāvas* to generate passionate feelings within the practitioner, based on the emotions of the original Kṛiṣhṇa devotees of Braj. The goal of the practice is the generation of a new identity—that of a handmaiden of Kṛiṣhṇa's consort Rādhā—composed of emotion (selfless love, or *prema*). For a detailed analysis of this practice, see Haberman 1988.

37. Kapoor 1977, 210.

38. According to the *Govinda-līlāmṛta* of Kṛishṇadās Kavirāj, the companions (*sakhīs*) of Rādhā are "like flowers and buds of the vine of love which is Rādhā," and when Rādhā experiences the joy of Kṛishṇa's love, her companions' experience of that joy is one hundred times greater than her own. See Kavirāj (463 *Gaurabda*). Because they are detached from ego and desire, they are more open to deeper forms of love, and can experience these intensely. Thus, detachment (from ego and desire) paradoxically leads to intensity.

39. There are special meditations which lead to experience of these intense emotional states. In the *mañjari sādhana*, the devotee identifies himself with one of Rādhā's handmaidens, while in the *gaur līlā sādhana*, he identifies himself with the servants of Caitanya Mahāprabhu, a fifteenth-century Bengali saint believed by devotees to be a joint incarnation of Kṛishṇa and Rādhā. See McDaniel 1989.

40. They differ in that the *sāttvika bhāvas* are composed only of *sattva guṇa*, and, as such, are purely spiritual emotions. There may be one or two at a time, or more than five may manifest themselves at once (in this case, the *sāttvika bhāvas* are said to be blazing, or *uddīpta*). While some of these may be caused by other events (such as sweating caused by heat or fear), the more of these bodily changes that appear, the greater the likelihood that the person is experiencing intense emotion.

41. A poem by Erfan Shah (Bhattacarya 1969, 55).

42. Quoted in Bose 1930, 76.

43. Cited in Dimock 1989, 168; from the *Śrīrādhār-krama bikāśa*.

44. Ibid., 195.

45. Probably the most famous example of *dveṣha-bhāva* is King Kamsa, the god Kṛishṇa's evil uncle and sworn enemy. He ended up going to Kṛishṇa's paradise because of his great passion for the god (even though that passion showed itself by threats on Kṛishṇa's life). The evil wet nurse Pūtanā was also blessed, though she put poison on her breast to kill the infant Kṛishṇa. When anger, pride, lust, and the like are directed toward the deity, they are purified and eventually transformed into love. The attention is more important than the ethical considerations.

46. There is a set of folk stories (told to me by several informants) that speak of a sage meditating in a cave who has tried for decades to gain intense love for the deity but leaves discouraged. A new young sage comes into the cave, begins to meditate, and is overcome by love and gains enlightenment in a short period of time. He has gained the love and dedication of the previous sage, who left them in the cave.

47. Marriott 1990, 18.

48. Ānandamayī Mā, in Bhaiji 1978, 68.

49. See Solomon 1976.

50. Ibid., 146.

51. In multiple-personality disorder, the selves are highly segregated dissociative states, developed during childhood as a response to severe trauma, usually repeated child abuse. Research indicates that the trauma must occur relatively early and that emotion and memory retrieval are bound to these dissociative states (thus protecting the child from a flood of painful memory and emotion). The most frequent alter-personalities are frightened children, though the most common chief complaint is depression. See Putnam 1988; Braun and Sachs 1985.

52. See American Psychiatric Association 1980.

Bibliography

Adigal, Prince Ilango. 1965. *Shilappadikaram (The Ankle Bracelet)*, trans. Alain Danielou. New York: New Directions.

American Psychiatric Association. 1980. *Diagnostic and Statistical Manual of Mental Disorders*. 3d ed. Washington, DC: American Psychiatric Association.

Arieti, Silvano. 1970. "Cognition and Feeling." In *Feelings and Emotions: The Loyola Symposium*, ed. Magda B. Arnold, 135-43. Academic Press.

Arya, Pandit Usharbudh, trans. and commentary. 1986. *The Yoga-Sūtras of Patañjali, with the Exposition of Vyāsa*. Honesdale, PA: Himalayan International Institute of Yoga Science and Philosophy.

Bhaiji. 1978. *Sad Vani*. Bhadaini: Shree Shree Ma Anandamayee Charitable Society.

Bhattacarya, Deben, trans. 1969. *Songs of the Bards of Bengal*. New York: Grove.

Bose, Manindra Mohan. 1930. *The Post Caitanya Sahajiyā Cult of Bengal*. Calcutta: University of Calcutta Press.

Braun, B. G., and R. G. Sachs. 1985. "The Development of Multiple-Personality Disorder: Predisposing, Precipitating, and Perpetuating Factors." In *Childhood Antecedents of Multiple Personality*, ed. R. P. Kluft. Washington, DC: American Psychiatric Press.

Dasgupta, Sri Birendramohan. 1983. *Samsad Bengali-English Dictionary*. Calcutta: Sahitya Samsad.

De, S. K. 1963. *Sanskrit Poetics as a Study of Aesthetics*, with notes by Edwin Gerow. Berkeley: University of California Press.

Dimock, E. C. 1989. *The Place of the Hidden Moon: Erotic Mysticism in the Vaiṣṇava-sahajiyā Cult of Bengal*. Chicago: University of Chicago Press.

Gerow, Edwin. 1977. *Indian Poetics*. Wiesbaden: Otto Harassowitz.

Haberman, David L. 1988. *Acting as a Way of Salvation: A Study of Rāgānugā Bhakti Sādhana*. New York: Oxford University Press.

James, William. 1902. *The Varieties of Religious Experience: A Study in Human Nature*. Many editions.

Kaelber, Walter. 1989. *Tapta Marga: Asceticism and Initiation in Vedic India*. Albany: State University of New York Press.

Kapoor, O. B. L. 1977. *The Philosophy and Religion of Śrī Caitanyai*. Delhi: Munshiram Manoharlal.

Kavirāj, Kṛṣṇadās. 463 Gaurabda. *Govinda-līlāmṛta*. Navadvīpa: Haribol Kutir.

Lutz, Catherine A. 1988. *Unnatural Emotions: Everyday Sentiments on a Micronesian Atoll and Their Challenge to Western Theory*. Chicago: University of Chicago Press.

Lynch, Owen, ed. 1990. *Divine Passions: The Social Construction of Emotion in India*. Berkeley: University of California Press.

McDaniel, June. 1989. *The Madness of the Saints: Ecstatic Religion in Bengal*. Chicago: University of Chicago Press.

Marriott, McKim 1990. "Constructing an Indian Ethnosociology." In *India through Hindu Categories*, ed. McKim Marriott. New Delhi: Sage.

Nelson, Andrew N. 1974. *The Modern Reader's Japanese-English Character Dictionary*. Tokyo: Charles E. Tuttle.

O'Flaherty, Wendy Doniger. 1982. *Women, Androgynes, and Other Mythical Beasts*. Chicago: University of Chicago Press.

Putnam, Frank. 1988. "The Switch Process in Multiple-Personality Disorder and Other State-Change Disorders." *Dissociation* 1: 24-32.

Schweder, Richard A., and Robert A. LeVine. 1984. *Culture Theory: Essays on Mind, Self, and Emotion*. Cambridge: Cambridge University Press.

Sharma, R. K., and Vaidya P. Dash, trans. 1983. *Caraka Samhita.* Varanasi: Chowkhamba Orientalia.

Siegel, Lee. 1983. *Fires of Love, Waters of Peace: Passion and Renunciation in Indian Culture.* Honolulu: University of Hawaii Press.

Sinha, Jadunath. 1961. *Indian Psychology, Emotion and Will.* Vol. 2. Calcutta: J. Sinha Foundation.

Sircar, D. C. 1948. "The Śākta Pīṭhas." *Journal of the Royal Asiatic Society of Bengal* 14(1).

Solomon, Robert. 1976. *The Passions.* Garden City, NY: Anchor/Doubleday.

Ethics of Emotion:
Some Indian Reflections

Purushottama Bilimoria

Jeffrey Moussaieff Masson, before he launched his even more controversial assault on the misdemeanours of psychoanalysis, claimed that the philosophical literature of India, with its tendency of world denying, professes a cultural version of "psychic fainting," a flight from emotions and from emotional entanglement. Great value was placed in ancient India, says Masson, on the ability to withdraw oneself from all but minimal involvement with the external world of human relations.[1] Masson compares this to the trend toward affectlessness in modern culture that psychiatry terms the "schizoid stance." This masochistic tendency to detach oneself from others and to exalt the detachment into a philosophical principle of sublime proportions was pushed to its limits in ancient Hinduism, Buddhism, and Jainism, Masson argues. Nevertheless, we can expect to find evidence, albeit veiled, of an original impulse which was so strong that it required this panicked flight.[2]

What might have been the "original impulse" from which the ancients sought to escape? Masson does not pause to answer this question directly. He hastily moves on to examine the presumed antecedent tradition of the solitary wanderer (*parivrājaka*), the man who renounces everything on account of the pervasiveness of pain (*duḥkha*). For example, Masson does grant, in half-scathing tone, that the Buddha's life reveals something about his concerns with emotions, insofar as the Buddha made *duḥkha* the cornerstone of his ethical teaching. But it took a severe depression, or melancholia, for this distorted recognition to arise; in other words, the "Buddha was able to perceive a basic fact of human experience correctly, even if he erred in seeking a direction for its provenance." Hence the sharp diagnosis: Much within Buddhism is "a manic defense against depression."[3]

In this essay I shall put Masson's analytic judgment to the test in the battlefield scenario moments before the *Mahābhārata* war erupts. My larger concern is the treatment of emotion, especially in relation to ethics, in the Indian thought tradition. As all inquiry has to have limits, I shall confine mine to the

Bhagavadgītā as a text that draws heavily on the broader narrative and the philosophical underpinnings of the culture in question. More importantly, one of my objectives is to offset the immense prominence given hitherto in the commentarial literature on the *Bhagavadgītā*, to the apparently guiding emotion of *bhaktibhāva* (love in devotion). I want to suggest that this particular preoccupation overlooks the equally significant role assigned in the narrative, especially in its deep ethics, to the more commonplace affects or emotions. Neither does the *Bhagavadgītā* (hereafter *Gītā*), a seminal text of Hindu orthodoxy in the classical years, dismiss the value of emotions in the sole interest of promoting a detached pursuit of duty. Rather, I want to demonstrate, the *Gītā* seeks to understand the phenomenological intricacies of emotion, its relation to propositional attitudes or judgments of the intellect, and its impact on a person's action or inaction. I want, finally, to show that the *Gītā*'s resolution is more sanguine, culturally sensitive, and philosophically circumspect than appears from the traditional perspective of asceticism.

Before I state my thesis more concisely, let me anticipate a rider to it. It is that there is a major lacuna in the *Gītā*'s handling of the challenging and difficult emotion, anger, or what others might call the "virtue of moral indignation." I propose that the *Gītā*, like the *Mahābhārata*, whose cultural discourse it continues, repudiates even the slightest trace of anger, regardless of the context or environment in which it might be experienced. In the wider tradition, anger is regarded with the greatest of suspicion and even fear, as in the wrathful potencies of Śiva's other form, Bhairava, or in the transcendentalized terror of the blood-thirsty Kālī.

Notwithstanding this blind spot, the thesis that I want to underscore is that the *Gītā* is exemplary in seeking to anchor ethical deliberations within the cultural sensitivities which make implicit reference to and signal the "unthought" in the tradition. The "unthought" in this context pertains to the universal emotionality germane to human existence which struggles to find expression through the cultural and moral repertoire of a people. In other words, I hope to show that emotion provides the bedrock for moral thinking, for emotion checks the excesses of an overprescriptive orthodoxy and helps to mirror the stark realities of the human condition. Outside of this, ethics reeks of a set of impersonal principles and axioms, much like geometry.

The paper is structured in five parts. Part 1 presents, by way of background, a brief profile of emotions in the Indian tradition. This is important, as without some acquaintance with the terminology and variety of emotions recognized by the tradition, the reader may fail to appreciate the breadth of affective states and attitudes being analyzed in the substantive body of the paper.

Part 2 sets up Arjuna's exquisite moral dilemma. Here we explore the nature of the moral issue confronting a troubled warrior, which is introduced, I want to stress, by Arjuna's sudden lapse into a profound state of depression.

The emotional narrative is an indispensable part of the moral analysis that ensues. Part 2 ends with some broad reflections on the reasons for Krishna's opposition to Arjuna's humanistic concerns.

After a consideration of the curious absence of anger or indignation in Indian moral discourse in part 3, part 4 casts the foregoing reflections in a tighter theoretical frame that alternates between two models—one, akin to the Kantian maxim of duty over passion, commanding cold prescription of caste (and "station-wise") duty; the other integrating a sensitive and appropriate emotional disposition in decisions leading to right action. My argument is that this tension, despite Krishna's sermon to take up arms, is resolved in the *Gītā* along the lines of the second model. This resolution is more subtle and implied than it is explicit.

The concluding part 5 returns us to consider the relative place and role of *bhaktibhāva* in the schema of emotion that emerges in this revised reading of the celebrated text. Indeed, the emphasis given to *bhakti* should be seen as reinforcing the argument.[4]

PART 1: THEORETICAL BACKGROUND

Although there is no single direct equivalence in Sanskrit or Pali for the Western term "emotion" (*ésmovoir*, with its Latin origin in *emovere*, "to move"), there is a general recognition of the distinction of affective states from cognitive and conative states (though how the three are related will, of course, vary between any two traditions of psychology).[5] In fact, there are several terms that cover the broad range of emotions and feelings, as we will see. The tendency on the part of some writers to settle for one blanket term, such as *bhāva* (sentiment) or *vikāra* (literally "mental excitement"), can be misleading.[6]

Caraka, the early medical cyclopedist, presented a somewhat Jamesian picture of emotion. He traced pleasure and pain to the harmony and disharmony, respectively, of the bodily humours (viz. flatus, bile, and phlegm) and also of the mental qualities, or mental modes of the *guṇas* (viz. *sattva*, *rajas*, and *tamas*, which I render as lightness, movement, and heaviness, respectively). Caraka further maintained that jealousy and envy (*īrṣyā*), grief (*śoka*), fear (*bhaya*), anger (*krodha*), pride (*mana*), hatred (*dveṣa*), and the like are affections of the mind (*manovikāra*) which arise as a result of perturbations of the intellect (*prajñaparādha*). In this account, emotions are characterized as errors of judgment and action.[7] Suśruta, the founder of Indian surgery, held a similar view about the perturbability of bodily humors, which results from violent obstruction to any kind of desire (including sexual).

The Jainas regard attachment, aversion, and delusion as the basic springs of action. Mirth, sentient pleasure (*rati*), sorrow, fear, disgust, sexual attraction, anger, pride, deceit, greed, and so on, are recognized as separate affective categories. Generally speaking, though, love or affection (*sneha*) is considered to be merely a kind of attachment, and does not constitute a distinct emotion. Noninjury alone appears to be a positive affect. Resentment is described as intolerance due to the thwarting of one's efforts toward an object of desire. Grief is mental agony evoked by the loss of something; dejection (*viṣāda*) is produced by grief, which is a result of delusion, and it hinders sense-organ function. Fear (*bhaya*) arises from the possibility of danger or threat to oneself, and anxiety (*udvega*) is bewilderment caused by fear and greed (*lobha*). Pride (*mada*) is conceit (*abhimāna*) due to inflation of mind or ego; boastfulness (*darpa*), haughtiness, and excessive pride are likewise due to ego inflation.

The Tantra tradition locates emotions inside the *chakras*, meridional energy centres residing in the subtle non-corporeal body, whose consciousness is more dormant than awake. This may be compared with the unconscious of Freudian psychoanalysis.[8]

The Yoga tradition regards emotions as intellectual disorders or, better, fluctuations of the mind (*cittavṛtti*), which are classified as afflictions (*kleśas*) and linked to *karma* or residual action potencies (*YS* II.3-11). Like the Buddha, Patañjali in the *Yoga Sūtras* regards *duḥkha* as the fundamental emotion in response to the contingency of existence (*YS* II.15). Prominent among the afflictions that trigger dissatisfaction are attachment, aversion, and the desire for continued existence (*YS* II.3). Attachment is defined as clinging to the pleasurable, and aversion, clinging to the unpleasant (II.7-8).

However, Patañjali proceeds to describe all suffering as due to fluctuations of the *guṇas* (the quality-agents of the body, senses, and mind). Since in any social intercourse all of the quality-agents are involved, whether in monitoring responses or instigating judgments and action, their subtly imbued shades inexorably impact on any kind of "motion of the soul." When the fluctuation of the mind is imbued with heavy or dark afflictions (from karmic demerits, etc.), the corresponding emotion is said to be one of pain or profound dissatisfaction; when the imbuing *saṃskāra* (psychic trace) is light (from merits, etc.), the emotion felt is that of joy and possibly pleasure (or at least absence of pain).

The Abhidharma Buddhist school has a similar theory about *kleśas* functioning as emotional predispositions or tendencies (*anuśaya*), which lie dormant or latent at the unconscious level. The *kleśas* are regarded as forms of psychic sedimentations that give rise to mental disturbances or excitations. Various English equivalents have been used to translate the term as "afflictions," "defilements," "affects," and "passions." However, among the *kleśas* the Indian theories include mental events—cognitive and conative and affective—that are not generally considered to be emotions in the West. Some examples from Yoga are languor, confusion, deceit, hypocrisy, doubt; and from the Abhidharma psychology we have, in addition, shame and embarrassment (and their opposites), concealment, spite, motivations, and wishes.

Again, in some respects, the concept of *kleśas* compares well with the postulate in psychoanalysis of the unconscious as the hidden ground in which certain more general as well as specific traits of neurosis are sedimented. And, accordingly, it would have to be accepted that, for certain seemingly spontaneous occurrent affects, the subject would be hard pressed to articulate a rational account of his or her beliefs, or even construals, correlative to the emotion experienced or manifested.

For example, when X breaks into a rage of anger and smashes a plate, he may later on confess that he did not know what had overcome him and why he smashed the plate. Did he have any belief about the plate as such? Certainly not, he might say; it was the nearest and most accessible inanimate object for him to, as it were, pour his anger out on. So how were anger and the object related in his mode of consciousness; that is, what was the precise intentional act in which anger or indignation and the plate featured? We may be forced to conclude that the relation was an entirely contingent one and, if anything, one that served to distract and divert attention from the pain or agony or sensation being experienced in that charged state. Thus, Yoga—and I believe Abhidharma, too—would argue that a reflex motor action is set off by an unconscious or latent disposition, which bypasses rational reflection altogether.

The Buddhist *Dhammapada* gives an interesting account of remorse (*anutapa*): The text avers that a moral action ought to be performed because to do so avoids remorse, and that an immoral action ought not to be committed because committing it would produce remorse. When a vile action has been committed, it excites remorse in the agent. Its characteristic is regret, and its function is to occasion sorrow about what has been done or what has not been done.[10]

The Mīmāṃsaka Kumārila Bhaṭṭa mentions a doctrine according to which an act is moral if it produces approbation in conscience and immoral if it produces remorse (*hṛdayakrośa*).[11] He criticizes the view and maintains that an act is moral if the *Vedas* prescribe it and that an act is immoral if they prohibit it. But he does not deny that a moral action produces moral approbation in conscience and that an immoral action produces moral disapprobation and remorse in it. Accordingly, remorse is recognized as one of the fundamental moral emotions: One who does not show any remorse for a vile act may be regarded as incapable of moral judgment and therefore incapable of refraining from similar behavior at a later time.[12]

Shame (*hrī*) is defined by the Vedānta as fear of social disapproval before committing an immoral action. Shame restrains a person from committing an immoral action. Some regard shame as disgust for immoral thoughts, words, and deeds, due to the apprehension that honest persons will condemn one if one so commits the act. For example, when one is about to utter a foul word or engage in a contemptible action, a sense of *vrīḍā* (shame), if it surfaces, would help to prevent the behavior.[13]

Time and again, the Indian systems analyze emotions and feelings in terms of the perturbations within the *guṇas* of the psychic apparatus. The ontology worked out by Sāṅkhya appears to undergird these analyses. The *Mahābhārata* presents a typology of emotions that follows closely the tripartite division of the *guṇas*: *sattva*, *rajas*, and *tamas* (lightness, movement, and heaviness). The states characterized by *sattva* are cheerfulness, joy, equanimity, pleasure, bliss, tranquillity, clarity, dispassion, forgiveness, nobility; by *rajas* are egoism, mendacity, lust, anger, desire, vanity, pride, hatred, discontentment, agony, grief, greed, and intolerance; and by *tamas* are delusion (or paranoia), indolence, oversight, nondiscrimination, and languor, among others. Pain is the consequence of *rajas* (*"rajasas tu phalaṃ duḥkham"*) (*BG* xiv, 16), while happiness (*sukha*) is a modification of *sattva*, which is constitutive also of good health or well-being (*ārogya*).[14] The *Upaniṣads* are not far off in their system of ordering the emotions, affects, and feelings, which revolve around the centrality given to desire (*kāma*). We shall deal with desire in more detail later.

We turn finally to the aesthetic school, which, in the course of developing forms of literary or dramatic criticism, exhibited comprehensive understanding of the range of aesthetic emotion or *rasa* (delight, *jouissance*). The aestheticians recognized forty-eight different emotions which people skilled in the arts are able to emulate in their respective performances and induce in the audience.

One issue debated by Mammata Bhaṭṭa, Daṇḍin, Abhinavagupta, Bhavabhūti, and other critics who have written on the aesthetic emotions is whether the induced emotion in an aesthetic experience depends on a preexisting emotional disposition in the audience. For example, Bhaṭṭa Lallota argued that, in the course of watching an exciting performance, the enduring sentiment of love (*rati*) is transformed into the erotic emotion (*śṛṅgāra-rasa*); while in another context, anger is transformed into the aesthetic emotion of rage.[15]

By and large, the Kantian view of a free-standing aesthetic sentiment, such as the sublime, is rejected. The general view is that aesthetic emotion has its basis in a predispositional emotion, which itself harkens back to some "raw" emotion in a real-life situation. The intensity and shade of the aesthetic emotion could indeed vary or be accentuated beyond the predispositional condition in ways that might take someone quite by surprise. Thus, a spectator may exclaim, while watching an enactment of Satī's fate, that she was not aware she could be overcome with such deep pathos.[16]

Culture and the arts help with the proper cultivation and maturity of *rasa*, which in turn stimulates creativity, both aesthetic and intellectual or literary. Kālidāsa, speaking through one of his characters in the play *Mālavikāgnimitra*, suggests that an art is esteemed on account of its intrinsic merit and that there is something of an element of universality about its appeal.[17]

Now if Masson still believes that the Indian tradition fled from emotions, he will have to account for the sensitivity the poets Bhartṛhari, Vātysayāna of

Kāmasūtra fame, and Kālidāsa expected their audiences to have. A cultivated predisposition for aesthetic emotions of various kinds is considered essential to an appreciation of their works, and that predisposition is based on feelings and affects that are part of the individual's native capacity to respond to life situations. As Pratima Bowes rightly observes, the distinctive contribution of these writers was a sophisticated theory of *rasa*, "a term coined to express the uniqueness of the aesthetic experience which is partly emotive and partly cognitive in nature. Aesthetic experience is a state of pleasure, but it is also a state of intuitive apperception of a structure or pattern that is based on human emotions."[18]

PART 2: ARJUNA'S MORAL DILEMMA

Let us now explore the opening scenario of the *Bhagavadgītā*. A major battle is about to commence. The bravest of the Pāṇḍava brothers, Arjuna, is perched on a chariot, which his friend and driver, Krishna, was asked to park between the opposing armies. Suddenly Arjuna loses strength and lets the powerful bow slip from his hand. He sinks down on the chariot seat, overcome with pitiful grief. Our task here will be, first, to highlight the emotive language used to describe this incident and, second, to draw out the relation between emotions and morals that begins to be outlined in these passages.

Arjuna, the hero, warrior, and prince, sees among both of the opposing armies arrayed in front of him "fathers, grandfathers, teachers, uncles, brothers, [their] sons, grandsons, . . . fathers-in-law and friends," and other kinsfolk (I.26f.). The sight throws him into confusion and deep pity (*kṛpayā*), and his mood is that of despondency (*viṣāda*). "Seeing my own kinsfolk assemble, eager to fight, my limbs become weak, [my] mouth dries up, my body trembles, my hair stands on end, . . . my skin has burning-sensation, I can't remain steady, and my mind wanders in confusion" (I.28-30).

Arjuna is outraged, and in this emotional fit he proclaims a moral perception: "I see evil (inauspicious) signs, and no real good in slaying my own people in battle" (I.31). He declares that he has no desire (*kāṅkṣe*) for conquest, "nor for kingship and pleasures, . . . for what joy (*bhogais*) is there—even of life?" (I.32). Imagining the death of his kinsfolk, Arjuna expresses intense fear that "evil (*pāpas*) would cling to us" (I.36), so he passes this moral judgment: "Therefore there is no justification in killing our own kinsfolk [*'tasmān nārhā vayaṃ hantuṃ . . . svabāndhavān'*]" (I.37).

Arjuna continues his sermonlike disquisition, appearing to offer tight arguments with consequentialist appeals to the evils of warfare: "the wrongs caused by the destruction of family, . . . lawlessness, leading to the corruption of women, . . . the intermixing thence of caste, . . . and the rescinding of family laws, ancestral rites, and timeless traditions, with the ultimate consequence of the collapse of society and descent into hellish chaos" (I.40-44).

What is presented here may be termed, pace de Sousa, a "paradigm scenario."[19] Everything about the scenario is significant; the meaning, structure, and context of the narrative run deeper than its rhetoric of ordinary language might suggest. For example, the chariot on which Arjuna is perched is itself a metaphor for the body; secondly, war itself suggests a moment of critical confrontation, in which the certainty and continuity of one's being are laid naked to the forces of contingency and upheaval. The body is the *locus classicus* of feelings, sentiments, and emotions, and the battle represents the challenges, exigencies, and stresses of the external world.

The first thing to notice is that Arjuna draws attention to his bodily identification; the body here marks the limit of the self. He reports a plethora of disturbing feelings and sensations overwhelming his body: quivering, shaking and jerking of the limbs, goose pimples erupting on the tissues, hair standing on end, the adrenaline running high through nervousness, heaviness of breathing, prickliness in the neck, flushing of the face, constriction of the knee, hand becoming limp, infirmity of posture.

The *Mahābhārata* had identified the body as the vehicle of pleasure and pain.[20] But the "feelings" in themselves are not, as Robert C. Roberts might also insist, emotions in a definitive sense. They are but symptoms of a mind in confusion, panicky, moody, paranoid, fickle, and indecisive. The feelings are not cognitive or intellectual states; rather, they are manifestations of "movements in the body," not unlike the thirst or hunger that accompanies depletion of fluid and solid in the body. And these feelings are transitory, as Krishna tells Arjuna: "Material touching [sense-object contact] that gives rise to cold or heat, pleasure (*sukha*) or pain (*duḥkha*), comes and goes, . . . is transient, and is to be endured" (II.14).

There sometimes develops, however, an attachment to pleasure or an aversion to pain. It is then that mere feelings become transformed into, or rather hook themselves onto, a corresponding state of the mind, a genuine emotion, such as excitability in the case of pleasure and perhaps fear in the case of pain. The point to be underscored is that the *Gītā* is quite categorical in its understanding of the distinction between feelings and emotions. And this has implications for the analysis of their differential nature and treatment.[21]

Moving on, the second point we notice is that emotion is characterized as intentional, that is, as being directed toward some object or event. A mere feeling may be an elementary sensation that is not intentionally directed toward any object at all.

The third point to note is that this affective directedness is marked by concern rather than some sort of abstract and detached apprehension, as in cognitive intentionality. This defines the ambience in which the object or situation is beheld by the subject. An example is the aura of romance surrounding the attention of a loved one. If the object of attention is threatened, one becomes afraid, perhaps even paranoid. And frustration of desire (*icchā* or *kāma*), in a context of attachment (*rāga*), results in dejection.

Furthermore, implicit in the emotions is an evaluative aspect or stance, from which certain judgments about good and bad, desirability and undesirability, are projected onto the object, event, or situation. One might call this evaluative aspect a "belief"; that is, the subject believes some state of affairs to obtain.[22] However, I don't see any compelling strict cognitive model of belief, with the strictures of truth conditions, has to be extended to emotions.

Belief in the sense of speech-act and judgment is more appropriate in this context. Indeed, the colloquial Indian term *viśvās* (or *Śaṇkā*) connotes a "soft conviction," a hunch or suspicion which, while a necessary constituent of an emotion, may nonetheless turn out to be false. This is so not because reflection is entirely absent but because the conditions that satisfy knowledge are not fully present. For example, while trekking through the forest and overcome by fear, I might say, "I have a suspicion that a tiger is approaching us from behind the bush," but I have not expressed any belief state.

In this regard, we notice that Arjuna's emotions reflect, wittingly or unwittingly, the moral repertoire of the community or culture of which he is a significant member. The principle of *ahiṃsā* (noninjury) was surely constitutive of his culture's self-understanding and its understanding of the moral order (*dharma*). But Arjuna feels an immense tension inside himself because his emotional response appears to be laced with a negative moral evaluation of the impending event, the value of which he thought his community had endorsed.

Arjuna immediately makes the connection between his emotional state and his inability to act in the expected or morally acceptable way. He has neither motivation nor energy to act, and he feels distracted from his real calling, his caste duty, namely, to engage in warfare. We see here that his emotional experiences are constitutive of his self-understanding; they are part of his judgment and belief.

Let us pause to consider what other hidden vistas his emotions may disclose. Arjuna finds himself challenging the norms of his warrior heritage, although he has no cognitive certainty about this, only doubts informed by counter-emotions that surface in his troubled consciousness. His concern does not seem to be part of any rational, purposeful project, and so he is not able to muster up convincing arguments for his lack of decisiveness. But if there is no argument, and reason is not responsible for the affective states that portend certain "evil omens," how does Arjuna expect to persuade himself, let alone anyone else, of the correct "point of view" and the proper course of action in the circumstances?

Arjuna is certainly aware of the impasse he has reached. He wonders if anyone, Krishna included, will be able to share and empathize with his perspective. The issue is a moral one, for whatever judgment he presently makes will have bearing on the course of action on which he decides. Befuddled, he cannot see his way clear to getting himself out of this sorrowful state, which he says dries up his senses (II.8).

Arjuna's dilemma is this: If he fails to fight, he betrays his noble caste duty as a warrior, but if he fights, he must share in the "guilt in the annihilation of the family" (I.38/39). Two passions or affects are in tension or utter contradiction to each other: the noble emotions of the warrior versus the strong ties of kinship. But if emotions do not have propositional status, then why should the contradiction matter? It matters, I believe, not because Arjuna finds himself thrown into some philosophical quandary, but because the tension is a source of unbearable existential fragility for him. Arjuna is unable to exert a direction for his action that would be right by the normative order he is committed to by dint of membership in a community.

And so the despondent warrior, fallen into self-pity, pleads to Krishna to help him make sense of his woeful plight. But, again, in this petition, is Arjuna appealing to the pristine virtue of reason over emotions, or is he instead asking Krishna to tell him if his emotions are serving him well? Can emotions prefigure morally appropriate, "objective," and reasonable responses, even if they appear to elude cognitive or rational discernment?

Krishna, seated by Arjuna's side in the chariot, turns to Arjuna in a friendly posture, but reprehends Arjuna for his unseemly timidity. With soft laughter, which can only be said to be sarcastic (a known ploy in countertransference), and almost as though to suggest that Arjuna's feelings are wicked, Krishna rebukes him for becoming despondent and embarrassed and for losing heart. The chariot here, if one can stretch the metaphor somewhat, takes on another significance: It can be compared to the couch of the analyst (which Masson, incidentally, failed to appreciate). On this "couch" rests a disturbed patient undergoing prolonged sessions of analysis, which, by some law of psychoanalytic magic, will result in a therapeutic healing of the dis-ease. The analyst encourages free association of thoughts, ideas, reactions, psychic feelings, and so on, which might provide clues or signs of the deeper structure of the client's unconscious.

Arjuna's objections to engaging in war are not based on well-thought-out and firm ethical grounds, except for some superficial consequentialist considerations; his arguments are scarcely coherent, and the appeal to his own conscience is minimal. But he is concerned that he is not able to see justice in the situation. His arguments appear to be rooted in his intense emotional reactions, the source of which he is not able to discern, for his intellect in this respect, too, is clouded by his negative affective states. At least, this is the message Krishna with his subtle innuendo and "body language" would attempt to impose on Arjuna.

We can wonder why Arjuna remains perturbed by his emotional condition despite Krishna's ironic attitude. On the other hand, why would Krishna want to dismiss his condition: Is it a socially improper or morally unworthy state to be in? Perhaps it is psychologically or psychosomatically painful and therefore bereft of utility? Or is such an emotional state simply irrational because it fogs well-intended judgment?

But is it not human to experience emotions, even negative affects? Haven't his emotions made Arjuna a little more reflective, muddled though he be, than he might otherwise have been? Is he not, as a result, at least "talking it out" with his friend, the charioteer-analyst? Indeed, might there not even be an obligation to have such emotions, just as there is a duty on Arjuna's part to engage in an action? Could duty itself be an emotion? The answers to these questions are never as simple as the Kantian, deontological approach suggests, as we shall shortly consider in more detail.

Indeed, Krishna's reticence aside, the text, in its own subtle way, is not blind to these possibilities. As a matter of fact, it delineates the contours of the problematic by deliberately setting up Krishna as a provocateur; his high moral brow is used as a ploy to accentuate the condition of the "poor lost soul" seated next to him. In the next section we shall take these reflections a stage further by looking at a theoretical development in the text itself, which will give us a keener insight into Krishna's initial reaction.

PART 3: ANGER

According to the *Mahābhārata*,[23] there are twelve negative emotions or vices that stand in the way of self-control and hence should be avoided: "Anger, desire, greed, delusion, possessiveness, compassion, discontent, pride, grief, lust, jealousy, and abhorrence." It is interesting to note that anger, followed by desire, heads the list. While Arjuna could be said to have harboured a desire for the kingdom in dispute (at least until the moment of his emotional collapse), he appears not to have expressed any anger. This is puzzling, given that he seems to have been overwhelmed by just about every other major negative affect. I want to dwell on this issue awhile.

It appears that the *Gītā*, here following the *Mahābhārata*, is open to alternative perspectives to the stark ascetic tendencies of the ancients. As we saw earlier, Krishna, although apparently denigrating, did not really deny or show utter disrespect for Arjuna's revaluations of his calling to war, his duty, and so forth. In point of fact, Krishna listened intently and recognized a touching concern. He only rebuked Arjuna, or, rather, questioned him, regarding the grounds on which he was making his revaluations, just as Arjuna could expect to be questioned were he making them in a perfectly "normal," rational state.

Furthermore, Arjuna proved right in the long run. Everything the beleaguered warrior suspected in his apparently confused, fearful, and besotted state—the destruction of the kingdom, the carnage of the elders, the collapse of family and tradition, and so on—did actually eventuate and was recognized to be so at the untriumphant, tragic conclusion of the war. Thus, the evil Arjuna had foreseen, and the reasons he gave for his fears in that most despondent and emotionally charged condition, played themselves out in the real world, although the moral judgment he ventured in his perturbed state was not what the society, in terms of the norms of the time, was prepared to countenance.[24] So why did Krishna believe that Arjuna's appraisal of the impending crisis, and not his own wisdom on the matter, was misguided, erroneous, and amoral?

To answer this question one must appreciate two presuppositions informing Krishna's assessment of Arjuna's condition. The first is derived from the following Upaniṣadic dicta:

> A person is what he desires;
> desires affect his resolve (*kratu*);
> this determines action . . .
> good action makes one good,
> bad action, evil.[25]

The other pertains to the relation between desire and karma or action. Karma is necessarily conditioned by an antecedent *kāma* (desire) and ineluctably followed by a corresponding *phala* (fruit), either in this or in a subsequent birth (*punarjanma*).[26] Hence, all actions bind, good ones to a pleasant fruit, bad ones to a painful one.

This view of karma can be rephrased in the *Gītā's* terms as follows: Let a person but think (*dhyāya*) of the objects of the senses, and attachment (*saṅga*) is born; from attachment springs desire (*kāma*); from desire comes indignation (*krodha*), when desire is frustrated; from indignation, bewilderment (*sammoha*); from bewilderment, wandering of the mind (*smṛti-vibhrama*); from wandering of the mind, destruction of the intellect (*buddhi-nāśa*); from destruction of the intellect, impairment of judgement . . . and the person is lost (II.62-63).[27]

Kāma with *krodha* is characterized as the "timeless foe (*nityavairiṇā*) of the wise man" (III.39). It lurks in subterranean regions of the self; "Senses, mind and intellect, they say, are the places where it lurks; through these it smothers wisdom, fooling the embodied self" (III.40-41). This is its link with suffering—the pervasive suffering which manifests variously as doubt, confusion, deceit, distracting thoughts, and, last but not least, erroneous beliefs. But what of anger in Arjuna's rupture?

Arjuna has been lured by *kāma*, desire that accentuates attachment to embodied existence. (Hence, Krishna tells Arjuna he should not lament the bodies of the living, whose death, in any case, is already in the hands of time, the great leveler.) Whilst renouncing all remaining desires for joy and power—desires to which he is entitled as a warrior—he retains other desires, or passionate attachments, which occlude his vision. By rights, the frustration of these desires should evoke a rage of anger, not just resentment.

Anger, it would seem in theory at least, should come naturally to Arjuna, for in his present constitution the quality-agents or "mood" (guṇas) of rajas and tamas overshadows sattva. This surely accounts in part for the weakness of his will and the lack of resolve in his determination (vyavasāya). However, nowhere in his introspective ruminations does Arjuna give any hint of being seized by anger.

There is one apparent exception: After having sketched the dire consequences of the war-to-be, and as if throwing his arms up in the air, he exclaims, "Ah! alas! mighty evil (pāpam) to perpetrate has been our resolve!" (I.45). But this posturing is followed immediately by those other revealing gestures of letting the bow slip from his arm and, saying it would be better if he is killed unresisting and unarmed, sinking back onto the seat of the chariot, his heart "overcome with sorrow" (I.46/47). This is not the way of an angry, livid being; rather, as Krishna points out, this is the posture of a timid, humiliated, and withdrawn man.

The explanation I favor is that anger, with the concomitant expression of aggression, is a greater embarrassment and threat than desire. For this reason, the tradition suppresses it at every opportunity. Also, anger, much like pain, is an occurrent state which need not last too long. True, there are numerous incidents and situations, before, during, and after the war, when rage and anger expressed by members of the feuding parties appear with some prominence. But these incidents merely exemplify the theory of self-control which the *Mahābhārata* adopts from the Yoga tradition. At no point does Arjuna's "blood boil"; he seemed too "cool-headed" and in a more pensive mood to suffer any indignation or afflict the same upon others. One cannot escape the conclusion: "Righteous indignation" fails to receive the regard in this tradition accorded it by, say, Aristotelian ethics.[28]

PART 4: DUTY AND DESIRE

Desire receives a great deal more attention than anger in the *Gītā*. Krishna, we may note again, has not denied Arjuna's inherent capacity to make a fair judgment of the situation; he has simply cast doubt on Arjuna's ability to reason and correctly evaluate his situation while in the grip of desire. Krishna, in his presumably higher wisdom or culturally privileged position, tells Arjuna that if he will rid himself of all desires and remain content within himself, he will be called "a person of balanced reason [sthitaprajña]" (II.55). Time and again, Krishna's sermon rehearses the evils of emotions such as anger, fear, passion, and egotism (vītarāgabhayakrodhaḥ [II.56]; kāmakrodhaviyuktānām [V.26]; vigatecchābhayakrodhaḥ [V.28]).

In practical terms, what Krishna expects of Arjuna or any adept is not to forfeit or relinquish these emotions in their entirety but rather to exercise equanimity toward their extremes. Krishna preaches even-mindedness toward pleasure and pain—in general, indifference toward pairs of opposites (I.57, II.38, II. 45)—as well as not being too excited when experiencing joy nor feeling ruffled when facing sorrow (V.20).

The seat of reason is *buddhi* (intelligence), and it is toward its stabilization and refinement that the qualities being inculcated are directed. While one can use yogic methods to withdraw from the objects of sense in order to prevent further sensations from arising—as the oft-used metaphor of the tortoise withdrawing its head suggests—it is not so easy to curb emotions. Tranquillity, achieved through prolonged practice of concentration of the mind, is necessary for the "cessation of all sorrows" (II.65). Nonviolence, veracity, absence of anger, compassion for all beings, and freedom from desire are among the highest virtues the art of yoga enables one to master. These are not achieved by rescinding anything or by the denial of one's inner being-nature (*svabhāva*).

If one cultivated the alternative emotion of detachment (*asakti*) (III.25), freeing oneself from the temptations of *kāma* (desire) and also anger, then one would achieve a state of reasonable intelligence (*vyavasāyātmika buddhiḥ* [II.41]) and, in this resolute state, be able to determine the best course of action. Such action would be *niṣkāma* (empty of desire). Actions carried out in this state do not bind one, that is to say, karma no longer accrues, for one no longer expects rewards from one's actions (II.39, VI.14). Desire and self-interest bracketed, one is left to perform actions from duty. In Arjuna's case, this would entail carrying out his caste duty, which is to take up arms and fight. This also accords with his own nature.

Interestingly, this locution about duty without regard to the fruits of action begins to sound like the Kantian maxim of duty over passion. I want to suggest, however, that this is not an appeal to a deontological imperative with a strong "ought" component. Rather, it involves a significant apprehension of a situation, with a strong "is" component.

It is one thing to say categorically, "Do X, according to your duty, without regard to desire," but quite another to say, appealing to prudence, "Do X, according to your duty, when you are at peace with desire." The former can lead to suppression of desire and pathological inclinations, for it ignores the impact on the subject's well-being as well as the subject's connections to a cultural system of values. (For Kant, as is well known, action motivated by desire, or even by our feelings of sympathy, love, and concern, does not count as morally worthy unless it also conforms to the moral law, which alone is indispensable [cf. Kant 1948]). The latter, on the other hand, clearly draws attention to, and challenges one to come to terms with, desire, recognizing that unless one is at peace, the mental life, which in turn affects the moral constitution, may not be firm (*dhṛti*) enough to guarantee a balanced harmonious judgment nor also, therefore, the goodness of the fruits or results of the ensuing action.[29]

The moral import of emotions is not, then, in this view, undermined in the interest of emphasizing the obligation in respect of duty. Indeed, duty is understood, appreciated, and reappraised through insightful emotional response. This response is modulated, on the one hand, by self-love and, on the other, by regard to the wider horizon of cultural sensitivities. Toward the very end of their enchanting though exhaustive colloquy, Krishna does not issue an unmitigated command to Arjuna; rather, he leaves it to his own better judgment, with these telling words: "Having reflected on this [my words] in all its ramifications, do as you desire" (XVIII.63).

PART 5: THE DENOUEMENT OF DESIRE IN LOVE

While desire is everywhere sought to be bracketed and sometimes even extinguished (a legacy of the ascetic tendency?) in the Indian approach to emotions, it is nonetheless acknowledged to be a significant component of the mental and spiritual lifeworld. And unlike in the earlier *śrāmaṇic* or ascetic traditions, the yoga praxis taken up in the *Gītā* does not aspire to the total eradication of desire; a complete dispassion, though desirable, becomes merely an ideal or a limiting concept after the Epics.[30] Instead, the *Gītā* offers a different avenue to dealing with desire, which admittedly has not been entirely uprooted and may never be. Here the Freudian insight of sublimation proves to be instructive.

The energy (*śakti*) of desire can be redirected to another object of concentration and thereby transformed into another passion, viz. love. When the intentional structure of this transfigured passion is constitutive of a transcendental object other than the subject's ego (*ahaṃkāra*), such as a divine representation, this particular passion is called *bhakti* (devotion). The transformative praxis requires minimal intervention by intelligence, for it is largely a matter of substituting for all and sundry objects of desire the image of "Me, the Imperishable"—the transcendental Subject-ive that exceeds all empirical embodiments, including the superego.

In this context, desire takes on a different dimension and colour. The symbiotic relationship between subject and Subject has the capacity to elicit much *jouissance* and a tremendous sense of *communitas*. Here is a challenge to the Buddhist-*śrāmaṇic* assumption that all suffering is rooted in desire.

The transformation may be effected by three interrelated disciplines. The first, as we have seen, is *yoga* (or better, *buddhi-yoga*), which seeks to restrain the mind, holding thoughts in check, and which culminates in *samatva*, a sameness-and-indifference with regard to all pairs of opposites (*dvandva*), or even-mindedness in the face of pleasure and pain, joy and sorrow, and so forth (VI.8). Indifference or even-mindedness, which I distinguish from complete dispassion, is considered to be an affect, for it is not the same as disaffection.

The second discipline is *niṣkāma karma,* which integrates *samatva* with the resolution to act with detachment (*asakti*). Again, one can argue that detachment implies not a severing of affect itself but a degree of aloofness, a bracketing or *epoché* performed on the intentional. Desire is not suppressed, nor its object obliterated; instead, the relationship between the subject and the other (*parataḥ*) is freed to transcend mundane expectations.

This brings us to the third discipline, *bhaktibhāva,* which instills the sentiment that all action is performed for some universal good. The individual is conceived as working for and collaborating with an agent who surpasses the individual ego. I suggest that this image of a *Paramātma* or transcendental agent is nothing more than a rhetorical slide show (as the great theophanic display in chapter 11 evinces). Or, in other terms, it is a heuristic move; psychoanalysis might recognize it as an act of positive transference and projective identification on the part of a fractured, fragile, and quivering personality, who looks up to another self, the not-very-other (*aparataḥ*), the idealized subject, as a better integrated personality.

In this identification, love, the most passionate of passions, is, as it were, boomeranged back to the individual; "I return my love in the same way that people bequeath theirs to me" (IV.11). The objective of this act of "grace" is to increase the individual's self-esteem and, hence, ability to be responsible for his or her own ethical guidance.

While this is in many ways different from a one-to-one relationship between two human individuals, the motivation is nevertheless not dissimilar. The net effect is that of transforming one passion (e.g., selfishness) into another (viz. love) which makes one "intent on" the other (cf. II.61), "trusting-and-loving" of the other, and so on (VII.16). Love (*bhāva*) also engenders firmness (*dhṛti*) in the mind, thus returning one, integrated in mind and body, to the field of *dharma* or the ethical life-world. Alternative to theistic images, the *bhāva* that is summoned up here bears comparison to the kind of loving attitude or deeply encompassing, self-effacing respect that some ecologists have called for in another context.

This, then, is the *Gītā*'s way of rekindling intellectual passion by arresting emotionally depleting passions and reorienting the perceptual field (*kṣetrajña*) toward a more balanced outlook on the world. The end result is to surrender neither to the dictates of a despotic orthodoxy, or orthopraxy, hitherto bridled to the fruits of sacrificial action (*yajña*), nor to the world- and self-denying tendencies of asceticism, with its diminution of the role of emotions and passions in the life-world. Rather, the *Gītā* settles for something of a middle position that attempts to reconcile the two opposing strands.

It should, however, be said in conclusion, that it is precisely in its sensitivity not to ride roughshod over either of the two strands that the *Gītā* also compromises the more sanguine *Mahābhārata*, Purāṇic, and aesthetic acceptance of emotions in human life—indeed, in all life. Notwithstanding its own qualification that desirelessness (*niṣkāma*) is only in respect of the fruits and not of desire itself, the *Gītā* clearly accedes to the thrust of *niṣkāma*, even regarding love.

Another final criticism, which has been made all too often but is worth repeating, is that the *Gītā*'s commitment is to a particular moral framework, established by the larger Epic, which remains bounded and is not open to radical revision. The only slightly modified or revised conception of a caste-based social order—with the concomitant power relations among the broad groupings, and the particularized expectations, privileges, entitlements, correlative duties, and so forth—continues to determine and give specific weight and nuance to what it is for something X (proposition, situation, felt-state, disposition, etc.) to be ethical and whatnot. This places certain constraints on the way emotions are linked to ethical concerns, which come under the rubric of *dharma*, its own culturally sensitive expression of the "unthought" (cf. Wittgenstein's "unsayable") undergirding all human strivings.

But to recognize this fact is also to recognize that reflection on emotions cannot proceed without paying specific attention to the general ethical framework or moral discourse of the culture in which they have their *bāshō* or *topoi*. Which emotions are to be cultivated and how these are to be used for adaptive and energizing purposes, and which are to be deemed wicked and how these, too, fare to be dealt with, depend on the mores of a culture.

Perhaps it is as Hildred Geertz has argued, that while the range and quality of emotional experience is potentially the same for all human beings, socialization selects, elaborates, and emphasizes certain qualitative aspects from within this range.[31] It follows that there may be certain emotions linked in certain ways to what is considered to be ethical (and aesthetic) life in one culture which are conspicuous by their absence from another culture. Thus, we end with a conundrum that has hovered over this inquiry: How is it that the Indian aestheticians identified some forty-eight (positive and negative) emotions, allegedly common in human life, while less than half of these are recognized or admitted as emotions, when distinguished from sensations, feelings, and peripheral affects, by Western theories of emotions?

Notes

*This paper owes a lot to discussions with Renuka Sharma and to the participants at the East-West Philosophy Conference (3rd Regional International) in Brisbane, July 1992, where an earlier version of the paper was read. Krysten Saunders provided invaluable help with data search; Joel Marks helped to tighten up the analysis with his skillful editing.

1. Masson 1981, 3.

2. Ibid., 5.

3. Ibid., 7.

4. Of course, Masson would dismiss the *Bhagavadgītā* as nothing more than a simple, popular poem, a composite of philosophical tidbits from the Great Epic, and some watered-down ideas from the *Upaniṣads*, therefore not warranting attention for the kind of inquiry we are interested in here. I am not daunted by this apparent dismissal, precisely because, as I want to show, the text gives us a vignette and an entry into the treatment of emotions, unobscured by the sterility of language to be found in the philosophical texts. Nor does Masson throw any light on this aspect of the text in his short piece, "Did Freud Comment on the *Bhagavadgītā*?" I cannot begin also to list the plethora of works in recent years that have emphasized beyond everything else the "bhakti structuralism" of the *Gītā*.

5. See, for example, the excellent discussion of Buddhist views in de Silva 1991, 1992.

6. Cf. Kaveeshwar 1971, 157, 160.

7. Sinha 1961, 101.

8. See de Silva 1992, 68ff.

9. See de Silva 1992, 56ff.

10. *Dhammapada* 1966, 158 (ch. 22, 9).

11. *SV* 2: 246.

12. Sinha 1961, 151. See also Sinha 1949, 293.

13. It may be mentioned in passing that emotions such as shame, guilt, and remorse are cultivated and may vary in intensity in relation to a particular situation from culture to culture. See, for example, Salman Rushdie's novel *Shame*, which is itself a commentary on the predominance and exploitation of shame in Islamic culture.

14. *MhB* (*Śāntiparva*) ch. 313, 17; *BG* xiv, 6.

15. Sinha 1961, 170.

16. Bhavabhūti describes the sentiment of pathos (*karuṇā*) as the fundamental emotion that dominates all others (Karmakar 1971, 64).

17. Kālidāsa 1966, act I, scene 4.

18. Bowes 1977, 147.

19. de Sousa 1987, 48, 181. I am using this concept in the sense he gives, but does not develop, of "a semantics of emotion."

20. *MhB* (*Śāntiparva*), ch. 174, 21-22.

21. Not all feelings divide neatly into pleasure and pain; some feelings, according to Buddhist psychology, are neutral (*upekṣā*). This kind of *vedanā* (neutral feeling), is said to be the absence of pleasure and pain (Sinha 1961, 79). But while the Buddhists identify feeling with cognition (Sinha 1961, 83), Nyāya makes a sharp distinction between the two, making cognition a function of apprehension (*grahaṇa*) and feeling the intentional content of certain apprehensions (*grāhya*) (see Sinha 1961, 79-83). Uddyotkara of Nyāya considers pleasure as simply the absence of pain—pain and pleasure being inseparable and interdefining—while other writers generally take them to be opposites; and pain is produced by an undesired object or circumstance (*Nyāyavārttika*, vi, 2, 34).

22. Cf. Roberts 1988, 159; Marks's introduction to this volume.

23. *MhB* (Chicago ed.) bk. 4/5, 289.

24. Although grief and remorse there were aplenty; see *MhB* (Calcutta ed.) bk. VI onwards.

25. *Bṛhadāraṇyaka Upaniṣad* IV, 3-4; II, 2, 12.

26. Borrowing an insight from De Smet (1977, 59).

27. See also related *BG* verses: VI.41-45, IX.20-21, XVI.19-21. This view is not unlike the Buddhist treatment of action, with the difference that the *Gītā* situates *kāma* and *krodha* as paradigmatic of the passions and holds them in mutual tension (*kāma eṣa krodha eṣa*) (III.37). In this latter respect, therefore, the *Gītā* is closer, on the one hand, to Aristotle and the European schoolmen's doctrine of desire and, on the other hand, to the psychoanalytic focus on the link between libido and aggressiveness (cf. De Smet 1977, 59).

28. See Matilal 1982.

29. For further discussion of the difference, see Bilimoria and Hutchings 1988 and Bilimoria 1992.

30. Cf. Marks's introduction to this volume.

31. Geertz 1974.

Abbreviations for Primary References

BG = Bhagavad Gītā

i) *Bhagavadgītā in the Mahābhārata: Text and Translation.* Trans. and ed. J. A. B. van Buitenen. Chicago: Chicago University Press, 1985.

ii) *Śrīmadbhagavadgītā* with the commentaries *Śrīmatśaṅkarabhāṣya* with *Ānandagīrī, Nīlakānthi, Bhāṣyotkarsadīpikā* of Dhanapati, *Śrīdhāri, Gītārthasaṅgraha* of Abhinavaguptacharya. Ed. Laxman Śāstrī Pansikar. New Delhi: Muhshiram Manoharalal, 1978.

iii) *Bhagavadgītā-Śaṅkarabhāṣya.* Ānandāśrama Sanskrit Series no. 34. Poona: Ananda Ashrama, 1981.

MhB = Mahābhārata

i) *The Mahābhārata,* Books I-V. 3 vols. Trans. J. A. B. van Buitenen. Chicago: Chicago University Press, 1972-1978.

ii) *The Mahābhārata.* Critical Edition. Poona: Bhandarkar Oriental Research Institute, 1933-1970.

SV = Ślovakavārttika

Ślokavārttika of Kumārila Bhaṭṭa, with commentary by Pārthasārathi Miśra. Varanasi: Tara Publications, 1978.

YS = Yoga Sūtras

The Yogasūtras of Patañjali, with commentary by Vyāsa. Anandasrama Sanskrit Series no. 47. Poona: Ananda Ashrama, 1919.

Up. = Upaniṣads

The Principal Upaniṣads. Trans. S. Radhakrishnan. London: Allen & Unwin, 1975.

Bibliography (Secondary References)

Baier, Annette C. 1987. "Getting in Touch with Our Own Feelings." *Topoi* 6: 89-97.

Balslev, Anindita N. 1991. "The Notion of Kleśa, and Its Bearing on Yoga Analysis of Mind." *Philosophy East and West* 41: 77-88.

Bilimoria, P. 1992. "Indian Ethics." In *A Companion to Ethics*, ed. Peter Singer, 43-57. Oxford: Blackwell.

Bilimoria, P., and P. Hutchings. 1988. "On Not Having Regard for Fruits: Kant and the *Gītā*." In *Religions and Comparative Thought*, ed. P. Bilimoria and P. Fenner, 353-68. Delhi: Indian Books Centre.

Bowes, Pratima. 1977. *Hindu Intellectual Tradition*. Delhi: Allied Publishers.

Calhoun, Cheshire. 1989. "Subjectivity and Emotion." Philosophical Forum 20: 195-210.

de Silva, Padmasiri. 1984. "The Ethics of Moral Indignation and the Logic of Violence: A Buddhist Perspective." V. F. Gunaratne Memorial Lecture. Colombo: Public Trustee Department.

————. 1991. *Twin Peaks: Compassion and Insight (Emotions and the "Self" in Buddhist and Western Thought)*. Singapore: Buddhist Research Society.

————. 1992. *Buddhist and Freudian Psychology*. Singapore: National University of Singapore.

De Smet, Richard, S. J. 1977. "A Copernican Reversal: The Gītākāra's Reformation of Karma." *Philosophy East and West* 27: 53-63.

de Sousa, Ronald. 1987. *The Rationality of Emotion*. Cambridge: MIT Press.

Dhammapada. Trans. and ed. S. Radhakrishnan. Madras: Oxford University Press, 1966.

Erlich, Vera St. 1974. "Regional Difference and Emotional Climate." *Sociologia* 16: 61-71.

Geertz, Hildred. 1974. "The Vocabulary of Emotions." In *Culture and Personality*, ed. R. LeVine. Chicago: Aldine.

Green, O. H. 1979. "Obligations Regarding Passions." Personalist 60: 134-38.

Greenspan, Patricia D. 1981. "Emotions as Evaluations." *Pacific Philosophical Quarterly* 82: 158-69.

Harrison, Bernard. 1984. "Moral Judgment, Action, and Emotion." *Philosophy* 59: 295-321.

Kālidāsa. 1966. *Mālavikāgnimitra*. Ed. C. R. Devadhara. Delhi: Motilal Banarsidass.

Kant, I. 1948. *The Moral Law: Kant's Groundwork of the Metaphysics of Morals*. Tr. H. J. Paton. London: Hutchinson University Library.

————. 1978. *Anthropology from a Pragmatic Point of View*. Tr. Victor Dowde. Carbondale: Southern Illinois University Press.

Karmakar, R. D. 1971. *Bhavabhūti*. Dharwar: Karnatak University Press.

Kaveeshwar, G. W. 1971. *The Ethics of the Gītā*. Delhi: Motilal Banarsidass.

Lauritzen, Paul. 1988. "Emotions and Religious Ethics." *Journal of Religious Ethics* 16: 307-24.

Lynch, Owen M. 1988. "Pilgrimage with Krishna, Sovereign of the Emotions." *Contributions to Indian Sociology* 22: 171-94.

Lyons, W. 1980. *Emotion*. Cambridge: Cambridge University Press.

Marks, Joel. 1982. "A Theory of Emotion." *Philosophical Studies* 42: 227-42.

Masson, J. Moussaieff. 1981. *The Oceanic Feeling: The Origins of Religious Sentiment in India*. Dordrecht: D. Reidel.

Matilal, Bimal K. 1982. *Logical and Ethical Issues of Religious Belief.* Calcutta: Calcutta University Press.

Myers, Fred. 1979. "Emotions and the Self: A Theory of Personhood and Political Order among Pintupi Aborigines." *Ethos* 7: 343-70.

Nussbaum, Martha C. 1990. *Love's Knowledge: Essays in Philosophy and Literature*. New York: Oxford University Press.

Nyāyavārttika. In *Nyāyadarśana* with *Bhāṣya* of Vātsyāyana. Ed. Anantalal Thakur. Mithila: Mithila Institute of Indological Research, 1967.

Oakley, Justin. 1992. *Morality and the Emotions*. London: Routledge.

Putnam, Daniel. 1987. "Sympathy and Ethical Judgments: A Reconsideration." *American Philosophical Quarterly* 24: 261-66.

Ramachandra Rao, S. K. 1962. *Development of Psychological Thought in India*. Mysore: Kavyalya.

Roberts, Robert C. 1988. "What an Emotion Is: A Sketch." *Philosophical Review* 97: 183-209.

————. 1991. "What Is Wrong with Wicked Feelings." *American Philosophical Quarterly* 28: 13-24.

Rorty, Amélie Oksenberg. 1982. "From Passions to Emotions and Sentiments." *Philosophy* 57: 159-72.

Rorty, Amélie Oksenberg, ed. 1980. *Explaining Emotions*. Berkeley: University of California Press.

Sankowski, Edward. 1977. "Responsibility of Persons for Their Emotions." *Canadian Journal of Philosophy* 7: 829-40.

Sinha, Jadunath. 1949. *Introduction to Indian Philosophy*. Agra: Lakshmi Narain Agarwal.

————. 1961. *Emotion and Will*. Vol. 2 of *Indian Psychology*. Calcutta: Sinha.

Solomon, Robert C. 1976. *The Passions: The Myth and Nature of Human Emotion*. Garden City, NY: Anchor/Doubleday.

————. 1988. "On Emotions as Judgments." *American Philosophical Quarterly* 25: 183-91.

Stocker, Michael. 1979. "The Schizophrenia of Modern Ethical Theories." *Journal of Philosophy* 73: 453-66.

————. 1987. "Emotional Thoughts." *American Philosophical Quarterly* 41: 59-69.

Wierzbicka, Anna. 1986. "Human Emotions: Universal or Culture-Specific?" *American Anthropologist* 88: 584-94.

Ecstasy and Epistemology

Leroy S. Rouner

East-West philosophical dialogue is possible because we all share some common ground. Within the realm of human experience, the fundamental emotions are part of this universal ground. When Golda Meir was Prime Minister of Israel, she once noted that Arab mothers, mourning their dead soldier sons, felt the same grief that Israeli mothers did in mourning theirs. Grief, love, fear, and anger are common to us all, despite the different cultural contexts in which these emotions take place, the different ways we have of expressing them, and the different meanings we attach to them.

This view has long represented the common wisdom in the West, but has recently been challenged extensively by Catherine A. Lutz.[1] Before I can proceed with my issue, I clearly need to engage hers.[2] I will propose two theses: one defends the universality of primary human emotions; the second compares and contrasts the way in which one such emotion—ecstasy—is a bearer of transcendental truth in both East and West.

I

There is much to criticize in universalistic pronouncements about human nature and culture. They came easily to those whose mindset was fashioned by the politics of Western colonialism. These universalistic assumptions either obscured significant cultural differences or declared other cultures "primitive" if they failed to reflect Western universalistic assumptions. As feminist scholars have pointed out, far from being genuinely universal, these were often only the tribal views of one sex from a certain social class and a single racial group—the dominant white Western male. The gift of cultural relativism to comparative studies—especially in philosophy, anthropology, and religion—is its openness to cultures significantly different from our own. That openness includes not only empathy with different worldviews but acceptance of different value systems.

For example, I had previously assumed that human rights was a universal value, only to discover that China has historically found this doctrine a divisive threat to its sense of community.[3] On the other hand, cultural relativism has its own pitfalls. One of the justifications used for brutalities against Vietnamese villagers by American troops during the Vietnam War was that the Vietnamese didn't feel about death "the way we do," and therefore lacked something in fundamental humanity. But this dehumanizing use of cultural relativism, while not incidental, is not the philosophical issue at hand.

There can be bad uses of good arguments. Pragmatists, of course, tend to disagree. For them, usage is the only route to meaning, so bad usage eventually means a bad argument. But I suggest the contrary. The fact that colonialists of all sorts use universalistic arguments for purposes of cultural domination doesn't mean that universality is therefore invalid, any more than my Vietnam illustration means that relativism is wrong. I agree that cultural practices *are* relative; that seems to me self-evident. The question is, Relative to what? I also agree that pragmatic "usefulness" is a good test of truth negatively, and in the short run I agree that if it *doesn't* work, it can't be true. And I agree further that "short views" best serve most practical needs of daily life. But for the meaning of life as a whole, we need something a little longer. Comparative studies are not possible without *some* "long view" element of universality. Relativ*ism* and plural*ism* are possible only on some universal ground; otherwise, one has only an unintegrated collection of unrelated ideas, values, and practices. For example, democratic theory could conceivably maintain its integrity without insisting on the universality of human rights, difficult as that is for Americans to imagine.[4] The reason for this is that human rights derive from a primary doctrine of democracy: the universal, coequal value of individual human beings. Democratic theory, however, cannot maintain its integrity without insisting on that primary doctrine.

This affirmation is not an empirical judgment. Indeed, as an empirical statement it is simply not true that "all men are created equal"—but neither is the affirmation just posited willy-nilly by those political communities that decide, for their own reasons, that they will treat all human beings as equal before the law. Democratic theory is an expression of belief in our common humanity. Classical Greek philosophy located that universality in human reason. Today, numerous philosophical efforts in the West to overcome the Cartesian dualism between mind and body have reemphasized the human significance of feeling.

My argument is that, along with human rationality, there are some elements of feeling which are part of our common humanity; and that these are inextricably intertwined with many aspects of our psychic life. Hence my thesis on the necessity of one emotion, ecstasy, for knowledge of rational yet transcendental truth in both East and West.

Lutz's concern is to counterbalance the prevailing Western view of emotion as a natural, precultural, private, yet universal phenomenon. This Western view is based on the dichotomies of modernity—body and mind, public and private, essence and appearance, irrationality and thought—and she deconstructs those dichotomies. At the same time, she presents a view of emotion as a social construct rather than a precultural element of human nature. Because it is social, emotion is therefore "unnatural." Emotions are a means of negotiating our social interaction. She presents this view through analysis of a premodern culture on Ifaluk, one of the Caroline Islands of the Pacific.

Since individuality is always derivative from the community of family and tribe in premodern societies, the social construction of emotional life is not hard to establish in these societies. But she argues that this is equally true of emotion in modern societies. Here I think she overstates her case, but she nevertheless makes an important point: Much of what we feel is not simply an inner, isolated emotion but the result of interaction with others and with our natural surroundings. And "emotion words" (she is studying our language about emotions) are, indeed, a cultural construct and not unproblematic tokens of an unchangeable inner essence that is the same worldwide.

Lutz's zest for deconstruction and for reshaping the conventional wisdom of the West is fair-minded, generous, and mindful of the need for balance. She is really challenging Western assumptions about the *importance* given to universality in emotional life, the weight we give it. She is proposing a different way of understanding that life and of weighting that issue. She is not arguing that there is no universality or that there is no "natural" or biological basis for emotion. She makes a case for looking at emotions in a different light than has been characteristic of Western thought since Descartes, but she acknowledges the need for *some* element of universality in order to make sense of our comparative study. "It is important to stress again in conclusion that the biological basis of human experience, including that termed emotional, is not denied here. Rather, the point has been to critique essentialism in the understanding of emotion and to explore the relatively neglected ways in which social and cultural forces help to give emotions their observed character."[5]

And again:

> One of the classic problems in ethnographic description concerns the degree to which we paint the members of another society as either 'just like us' or as 'not at all like us.' The former strategy tends to be associated with an anthropologist's assumption of a *basically universal human nature*, while a more exotic rendering of others is often correlated with a more relativistic or culturological stance. The dilemma in cultural description is how to *balance the competing demands* of these two tendencies such that these other people can be portrayed as *recognizably human* without 'human-ness' being reduced to the terms of a Western and hence culturally provincial definition.[6]

I differ from Lutz largely in emphasis. I am primarily concerned with cross-cultural community building, so elements of universality have special appeal for me. But on the historical issue I am prepared to be somewhat less genial. The communalism of the Ifaluk people is admirable in itself and a fine illustration of her clearly stated Marxist sympathies; but it strikes me as largely irrelevant to the contemporary world, which is rapidly modernizing. The great achievement of modernity in the West has been to break through those communal constraints which bound individuals to the totalitarian expectations, however benign, of tribe and clan. It freed them for hitherto unknown possibilities of personal fulfillment. Yes, we moderns are lonely and homeless and afraid; but we are free. The nineteenth-century liberal idea of progress may have been simplistic; but there is a ratchet of sorts built into the twists and turns of history. Some discoveries, both on the level of technic and of morals, are lost; but others, once discovered, remain with us. The current spread of democracy, I suggest, is a case in point. We can't go home again to the comforting constraints of the old premodern communalism.[7] More than that, we have an experience of emotion as belonging to us as individuals which remains even after we have given social influences their due. Lutz admits that we do indeed "experience emotion as something that rises within the boundaries of our bodies," but she counters that "the decidedly social origins of our understanding of the self, the other, the world, and experience draw our attention to the impersonal processes by which something called emotion or some things like joy, anger, or fear come to be ascribed to and experienced by us."[8] I may have missed something, but I find no definitive argument that this personal experience is totally replaced by an experience of "decidedly social origins of the self."

But Lutz is no dogmatist. She presents her work as a "temporary truce among contending forces"[9] in the good hope that her research "more clearly illuminates some of the alternative ways people can become passionately involved in the world."[10] Her study is a major contribution toward recognizing the need for community in a modern world that is indeed lonely, homeless, and afraid and for overcoming the dichotomy between thought and emotion that has become a modern sickness. The reflections on ecstasy and epistemology which follow seek to overcome that dichotomy.

II

Ecstasy is "the state of being 'beside oneself,'" or "standing outside one's self." *Exstasis*, in classical Greek, meant "insanity" or "bewilderment," but in late Greek it came to mean "withdrawal of the soul from the body, mystic or prophetic trance." From the sixteenth century onward, the English word *ecstasy* indicated "intense or rapturous delight."[11] Numerous forms of ordinary experience are familiar to us all in which we would describe ourselves as "being ecstatic." The moment of athletic victory, the height of sexual orgasm, the actor's or politician's reception of applause, the mother's bliss after the pain of childbirth. This is all human stuff we share in common, and provides a window on the deeper dimensions of ecstatic experience and its philosophical significance.

Philosophically, ecstasy is a special case among the emotions, for two reasons: first, because it is a bearer of the distinctively human experience of self-transcendence; second, because ecstasy is the intense expression of happiness, and philosophers East and West have regularly argued that happiness is the primary goal of human life.

Self-transcendence is that distinctive capacity of the human mind (as opposed to animal mentality) of "standing outside," or "being beside," ourselves. This capacity of a subject to see itself as object—a self observing itself—makes self-knowledge possible. My dog is very smart, has a certain self-awareness, and can be intensely happy; but she lacks self-knowledge, and is not capable of ecstasy in the philosophical sense. She cannot "stand outside" herself, observing herself in the act of being herself. So she cannot know herself. I know that I am a man. She does not know that she is a dog.[12]

The various popular definitions of humankind are all based on this distinctive human capacity for self-transcendence, or standing outside ourselves. Whether one defines humankind as the rational animal or the animal who laughs or the animal who goes to school, one presupposes the capacity to stand outside oneself and the self-knowledge that is possible as a result. Human rationality is the capacity for abstraction and generalization, which "stands outside" the particularities of immediate experience. The capacity for laughter is the capacity to stand outside an immediate situation and, from a vantage point "above" it, perceive incongruity, the basis of humor. Openness to education requires a self-transcendent vantage point from which the self knows that there are things it does not know and conceives a future in which these things can become known. The emotion that transmits this experience of self-transcendence is a weak and preliminary, but nevertheless authentic, form of ecstasy, whether the feeling is the grand "aha!" of intellectual insight or the more modest "ho ho!" of humor.

The relation between ecstasy and ultimate human happiness is more significant but more difficult to articulate, because any description of "ultimate human happiness" stretches the limits of language. Philosophers East and West have regularly argued that happiness is the goal of human life. Ecstasy is the definitive emotional form of happiness. In this case, however, the experience of standing outside oneself is one of freedom from the ambivalences, incongruities, and uncertainties of human contingency. Religious mystics in both Eastern and Western traditions speak of "peace" at the conclusion of this traumatic ecstatic experience. One has escaped the inherent conflicts and pain of human finitude. Whether one conceives of it as *moksha* in the Hindu tradition or the "Peace which passes all understanding" in the Western Christian tradition, the result is release, however briefly, from the dualistic conflicts of finite existence, and fulfillment in a transcendental unity.

C. S. Lewis has written extensively about this ecstatic experience, which he calls simply "joy." He argues that it is the meaning of the human search for happiness.

> It is the secret signature of each soul, the incommunicable want, the thing we desired before we met our wives or made our friends or chose our work, and which we shall still desire on our deathbeds, when the mind no longer knows wife or friend or work.[13]

In religious experience, ecstasy is the context in which both the insight of the mystic vision and the proclamation of the prophetic word are received. It is the state in which humankind is touched by the divine. Modern Western thought has tended to distinguish between this kind of esoteric ecstatic insight ("revelation") and sober exoteric reflective judgments ("reason"). While there is often a distinction between religious and scientific ways of knowing, this distinction seems to me to have regularly been overdrawn. Reason, East and West, relies on a degree of intuitive insight that becomes self-confirming through the ecstatic emotion that bears it. Reason must stand outside itself at two critical points. One is at the moment of the inductive judgment, when disparate facts are illumined by the universal which gives them meaning; the other is at the moment when one "sees" that the universals governing the inductive process are true.

Aristotle's *Posterior Analytics*, for example, presents the view—still true of modern science—that reasoning proceeds inductively from "facts" (whatever one may take them to be), or "particulars," to "universals" (*archai*), or "reasons why" these facts are as they are, and then deductively from these universals back to new facts. Universals are discovered through repeating the original examination of "facts" until we recognize the universal that gives them meaning because it is implicit in them. "When the observation of instances is often repeated, the universal that is there becomes plain."[14] The process of repetition winnows the "accidental" elements in each instance, so that the "universal" can be seen. So in medical experiments, one examines the facts under different conditions, and in different relations, to find what is causing the illness or effecting the cure. Numerous possibilities present themselves in the course of this process, many of them viable. How do we know which one is correct? Aristotle does not explain how the *archai* "become plain," but the conventional cartoon image of the scientist "seeing" the solution is of one ecstatically shouting "Eureka!" The image is appropriate. The scientist knows he or she has a solution, because, among a number of rational possibilities, the explanatory power of the emerging universal implicit in this one possibility has struck the mind with such self-confirming force as to make him or her ecstatic.

But how does one know that this universal principle is true? Here the ecstatic/intuitive element in knowing is more clearly evident, since the truth of the *archai*, in Aristotle, is not validated by reasoning but by *nous* (intelligence). In his *Aristotle*, Randall notes,

> We find universals in experience. We add two apples to two apples and find we get four apples; we add two marbles to two other marbles, and we get four marbles. In this way we come to learn that two and two are four; we "see" it in a kind of intellectual vision, we "recognize" its truth. But two and two are not four *because* of the apples, or *because* of the marbles: the apples are clearly irrelevant to the truth of the arithmetical proposition.
>
> Plato had put this, it is "like remembering," like "being reminded" of the truth, by experience, by observed facts. Aristotle puts it, we "recognize" the universal, the *arche*, by *nous*, by an intellectual seeing. These are two different ways of trying to express the element of recognition, of insight, in knowledge. We "see" the point, we say: it now "makes sense." This function of *nous* is like "seeing the point" of a story or joke. We either see it or we don't. . . . We grasp its truth by *nous*, by intellectual intuition, by insight.[15]

Since it is, indeed, like getting the point of a joke, Randall's illuminating account is too dispassionate. Anyone who has ever taught a small child that two plus two is four knows the difficulty experienced in making the leap from apples and marbles to abstract numbers. And because of that difficulty, the moment in which the child finally "sees the point," breaks free of the difficulty and finally "gets it," is inevitably a moment of delight. Once again, a preliminary form of ecstasy is the confirming context of intellectual insight.

The most profound ecstatic experiences, however, have always been associated with moments of religious insight. Rudolf Otto's *The Idea of the Holy* (New York: Oxford University Press, 1950) is probably the best known study of this issue, but Otto's book is primarily a phenomenology of religious experience. He explores the experience of receiving a religious revelation, but makes relatively little connection between this experience and traditional conceptions of reason, or epistemological theory. That connection is central to Paul Tillich's philosophy of religion. In volume 1 of his *Systematic Theology*, Tillich proposes a doctrine of "ecstatic reason" as a bridge between conventional theories of "reason" and "revelation" and, hence, on a broader scale, between religion and science.

Ecstasy—which Tillich defines as "standing outside oneself"—is the state in which religious revelation is received, but it does not destroy the rational structure of mind. "The reports about ecstatic experiences in the classical literature of the great religions agree on this point—that while demonic possession destroys the rational structure of the mind, divine ecstasy preserves and elevates it, although transcending it."[16] What is transcended is "the basic condition of finite rationality, the subject-object structure."[17]

This distinction is not unlike the distinction Aristotle makes between "reason" and *nous*. The truth of the *archai*, the universals of any science, cannot be confirmed by reasoning: Their truth is beyond reason. But the truth of the *archai* cannot be irrational, since this truth is grasped by *nous* and reason is a function of *nous*. So, also for Tillich, ecstatic reason is not irrational, it is only beyond the finite condition of rationality, which is the duality of subject-object relations. Ecstatic reason is the opening of reason to the infinite, the transcendent, the divine.

Tillich notes that this is the state of mind which mystics try to reach. The religious motivation for both the Christian philosopher C. S. Lewis and Indian philosophers in both the Hindu and Buddhist traditions is transcendence of the pain attending the dualistic clash between all subjects and all objects in the contingent world of reason. To experience Joy is to be beyond this conflict. The difference between Tillich and Lewis, on the one hand, and, on the other, many Hindu and Buddhist philosophers is that religious philosophy in the East has trusted that discipline and/or reflection could produce a historical condition in which humankind could be free of contingency and the pain of mortality, including the inherent subject-object conflict, which dogs human reason.

Christian philosophers in the West, however, have noted a persistent inability of humankind to transcend what Tillich calls "the human situation." The reason is that the Eastern notion of freedom anticipates that we can give up the subjectivity that, among other things, initiates the polar tension between subject and object in Western thought. Much Buddhist and Hindu thought either specifies or implies that "selflessness" is an achievable human goal. Most Christian reflection on the human condition finds "selfishness" ineradicable.

But, for Tillich, there can be moments of breakthrough to transcendent insight, when the ineradicable selfishness that Christians call "original sin" can be negated. No one can live permanently in an ecstatic condition, but "ecstatic reason" can give us a glimpse of what Lewis meant by that "secret signature of each soul, the incommunicable want" for what human happiness might be like. For Tillich, only the divine reality can satisfy that incommunicable want, and therefore, ecstasy is real only in a genuinely revelatory experience. "Ecstasy occurs only if the mind is grasped by the mystery, namely, by the ground of being and meaning. And, conversely, there is no revelation without ecstasy."[18]

The "ground of being" is Tillich's definition of God. Religious ecstasy is therefore genuine only if the ecstatic experience is of the divine reality. This is a necessary distinction because there is much intense religious emotion that does not qualify as ecstasy. "Enthusiasm," for example, means only the passionate emotional support of an idea, person, or value, and does not have metaphysical significance. By the same token, "ecstatic" movements among religious groups regularly confuse overexcitement with the presence of the divine. The storefront preaching services in East Harlem, the rural prayer meetings in Appalachia, the sophisticated enthusiasm of mega-churches across America— all are "enthusiastic" in Tillich's vocabulary, not genuinely ecstatic.

Nor is ecstasy simply a psychological phenomenon. It has a psychological side, but "it reveals something valid about the relation between the mystery of our being and ourselves. Ecstasy is the form in which that which concerns us unconditionally manifests itself within the whole of our psychological conditions. It appears through them. But it cannot be derived from them."[19] However, the phenomenon of overexcitement leads Tillich to a metaphysically valid experience, beyond excitement, which is that of "ontological shock."

God, for Tillich, is the ground of being-itself. God is experienced by each person as one's "ultimate concern."[20] Over against God, yet somehow also *within* God as being-itself, is the "threat of non-being." Human life is always divided against itself: time and eternity, here and there, now and then, you and me. And that reality of dividedness is rooted in the threat of non-being, symbolized for us in the inevitability of death. Human life is therefore "fallen," as symbolized by the story of Adam and Eve in the book of Genesis and articulated in the Platonic myth of the fall from essence into existence. In his *Confessions*, Augustine speaks of humankind's "restless heart," yearning for reunion with God. Tillich interprets this as the desire of the "existent" to be restored to its "essential being." The awareness of this fall is experienced as "ontological shock."

> The threat of non-being, grasping the mind, produces the "ontological shock" in which the negative side of the mystery of being—its abysmal element—is experienced. "Shock" points to a state of mind in which the mind is thrown out of its normal balance, shaken in its structure. Reason reaches its boundary line, is thrown back upon itself, and then is driven again to its extreme situation. This experience of ontological shock is expressed in the cognitive function by the basic philosophical question, the question of being and nonbeing. . . .

> In revelation and in the ecstatic experience in which it is received, the ontological shock is preserved and overcome at the same time. It is preserved in the annihilating power of the divine presence (*mysterium tremendum*) and is overcome by the elevating power of the divine presence (*mysterium fascinosum*). Ecstasy unites the experience of the abyss to which reason in all its functions is driven with the experience of the ground in which reason is grasped by the mystery of its own depth and the depth of being generally.[21]

W. H. Auden's *Christmas Oratorio* describes this "annihilating power of the divine presence" in lines spoken by the Star of the Nativity, announcing the meaning of Jesus' birth:

Descend into the fosse[22] of Tribulation
Take the cold hand of Terror for a guide;
Below you in its swirling desolation
Hear tortured Horror roaring for a bride:
O do not falter at the last request
But, as the huge deformed head rears to kill,
Answer its craving with a clear I Will;
Then wake, a child in the rose-garden, pressed
Happy and sobbing to your lover's breast.[23]

Tillich is careful not to reduce ecstasy to emotion, even though it clearly has a strong emotional side. "In every ecstatic experience all the grasping and shaping functions of reason are driven beyond themselves, and so is emotion. Feeling is no nearer to the mystery of revelation and its ecstatic reception than are the cognitive and ethical functions."[24] And he is cautious about equating the cognitive side of ecstasy with "inspiration." He notes that "inspiration, if it is the name for the cognitive quality of the ecstatic experience, cannot mediate knowledge of finite objects or relations. It does not add anything to the complex of knowledge which is determined by the subject-object structure of reason. Inspiration opens a new dimension of knowledge, the dimension of under-standing in relation to our ultimate concern and the mystery of being."[25]

Tillich is an existentialist who writes in the metaphorical and symbolic language of German Romanticism. This is not Aristotle's language, but the *structure* of the two views is comparable. For both, reason needs something from beyond itself to confirm its own validity. *Nous*, for Aristotle, is the tran-scendent power enabling his functional and naturalistic conceptions of life, reality, and rationality. The experience in which the truth of the *archai* of any science are confirmed in the mind is an experience, as Randall once put it, "of the divine *Nous, nousing nous* in us." We would say that we know the truth because the World Mind thinks the thought of truth in our minds. For Aristotle, as for Tillich, this event does not mediate knowledge of finite objects or rela-tions. For both Tillich and Aristotle, we don't know any *particular* thing that we didn't know before; we just know that what we already thought to be the case is, indeed, really true. For Tillich, the ecstatic religious experience simply confirms the reality of God. For Aristotle, *Nous* simply confirms the truth of the *archai*.

Aristotle's "God" is the Unmoved Mover, the first principle in a dynamic universe of becoming, who was later known as "the God of the philosophers." Tillich's God is both the God of the philosophers—the Ground of Being—and "the God of Abraham, Isaac, and Jacob" who is the ground of the per-sonal as well as the ground of being. Aristotle was interested in virtually every-thing, it seems, except religion. This omission is as odd as it is inexplicable, since religion is so widespread, so powerful, and so curious, and since Aristotle had so much creative curiosity. Without religious sensibilities, however, Aristotle was content with a minimal, and highly abstract, explanation of how we know the truth of the *archai*.

But if *Nous* is *nousing nous* in us, surely this is a major epistemological event, not comparable to ordinary empirical judgments. For all his murky language, Tillich's doctrine of ecstasy is at least a more comprehensive explanation of this fundamental knowledge event than Aristotle's. The rational examination of experience requires confirmation that the principles governing that examination are valid. That validation cannot come from within the process itself. Aristotle and Tillich are agreed that it comes from beyond rationality. But Aristotle describes the event in the ordinary language of rationality. Tillich is aware that the ordinary language of rationality will not be adequate to describe a transrational process. So he invents a new, metaphorical language that has its own pitfalls but that nevertheless takes seriously the dimension of transcendence in a way that Aristotle does not.

The phenomenon of ecstasy also functions in epistemological theories in the East, and is of special interest in the tradition of *Advaita Vedanta* in Hindu philosophy. A contemporary of Tillich's in this tradition, Sri Aurobindo, proposed a philosophy of *The Life Divine*, which proposes a somewhat different epistemology of ecstasy. Aurobindo believes in the possibility of a divine life for human beings. His opening chapter is a brief analysis of "The Human Aspiration," which he understands as "an impulse towards perfection, the search after pure Truth and unmixed Bliss, the sense of a secret immortality."[26] This is not unlike C. S. Lewis's preoccupation with "Joy," but it is cast in the classic *Advaita Vedanta* conviction that ultimate reality is *sat, cit, ananda* (being, intelligence, bliss). Bliss (*ananda*) is an ecstatic state, and, for Aurobindo, it is a permanent condition. For Tillich, on the other hand, ecstasy was a vehicle of revelation which came only from time to time. This reflects Tillich's Western Christian conviction that, while we can and must be briefly touched by the reality of God so that we know who we are, what our experience means, and what we are to do, it is not true to say that we *are* God. So the soul strives to overcome the ambivalence of finitude, and yearns for an existence that has recovered its essence, knowing that one must forever be a stranger and sojourner in this life, because we are different from God and prisoners of our finitude. We cannot escape "the human condition." The finite human condition is finally overcome only in the Kingdom of God. In this sense, the Christian philosophy of history is a tragic view of life.

For Aurobindo, however, *ananda* is primarily a metaphysical category, so it cannot mean primarily standing outside oneself in the literal sense in which Tillich uses the term. Because Christianity defines God as, *in some sense*, other than humankind, it is committed to some form of metaphysical dualism, however modified it may be in those philosophical theologies, such as

Augustine's and Tillich's, where God is defined as Being. Because of the gap between the reality of God and the reality of humankind, a Christian epistemology must explain how it is possible for us to know God. Christian theology regularly replies that, strictly speaking, we don't know God; God makes himself known to us—that is, God "reveals" himself through his Word, in the prophets, the scriptures, and definitively in the person and work of Jesus, the Word of God who has "become flesh and dwelt among us." The doctrine of Revelation has therefore been the foundation of traditional Christian doctrines of our knowledge of God.

But how is it possible for us to "hear" the "Word of God"? This question has gone unanswered in much twentieth-century Christian theology, perhaps most notably in the magisterial work of Karl Barth. Tillich addresses this issue directly, as part of his doctrine of Revelation, with the notion of ecstatic reason. We are able to hear the Word of this God who is radically different from us because we are able to stand outside ourselves. In so doing, we do not *become* God, but we do inhabit a mysterious and fearsome epistemological no man's land outside ourselves where, in a moment of ecstasy, the Revelation of the *mysterium tremendum* can be received. And "there is no revelation without ecstasy."[27]

For Aurobindo, the epistemological problem is different, because his metaphysical position is nondualistic. There is no radical difference between ourselves and what Heinrich Zimmer calls "the Transcendent Holy World Power" of *Brahman*, so the question is not How is it possible to know God but Why is it that we seem *not* to know God? Since the Self (*atman*) is identical with the Transcendent (*Brahman*), knowledge of the Transcendent must be presupposed in our knowledge of anything at all. And the place where we know this cannot be some epistemological wilderness "outside" the true Self, since the notion of "outside" is metaphysically meaningless for nondualism. The place of knowing is in the deepest dimension of that Self.

The characteristic human problem, as the *Advaita* tradition sees it, is that we are ignorant regarding the true nature of the Self. What we need to stand outside of, or escape from, are our ignorance and the unreal illusions with which it has clouded the mind. This knowledge event will not produce something new, like the content of Christian revelation. In a manner not unlike Plato's "remembering," it is a moment in which we "realize" a truth that was always in us, awaiting recognition. The moment of Christian insight is—to borrow the title of one of Tillich's volumes of sermons—"a shaking of the foundations." The moment of *Advaitic* insight has comparable spiritual significance, but is more like the lifting of a veil, release from the bondage of ignorance.

This moment of insight, however, then becomes much more personally empowering than anything in Christianity. Since one has finally discovered divinity within, the result is a release of divine power. Heinrich Zimmer, in his *Philosophies of India*, illustrates this point with the traditional fable about a tiger cub, brought up among goats, who ate grass and bleated until an old Tiger found him and forced him to see, in their two reflections in a pond, that he had "the pot-face of a tiger." Next he forced him to eat raw meat, and when the little fellow finally got the taste of the blood, he lashed his tail and roared "the full-throated roar of a tiger." His guru-tiger then asked, "*Now* do you know who you are?"[28]—the quintessential question of the Indian philosophical tradition.

Aurobindo's philosophy of the life divine is therefore a philosophy of empowering a new kind of human, a "gnostic being." "As there has been established on earth a mental Consciousness and Power which shapes a race of mental beings and takes up into itself all of earthly nature that is ready for the change, so now there will be established on earth a gnostic Consciousness and Power which will shape a race of gnostic spiritual beings and take up into itself all of earth-nature that is ready for this new transformation."[29] Unlike Tillich, for whom ecstasy is an epistemological principle and a momentary event, Aurobindo foresees an ecstatic life lived permanently in the metaphysical power of *ananda*.

But ecstasy is also crucial to Aurobindo's epistemology in describing the transition from ignorance to the state of blissful empowerment. This transition is essentially psychological. What changes is one's point of view. One can learn or "realize" the truth in the different schools of Indian philosophy through various disciplined ways, or *yogas*, such as the devotion of loving faith (*bhakti-yoga*). But *jnana-yoga*, the "way of knowledge" in *Advaita* philosophy, is the intellectual/spiritual realization that the "empirical" self is part of the world of *maya* (illusion). The true Self is the spiritual self, or *atman*. But the event of *Advaita* "realization" is ecstatic in the same way that the event of Christian "revelation" is, because the *atman* must stand outside its "empirical self" in order to realize its true spiritual self.

For Aurobindo, the transition from ignorance to realization is not a single radical occasion but an evolutionary process in which the world of illusion and the dominance of the empirical self is gradually left behind as insight and ecstasy increase. "Our gain in becoming more perfect mental beings is that we get to the possibility of a subtler, higher and wider existence, consciousness, force, happiness and delight of being."[30] *Purusha* (spirit) gradually overcomes *Prakriti* (nature or matter) in the emergence of the life divine. Self-discovery "can even put aside all relation to form or action of Nature."[31] And, just as for Tillich, this is not a state of "exalted emotional fervor." In discovery of the true Self,

> peace and ecstasy cease to be different and become one. The supermind, reconciling and fusing all differences as well as all contradictions, brings out this unity; a wide calm and a deep delight of all-existence are among its first

steps of self-realization, but this calm and this delight rise together, as one state, into an increasing intensity and culminate in the eternal ecstasy, the bliss that is the Infinite. In the gnostic consciousness at any stage there would be always in some degree this fundamental and spiritual conscious delight of existence in the whole depth of the being.[32]

Rationality, pure and simple, does not bear on its face an adequate explanation of how we know what we know, in either the West or the East. The problem, if I may appeal to a controversial principle, is one of foundations. How do you know that the principles on which your rational exploration is based are true? There is wide agreement that the rational process itself is not self-confirming. One can then say that there is no confirmation, and drift off toward other intellectual interests. Or—as I have suggested—one can take seriously the need for confirmation, since most of us believe in truth and seek it in some insight, event, or process which must necessarily transcend reason itself.

If we choose to take that route, there are resources in the philosophy of religion, and its various doctrines of ecstasy, explaining how we know what we know.

Notes

1. Catherine A. Lutz, *Unnatural Emotions: Everyday Sentiments on a Micronesian Atoll and Their Challenge to Western Theory* (Chicago: University of Chicago Press, 1988).

2. I am grateful to my friend and colleague Eliot Deutsch of Hawaii for questioning the universalistic assumptions in an earlier draft of this paper and for referring me to Lutz's book.

3. Roger Ames, Theodore deBary, and Henry Rosemont were my instructors in this matter. See their respective essays in my *Human Rights and the World's Religions* (Notre Dame: University of Notre Dame Press, 1988).

4. The coming democratic revolution in China will probably not speak of individual rights. It will speak instead of the individual's relation to the community; and the inherent dignity and value of the individual, which is fundamental for democracy, will be rooted in his or her participation in the community.

5. Lutz, *Unnatural Emotions*, 210.

6. Ibid., 11 (italics mine).

7. See my *To Be at Home: Christianity, Civil Religion, and World Community* (Boston: Beacon Press, 1991).

8. Lutz, *Unnatural Emotions*, 5.

9. Ibid., 228.

10. Ibid., 225.

11. "Ecstasy," in *A New Dictionary of the English Language* (Oxford: Clarendon, 1893), vol. 7, sec. E, p. 36.

12. This illustration is unpopular with my students. My German Shepherd, Maya, comes to class with me, the students are quite fond of her, and they

resent this philosophical put-down. "How do you know she doesn't know she's a dog?" I reply, "If she knew, she would have said so." This prompts a long discussion about whether knowing *has* a language or *is* a language. Then someone familiar with the dolphins-language literature asks, "How do you know she isn't telling you and you just don't get it?"

13. C. S. Lewis, *The Problem of Pain* (New York: Macmillan, 1962), 146-47.

14. *Posterior Analytics* II. xix. 100a5, 6, 100b4, 5. Quoted in John Herman Randall Jr., *Aristotle* (New York: Columbia University Press, 1960), 42-43.

15. Randall, *Aristotle*, 45.

16. Paul Tillich, *Systematic Theology* (Chicago: University of Chicago Press), 113-14.

17. Ibid., 112.

18. Ibid.

19. Ibid., 113.

20. For Tillich, as for biblical religion, the fundamental spiritual distinction in human experience is not between those who believe in God and those who do not. The distinction is between those who believe in the true God and those who believe in "false gods." Hence, the great sin for the religion of Israel was idolatry, not atheism.

21. Tillich, *Systematic Theology*, 1:113.

22. "Ditch" or "pit."

23. W. H. Auden, "For the Time Being, A Christmas Oratorio," in *The Collected Poetry of W. H. Auden* (New York: Random House, 1945), 431.

24. Tillich, *Systematic Theology*, 1:114.

25. Ibid., 1:114-15.

26. Sri Aurobindo, *The Life Divine* (New York: India Library Society, 1965), 3.

27. Tillich, *Systematic Theology*, 1:112.

28. Heinrich Zimmer, "The Roar of Awakening," in *Philosophies of India*, ed. Joseph Campbell (New York: Pantheon Books, 1951), 1-14.

29. Sri Aurobindo, *The Life Divine*, 859.

30. Ibid., 650.

31. Ibid., 762.

32. Ibid., 879-80.

Theoretical Perspectives on Emotions in Early Buddhism

Padmasiri de Silva

This study will focus on the concept of emotions in early Buddhism and how it integrates different theoretical strands like feelings, desires, cognitions, and bodily factors. It will also be concerned with the place of emotions in the good life and the moral dimensions of emotions according to Buddhism.

The Pali term *vedanā* (feeling, sensation, or hedonic tone) has to be distinguished from the term "emotion" as used in the English language. In fact, in the psychology of Buddhism, there is no generic term for emotion, though there are varied discussions of specific emotions, such as anger, fear, sadness, joy, and compassion. As Nyanaponika Thera says, "It should be first made clear that, in Buddhist psychology, 'feeling' (Pali: *vedanā*) is the bare sensation noted as pleasant, unpleasant and neutral. Hence it should not be confused with emotion which, though arising from the basic feeling, adds to it likes or dislikes of varying intensity, as well as other thought processes" (Nyanaponika 1983, 7).

Feelings can be understood in terms of the five aggregates (*khanda*), which go to make up what we conventionally refer to as a person:

1. Body (*rūpa*)
2. Feelings (*vedanā*)
3. Perceptions (*saññā*)
4. Dispositions (*sankhāra*)
5. Consciousness (*viññāna*)

Of these five factors, the concept of *sankhāra* provides a framework for placing the operative factors of emotion together. In the context of Buddhism, an emotion may be described as an interactive complex or construct emerging within a causal network. Thus, we should not expect to find an attempt to perform some reductive analysis into elements. Within this network, feelings, desires, beliefs, appraisals, and bodily sensations may be variables that generate fear, anger, sadness, and so on.

Negative emotions are fed by cognitive distortions and unwholesome desires. Positive emotions emerge on the path of liberation from these distortions and unhealthy desires. As I have shown in greater detail elsewhere, the emotion of anger in Buddhism (*dosa, paṭigha, vyāpāda, kodha, kopa*) is a completely negative emotion, while certain fears may be negative or unwholesome and certain other fears positive or wholesome (de Silva 1992c).

The concept of *sankhāra* also embodies the notion of intention and responsibility, so that emotions are susceptible to moral criticism. The notions of complexity, intention, aboutness (intentionality), and responsibility are evident qualities of the emotions discussed in Buddhist texts. Emotions can be understood in a *dispositional* or an *occurrent* sense. If we describe a person as conceited, we can refer to a special display of this feature in a certain context (refusing to recognize a former friend or boasting about his job), or we can consider conceit (*māna*) as a deep-seated propensity which can be triggered in a specific situation. The Buddhist terminology for such a propensity is *anusaya*.

Buddhist perspectives on emotions also have a focused relationship to the Buddhist analysis of the "self" (de Silva 1992c, 75-96; de Silva 1994). It is the relationship between the emotions and the doctrine of egolessness (*anatta*) that helps us to distinguish between "egoistic" and "nonegoistic" emotions and understand the logic of self-transcending emotions such as loving kindness (*mettā*), compassion (*karunā*), gladness at the success of others (*muditā*), and equanimity (*upekkhā*).

Now that I have outlined briefly the framework for understanding the nature of emotions as well as their moral assessment, I will present a review of the different facets of an emotion in terms of the Buddhist perspective.

FEELINGS

Feeling arises when there is a meeting of three factors: the sense organ, the object, and consciousness. This is called contact (*phassa*) (*M* I.111). It is said to be sixfold, as it is conditioned by the five physical senses and the mind. In the series of dependent origination, contact conditions feeling, and feeling conditions craving. The Buddha's saying that "all things converge on feelings" (*A* IV.339) shows the significance of the affective dimension of life in the context of the Buddhist philosophy of *dukkha* (human suffering, unsatisfactoriness).

Feelings may be pleasant, painful, or neutral. Pleasant feelings, if not properly understood and managed, may turn into lust, greed, and infatuation; painful feelings, if not properly understood and managed, may manifest as anger, destructive forms of fear, and depression; neutral feelings (which are different from states of equanimity), if not understood and properly managed, can degenerate into boredom. Pleasurable feelings due to the attachment to pleasant objects can rouse latent sensuous greed (*rāgānusaya*); painful feelings can rouse latent anger and hatred (*paṭighānusaya*); the delusion of the attachment to the ego may rouse the latent proclivity toward ignorance and conceit (*diṭṭhi-mānānusaya*).

As feelings provide a crucial starting point for behavior and thinking which may be wholesome or unwholesome, the Buddhist practice of mindfulness in the development of meditation gives a crucial place to the *practice of mindfulness on feelings*:

> This, therefore, is a crucial point in the conditioned Origin of Suffering, because it is at this point that Feeling may give rise to passionate emotions of various types, and it is, therefore, here that one may be able to break that fatuous concatenation. If in receiving a sense impression, one is able to pause and stop at the phase of Feeling, and make it, in its very first stage of manifestation, the object of Bare Attention, Feeling will not be able to originate Craving. It will stop at the bare statement of "pleasant," "unpleasant," or "indifferent." (Nyanaponika 1975, 69)

By practice of bare attention, the possible transition from feelings to negative emotions is watched with great vigilance and alertness.

A very complex point about both the psychology and the epistemology of Buddhism is that concepts such as feelings are part of a synthetic process, and it is only by abstraction and analysis that we can speak of feelings as different from perception. The slowing-down process helps one to focus on feelings in their unalloyed form in meditative practice. It is said in the discourses that consciousness, feeling, and perception are inseparable (*M* I.293). But yet, in the process of dependent origination, visual consciousness arises because of eye and material shapes; the meeting of the three is sensory impingement, and because of sensory impingement arises feeling (*M* I.111).

It was characteristic of the Buddha's methodology that he did not push these distinctions into their absolute realm but used them within context. In fact, there was a famous debate as to the number of feelings, and he said there are two feelings in one way of analyzing (bodily and mental), three feelings in another way of analyzing (pleasant, painful, neutral), six feelings in another (related to the five sense organs and the mind), and so on, up to 108 feelings (*M* I.393-401). Thus, from one perspective these contextual distinctions are important, but from another perspective the relative, constructed, "designation only" character of these terms is emphasized. Both in philosophical analysis and in meditation, a contextualism of this sort brings sanity and pragmatism into Buddhist practice.

In the *arahant* (perfected one) we find the person of "refined sensibility," in whom all the gross aspects of the cognitive process have been eliminated. While the ignorant worldling (*puthujjana*) is often subject to an action-reaction or even compulsive response to the emergence of feeling, the perfected one responds differently. The crucial term is *phassanirodha*. The term *phassa* has been rendered as "contact," and *nirodha* literally means "extinction." Contact is generally designated as the coming together of sense organ (eye), form, and consciousness, as I have already indicated, but in a deeper sense the "contact between me and things is *phassa*." So long as there is ignorance (existential confusion about my identity), which is referred to by the Pali word *avijjā*, all things are inherently in subjection, they are appropriated, they are mine (Nanavira 1987, 89–90).

All normal experience has this duality, but only the one who has attained right view sees it for the deception it is. Though the one with the right view is not deceived, correct view regarding the self is only the first stage on the path of perfection. He is still subject to the "I am" conceit (*asmi māna*), and, as Nanavira says, this "aroma of subjectivity" hangs about all his experience, until the attainment of perfection. It takes a substantial form in the experience of negative emotions.

When it is said that the arahant is not assailed by "contact," it does not mean that he is like a man who cannot hear, see, or smell. If this were the case, a blind person or deaf person would be perfected. What it implies is a more refined and sensitive person. In describing a liberated monk, it is said that he is completely calmed and freed; the sight, tastes, sounds, smells, and touches which are normally "longed for and loathed for" by the worldling do not disturb the arahant. The arahant is like a massive rock unmoved by the winds: "imagine, lord, a mountain crag, cleftless, chasmless, massive; and a squall to come from the east: it would not shake, nor rock, nor stir that crag" (*A* III.377).

It is also said about the arahant that he may experience painful feelings but they are different from the worldling's experience. The point is that there is only a bodily feeling and not a mental feeling; he does not wail, lament, grieve, beat the breast, fret, or faint. The ignorant worldling is struck by two arrows—the bodily and the mental; the arahant is struck by only one arrow—the bodily (*S* IV.208). The following stanza from the *Kindred Sayings on Feelings* is worth quoting:

> Not swayed by feeling is the sage. Nor ease
> Nor pain affecteth him of knowledge wide.
> Betwixt the wise man and the worldly one
> Vast is the difference in goodliness. (*S* IV.209)

This does not mean that Buddhist detachment should be identified with "the destruction of emotion." As will be emphasized in our concluding section on compassion, the Buddhist sage is capable of a wide range of rich and wholesome emotions. In Buddhism, wholesome emotions are an integral part of refined sensibility, and provide fertile soil for clear judgment and the generation of moral and spiritual insights.

DESIRE AND CRAVING

Some of the motivational theories of emotion in the western tradition see a close link between feeling and desire as well as between desire and emotions. However, in recent emotion studies in the West, the strong focus on the cognitive factor has led to the relative neglect of desire. Joel Marks claims that desire is *intentional*, but in an interestingly different way from belief (Marks 1986). These points should make the Buddhist analysis of the role of desire and craving in the generation of emotions a subject of current interest. In fact, in the Buddhist analysis, one of the dimensions for the moral criticism of emotions is their motivational base and related desires.

According to the discourses of the Buddha, a person feels attraction (*sārajjati*) for agreeable objects and feels repugnance toward disagreeable objects (*byāpajjati*). An individual thus possessed of like (*anurodha*) and dislike (*virodha*) approaches pleasure-giving objects and avoids painful objects. In the Buddhist formula of dependent origination, feeling conditions craving; thus, there is a close link between feeling and desire, as craving may be considered excessive and an unwholesome desire.

Craving in turn conditions clinging (*upādāna*). It is the word *taṇhā* that is translated as "craving," and its etymology suggests an unquenchable thirst. *Clinging* implies a certain strong bonding with the object, as in greedy possession or anxious obsession. A desire to destroy (hatred) is also paradoxically related to clinging. Though the word *clinging* (*upādāna*) refers to things we like, in a deeper sense it means entanglement with things we like or dislike. It is the notion of clinging that adds the ingredient of adhesiveness to craving and certain desires. A concept close to clinging has been introduced to the western philosophy of emotions by Ronald Alan Nash (1989), who refers to "overevaluation" and intensive attentional focus. In general, a distinction can be made between the satisfaction of a desire and holding onto the object of desire. The distinction between appetitive emotions and possessive emotions is made clear by C. C. W. Taylor (1986), where the former emphasizes the elements of appetite, greed, and craving, and the latter, the elements of adhesiveness, fixation, and clinging.

On the analogy of sexual desire or the simple physiological drive of thirst, it can be said that these desires are temporarily satisfied; but they emerge from time to time, and it is an unending process, which is referred to in the Buddhist context as "becoming." On the one hand, there is a strong fixation on the object of desire, but there is also a search for variety and change, finding delight "in this and that, here and there" (*tatra tatra abhinandini*) (*S* V.421).

It must be noted that desire (*chanda*), as opposed to craving (*taṇhā*), is considered virtuous or vicious, depending on context. The word is also translated, depending on context, as "impulse," "excitement," "intention," or "will." It is sometimes considered the desire to do the right and the zeal for righteousness (*A* III.441; *S* I.202). At other times, it is a vice: The four desires that generate evil are partiality, enmity, stupidity, and fear (*D* III.182). Compared with the term *desire*, *craving* has a negative connotation, with a few exceptions. One example is where the craving to end craving is recognized. Venerable Ananda instructs a nun by saying that "dependent on craving is craving abandoned" (*A* II.144).

In general, when the issue of moral assessment emerges, one looks at the bases of behavior and action. In Buddhist psychology, the springs of human behavior are found in the six roots: greed, hatred, and delusion for the immoral actions, and generosity, compassionate love, and wisdom for the moral actions. Greed (*lobha*) manifests either as the craving for sensuous gratification (*kama taṇhā*) or as the craving for egoistic pursuits (*bhava taṇhā*). Hatred (*dosa*) emerges as types of aggression and self-destructive behavior (*vibhava taṇhā*). Delusion (*moha*) is a primary root which, in the context of the present analysis, may be described as the existential confusion pertaining to the nature of "self."

These bases of craving, in fact, provide a kind of framework to plot some of the basic negative emotions. Attachment emotions are very much related to greed; aversion emotions, to hatred; and the emotions linked closely to the self (conceit), to delusion. Greed, lust, fear of certain types, grief, and anxiety fall into the first group; anger, indignation, resentment, envy, self-hate, and malice fall into the second group; conceit, inferiority feeling, certain forms of depression, shame, and guilt fall into the third. An emotion such as jealousy would be nourished by several other emotions: excessive love toward a person, hatred of the rival, fear that something precious may be lost, pride as a threat to prestige, and ambivalence (love and hatred toward the beloved).

Like the six springs of action, concepts of craving, desire, and clinging shed a great deal of light on the logic and psychology of emotion. The Buddhist analysis of craving is very rich for understanding human emotions and the affective dimension, though space does not permit a detailed analysis (see de Silva 1991a, 1992a, 1992c). The three forms of craving provide some of the finest insights into the desire-emotion linkage in Buddhism.

EMOTIONS AND THE COGNITIVE ORIENTATION

The Buddhist perspective on emotions is strongly cognitivist. While thoughts and beliefs are considered an important ingredient in the making of emotions, the greater focus is on what may be called a "cognitive set," after Calhoun:

> Our cognitive life is not limited to clear, fully conceptualized, articulated
> beliefs. Instead, beliefs constitute only a small illuminated portion of that
> life. The greater portion is rather a dark, cognitive set, an unarticulated frame-

work for interpreting our world, which, if articulated, would be an enormous
network of claims not all of which would be accepted by the individual as his
beliefs. (Calhoun 1984, 338)

Unwholesome behavior is traced to the three roots of greed, hatred, and
delusion by the Buddha. The term *delusion* is a translation of *moha*. Similarly,
the term *avijja* is translated as "ignorance" (generally understood as ignorance
of the Four Noble Truths). But what delusion and ignorance convey is the
deep state of existential confusion regarding one's identity. The term *ditthi*
refers to wrong cognitive sets, and *sakkāya-ditthi* in particular to wrong personality belief. Thus the illusion of ego provides the basis for philosophical and
intellectual puzzlement, as well as emotional discontent and anxiety. At the
philosophical level, it is said that the sage has abandoned all views. "He has no
view because he has got rid of the *point of view*, that is, the illusion of the
ego" (Nanananda 1971, 36). Breaking through the barrier of the ego is Buddhist
insight (*paññā, vipassanā*); compassion (*karuṇā*) is its emotional equivalent. It
is in this deep sense that we can talk of a cognitive orientation in Buddhism, but
then it is a little different from the reigning cognitive theories of beliefs, judgments, and propositions in the West.

Of course, at a more prosaic level, the Buddha refers to thoughts and
beliefs which have links with emotion. One of the discourses, "On the Twofold
Thought," indicates the role of thought (*vitakka*) in relation to the generation of
sensuality, malevolence, and harming others (*M* I.115). Another, related discourse, "Forms of Thought," deals with the five techniques of handling
thoughts associated with greed, aversion, and confusion (*M* I.119). In the practice of mindfulness, apart from the emphasis on feelings and the body, states of
mind and mental contents are selected for meditation. There is no attempt to
reduce these thoughts to propositional attitudes, but, in a very loose sense, the
link between thought and affectivity is emphasized in the discourse.

I have discussed elsewhere the role of cognitive theories in therapeutic
contexts and the management of emotions (de Silva 1980). This examines cognitive theory as different from behavior therapy, but I do not wish to pursue this
question here.

THE BODY AND PHYSIOLOGY IN EMOTIONS

The material on the linkage between affective experience and the body is unsys-
tematic and dispersed in the discourses, but if one studies the contexts with
care, the importance of the body in emotions from a Buddhist perspective is evident. The body is one of the five aggregates, and it is differentiated from the four
nonbodily factors that go to make our conception of a "person." The term *rupa*
refers to the body, and the term *nama*, to the mind, and they form an integral
complex. There is mutual dependency of the body on mind and mind on body.

The finest context where the body in affective experience may be identified and understood according to Buddhism is in the practice of meditation. The contemplation of the body (*kāyānupassanā*) is the first of the four objects of mindfulness. In the practice of the mindfulness of breathing and bodily postures, one discerns the intrusion of irritability and resentment into our routine lives.

In the way that meditative experiences and the practice of mindfulness give one a close understanding of the interplay of body, feelings, thoughts, and desire in negative emotions, there are also physiological facets linked to tranquility and joy. William Lyons (1980), who has written a sustained account of the role of physiology in emotions, says that though physiological changes may not help us to distinguish one emotion from another, as they are not *conceptually tied with particular emotions*, yet physiological changes are part of our occurrent emotions. When we refer to physiological changes, we refer not only to increased heartbeat and the like, which are disturbances, but also to decreased pulse rate and decreased respiratory rate, as in the experience of calmness and tranquility.

There are interesting references in the discourses to emotions and physiognomic features and bodily postures. The spiritually developed person is associated with pleasing features, joyousness, "looking contented," and cheerfulness, whereas those with evil dispositions are wretched, "their color bad, yellowish, their veins standing out in their limbs . . . not at all pleasing to behold" (*M* II.121-22). The perfected ones are always associated with a pleasing deportment, amiable eyes, gentle speech, and relaxed rhythms of the body and mind. The body is one of the avenues through which both evil and good may be expressed.

An interesting episode cited in the discourses is the debate between the Buddha and Saccaka the Jain. While the Buddha maintained an unruffled countenance and relaxed body and mind and disclosed his golden body to the audience, Saccaka was so excited that sweat was pouring from him, soaking his robes. The Buddha remarked, "But it is from your brow . . . that drops of sweat are pouring, and having soaked through your upper and inner robes, are falling to the ground" (*M* I.228-51). It is said that at the end of the debate Saccaka felt ashamed, his shoulders drooped, his head was cast down, and there was "loss of face" for him. This context shows the facial and behavioral expression of the experience of shame.

The practice of mindfulness is directed to both breathing and bodily postures. Complete awareness of bodily movements makes one careful of bodily distortions, nervous haste, and aggressive movements. Most important, one avoids physical disorders emerging from improper breathing patterns, diminished blood supply, and interference with the regular digestion of food. Bodily postures grounded in the fight-or-flight syndrome emerge naturally from the human system, but the cultivation of mindfulness will keep the body and mind healthy. A strong therapeutic orientation colors the Buddhist understanding of affectivity and the body (de Silva 1980).

THE EPISTEMIC QUALITIES OF EMOTIONS: INSIGHT AND COMPASSION

I have concentrated on drawing a theoretical profile of the concept of emotions in Buddhism, examining the relative place of feelings, desire, cognition, and the body. A final dimension I shall now consider is the epistemic, which also has moral implications.

I have emphasized that, at a prosaic level, there are thoughts and beliefs associated with emotions, so that one can make some sense of these emotions. But, at a deeper level, negative emotions are influenced by cognitive distortions, whereas positive emotions are experienced through a right conception of the world and "self."

Buddhism goes beyond any mere "intellectual assent." By the dual process of the transformation of insight and understanding (*paññavimutti*) and that of emotional transformation (*cetovimutti*), there is an interactive pattern; cognitive purification stabilizes emotional standing, and emotional transformation provides the ideal soil for the emergence of insight and understanding. I have symbolized this by the metaphor of the twin peaks, compassion and insight (de Silva 1992c); insight is a peak a little higher than compassion.

Loving kindness, compassion, sympathetic joy, and equanimity provide a basis for morality and social conduct. But they are also prescribed meditations that pave the way for the release of the heart. The ultimate purpose of these sublime states is to provide for the development of insight (*vipassanā*). The insight gained is an insight into the nature of impermanence and the notion of no-self. The term *paññavimutti* indicates those who have been liberated on the basis of the *vipassnā* techniques, while *cetovimutti* are those who have practiced meditation and the *brahmaviharas* as well as insight meditation.

In a sense, the doctrine of compassion is the emotional equivalent of the truth of the non-self doctrine. What we call *paññavimutti* is deliverance through insight into the truths of impermanence, unsatisfactoriness, and impersonality. The compassion of such a person who has reached the highest peak is truly boundless, for that person has, with insight, rejected the artificial barriers that divide one person from another or, in the words of Derek Parfit, removed the "glass wall between me and others" (1984, 282).

From a Buddhist perspective, intellectual clarification is necessary for intelligent practice, but if we do not "test the meaning of these things by intuitive wisdom" (*M* I.133) and instead make intellectual debate an end in itself, reproach others in a battle of scholarship, and use our knowledge of the *dhamma* for adornment, we come very close to being like the man who carried the raft on his shoulders after crossing the river (*M* I.135). When excessive rationality and abstraction from the human predicament need a shaking, it can come from the realm of human emotions. It was such an encounter with the tangle of human suffering (*dukkha*) that generated the search for solutions in the mind of young Siddhartha. Emotions such as the tragic sense (*saṃvega*) (*A* II.13), the encounter with suffering, stir up a person towards liberation.

Even in the case of negative emotions such as anger, one could (in the words of a meditation teacher of my acquaintance) make friends with anger. The nonjudgmental observations of negative emotions is a technique of self-understanding as well as of understanding the nature of emotions. This is what is meant when we say that emotion has the quality of being thought dependent and thus has a certain epistemic quality. In the context of Buddhism, this is merely a window to exploring the deeper cognitive net that catches us up in an emotion, when, according to the Buddha, we should liberate ourselves from such negative emotions.

But beyond understanding your own negativities by "making friends with anger" or being struck by the tragic sense of life (*saṃvega*), which can awaken you to the world of human suffering, in the ultimate analysis, the Buddhist path takes you to the most fundamental realities of suffering, impermanence, and the non-self. Of these, the doctrine of non-self (*anatta*) is most crucial, and the crowning emotion in Buddhism, which takes us closest to this insight, is compassion.

In fact, Buddhist compassion plays a double role: It produces both insight (*pañña*) and right conduct (*sila*). The latter dimension emphasizes the value of compassion as a moral emotion. In fact, though there has been a popular opposition between the deontological ethics of Kant and the teleological consequentialism of utilitarianism, a third alternative emphasizing the altruistic emotions is a possibility. It may not be a complete alternative but rather a supportive strand of the web of morality. (Schopenhauer, under the influence of Buddhism, charted out the path to such a view.) Thus, compassion, in the Buddhist context, can both deepen and enlarge our understanding of the world.

Bibliography

Calhoun, Cheshire. 1984. "Cognitive Emotions?" In *What Is an Emotion?*, ed. Cheshire Calhoun and Robert Solomon, 327-42. New York: Oxford University Press.

————. 1989. "Subjectivity and Emotion." *Philosophical Forum* 20: 195-210.

de Silva, Padmasiri. 1980. *Emotions and Therapy: Three Paradigmatic Zones*. Colombo: Lake House Investments.

————. 1991a. "Buddhist Ethics." In *A Companion to Ethics*, ed. Peter Singer. London: Basil Blackwell.

————. 1991b. *An Introduction to Buddhist Psychology*. London: Macmillan.

————. 1992a. *Buddhist and Freudian Psychology*. Singapore: National University of Singapore.

————. 1992b. *Tangles and Webs*. Singapore: Buddhist Meditation Centre.

————. 1992c. *Twin Peaks: Compassion and Insight*. Singapore: Buddhist Research Society.

————. 1994. "Emotion Profiles: The Self and the Emotion of Pride." In *The Self in Theory and Practice*, ed. Roger Ames, Thomas Kasulis, and Wimal Dissanayake. New York: State University of New York Press.

Lyons, William. 1980. *Emotion*. Cambridge: Cambridge University Press.

Marks, Joel, ed. 1986. *Ways of Desire*. Chicago: Precedent.

Nanananda Bhikku. 1971. *Concept and Reality*. Kandy: Buddhist Publication Society.

Nanavira Thera. 1987. *Clearing the Path*. Colombo: Path Press.

Nash, Ronald. 1989. "Cognitive Theories of Emotion." *Nous* 23: 481-504.

Nyanaponika Thera. 1975. *The Heart of Buddhist Meditation*. London: Rider.

————. 1983. *Contemplation of Feelings*. Kandy: Buddhist Publication Society.

Parfit, Derek. 1984. *Persons and Reasons*. Oxford: Clarendon.

Taylor, C. C. W. 1986. "Emotions and Wants." In *Ways of Desire*, ed. Joel Marks, 217-31.

Taylor, Gabriele. 1975. "Justifying the Emotions." *Mind* 84: 390-402.

Abbreviations for Buddhist Sources

A: *Anguttara Nikāya*
D: *Dīgha Nikāya*
M: *Majjhima Nikāya*
S: *Samyutta Nikāya*

The Emotions of Altruism, East and West

Joel J. Kupperman

In colloquial English, *altruism* means concern for other people, especially concern that is expressed in helpful behavior. Some philosophical studies mirror this usage. Thomas Nagel, for example, means by *altruism* "*any* behavior motivated merely by the belief that someone else will benefit or avoid harm by it" (Nagel 1970, 16, n.1). One sense of the word, in its ordinary usage, equates altruism with giving more weight to the preferences of others than to our own (Hare 1981, 129). In this essay, I will use *altruism* in a somewhat different (and technical) sense, to stand for the policy of giving equal weight to the well-being of all sentient beings, including oneself as counting for one. Altruism in this sense is a feature of a good deal of utilitarian philosophy, including recent work by R. M. Hare and Derek Parfit. Something like it is a feature of Buddhism. This essay will be concerned with understanding altruism as part of the structure of the life of the altruist, especially in relation to such a person's emotions.

I

Ernest Albee (1957), in his classic *History of English Utilitarianism*, notes a shift between Hume's grounding of morality in his *Treatise of Human Nature* (1739) and its grounding in his *Enquiry Concerning the Principles of Morals* (1751). The springs of action in the *Treatise*, Albee says, are egoism, altruism (limited largely in its objects to those close to us), and "sympathy" (in which our idea of another's emotion may become so vivid as to give rise to the same emotion in ourselves). In the *Enquiry*, Albee suggests, "sympathy" comes to mean "nothing essentially different from the general benevolent tendency" (Albee 1957, 95-96). Francis Hutcheson, meanwhile, had arrived at a very similar view; in his *System of Moral Philosophy*, published posthumously in 1755, he speaks of "the notion of the greatest possible system of sensitive beings" and a "calm, stable, universal good-will to all, or the most extensive

123

benevolence" (Hutcheson 1968, 50, 69). This universal benevolence is not, as Hutcheson acknowledges, an element of "the ordinary condition of mankind . . . but of the condition our nature can be raised to by due culture." Doubtless, he says, "some good men have exercised in life only the particular kind affections, and found a constant approbation of them, without either the most extensive views of the whole system or the most universal benevolence" (Hutcheson 1968, 77-78).[1]

It is important that we be clearly aware of the difference between "particular kind affections" and "the most extensive benevolence," which latter is an aspect of altruism in the sense of this essay. The great majority of human beings experience particular kind affections, and are able to feel sympathy for some human beings (especially those close to them or those who are like them) and for some animals (especially household pets). It might seem at first that there is a scale here that admits of degrees, in that some people are more affectionate and have wider sympathies than others, and that "the most extensive benevolence" simply represents the top of the scale. I wish to argue the opposite, that what Hutcheson describes is a very different kind of thing from particular affections and sympathies, that it is (as he suggests) fairly uncommon, and that when it occurs it is very likely (as he also suggests) the result of a shaping and refining of attitudes that is a peculiar form of cultural enrichment.

The last part of this argument will appear in the final section of this essay. We may turn our attention now, though, to the differences between altruism ("the most extensive benevolence") and particular affections and sympathies. A clear view of the differences will show also how uncommon a thing is altruism (in the sense under discussion).

Familiar examples of particular affections include those of romantic love and those directed toward one's parents or one's children. We care about these people, and, indeed, whether we really do care would come into question if we did not feel satisfaction at their well-being and apprehension at dangers to them. Such "significant others" are thus, in the words of Shakespeare's *Macbeth*, "hostages to fortune": They represent areas of vulnerability in our lives. They are, if we are fortunate in our connections, sources of positive experiences, such as joy, delight, various pleasures, and even happiness. Because nothing in life is certain, they are also potential sources of uneasiness, fear, grief, distress, and suffering. In short, particular affections are sources of emotional agitation. The more people, animals, and the like we care about in this way, the more hostages to fortune we have and the more agitated our emotional life is likely to be. Could someone sleep at night who cared about every member of the human race the way we care about our loved ones? If the emotions of particular affections and sympathies were spread as widely as possible, the result (given the limitations of human psychology) would be psychic overload, benevolence burnout.

It might be objected that this is too quick and simple. If the emotions of particular affections and sympathies were spread as widely as possible, why can we not assume that their intensity would be dimmed proportionately? We can imagine two forms this might take. One is that some affections (e.g., for spouses, parents, children) would retain some moderately high intensity, whereas others would be of suitably low intensity. The other is that all affections would be of suitably low intensity. We may dismiss the first possibility immediately, for the purposes of this essay, simply in that it does not amount to altruism in the sense under discussion (or the sense in which altruism is implicit in Buddhist and utilitarian philosophy). The second possibility, though, points toward a plausible reconstruction of altruism, and corresponds to the respects in which the Buddhist perfect way "refuses to make preferences" and is "freed from love and hate" (Seng Ts'an, "On Believing in Mind," trans. D. T. Suzuki, in Conze 1959, 171). Indeed, this possibility amounts to altruism if the intensity (which would have to be very low indeed) of affection for all sentient beings were equal. But would this extremely low-intensity affection qualify as what we normally call "affection"? Differences in degree can amount to differences in kind; and I suggest that, if one divided all concern for others among the trillions of sentient beings, one's spouse and children would judge that one no longer "cared" for them.

The second model of altruism, of concern for others divided equally among a very large number of objects, is a useful way of beginning to think about what altruism is. But it can be criticized as being too hydraulic, treating concern as if it were a quantifiable and divisible liquid. Indeed, if the number of those whose well-being matters is in the trillions, the concern per being (on this model) is infinitesimal, and looks very much like indifference. The truth is that the altruist, unless she or he has some administrative or political role, is usually not confronted with the needs and problems of very large numbers of beings at any one time. Hence, a significant degree of warmth and compassion will be possible. But the realization that there are others whose needs and problems are equally important—especially if it is coupled with a belief that it is part of the order of things that those who are not enlightened will often suffer—should prevent grasping onto the welfare and absence of suffering of any particular being or beings as a requirement of life. The popular saying "You win some and lose some" will apply, and will shape the attitudes of the altruist. There will be (at least in theory) significant concern without attachment; the concern will be genuinely felt but also will be guarded and limited in intensity, as it were with strings connecting it to the realities of disappointment and suffering.

Thus, another way to look at the difference between particular affections (unguarded and, in some cases, unlimited in their intensity) and altruism as a state of mind is to contrast the emotional ups and downs and disturbances of the person who has particular affections with the evenness and lack of emotional disturbance of the genuine altruist. This implies a transformation of both social and psychological conditions. The two are illustrated well in the Buddhist poem "The Rhinoceros." The enlightened person "fares lonely as a rhinoceros," with "mind that festers not, nor burns" (Conze 1959, 79-82). This is a natural consequence of the Buddhist recommendation of "a boundless good will towards the entire world" (Conze 1959, 186). Whether it is equally a consequence of utilitarian altruism will be examined in the final section of this essay.

II

First, though, we need to look at what emotions are. A skeptical reader might ask whether altruists, as I have been describing them, have emotions. Possibly the title of this essay reflects a confusion. Perhaps it should have been "The Non-emotions of Altruism, East and West"?

Plainly much depends on what we count as an emotion. Motivational force would seem to be linked to the idea of emotion, and there is a traditional argument (a classic formulation of which is found in Hume) to the effect that human action presupposes a motivational element. Reason, Hume says, "being cool and disengaged," is no motive to action, and "directs only the impulse received from appetite or inclination" (Hume 1975, 294). Hence, "taste" is "the first spring or impulse to desire and volition."

Hume took care with language, and we should take him seriously when he speaks of the impulse "received from appetite or inclination." We may take it that "appetite" and "inclination" here represent alternatives; otherwise, he would have used one word instead of two. What is the difference between an impulse received from appetite and one received from inclination?

The ordinary meaning of "appetite" is close to that of "felt want." Can someone be hungry or thirsty without *feeling* hungry or thirsty or without (at least) having such feelings close to the surface? If someone says, "I had no idea that I was hungry at all until I sat down and began eating," it would be tempting to interpret it as meaning that he or she began to feel hungry while eating, and that this was a matter of feelings of hunger surfacing that had been latent all along. Other appetites, such as for sex, power, or love, may be less closely tied to feeling than are hunger and thirst. Even so, the central, paradigmatic cases of appetite for sex, power, or love are ones in which the subject, if induced to be candid, could report feelings that are expressive or indicative of the appetite. Appetites that are not felt will be considered appetites, in large part, because they function, both in patterns of behavior and in associated thoughts and utterances, very much like the familiar cases of appetites that are felt.

There are cases, on the other hand, in which someone stands ready to choose one thing over another without any felt or latent craving for what is (or will be) preferred, without any noticeable feeling at all, and without any of the behavior, thought, or utterances that normally would be associated with felt cravings. Bloggs simply picks X over Y, and perhaps remarks in a calm, dispassionate way that X is better than Y. It may be that Hume used the word "inclination" with reference to cases like this.[2] There does not appear to be any logical or psychological reason why someone could not, as a bare fact, be inclined toward one thing rather than toward another thing without having the stirrings of appetite for what is preferred and without exhibiting behavior or reporting thought that we would associate with appetite. We need not look at Buddhists and utilitarians in order to find such cases. Many everyday situations in which a person says, "If it's all the same to you, I think I'd rather have X than Y," serve quite well.

We thus can draw from Hume's language the suggestion, I think, that motivational force in some cases is generated by feelings and in some cases does not require feelings. (In what follows, I will use *motivation* as a technical term that straddles both these possibilities.) One has to be cautious here, in that our introspective reports are generally not precise; and while sometimes we are able to say readily enough whether we have strong feelings or not, the boundaries within territory that includes hardly any feelings at all about X, no noticeable feelings about X, and no feelings about X are somewhat blurred. It may be that the stoic ideal of *apatheia* was meant to encourage an emotional life within that territory, allowing for very slight feelings, or ones of negligible intensity, about this or that. We can similarly interpret the ideal proposed by the seventeenth-century poet Henry Vaughan when he says, "Incite and use thyself to a gallant apathy." Vaughan was praising the courage and effort required to make one's feelings very slight.

An ambiguity in phrases such as "no feelings" also needs to be noted. It can mean no feelings whatsoever, period, or it can mean no feelings of the sort that involve intentionality (i.e., that implicitly refer to and require objects). If we interpret stoics and Buddhists as recommending that we have no feelings, it has to be in the second sense. Otherwise, it will be hard to understand Philip Hallie's linking the ideal of *apatheia* with "spiritual peace and well-being"; it also will be hard to follow Buddhist discussions of "the joy of quietness" (Hallie 1967; *The Dhammapada*, no. 205, p. 64). The distinction is apparent in ordinary English: Someone who truthfully says, "I have no feelings in the matter," may be feeling very relaxed.

There is a parallel ambiguity involved when someone is spoken of as "unemotional" or (which is not entirely the same thing) as "having no emotions." Someone may be spoken of as having no emotions who is possessed of a calm, quiet inner joy, as can someone who feels no joy and indeed feels nothing (qualifying as "affectless"). Either could be spoken of as "unemotional," although I judge that the term also could be applied to someone who has discernible but mild emotions of the sort that involve intentionality, as long as these emotions were not disturbing.

To return to feelings: There is a tradition in recent analytic philosophy of equating feelings with disturbances, which goes back to Gilbert Ryle's *The Concept of Mind* (1949). Some will think of Ryle's famous list: thrills, twinges, pangs, throbs, wrenches, itches, prickings, chills, glows, loads, qualms, hankerings, curdlings, sinkings, tensions, gnawings, and shocks (Ryle 1949, 83-84). With the possible exception of glows, these are all disturbances, and, indeed, Ryle's bias is made explicit later when he claims that "feelings are intrinsically connected with agitations" (Ryle 1949, 104). It is not difficult to see the appeal of this claim. Not only are most feelings (including the most noticeable ones) connected with agitations, but it can be argued that feelings (like perceptions) can be registered only if there is some element of contrast. Just as a uniform perceptual field that lasted an entire lifetime would not allow any perception, a uniform psychic state that lasted an entire lifetime would not allow for the experience of feelings. Agitation is the most obvious way to introduce contrast into someone's psychic states. But it is not the only way, and, indeed, the *absence* of tension and apprehension that one used to suffer from can be felt. It cannot be emphasized too strongly that some feelings are calm, undisturbed, and do not involve appetites.

A similar point can be made about emotions. Hate, fear, and erotic love are emotions, but is there any reason not to include *agape* and compassion as emotions? Jerome Shaffer's influential discussion of emotion takes emotion to be "a complex of physiological processes and sensations caused by certain beliefs and desires" (Shaffer 1983, 161). It is natural to think of Ryle's list in connection with the phrase "physiological processes and sensations." But much of the literature of Buddhism—Zen Buddhism especially—stresses that there are physiological processes and sensations characteristically associated with a calm enlightenment. Are these caused by beliefs and desires? Philosophical beliefs, including metaphysical beliefs about the self, certainly are at work. Every schoolchild knows that Buddhists eschew desire but this does not mean that their lives are utterly devoid of motivational elements: They are not, in every situation, entirely suspended between available alternatives. In fact, as Annette Baier (1986) has pointed out, the word *desire* is used, in the recent philosophical literature on the emotions, in a very broad technical sense rather than with its ordinary meaning. In this broad, technical use of *desire*, any motivational element (no matter how gentle and no matter how free of appetite) qualifies one as having a desire; and in *this* sense, even Buddhists have desires. Their beliefs and "desires" cause physiological processes which are such that enlightened Buddhists, as one Zen text puts it, can like thieves recognize each other without any introduction (*Zen Flesh, Zen Bones*, n.d. 129).

There is no clear reason, then, to deny that altruism can involve emotions.[3] If someone pursues an altruistic policy because of certain ethical beliefs which are linked with appropriate motivational elements, and if the altruist at the same time feels calm and dispassionate (as well, perhaps, as having other, associated feelings), what is missing? This is not to say, though, that what is present will be the same in all traditions of altruism. In the remaining section, we need to look at some East-West differences.

III

Up to this point, no distinction has been made between utilitarian altruism and Buddhist altruism. Indeed, there is a remarkable congruence in formulas. Besides the utilitarian assertions that each sentient being should count equally and Hutcheson's "calm, stable, universal good-will to all" we may place Buddhist affirmations of the ideal of "a boundless good will towards the entire world" (Conze 1959, 186).

This does not mean, of course, that altruism functions, or is meant to function, in the same way in the lives of Buddhists and utilitarians. For that matter, not all Buddhists will be alike, nor will all utilitarians be alike, either in doctrine or in personal lives. But there are characteristic Buddhist forms of altruism, nevertheless, and persistent utilitarian patterns—which are quite different from the Buddhist ones—of attempts to integrate altruism into a life. To explore the differences is to glimpse two different sorts of emotional life.

The Buddhist literature is full of examples of people who have taken the altruistic ideal to its logical conclusion, in the sense of leading calm, even lives with no personal attachments. There is no comparable literature of utilitarian saints. I can record that the prominent utilitarians that I have known have seemed, in my experience, extraordinarily considerate people; but that is not quite the same thing. Is it just that the West, since the Reformation, has not gone in much for saintliness? The explanation runs, I think, much deeper, and is, in fact, mirrored in many of the polemics of recent Western ethical philosophy.

Many ongoing debates take this form. An ethical philosophy (it may be utilitarianism, but Kant is also a favorite target) seems to offer no room for special obligations or responsibilities that we have to others (either because they are close to us or because we care about them).[4] The philosophy's defenders *might* take the line that the special obligations or responsibilities that are appealed to are symptomatic of a lower state of human life, and that ideally they would not (need not) play a role in one's choices. Something like this could be argued to be implicit in Kant's writings and in R. M. Hare's (1976, 1981) recent discussions of two levels of morality. But, in fact, I have not seen a thoroughgoing development of this in order specifically to discredit (or relegate to lower or provisional status) special responsibilities to those close to us. One often does see Kantian or utilitarian accommodationist responses, in which it is argued, for example, that Kant has room for emotional attachments as ancillary to, or merely regulated by, the workings of the categorical imperative, or that pursuing particular loyalties is conducive to the greatest happiness of the greatest number.[5]

Do utilitarians, then, in their everyday lives interpret utilitarianism so that they can cheerfully favor their nearest and dearest over others? The short answer that I wish to suggest is that many do so for some parts of their lives and not for others.[6] Utilitarian altruism (along with its cousin, Kantian ethics, in which the emphasis is on respect as well as concern for well-being, and the domain is limited to rational beings) is alive and well, but only within the context of a compartmentalization of human life. This means that the emotions of the most prominent form of Western altruism will be very different from the emotions of Buddhist altruism.

The major division that allows altruism to be combined with particular affections is between the public and the private. It roughly corresponds to the division between what is subject to moral judgment and what is not.[7] A number of lines of thought converge on these divisions. If something is a public matter, then standards of fairness apply. We cannot discriminate; equal cases must be treated equally. Poor decisions are subject to the communal pressure that is characteristic of morality, which itself appeals to standards that should be apparent to all (and hence must be independent of any particular point of view).

If something is a private matter, on the other hand, it is not subject to (or should not be subject to) communal pressure. (See J. S. Mill, *On Liberty*.) It then can be put under the heading of "expediency" (Mill) or viewed as subject merely to hypothetical imperatives (Kant). The degree of one's concern for, or involvement with, others then becomes relevant to the question of how best one should behave toward them. The cases of those who are strangers or otherwise unconnected are, then, in these matters, not equal cases with those of our nearest and dearest, and there is no requirement of equal treatment.

What is generally a private relationship can, of course, become a public matter if there is an abuse serious enough to warrant communal pressure or to rule out what was done as ineligible to be universal practice. Apart from such abuses, though, the division between public and private corresponds to a division between two spheres of one's life. It may be helpful to think of an area of life in which one is "on duty" and an area in which one is "off duty."

One aspect of the public/private division is that we expect people to be impartial in decisions relating to such matters as promise keeping; adherence to agreed-upon conventions that govern property rights; business and educational hiring, firing, and preferment (nepotism is obsolete); judicial actions; and so on. It is all right not to be impartial among the members of one's society in deciding to whom to give Christmas presents but not in one's activities as a judge, employer, banker, or concerned citizen.

What I have been drawing with a broad brush is a cluster of attitudes and habits of mind that are characteristic of modern Western civilization and that influence educated and responsible people generally as well as utilitarians in particular. This cluster of attitudes and habits of mind allows utilitarian altruism to be an altruism limited in the range of occasions on which it comes into play. (In what follows, I will refer to altruism that is limited in this way as "limited altruism."[8]) In a way that might bewilder someone who is unfamiliar with modern Western civilization, it is as if the altruism is turned on and off.

The limited altruism of the West under discussion might be held to be connected with a Western philosophical tradition one of whose major constructs is an individualistic self. There is a contrast here with the Confucian view of the person in which social context and connections assume a much more essential role. (See Ames 1991 and Fingarette 1991.) Confucian altruism, though, is a *tertium quid*, sharply distinct (in taking account of gradations in our connectedness) from Buddhist altruism and (in not relying on a compartmentalization of life) from what I have been characterizing as a widespread modern Western form of altruism. The individualistic Western construct of self does play a part in the contrast I am drawing between Buddhist and Western altruism, but so does Buddha's insistence that the network of special relationships is part of the sickness from which we must escape.

Buddhist altruism, operating in an unlimited range of circumstances, requires an emotional development that is also required for Buddhist enlightenment: David Kalupahana speaks of "pacification (*vupasama*) of craving and desires" (1976, 60). Unpacified desires are disturbing and also lead to partiality of various kinds. A utilitarian who pursues a strategy of limited altruism, on the other hand, need not pacify her or his craving and desires. In certain contexts (by and large, those of private life) their expression is licit, and may, indeed, promote the greatest happiness of the greatest number. On the other hand, in the public decisions that are governed by morality, they must be out of play.

When a culture, or a segment of a culture, develops a unified worldview, one usually can expect that the attitudes and beliefs that form the worldview will be, on the whole, mutually reinforcing. That is, each element of the worldview will be such that if it is accepted many of the others will seem more reasonable than otherwise they might have seemed. The connections normally will not be as tight as logical implication, and might be very difficult to analyze in terms of formal logic; but they will be apparent to most students of the culture.

One element of modern Western culture which supports limited altruism is the persistent claim, found in the eighteenth century in Mandeville and in Adam Smith, that private affections and selfishness are (if regulated or limited in appropriate ways) conducive to the public good.[9] It should be noted that the public good is construed, in these arguments, largely in terms of economic prosperity and the freedom to engage in various desire-laden activities. Thus, the arguments would be unlikely to satisfy any strict Buddhist. But they do have the force, if one accepts the value system embedded in them, of dissolving what looks like a contradiction: between, on one hand, the ideal of altruism and, on the other hand, the claim that in many of the elemental transactions of life it is quite all right to favor oneself or one's loved ones. The arguments suggest that *indirectly* this is as good as—indeed, better than—altruism.

What are the emotions of limited altruism? It may seem that the answer points toward the range of emotions to be found in one's culture, in that it is all right to have such emotions and to express them, although in some cases the expression is to be restricted to a portion of one's life. This is largely right, but does not do justice to the emotional adaptation that is required if someone is to function effectively as an altruist in moral, social, and political decision making. It might seem that we could borrow an analogy from current computer technology: thinking of the limited altruist—or, for that matter, anyone who is scrupulously impartial in a limited sphere—as opening a Buddhist "window" on her or his emotional screen. But this does not fit the reality around us. Judges, politicians, educators, and administrators who succeed in pursuing a policy of one of these sorts are not, typically, like Buddhists in their emotions while they are at work. The typical American law court or office, even if it is staffed by the most high-minded people, is not lit up by a host of gentle, compassionate smiles.

Basically, there is a huge difference between denial of self and holding "dear self" (as Kant puts it) in check in part of one's life. The latter requires emotional mechanisms more closely linked to puritanism than to compassion. In one's private life, the part of life in which one most essentially lives, of course one prefers one's own interests and those of loved ones to those of strangers. But in one's public/moral and political capacity one tries to be fair, recognizing that they are human beings and that they count equally, and so forth. A utilitarian may remind herself or himself that even rats and cockroaches are sentient and presumably can experience pain, and this will condition life-or-death decisions. The "window" that comes up on the utilitarian's emotional screen, though, will be not compassion but rather a stance of impartiality, an impersonal distancing from emotions that are at the heart of our being.

This is one reason why extremely fair-minded people in our culture often seem cold, even to each other. The distancing from personal emotion that one sees can look very much like an absence of emotion. Indeed, that is a possibility, especially for someone whose work (or whose moral and political activities) is, as we say, his or her life. We also need to confront the possibility that the compartments of the limited altruist's life may not be as sharply separated as in theory they might be. An element of impersonality may seep into private life. A degree of warmth may seep into public life, leading to the occasional smile of gentle compassion.

In the end, of course, it is impossible to arrive at generalizations about what the emotional life of all, or, indeed, almost all, sincere utilitarian altruists will be like. We can gesture at likely patterns of emotions, and think that we can recognize them in some of the people around us (as well, perhaps, as in ourselves). One further general difference between utilitarian altruism and Buddhist altruism should be remarked upon. By and large Buddhists, especially in the classic period of Buddhist philosophy, have not been drawn to social and political remedies for the problems of the world. It is easy to see why, given the Buddhist value system: The loss of desire (which is paramount) is a matter of individual effort. Utilitarians, on the other hand, have been strongly drawn, almost from the outset, to social and political reform and organizational programs. It is easy to see why this should be, given not only the values of utilitarians but also the complex social, economic, and political networks characteristic of modern "developed" countries. Utilitarians can plausibly believe that the right kind of social, political, and economic activities can bring great benefits to the general population. They also can plausibly believe that technical knowledge and the ability to calculate consequences (especially in the long run) of various policies are required to know what is for the greatest good of the greatest number. Some utilitarian technocrats thus can practice limited altruism much more effectively than the average person could. Inevitably, this imports a paternalistic (or maternalistic) tinge into limited altruism. It also is easily mocked, as when the anti-utilitarian Bernard Williams speaks of "Government House utilitarianism" (Williams 1985, 108-10).

Philosophies can be forms of life. As such, they can change and develop, even while retaining their link to a core of classic texts. Philosophers typically concentrate on the texts, along with the logical implications of what is in them. But there is room also for inquiries conducted by philosophers, historians, and psychologists into the role of philosophies in structuring and orienting human lives. This essay should be read as a crude, early attempt to move in that direction.[10]

Notes

1. Hutcheson, it should be noted, is not usually listed as a utilitarian, mainly because his utilitarian-like formulas are intended to capture what a well-educated moral sense would judge and are not intended as decision procedures for agents making choices in the world. But (a) he is part of the broader Western movement of thought that includes utilitarianism, (b) most utilitarians would agree with his points that have been cited, (c) it is highly debatable whether utilitarianism must be treated as primarily a decision procedure, and thus (d) the fact that Hutcheson does not treat "the greatest happiness of the greatest number" (a phrase that he invented) as a decision procedure shows at most that he is not a utilitarian if one employs a narrow meaning of the term.

2. In Hume's terms, such an inclination could qualify as a "mild passion." We would have an impression of it, much as Hume says (in his discussion of causality) that we have an impression of "a determination of the mind to pass from one object to its usual attendant" which gives us our notion of causal necessity. See Hume 1978, 165. I am indebted to Donald Baxter for discussion on this point.

3. I have argued this claim in relation to Shaffer's definition of *emotion*. But the claim can stand apart from the definition, and, indeed, is compatible with the view that there can be no entirely adequate definition. We should bear in mind that often a word can be used in a variety of ways, which may (as Wittgenstein observed in *Philosophical Investigations*) be linked by "family resemblances." This inclines me to side with Ryle when he suggests that the word *emotion* is used to designate at least three or four different kinds of things. His tentative list includes inclinations (the meaning of which is close to what I am calling "motivations"), moods, agitations, and feelings. The first three, Ryle says, are propensities rather than occurrences (Ryle 1949, 83). When I speak of the emotions of altruism, I will not be concerned with moods or with feelings or agitations that do not have a strong real-life connection with motivations. (Feelings that do not have a strong real-life connection with motivations, though, constitute a fascinating topic that needs further investigation. For an interesting approach to it and related matters, see Tanner 1976-1977. The "emotions" with which the final section will be concerned will be causally connected complexes of feelings, real-life motivations, and ethical beliefs. The causality will operate in one or both of two directions: The motivations and eth-

ical beliefs may cause or reinforce the feelings, but it is also possible for someone to start out with feelings characteristic of altruism and to develop appropriate beliefs and motivations as a result.

4. An especially good general formulation of the line of thought that there has to be this room is in Sommers (1986). She contends that we need a model of obligations that allows for "differential pulls."

5. The best utilitarian development of this is in Smart (1977). Smart contends that "there are good utilitarian reasons for discouraging a too calculating bent of mind" (p. 128) and for allowing play to our ordinary motives of affection for our friends or those we love. Much of the journal literature on this topic in the last fifteen years has been inspired by Stocker (1976). A very effective Kantian account is contained in Herman (1983). See also Louden (1991). An illuminating discussion that is not anchored to a particular theory is contained in Pettit (1988).

6. There may well be exceptions to this pattern of divided lives. Anecdotal evidence suggests that Peter Singer is a prominent exception. The stringent morality that this points towards is suggested in his *Practical Ethics* (1979).

7. David Lyons (1973) has interpreted Bentham as espousing a dual standard, one for public matters and another for private ones. I am indebted to John Troyer and Diana Meyers for calling this to my attention. For Mill's distinction between the moral and nonmoral, see his *Utilitarianism*, ch. 5, para. 14.

8. It may help some readers to review the variety of ways in which something that looks like altruism can be limited. It can be limited in the range of its objects; for example, someone can be altruistic only within her or his immediate family or clan. It can be limited in the intensity of the feelings it permits (and by not allowing any attachments) as, in most interpretations, Buddhist altruism is. Finally it can be limited in the sense under discussion, in the occasions where it comes into play. Part of my argument is that altruism that is limited in this last sense is characteristic of much modern Western ethics, and can be contrasted with Buddhist altruism.

9. A very interesting recent exploration of this theme is Ci (1991).

10. The final version of this paper has benefited from the efforts of some colleagues who forced me to think harder about key constructs: Joel Marks about altruistic emotion, Roger Ames about the self, and Loren Lomasky about altruism.

Bibliography

Albee, Ernest. 1957. *History of English Utilitarianism*. [1901.] London: Allen & Unwin.

Ames, Roger. 1991. "Reflections on the Confucian Self: A Response to Fingarette." In *Rules, Rituals, and Responsibility*, ed. Mary Bockover, 103-14. La Salle, IL: Open Court.

Baier, Annette. 1986. "The Ambiguous Limits of Desire." In *The Ways of Desire*, ed. Joel Marks, 39-61. Chicago: Precedent.

Bockover, Mary, ed. 1991. *Rules, Rituals, and Responsibility: Essays Dedicated to Herbert Fingarette*. La Salle, IL: Open Court.

Ci, Jiwei. 1991. "Freedom and Realms of Living." *Philosophy East and West* 41: 303-26.

Conze, Edward, ed. 1959. *Buddhist Scriptures*. Harmondsworth, UK: Penguin.

The Dhammapada. 1973. Trans. Juan Mascaro. Harmondsworth, UK: Penguin.

Fingarette, Herbert. 1991. "Comment and Response: Roger T. Ames." In *Rules, Rituals, and Responsibility*, ed. Mary Bockover, 194-200. La Salle, IL: Open Court.

Hallie, Philip. 1967. "Stoicism." In *Encyclopedia of Philosophy*, ed. Paul Edwards, 8: 19b-22b. New York: The Free Press.

Hare, R. M. 1976. "Ethical Theory and Utilitarianism." In *Contemporary British Philosophy*, 4th ser., ed. H. D. Lewis, 113-31. London: Allen & Unwin.

——. 1981. *Moral Thinking*. Oxford: Clarendon.

Herman, Barbara. 1983. "Integrity and Impartiality." *Monist* 66: 233-50.

Hume, David. 1978. *Treatise of Human Nature*. [1739.] 2d ed. Ed. L. A. Selby-Bigge, rev. P. H. Nidditch. Oxford: Clarendon.

———. 1975. *Enquiry Concerning the Principles of Morals*. [1751.] In *Enquiries*. 3d ed. Ed. L. A. Selby-Bigge, rev. P. H. Nidditch. Oxford: Clarendon.

Hutcheson, Francis. 1968. *A System of Moral Philosophy*. [1755.] New York: Augustus M. Kelley.

Kalupahana, David. 1976. *Buddhist Philosophy: A Historical Analysis*. Honolulu: University Press of Hawaii.

Louden, Robert B. 1991. *Morality and Moral Theory: A Reappraisal and Reaffirmation*. New York: Oxford University Press.

Lyons, David. 1973. *In the Interest of the Governed: A Study of Bentham's Philosophy of Utility and Law*. Oxford: Clarendon.

Mandeville, Bernard. 1714. *The Fable of the Bees*.

Marks, Joel, ed. 1986. *The Ways of Desire*. Chicago: Precedent.

Mill, J. S. 1859. *On Liberty*.

———. 1861. *Utilitarianism*.

Nagel, Thomas. 1970. *The Possibility of Altruism*. Oxford: Clarendon.

Pettit, Philip. 1988. "The Paradox of Loyalty." *American Philosophical Quarterly* 25: 163-71.

Ryle, Gilbert. 1949. *The Concept of Mind*. New York: Barnes & Noble.

Shaffer, Jerome. 1983. "An Assessment of Emotion." *American Philosophical Quarterly* 20: 161-73.

Singer, Peter. 1979. *Practical Ethics*. Cambridge: Cambridge University Press.

Smart, J. J. C. 1977. "Benevolence as an Over-Riding Attitude." *Australasian Journal of Philosophy* 55: 127-35.

Smith, Adam. 1776. *An Inquiry into the Nature and Causes of the Wealth of Nations.*

Sommers, Christina Hoff. 1986. "Filial Obligation." *Journal of Philosophy* 83: 439-56.

Stocker, Michael. 1976. "The Schizophrenia of Modern Ethical Theories." *Journal of Philosophy* 73: 453-66.

Tanner, Michael. 1976-1977. "Sentimentality." *Proceedings of the Aristotelian Society* 77: 127-47.

Williams, Bernard. 1985. *Ethics and the Limits of Philosophy.* London: Fontana.

Wittgenstein, Ludwig. 1958. *Philosophical Investigations*, 3d ed. Trans. G. E. M. Anscombe. New York: Macmillan.

Zen Flesh, Zen Bones. N.d. Ed. Paul Reps. New York: Doubleday Anchor.

Dispassion and the Ethical Life

Joel Marks

> Those hard and flinty philosophers, who talk'd of an utter dispassion.
>
> —Cited ur der "Dispassion" in the *Oxford English Dictionary*

> Philosopher commits crime of passion.
>
> —Newspaper headline

Dispassion is the stereotypically philosophic virtue worldwide. As such, it has tended to be put forward by those same philosophers—who, after all, value their way of life—as a virtue to be commended to everyone. A typical line of thought in the West goes like this:

1. Philosophers are those who (should) value Reason above all (and probably everyone else would do well to model themselves on the philosophers in this regard).
2. Reason is the antithesis of Passion.

Therefore, philosophers (and probably everyone else) (should) value dispassion.

Yet, despite its impressive influence on the history of thought, dispassion is today out of favor in certain philosophic circles. On the one hand, Premise 1 above has been denied; for example:

> Visceral fear, as Robert Kraut has pointed out, may be, in a wise animal or person, an appropriate response to a situation which does contain danger, but not danger to which one has intellectual access. . . . So feeling when we cannot see at the time what the reasons are to have that feeling may be not weaknesses but strength of the heart. (Baier 1985, 117f.)

Feminists in particular have championed the value of emotion as a way of knowing.[1]

139

On the other hand, premise 2 is denied by the dominant ideology among emotion theorists today, viz., cognitivism.[2] Emotions are not mere feelings, akin to sensations such as tickles and pains, but instead contain *cognitive* content; for example:

> If I evaluate the dog's approach as threateningly dangerous, then I have reason
> to get worked up about the situation, and my beliefs have become the plausi-
> ble cause for my ensuing physiological upset. (Lyons 1980, 58)

It is perfectly rational to be afraid if danger is imminent; thus, emotions themselves partake of the stuff of Reason, viz., cognition.

In addition to these contemporary philosophical/epistemic critiques, there is, of course, the traditional and popular view of emotion as the very stuff of life: that which makes us human, that which makes us caring, that which motivates us, that which is the source of our happiness. These ideas continually find their expression in literature; as Marlow puts it succinctly in Joseph Conrad's *Lord Jim*: "[T]hose who do not feel do not count."

Faced with these formidable expressions of dissent, I shall undertake in this essay a defense of the virtue of dispassion. I believe that the ("traditional") philosophers—East and West—have been onto something all along. But the discussion has been confused by a failure to clarify what is being proscribed, that is, what an emotion is.

Right at the outset, I believe, it is possible to block the double-whammy contemporary philosophic critique of dispassion—from feminism and cognitivism—by a simple stipulation in the definition of emotion: Emotions or passions are *strong* feelings. Thus, dispassionate does not mean affectless, without feeling(s); dispassionate means without passions, which are strong feelings.

More specifically, emotions or passions have a strong-desire component. As noted above, recent analyses of emotion have stressed their cognitive aspect, usually in terms of a belief-component. The emphasis on belief is justified by the clearly intentional content of emotions; for example, one is afraid *of the dog*, and is not merely in some sensationlike state, as when experiencing an itch or a burn.

But the intentionality of emotion is not fully captured by belief; a desire component is required as well.[3] Thus, one would not fear the dog if one did not also desire not to be bitten. Furthermore—and this is the point most related to our present concerns—the desire component of an emotion or passion (as opposed to a mere "attitude") is *strong*. One will not have an *emotional* fear of the dog if one does not *strongly* desire not to be bitten.

The general argument for the "strong desire" qualifier goes like this:

> Without the qualifier, *every* belief/desire set—where "set" connotes a
> shared intentional object[4]—would constitute an *emotion*.

But it is clearly at odds with usage to regard *every* instance of *entertaining a belief and a desire about something* as an emotion; for example, it is not an emotion to have a run-of-the-mill desire for some groceries and believe they are at the food store.

Therefore, Q.E.D.

Thus, it is necessary to deny neither the value of feelings nor the cognitive content of emotions, in order to defend dispassion as a virtue. Hence, neither feminism nor cognitivism counts as an objection to the virtue of dispassion, at least not without further argument.

Now, someone might object at this point that the argument smacks of the *ad hoc*.[5] One can save any hypothesis whatsoever by the simple expedient of defining terms to one's liking; for example, unicorns exist if "unicorn" means "mammal with one horn on its forehead." *Emotion* and *passion* are words that have been used in many ways. Perhaps *one* of those ways does correspond to the analysis just given. But why assume that that is the way the word has been intended by cognitivists and feminists?

My reply is this. It is true that the proffered analysis seems tailor made to meet the cognitivist and feminist objections to dispassion. One would have thought that was its strength! For what it is worth, I will say that this use of the analysis was a genuine discovery; the analysis arose in independent circumstances, having to do strictly with issues in the philosophy of mind.

But the objection still calls for a reply on its own terms. I certainly grant that "emotion" has several meanings and also that it has been employed variously by other theorists. What justifies my restriction (1) to a single usage and (2) to the "strong desire" usage in particular is precisely that it sustains the viability of a traditional ethical thesis about emotion in the face of two contemporary critiques. This may seem a circular argument, but I see it as exemplifying the way concepts are established, viz., by a process of adjustments that attempts to make consistent as much as possible of our thinking.

I do not think it does violence to our everyday notion of emotion to parse it as involving strong desire; in fact, this captures much of its essence and still leaves plenty of alternative terminology, such as "feeling" and "affect" and "attitude," for other purposes. If, then, it is possible in addition by means of this analysis to salvage a significant ethical thesis about emotion, which has had its eminent defenders in all times and climes, the case has been made, I submit, to give that ethical thesis, based on that analysis, a new day in court; hence, this essay.

The plan of the essay conforms to certain distinctions among ethical concepts. I understand *ethics* to encompass the whole of norms that pertain to human behavior and well-being. "Behavior" here includes all aspects of human being that are subject to voluntary control, however indirectly or over the long term; thus, not only specific, overt acts but also patterns of thought and feeling and even character and personality are arguably forms of behavior in this sense.

A typical starting point for the investigation of ethics is *the good life*. This is the life that is best for the individual. This is not intended to imply a separate investigation for each individual (although every individual is encouraged to extend or "apply" the investigation to his or her own case); the inquiry concerns the most general features of such a life, the presumption being that *at some level* it is possible to find common ground among all human beings in regard to what has real value, what is truly worthwhile, what gives life its "meaning."

As profound as such an investigation is, it is not the end of ethics. At least, it is not *necessarily* the end of ethics if, in the process of reflecting on the nature of the good life or "prudence," one has neglected to consider one's obligations toward the rest of the universe. The domain of *morality* is precisely these relations of obligation toward others.

Running the gauntlet of these categories in this essay will be *the dispassion thesis*, to wit: The ethical life is dispassionate. Thus, first to be considered is whether the good life is dispassionate; that is, whether it is, as a rule, prudent to be dispassionate. As already noted, this philosophical prescription for contentment faces formidable opposition from the popular attitude that strong feeling is, in at least some of its forms, what life is all about.

Next to be considered is the morality of dispassion. On the one hand, should the proponents of passion prevail with respect to the good life, there may still be moral reasons for preferring dispassion as a general ethics. On the other hand, should dispassion win the day in terms of prudence, there may still be moral objections to its adoption as a general ethics; for example, is not compassion, as its very name suggests, a passion?

Finally, even if it passes this substantive ethical examination, the dispassion thesis may falter on more "formal" grounds. For example, is it even possible for human beings to assume a settled disposition of dispassion? On the general principle that "ought" implies "can," an ethics based on an impossible attainment is really no ethics at all.

My approach to all of these issues will be analytic, by which I mean simply that I will consider the arguments. However, I intend also to incorporate non-Western thought as source material; in particular, the Buddhist Middle Way has been an inspiration throughout. I wish to clarify, however, that this essay is not intended as a scholarly contribution to Buddhist philosophy. But, then, neither is it intended as a scholarly contribution to Greek philosophy, German philosophy, and so on. It is intended to promote truly comparative philosophy, by which I mean that *all* cultural traditions are our philosophical oyster. And so we may allude to the Buddha or the *Gita* or *karma* or *samkhya* as—dare I say—*casually* as to Plato or the *Grundlegung* or the principle of utility or idealism . . . even if in so doing we occasionally raise the hackles of a Buddhist or Kantian scholar.[6] But our main intent is to philosophize.[7]

I. THE GOODNESS OF DISPASSION

Let us begin the defense of dispassion with a traditional Buddhist argument against passion:[8]

1. Suffering is bad.
2. The singular cause of suffering is strong desire.
Therefore, strong desire (i.e., passion or emotion) is bad.

The second premise is the crucial one. Life is full of hardships, so it is apparently full of causes of suffering: illness, injury, pain, war, bereavement, and so on, *ad infinitum*. But it was the great insight of the Buddha that there is a common denominator to all human suffering, namely, the desire for what has occurred not to have occurred or the desire for what has not occurred to have occurred or the desire for what may occur not to occur or the desire for what may not occur to occur . . . in a word, desire.

There is a persuasive argument for this claim. Consider any supposed cause of suffering,. for example, illness. Normally, illness does bring suffering, or unhappiness, in its train; but this is only because normally we desire not to be sick. There is nothing necessary about this attitude. We all recall our joy as a child to discover that we "had a temperature" and therefore did not have to go to school. What matters for suffering, then, is not illness per se, but our state of desire with respect to it. Illness is not the cause, but only an occasion, of suffering.

Now, it may seem that the appropriate conclusion to draw is that *desire* is bad. And this is often the phrasing used in translations from Buddhist sources. However, the word *desire* can, itself, connote an intensity of attitude; to avoid ambiguity, therefore, I prefer to speak of "strong desire." But *is* strong desire intended in the Buddhist usage of "desire"? I think the answer must be Yes, for in this way Buddhist ethics is saved from absurdity. A total condemnation of desire would leave no basis for feeling and action, but these are necessary for life. Furthermore, it does seem plausible that *suffering* would result from, or be a form of, *intensity* of feeling and not just any degree of feeling.

Objection 1. The Buddhist argument is invalid. Let us grant the Buddha his "great insight" that the common denominator of all human suffering is (strong) desire or passion. It still does not follow that passion is bad, that is, bad *tout court*. For passion may also cause happiness and joy, and therefore, its absence would itself be bad.

And when we consider the analysis of passion as strong desire, it does seem that the tables can be completely turned on the Buddha. For just as a person will be unhappy if what is desired does not come about, so a person will be happy if what is desired does come about, etc. And, again, just as with unhappiness or suffering, the stronger the desire involved, the greater the happiness. So strong desire is the singular cause of joy.

Another way to explain the fallacy in the Buddha's thinking is to clarify that it is *frustrated* (strong) desire that is the true cause of suffering. But, by the same psychology, *satisfied* (strong) desire is the true cause or source of all joy. Therefore, to condemn desire itself is to throw the baby out with the bath water.

Reply. Let us grant that strong desire is part and parcel not only of suffering but also of joy; does it follow that we are stuck with it? No, there are alternatives; for example:

1. The likelihood of suffering is greater than the likelihood of joy.
2. Moderate happiness is sufficiently rewarding.

1. The Buddha seems to have maintained this, for the Second Noble Truth—that strong desire is the source of all suffering—follows upon the First Noble Truth, which is that suffering predominates in life. There are different ways one might attempt to argue for this. For example, John Stuart Mill, in a stirring rendition of the Problem of Evil, inventories the ravages of nature on human existence: pestilence, flood, famine, fire, and so on.' But this is not really in the Buddhist spirit, for it ignores the basis of suffering in *desire*.

Once again, Buddhism itself offers a forceful argument: Joy is *systematically* elusive. This follows from the nature of desire and the contingency of the world. Suppose that *j* is something you desire very much, and so is, potentially or actually, an object of joy for you. You will then be in one of several possible relations to *j*; for example:

- You are not yet in possession of *j*, and believe you never will be.
- You are not yet in possession of *j*, but believe you someday will be.
- You are in possession of *j*.

It may seem that the three possibilities listed are in the order of increasing happiness. But this is not at all necessarily the case. With regard to your actually being in possession of *j*, there is the distinct possibility that a new desire will arise. For let us take the best case, where the possession of *j* *does not* disappoint you; *j* turns out to be exactly what you expected it to be; that is, it really was *j* that you desired and not some "apparent *j*." And now you have it.

But your knowledge of the world must fill you with dread. For now that you have your heart's desire, you are mortally afraid that it will be taken from you. This can happen in so many ways. For example, if *j* is a person, *j* may die. Or *j* may simply change in such a way that he or she ceases to be *j* in the way you desired him or her. Or *j*'s change, or some change in yourself, may cause *j* to lose interest in *you* and therefore leave you.

Each of these possibilities is, itself, an occasion of suffering that may await you, and so this is one way that joy itself promotes suffering. But the more immediate canker in joy is the mere knowledge that these possibilities exist and, indeed, in this world of flux, that *one* of them is *likely* to occur.

Thus, although now you are in possession of *j*, your general state of desire is still one of frustration; for now it is to retain, rather than obtain, *j* that you pine, and so you are in pain. And this new desire is, if anything, less likely to be satisfied than the original desire; for however difficult it may be to acquire a desired object, it is surely impossible to be able to count on its indefinitely continued possession.[10]

2. Nonetheless, one might suppose, as Tennyson says in *In Memoriam*, "'tis better to have loved and lost than never to have loved at all." No matter how rare, shortlived, or adulterated joy may be, it is what makes life worth living. To forsake it altogether so as to avoid the admittedly equally intense and even predominant suffering of life is, once again, to throw the baby out with the bath water.

Another reply to this charge, therefore, is that an alternative source of happiness has been overlooked, viz., satisfaction of desires of moderate strength. Cease to overwhelm the palate with soda pop, and how sweet a strawberry will taste! Cease to flush the psyche with passions, and more refined sensibilities will be able to operate (and this is "more" in both a qualitative and a quantitative sense). It is true that desires of moderate strength don't get the same "press" as indulged emotions, but might they not, nonetheless, prove just as satisfying—dare I say, more so?—in the long run? (And this, recall, would be combined with one's relative immunity from extremes of unhappiness if one were dispositionally dispassionate.)

I would go so far as to identify passion—that is, strong desire—with addiction. The parallels between such things as anger, sexual desire, and chemical dependency are striking and instructive. This is true of these phenomena in all of their aspects which are being treated in this essay—prudential, rational, moral, phenomenological, motivational, and so forth.

Thus, if the high of a drug is compelling enough, the experience may be desired to the point of irresistibility.[11] And yet it is a commonplace that the pursuit of this high can wreck a life—not because the high is not a high (let us grant that it is truly supremely pleasurable), but because its pursuit and enjoyment interfere with the pursuit and enjoyment of the multitude of perhaps less intense satisfactions that constitute a good life.[12]

Objection 2. Emotion is not only something we feel, hence enjoy (or suffer), but also something that motivates us. "Nothing great in the world has been accomplished without passion."[13]

Reply. To put the objection in the terms of our own analysis of emotion: Desire is a component not only of emotion but also of motivation. Hence, the elimination of strong desire will preclude not only extremes of feeling but also forceful and/or sustained action.

In reply let me first acknowledge the dual role of desire in our psychic life. I do accept that not only emotion but also motivation and hence action require the presence of desire; thus, I cannot evade the objection by holding out for some purely cognitive basis for action. For example, some philosophers would argue that a particular behavior (say, running away from a dog) can be motivated solely by a belief (say, that the dog is about to bite). But I would counter that even such a belief would be motivationally idle if not accompanied by a desire (say, to avoid pain and injury).[14]

Furthermore, let me acknowledge the corollary that the elimination of passion, that is, strong desire, would eliminate a class of motivation as well, viz., "strong motivation," and hence also actions of a certain type. This I consider to be just as good a consequence as the elimination of passion (-ate feeling) itself. (I shall say why at the end of this section.)

Nonetheless, the objection as it stands is invalid. The reason is that it ignores *relative* strengths of desire. For suppose you have achieved a general state of dispassion. This does not mean that all of your desires are of the same strength; there is still possible a wide range of "moderate strengths" (not to mention weak ones). Thus, if your desire to achieve some difficult goal is moderate, but also the strong*est* desire in your conative repertoire, are you not likely to be sustained on the arduous path?

Might we not even question whether, under the circumstances, the path should be conceived as arduous? Absent a conflicting strong desire, the task itself may cease to be a difficult one; in other words, perhaps it is only our own desires that make things difficult.[15] If no strong desire opposes our intention, do we require a strong desire to implement it?

One might counter that the reply depends on a distinction without a difference: If *relative* strengths remain, then strong desire itself remains. There are no *ergs* of desire by which to measure its absolute strength. Strong desire just is strong*est* desire. Thus, if no other desire is strong enough to stand in the way of your desire to accomplish some task, then the latter is strong simpliciter; what more could be expected of a strong desire than irresistibility?

However, I think it does make sense to distinguish relative from absolute strength of desire. Suppose there are two persons, *A* and *B*, on their deathbeds who desire nothing so much as to continue to live; thus, for each, the desire to live is his strongest desire. Both have a "clear conscience"; they are not in physical pain; and so on. Nonetheless, we can imagine that *A* and *B* cope very differently with the situation. For *A*, there is despair, torment, terror at the thought of soon ceasing to exist; *A* is also highly susceptible to come-ons from salespersons offering miracle cures, televangelists, and the like. Meanwhile, *B* does not exhibit these feelings and behaviors; *B* maintains an interest in what life still has to offer and attends to affairs in a responsible manner. This seems to me to be the kind of evidence that would entitle us to attribute different *absolute* strengths of desire to A and B.

Perhaps we may sum it up by saying that strong desire is that strength of desire which makes one liable to both extremes of feeling and irrationality of behavior. A strong desire that is (believed to be, or eventually to be) satisfied yields joy, while one that is frustrated yields suffering; but, whether satisfied or frustrated, a strong desire makes one liable to irrationality. We may suppose, in keeping with our belief/desire analysis of both feeling and motivation, that a *strong* desire is precisely one that oversteps its bounds and intrudes on the domain of belief, in the sense that the desire substitutes for evidence. For example, the strong desire to live may induce one to enlist the services of a faith healer, whom one has come to believe is the epitome of good sense and sound science, absent evidence to persuade one of these things when one considers them in the "cool light of reason."

In other words, the roles of belief and desire are reversed under the influence of strong desire. We would normally expect belief to take the lead and desire to follow; for example, you believe that the dog is about to attack and, on that basis, desire to relocate. But if your desire not to be bitten is strong enough (e.g., due to some early childhood experience), then, upon seeing a friendly-looking dog lying peacefully in your path, you may be seized with the conviction that it is primed to attack, and run away. In this way, irrationality arises in both thinking and action; and this not only supports the notion of absolute strength of desire and thereby rescues the dispassion thesis from the charge of unintelligibility, but also constitutes in its own right a defense of that thesis.[16]

II. THE MORALITY OF DISPASSION

Objection 3. The preceding discussion has dealt with the prudential aspects of dispassion. Very often this is *all* one hears discussed. Countless treatises, both popular and traditional, regale us with the advantages to ourselves of a tamped-down feeling life. But even if we grant these advantages, they are not the last word on the *ethical* life, for this must be sensitive to *moral* considerations as well.[17] And these require that one be capable of full-blooded responses to happenings in the world.

This is true in two ways (which may or may not merge, depending on one's moral theory): First, one must have sufficient feeling capacity to be morally sensitive; that is, one must have moral sensibility, the ability to care (about others, or about moral principles[18]), the ability to form moral judgments. Second, one must have sufficient feeling capacity to act on those judgments; that is, one must have moral motivation. The dispassionate individual will be lacking on both counts. Thus, the dispassionate life cannot be recommended.

Reply. This moral objection to dispassion is similar to the earlier, prudential ones in that dispassion is faulted in the two respects of feeling and motivation. As before, it is because desire plays a role in both that *strong* desire is considered essential to their proper functioning in certain situations.

My reply consequently runs parallel to those in the preceding section. First, with respect to feeling: Before, it was argued that strong desire is the root cause of suffering and is therefore (other things being equal) ill-advised on prudential grounds. The analogous argument in the present context is that strong desire *directed toward moral ends* is at least as likely to generate suffering in the desirer as is strong desire directed toward personal ends.

This follows from the analysis of emotion as consisting (in part) of (strong) desire; a frustrated desire is a frustrated desire, no matter what its object, and hence is an instance of suffering. And in the moral arena, desire is, if anything, more likely to be frustrated, for one has cast one's lot with others (presumably the likelihood of disappointment with respect to n entities is, other things equal, n times that for just one, i.e., oneself).[19]

Strong moral desire, therefore, will be associated with suffering. This is a significant observation, because one might have supposed that the onus of moral responsiveness had to do with our innate egoism, that morality is difficult for us precisely because it interferes with our selfish tendencies. But the present argument demonstrates that morality can be difficult *in its own right*—specifically, when it involves *strong* moral desire.

The argument continues: Is this a situation that is likely to sustain moral concern and sensibility? Here I appeal to commonsense psychology. It seems patent that, human beings being what they are[20]—among other things, averse to suffering—their tendency to shy away from morality will increase as the pain associated with morality increases.

A second prudential argument against emotional feeling was that strong feelings tend to crowd out moderate ones, both qualitatively and quantitatively. This is equally true in the moral realm and is just as likely to lead to *moral* impoverishment. An example would be the person who is so caught up in her important job, on whom hinges many people's very survival, that she habitually neglects her family.

Yet another prudential argument was that strong desire is prone to irrational thinking and action. This is applicable in a straightforward way to moral contexts; one does not want an irrational agent for the attainment of moral ends any more than for prudential ends.

Finally, it was argued earlier that relatively strong desire is possible even in the absence of absolutely strong desire. This needs to be elaborated in the present context. An especially germane example is the Paradox of Compassion in Buddhism.[21]

"Compassionate" is an epithet that is commonly applied to the Buddha. And yet calmness is certainly another of his inseparable qualities. How are these to be reconciled? Does not a universal calmness necessarily undercut the capacity to care about and act on behalf of others? Does this not follow from the very analysis of feeling and emotion that has been put forward: To care is to desire strongly, but to be calm is not to?

My reply (on behalf of the Buddha, although the interpretation is my own) presupposes two psychological truths about human beings: (1) Our strongest desires tend to be egoistic ones,[22] but (2) we are naturally possessed by altruistic desires as well. I will not spend any time attempting to persuade the reader of these truths (hypotheses?); I refer you to your own knowledge of the world and, if need be (especially for the second one), the conceptual clarifications of C. D. Broad (1952).

Now add to this brew the possibility of relative strengths of desire and the injunction to eliminate passion: The result, I maintain, is a heightened compassion, both in terms of feeling and action. This is because the elimination of passion, given the original preeminence of egoism, will not only reduce egoism "absolutely" but also relatively to altruism, for the latter was (*ex hypothesi*) "moderate" to begin with, and so will not be reduced absolutely. Hence one's altruistic feelings will move more to the fore in one's consciousness (or "feelings") and also become more influential in one's motivations.

For example: A child needs to be rescued from the rapids. Does the Buddhist jump into the water, at some risk to herself, to try to save the child? A person who is strongly egoistic might be daunted by concern for her own welfare. But the Buddhist would have *less* concern for herself and so would be *more* likely to attempt the rescue.[23]

Does the present argument undercut the earlier one that strong moral desire inhibits moral responsiveness by inducing suffering? After all, if one's egoist desire diminishes in strength, won't moral suffering itself be less aversive? One would simply care less that one is suffering. Therefore, one could, with good effect, retain strong moral desire so long as one moderated one's egoist desire.

But I think the present argument complements rather than undercuts the earlier one. The mental or emotional suffering I have identified with frustrated strong desire is *intrinsically* aversive; that is, it does not depend for its aversiveness on being the object of yet another desire, viz., the desire that one not suffer.[24] Otherwise, the very meaning of "suffering" would be empty; if only the (strong) desire not to *s* defined what *s* is, what would *s* be? (Cf.: One need not believe one is in pain to be in pain.)

Of course, I do not deny that one's own suffering could be an object of one's own desire—since anything can be—and hence, on account of the second-order desire, a source of compounded suffering. It's just that it need not be the object of another desire in order to be what it is (i.e., suffering).

I conclude, therefore, that the prescription for enhanced compassion need not be to strengthen one's concern for others. Especially if one is concerned about action, and hence that one's compassion function rationally, one may well be advised to leave compassion at its present strength and work on the *reduction* of *egoism instead.*[25]

III. THE ETHICS OF DISPASSION

Objection 4. Suppose it were true that dispassion is desirable. This still does not provide an *ethics* unless dispassion is *possible*, on the general ground that "'ought' implies 'can'." Indeed, the very person who gave us that idea, Immanuel Kant, maintained that his Categorical Imperative, which enjoins us to *act* in a certain way, is superior to (or at least is the proper interpretation of) the Second Commandment (Matthew 22: 39)—"Love your neighbor as yourself"—for precisely this reason: Emotion is not subject to voluntary control.[26]

Reply. The sense of "voluntary" in which emotions are not subject to voluntary control is a very narrow one. In fact, there are countless ways—many of them quite commonplace—to control—and, specifically, to diminish—emotion. In the short term: If you are angry, count to ten. The time you give yourself can serve to moderate emotion in several ways: (1) There is time to reflect upon, to recollect, the reasons you have for not expressing your anger and even for not *being* angry; (2) avoidance of expressing and otherwise "indulging" in the anger is a way of not "feeding the fire," both in terms of not inciting another party to the dispute to further inflammatory acts and not artificially reinforcing your own perception of the situation; (3) the passage of time allows for new developments that may short-circuit the anger (e.g., the other person offers an apology, or new information is forthcoming that removes the grounds for anger).

By and large, the available methods depend on the cognitive nature of emotion. Since belief is an essential component of emotion, the alteration of a belief can change the nature of an emotion or alter its intensity or even eliminate it entirely. For example, if you are angry because you believe someone has insulted you, then coming to believe that you misheard or misinterpreted that person and that, in fact, he intended to praise you will, other things being equal, eliminate the anger (and could even "transform" it into affection).

I say "other things being equal" because emotion tends to breed emotion. But, again, the process can be understood cognitively. In the example given, suppose a long time elapses before you are disabused of the mistaken belief that this person insulted you. Now, since the context is, *ex hypothesi*, an emotional one, we must suppose that you also harbor a *strong* desire not to be insulted. This combination of belief and desire, which constitutes anger and resentment, naturally leads to a certain critical alertness with respect to that person. (Thus, note the crucial function of *strong* desire in the typical functioning of the emotion; merely to believe oneself insulted does not—*cannot* I would say—result in emotional behavior if one simply does not care very much.)

And so, over time, you (think you) become aware of other slights from this person. You may even begin to dish out some of the same to him, eventually eliciting from him thereby *genuinely* disdainful behavior. Then comes the day when you realize your original umbrage was ill-founded. But by then you have built up such a strong "case" for this person's poor treatment of you that your anger may be relatively immune to alteration.

Now, granting that the argument so far has shown the task of controlling, and specifically extinguishing, emotion to be a cognitive one, the objection may be pursued that emotion control is still by and large impracticable. Three reasons may be cited:

1. Reducing the problem of emotion control to belief control hardly establishes the voluntary nature of emotional control, since beliefs are themselves immune to voluntary control (e.g., you cannot simply will yourself to believe in Santa Claus).

2. The beliefs that constitute an emotion may be *true*, and so be ineradicable in the sense that they fully justify the emotion.

3. An emotion may be so buttressed by beliefs, as in the last example, that it will elude every effort to dislodge it.

Reply to (1): Here again, the conception of the voluntary that has been put forward is too narrow. It is true that one normally cannot simply will a belief into or out of existence. But countless ways exist to alter belief, in which one may voluntarily and intentionally engage.[27] For example, if you decide to read a book on physics, are you not knowingly and willingly embarking upon a course of action that will likely produce many beliefs in you and even eliminate some existing ones?

Reply to (2): I must, of course, grant the justice of the argument that, often, the belief that constitutes an emotion is true. However, it does not follow that the emotion is thereby justified. Here, yet again, the importance of the *desire* component of emotions comes to the fore.

Recall the example of anger due to perceived insult, and suppose that the insult was, indeed, real and intended. But this in itself does not constitute, and certainly does not justify, anger. One must *strongly desire* not to be treated in this fashion in order for *emotion* to be present. But even then, a *justification* for the emotion may be lacking. That is because in order for an emotion to be *justified* (and not merely present), not only the component belief requires validation *but also the component desire* AND ALSO ITS STRENGTH.

Thus, in the insult example, we must ask, Was there justification for the strong desire that one not be insulted? The answer to this question calls for tracing out the roots of the desire and its strength. Pride may be uncovered. Is *pride* justified? The answer to this question depends on what pride is. Perhaps it is just a good opinion of oneself (and not, for example, conceit). So we may grant the propriety of it, at least in the normal case (although Christianity might balk and Buddhism definitely would). Even so, we may question whether *excessive* pride is involved: Is one's opinion of oneself perhaps too high, hence too insistent upon prerogatives, such as immunity from public judgment by others?

Observe that, once again, a process of rational reflection has been engaged in for the purpose of influencing, perhaps eliminating, an emotion. But this time the process has been applied not to the component belief of the emotion but to the component desire, and particularly to that desire's intensity.[28] The process is rational because, once again, beliefs have been examined; but this time the beliefs are those which support the desire component of the emotion (e.g., the belief that I am so wonderful, which is the basis of the desire that everyone recognize my greatness) rather than those which help constitute the emotion (e.g., in this case, the belief that this person has insulted me).[29]

Reply to (3): More sophisticated means than counting to ten exist for exploiting the cognitive nature of emotions. Indeed, a great deal of the history of psychotherapy can be understood in cognitivist terms.[30] One may need to trace whole networks of belief and desire and behavioral history in order to reach the sources of one's emotionality, and so it is true that a great deal of work may be needed.[31] But it can be done, and the effort to do so is a voluntary act of the client's.

Furthermore, besides working on specific emotions (e.g., your ill will toward this person) or emotional hangups (e.g., your proneness to "love too much"), there are methods for cultivating dispassion as a general disposition. These also exploit the cognitive nature of emotion. Thus, one could reflect upon the general arguments in this essay and bring them, and variations thereon, before the mind on occasions where emotion threatens (which is almost always); for example:

> When anything, from the meanest thing upwards, is attractive or serviceable or an object of affection, remember always to say to yourself, "What is its nature?" If you are fond of a jug, say you are fond of a jug; then you will not be disturbed if it be broken. If you kiss your child or your wife, say to yourself that you are kissing a human being, for then if death strikes it you will not be disturbed.[32]

Another technique involves repeating a word in the mind.[33] This may seem to be the epitome of noncognitive control, because one is not entertaining any particular beliefs (such as "It is silly to get upset about his comment"), but, quite the opposite, one is attempting to banish from one's mind all thoughts whatsoever (other than the word).

But consider it more closely. Should some thought arise during this process—for example, "I wonder if she really meant that"; "I'm cold"; sound of ticking wristwatch; and so on—one "gently" brings one's attention back to the word. In this way, one cultivates a mental skill, viz., how to direct one's attention where one wants it.

If, therefore, on some other occasion (i.e., when one is not explicitly practicing this technique) a potentially emotional situation arises, one is in a better position to defuse it. For example, when your child won't stop crying, such thoughts as these may begin to crowd your mind: "Why must he be so selfish? He exaggerates everything. He is trying to rule my life." But if one has practiced the technique enough, one will be able to assimilate the situation to it: First one will notice the similarity, and then one will act by gently bringing the mind back to (the present moment, the actual situation) and away from the troubling, distracting thoughts. One thereby denies to emotion the cognitive seed on which it would condense.

Now there is room to entertain other perceptions and thoughts; for example, "I wonder what is really troubling him. Actually, this whole situation is kind of funny: I'm seeing him as selfish and exaggerating and trying to take control, when, in fact, I'm just a child myself who is trying to get my own way and blowing the whole thing out of proportion. (Hmmm . . . I wonder if his behavior is in some way a reflection of mine . . . ?)"

In this way one dampens emotion and enhances perception and cognition, sensibility and rationality, heart and mind.

Notes

I am grateful for a sabbatical leave and research grant from the University of New Haven which made possible the writing of this essay. A number of refinements are due to the proddings of my co-editor and of Harvey Green, both of whom have indicated in the friendliest of ways that they think my thesis is dead wrong.

1. See the introduction to this volume for a review of the recent literature.

2. See the introduction to this volume for a review of the recent literature.

3. This thesis is defended at length in Marks (1982).

4. I owe this stipulation to O. H. Green.

5. E.g., Amélie O. Rorty (1980).

6. Another way to put this is that whatever is attributed herein to Buddhism (etc.) should be taken to be my interpretation thereof.

7. No disrespect intended. The scholar and I are simply about different tasks (or subtasks, if we consider the interrelations of our work).

8. Buddhism is no more of a piece than any other major philosophic tradition. It is possible even to find passion (suitably interpreted, as always) in Buddhism; witness, for example, Parkes's contribution to this volume. It is my belief that the argument I here adduce represents a main component of the tradition. I can certainly attest that *my own thinking* on the subject of emotion has been influenced by my readings in Buddhism (however well or ill I have interpreted them), and it is in this sense only that I would call this essay a work in comparative philosophy. In the end, what concerns us is the strength of the argument in its own terms (i.e., in terms that engage the reader, whether Western or Eastern), even if *no* scholar were to sanction it *as Buddhist*.

For what it is worth, then, let me cite as a relevant source the central Theravāda text, *The Dhammapada*, according to which the model personage, the

Brahmin, "has no craving desires, either for this world or for another world, who free from desires is in infinite freedom" (Mascaró 1973, verse 410). In the crucial second premise of "my" argument, "strong desire" is a rendition of the Pali term, *taṇhā*, which Rahula (1974) translates as "thirst, desire, craving" (p. 146) and about which he says, "[while] not the first or the only cause of the arising of *dukkha* [suffering], . . . it is the most palpable and immediate cause, the 'principal thing' and the 'all-pervading thing'" (p. 29).

9. *Nature and Utility of Religion.*

10. "[T]he dearest and most attractive dwelling-place of despair is in the very heart of immediate happiness" (Kierkegaard, *The Sickness unto Death*, W. Lowrie, tr.).

11. I do observe a distinction between pleasure and desire satisfaction, and even an intense pleasure may be desired only moderately, if at all. However, as in the present example, intense pleasure and strong desire are naturally paired, other things equal. (*Mutatis mutandis* for pain and aversion.)

12. Yet a third alternative to dependence on strong desire for the good life is the mystical notion that the attainment of dispassion is—to use but one of many similes in the world's mystical literatures—like the calming of a pond's surface so that the sun's image may shine forth. While almost certainly on the agenda for a great deal of Buddhism, as well as for other dispassionate philosophies, I omit further discussion of the mystical life because I am concerned to see how well the dispassion thesis can be defended in mundane terms.

13. Hegel, *Philosophy of History*, J. Sibree, tr.

14. See Marks 1986.

15. As it says in my stepson's "Karate Club" reader, citing Nakamura, "It doesn't matter whom you're paired against; your opponent is always yourself."

16. I would like to thank Jerry Shaffer and Mitchell Silver for help in formulating the foregoing reply (and absolve them of responsibility for any inadequacy it may still possess).

17. Arthur C. Danto (1988) makes this point most articulately, especially ch. 4.

18. That the latter is also a form of caring is argued persuasively by Blum (1980).

19. A Kantian concern for duty rather than people per se may escape this quantitative objection but is still subject to the qualitative objection that excessive concern makes one liable, indeed, prone, to suffering. For simplicity's sake, I shall continue to treat morality as implying altruism.

20. And suffering being what it is; see the argument at the end of this section.

21. So far as I know, I coined this term in a paper presented at the Radhakrishnan Centennial Conference, Miami University, Oxford, Ohio, April, 1988; I had in mind the Paradox of Desire, discussed by Alt (1980) and Herman (1980). The two "paradoxes" are formally identical, for both have to do with the motivation to achieve Nirvana, the one on behalf of everyone or -thing, the other just oneself. Cf. also Kaplan 1961, 261-63.

22. Or at least not altruistic ones. As Bishop Butler demonstrated in his *Sermons*, it is a mistake to suppose that a desire is egoistic just because it is *one's own*. It is the *object* of a desire that determines whether it is egoistic; hence, your desire to thrive is egoistic, but your desire to experience maximal pleasure may be only hedonistic (and quite detrimental to your long-term well-being), and your passion for stamp-collecting, merely philatelic. Thus, there is a potentially infinite array of nonaltruistic desires, of which egoism is just one.

23. To quote Mary Shelley's blind man DeLacey (when he was speaking to Frankenstein's monster): "The Hearts of men, when unprejudiced by any obvious self-interest, are full of brotherly love and charity."

24. Indeed, this seems to be what distinguishes suffering from physical pain, for the latter *need not be aversive*; see Shaffer 1976.

25. Thus, I am offering a strictly ethical interpretation of a central Buddhist doctrine: "this 'thirst' [*taṇhā*, strong desire] has as its centre the false idea of self" (Rahula 1974, 30). The standard Buddhist prescription, then, is to recognize the illusoriness of the self; desire will perforce lose its grip. But I am suggesting a more commonsensical approach, which retains the notion of (one-)self as the subject of one's desires and counsels only its diminution as the object of one's desires. (This also seems to have the ethical advantage over the more metaphysical doctrine of the illusoriness of self that *other* selves remain possible objects of one's concern.)

26. See the first section of the *Grundlegung*.

27. Robert C. Solomon has stressed this point, at least by implication, in his many works on passion. E.g., see Solomon 1976.

28. Brandt (1979) develops a procedure of "cognitive psychotherapy" for precisely this purpose. See also Marks (1983), who emphasizes that there are both qualitative and quantitative aspects to desire therapy: One wants to know *which* desires to retain and also *at what intensities*.

29. Schematically:

BELIEF (A insulted me) + DESIRE (to be appreciated) = EMOTION (umbrage)

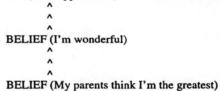

BELIEF (I'm wonderful)

BELIEF (My parents think I'm the greatest)

30. A therapeutic method such as Albert Ellis's rational-emotive psychotherapy recognizes this explicitly. See, e.g., Ellis 1962.

31. Alternatively, one can attempt to bypass history and undergo a process of desensitization, which is also cognitive; for example, an object that disgusts one can be repeatedly cognized as composed of inoffensive molecules.

32. Epictetus, *Enchiridion*, P. E. Matheson, tr. I take the examples to be advising the tempering of concern about *one's own* welfare (albeit for the sake of one's own welfare); this is in keeping with my argument that a dispassion program will, by and large, be concerned with reduction of egoism, not altruism. I would not, therefore, go along with Epictetus on the following bit of advice, for here, I take it, he advises the tempering of one's concern about *another's* welfare (for the sake of one's own welfare):

> If you wish to make progress, abandon reasonings of this sort: . . . "If I do not punish my son, he will be wicked." . . . It is better for your son to be wicked than for you to be miserable.

33. Cf. Benson and Klipper 1976, which was inspired, of course, by *japa* yoga, or meditation that employs a mantra.

Bibliography

Alt, Wayne. 1980. "There Is No Paradox of Desire in Buddhism." *Philosophy East and West* 30: 521-28.

Baier, Annette C. 1985. "Actions, Passions, and Reasons." In *Postures of the Mind: Essays on Mind and Morals*. Minneapolis: University of Minnesota Press.

Benson, Herbert and Miriam Z. Klipper. 1976. *Relaxation Response*. New York: Avon.

Blum, Lawrence A. 1980. *Friendship, Altruism, and Morality*. London: Routledge & Kegan Paul.

Brandt, Richard B. 1979. *A Theory of the Good and the Right*. Oxford: Clarendon.

Broad, C. D. 1952. "Egoism as a Theory of Human Motives." In *Ethics and the History of Philosophy*, 218-31. London: Routledge & Kegan Paul.

Danto, Arthur C. 1988. *Mysticism and Morality*. New York: Columbia University Press.

Ellis, Albert. 1962. *Reason and Emotion in Psychotherapy*. New York: Lyle Stuart.

Herman, A. L. 1980. "Ah, But There Is a Paradox of Desire in Buddhism." *Philosophy East and West* 30: 529-32.

Kaplan, Abraham. 1961. *The New World of Philosophy*. New York: Random House.

Kraut, Robert. 1986. "Feelings in Context." *Journal of Philosophy* 86: 642-52.

Lyons, William. 1980. *Emotion*. Cambridge: Cambridge University Press.

Marks, Joel. 1982. "A Theory of Emotion." *Philosophical Studies* 42: 227-42.

————. 1983. "The Rationality of Dispassion, or Why Richard Brandt Should Be a Buddhist." In *Emotions: Philosophical Studies*, ed. K. D. Irani and G. E. Myers, 57-71. New York: Haven.

————. 1986. "The Difference between Motivation and Desire." In *The Ways of Desire: New Essays in Philosophical Psychology on the Concept of Wanting*, ed. Joel Marks, 133-47. Chicago: Precedent.

Mascaró, Juan, trans. 1973. *The Dhammapada*. New York: Penguin.

Rahula, Walpola. 1974. *What the Buddha Taught*. New York: Grove.

Rorty, Amélie Oksenberg, ed. 1980. *Explaining Emotions*. Berkeley: University of California Press.

Shaffer, Jerome A. 1976. "Pain and Suffering." In *Philosophical Dimensions of the Neuro-Medical Sciences*, ed. Stuart F. Spicker and H. Tristram Engelhardt, Jr., 221-33. Dordrecht, Holland: D. Reidel.

Solomon, Robert C. 1976. *The Passions. The Myth and Nature of Human Emotion*. Garden City, NY: Anchor/Doubleday.

The Concept of Emotion Revisited: A Critical Synthesis of Western and Confucian Thought

Mary I. Bockover

Western philosophy has entertained various, even antithetical, views of emotion. In section 1 of this article, I will explain two prominent ways the emotions have been understood in the West in this century which exemplify this disparity. First, though, a brief description of the subjective/objective distinction will provide background for all of the discussions that follow. Next, in section 2, some Confucian insights into the nature of human "goodness" will be examined. Finally, I will offer my own view of the emotions in section 3, and then will conclude by bringing Confucian thought to bear on the concept of emotion. My overall aim is to present a critical synthesis of current Western and ancient Chinese lines of thought, in light of a new way of understanding the emotions.

I

The subjective/objective distinction that has been prominent for the last few centuries grew largely out of the work of Descartes and Kant. Roughly, according to this distinction, "subjective" refers to a kind of perception, knowledge, or understanding that is unique to a specific person's experience of the phenomenal world—one dependent on time, place, context, frame of mind, and various other factors. "Objective," on the other hand, refers to that which is known to exist regardless of one's unique individual experience or conception of it. To know something objectively is to know precisely what any other rational person with intact faculties would know about the same thing. To the contrary, to know something subjectively is to know it in a way that presumably cannot be adequately defined or justified for another person, for the very reason that it is a product of one's own unique experience. As a result, subjective experiences are considered private and even inaccessible to others, since we cannot get into the consciousness of another to know exactly what she is experiencing. We can only speculate that the experience may be analogous to our own. The difficulty that results is that "subjective truths" may be justified for one person but not for another, even though both are of the same rational nature.[1]

The West now heavily relies on "subjective" concepts while trying to resolve some of its main philosophical questions. In fact, our tradition has taken the subjective/objective dichotomy to the point of perfect abstraction, where "subjective" squarely refers to *intrapersonal* phenomena and "objective" refers to phenomena presumed to have a reality not dependent on the experiential idiosyncrasies of any given person. To reiterate, something deemed "objective" is taken to be knowable in accordance with the dictates of human experience and reason. Something "subjective," on the other hand, is taken to be particular to a person and to inhere *inside the person*; it is a matter of thought and experience that cannot be precisely known by or communicated to others, even though we may presume that subjective experiences are similar in certain cases. Such a subjective analysis has been employed to describe even the most basic human phenomena. Emotions are paradigmatic examples of this, in being defined typically as subjective, internal psychological states of one kind or another.

Emotions have been described as subjective states in many ways. One of the most prominent descriptions was offered by William James and Carl Lange, who defined emotions as *feelings* or the perception of bodily disturbances. In order to counter "our natural way of thinking" about the emotions, which wrongly assumes that "the mental perception of some fact excites the mental affection called the emotion" and, in turn, gives rise to the bodily "manifestations" of emotion (James and Lange 1967, 13), James offered the following:

> My thesis on the contrary is that the bodily changes follow directly the PER-CEPTION of the exciting fact, and that our feeling of the same changes as they occur IS the emotion. Common sense says, we lose our fortune, are sorry and weep; we meet a bear, are frightened and run; we are insulted by a rival, are angry and strike. . . . The more rational statement is that we feel sorry because we cry, angry because we strike, afraid because we tremble, and not that we cry, strike, or tremble, because we are sorry, angry, or fearful as the case may be. (James and Lange 1967, 13)

Although this may seem like a counterintuitive way of thinking about the emotions, one must remember that the James-Lange theory of emotion makes no sharp distinction between feelings qua perceived bodily disturbances that occur internally or physiologically and those expressed externally or behaviorally. The location of the disturbance is irrelevant, as "manifestations" of emotion are "strongly characterized from within and without" (James and Lange 1967, 12-13). Thus, "external" or behavioral bodily disturbances such as crying, trembling, and striking may be considered manifestations of sorrow, fear, and anger, respectively, in the same way that "internal" or visceral disturbances such as having one's face redden and one's throat tighten may be considered manifestations of embarrassment and shame. However, there is no real difference between the perception of internal and external bodily disturbances regardless of how much or how little they are extensions of the nervous system, for, as James states the matter, every one is "a bundle of predispositions to react in particular ways upon the contact of particular features of the environment" (James and Lange 1967, 13).

Again, the James-Lange theory of emotion defines one's perceived behavioral changes, such as crying, trembling, and striking, as emotions or *feelings*, for "every one of the bodily changes, whatsoever it be, is felt, acutely or obscurely, the moment it occurs" (James and Lange 1967, 16). These more overt manifestations of emotion are feelings for the same reason that internal, visceral events that go undetected by others (at least under normal circumstances) are—because they are felt by the one experiencing them. In line with James's view, I submit that drawing the line between internal and external bodily feelings is actually somewhat arbitrary. For instance, is feeling one's face redden internal or external? This feeling was described earlier as a more internal, or "visceral," manifestation of embarrassment or shame, at least when compared to more behavioral manifestations of emotion, such as crying or running. But feeling one's face redden can also be described as being external, especially in comparison to the less observable experiences of feeling "butterflies" in the stomach or feeling one's throat tighten. The main point, according to James, is that the one having the emotion will feel all of its manifestations, regardless of whether they are below or above the bodily surface, or regardless of whether they can somehow be observed by others.

For James and Lange, then, it should be clear that emotions are defined in subjective terms—as being intrapersonal experiences that may be observed by others in various contexts but as essentially being subjectively *felt* experiences. More specifically, emotions were thought to be feeling qua perceived internal and/or external bodily disturbances. At best, then, we can only presume that the emotions of another are analogous to our own.

A more recent view, expressed most prominently by Robert Solomon, is that emotions are essentially normative judgments. Solomon spells out the connection between *intentionality*[2] and emotion, defining emotions as "cognitive"; in turn, he points out that they are amenable to rational evaluation and control, and are therefore a lot like actions. For this reason, his writings were pivotal in reanimating philosophical dialogue about the emotions starting roughly in the mid-1970s. I will begin this discussion, then, by explaining how Solomon's treatment of the emotions is antithetical to the "perceived bodily disturbance" view that had been predominant and that effectively relegated the whole investigation to the discipline of psychology.[3]

In articles such as "Emotions and Choice," Solomon expresses the view that, unlike (perceived) physiological occurrences, emotions are rational, purposive, and so can be chosen in much the same way we choose many of our actions. Moreover, emotions do not conceptually entail bodily feelings at all. He states the issue this way:

> An emotion is neither a sensation nor a physiological occurrence. . . . Emotions are judgments—normative and often moral judgments. . . . Anger is not a feeling; neither is anger a feeling plus anything else . . . but my anger-at-John-for-stealing-my-car is inseparable from my judgment that John in so doing wronged me. (Solomon 1984, 306-13)

How did this view allow emotions to be regarded as philosophical subject matter once again? The answer is not hard to surmise: Normative judgments can be conceptually analyzed—or, to be more specific, they can be evaluated as being rational or not, justified or not, appropriate or not. Most fundamentally, the intentionality of emotion is that very feature which felt bodily occurrences lack and which therefore serves to distinguish them.

Looking more closely at the significance of intentionality, then, one finds that intentional events must "have direction" or must be *about* something, unlike sensations or bodily feelings, which are not "about" anything at all. In effect, intentional events have "cognitive content," comprised of the objects they are about. Solomon's point is that emotions themselves have such content and direction; they must be about things appraised critically or approvingly—which is why he defines emotions as normative judgments. I will stress, however, that *intentionality* is what endows emotions with content and direction, while judgments are only one kind of intentional event.[4] In any case, because emotions are intentional, they must be differentiated from bodily feelings, which lack this referential quality. In Solomon's words, "feelings do not have 'directions'" (1984, 307).

At this point, we must be sure to understand that the content or object of any intentional event—be it a belief or judgment, emotion, desire, attitude, wish, prejudice, dream, or speculation—is conceived. Intentional events are called "mental" or "cognitive" for this reason. This may seem an obvious point, but we will see in greater detail, shortly, that it is one of the reasons that an emotion qua intentional event can be said to be justified or unjustified, reasonable or unreasonable, appropriate or inappropriate. And we shall also assess these features of emotion in much the same way we would evaluate any other intentional event—for example, a belief or judgment—which first requires that we identify its (conceived) object.

Before discussing how emotions can be evaluated, we must also fully understand that they cannot be identified independently from their objects, just as beliefs cannot be identified independently from what they are beliefs about.

Now, from the fact that emotions are intentional, Solomon straightforwardly concluded that they are normative judgments. He did not argue that emotions may comprise some other—perhaps unique—kind of intentional event, a view I will discuss at length in section 3 of this essay. He did explain, however, that in virtue of their intentionality, emotions "can only be identified under certain descriptions, and those descriptions are determined by the emotion itself" (Solomon 1984, 308). In other words, emotions *entail* their intentional objects; these objects are essential features of emotion which constitute their cognitive content. To follow Solomon's example: "To be angry is to be angry 'about' a peculiar sort of object, one that is distinguished by the fact that it is what I am angry 'about'" (1984, 308). Being angry would make no sense without being angry about something; thus, one's anger could never be adequately understood without reference to its object or content (i.e., to what one is angry about) any more than a belief could be adequately defined without reference to its object or content (i.e., to what it is a belief about).

Emotions and beliefs are intentional events that entail objects or cognitive direction. This does not mean that emotions are about beliefs. Again, Solomon stresses this point to argue that emotions are normative judgments instead of being about normative judgments: "The (moral) judgment entailed by my anger is not a judgment about my anger, my anger *is* that judgment" (1984, 312); moreover, "what I am angry 'about' is clearly not that I believe that John stole my car, but rather *that John stole my car*. . . . I am angry about the intentional object 'that John stole my car'" (1984, 307). So now we can begin to see how emotions are "rational and purposive," or how they can be evaluated in terms of their justifiability and appropriateness. For what if the conceived object of my anger is mistaken? What if I come to realize, for example, that John did not steal my car but is just driving a car that looks like mine? Solomon answers this by saying that a change in an emotion's intentional object requires a change in the emotion itself. This follows neatly from the fact that emotions entail their intentional objects and so cannot be defined independently from them. Solomon therefore explains, "A change in what I am angry 'about' entails a change in my anger; if I no longer feel wronged by John, who only bought a car that looks like mine, I cannot be angry at John (for stealing my car) any longer" (1984, 308).

Because emotions have intentional content, they can be rationally evaluated in the way exemplified above. First, the content or object of intentionality is identified—for example, "John stole my car" is an object of anger. Then the object's truth or falsity is established—for example, if I am angry that "John stole my car" and he, in fact, did not, then my anger is not justified; but if true, then presumably my anger would be justified. One could also argue that my anger would be even more clearly unjustified after I was given good reason to believe that its content is false or that John did not steal my car and I continue to be angry at him. However, evaluating some intentional events may be very difficult in practice.⁵ Just consider the difficulties emotions may present, with respect to accurately identifying their objects as well as assessing their truth or falsity. For example, identifying and reflecting on what one is angry about or what one is jealous about can be quite a task. Another central factor bearing on the evaluation of emotions is that experiencing certain emotions may be inappropriate, even if the respective content is undeniably true. It may be inappropriate to feel embarrassed about one's misfortunes, for instance, or to feel angry about the death of a loved one.⁶ Of course, analyzing the way in which emotions may or may not be justified or appropriate is an interesting topic, but it need not be investigated at length here. The point here is just to give an outline of what sort of thing such an analysis would involve, to show how emotions are indeed amenable to rational evaluation.

A major implication of the fact that emotions can be rationally evaluated is that they cannot be passed off as being beyond purposive control—as being things that often cause us to act in "irrational and disruptive" ways for which we cannot be held accountable or responsible. On the other hand, this may be true of bodily occurrences that do "just happen" to us; we are not ordinarily praised or blamed, for instance, for fainting or blushing. Because emotions are intentional events, however, we can be motivated to act irrationally by them only for the same sort of reason that we can be motivated to act irrationally by (false) beliefs. The fundamental advantage that accrues from seeing emotions as intentional—despite the fact that this may not always be an easy task—is that we can examine them and change them if we will. This is why emotions are like actions: They are purposively directed at objects, and so are amenable to evaluation and control.⁷

To be sure, the cognitive view of emotion is certainly a different (and far more accurate) description of emotion than the nonintentional "bodily disturbance" view that James offered. That James's view of the emotions is inaccurate, and that emotions are indeed intentional, has been sufficiently argued here and elsewhere.⁸ A central advantage of viewing emotions as intentional is that it pulls the emotions out of a purely subjective, intrapersonal framework. Insofar as emotions are intentional, and therefore open to rational evaluation, they are not just subjectively felt experiences; emotions are "objective" subject matter to the degree that they have content and are therefore falsifiable.

More accurately, though, I maintain that the subjective/objective distinction does not apply very well at all here, nor does it nonarbitrarily apply to much of what we have been led to believe, despite its widespread employment. In this context, the distinction does not straightforwardly apply to emotions, since they are items of personal consciousness which conceptually entail objects. To be more precise, if "objective" means "true in a way that is not dependent on one's personal experience," then *all* intentional events are objective, just as long as their conceived content is true. Their *justifiability* does not depend on one's personal experience in turn, and so if they are justified for one person, they would be justified for another in the same sort of situation. This is not to deny that they are still "personal" events or products of one's own mind, as anything must be in order to be known or consciously experienced by any given individual. The upshot is this: Taking into account all the relevant factors that would allow for a proper evaluation, intentional events are justified independently of one's personal experience or regardless of whether they are yours or mine. In effect, they may be considered "objective." On the other hand, as products of one's "psyche" or personal consciousness, intentional events may also be considered "subjective."⁹

The fact is that intentional events have features that preclude accurately thinking of them in such terms, for a neat application of the subjective/objective dichotomy is just not possible. Moreover, the distinction is misleading and question begging with respect to the features intentional events actually do involve. This point will be brought out further in the sections that follow.

II

To take what may appear to be a major shift of focus, we will now look at a philosophy from approximately two and a half millennia ago, set in ancient China. After this discussion, I will offer my own view of emotion in Section 3, showing how it has been informed by the philosophy of Confucius.

By way of general introduction, Confucius's teachings are not abstract and theoretical; couched in language that is "down to earth" and primarily concerned with human relationships and interaction, he was nonetheless able to provide a profound teaching on living a good life. Without abstraction, Confucius gives us a way of understanding how to interact with others *humanely*, or in a harmonious, civilized way. This will be explained in light of two ideas that are central to Confucian philosophy: *li* and *jen*.¹⁰ I will end this section by explaining how the subjective/objective distinction is useless in understanding these ideas as well, ideas which, taken together, refer to a kind of intentional event that, for the Chinese, is essentially manifest in interpersonal conduct.

To be more specific, *li* has been translated as "rite," "ritual," "ceremony," "propriety," and "right conduct." By comparison, *jen* has been translated as "goodness," "nobility," "benevolence," and "humaneness." Crucially, though, it has been argued that the concepts of *li* and *jen* are essentially related, and cannot be fully understood independently from each other.¹¹ Confucius sometimes speaks of them separately, however, in various passages from the *Analects*. For this reason, I will examine *li* and *jen* as independently as possible by discussing the major themes of each, derived from that work. I will then show how *li* and *jen* are related, by providing a key insight introduced by Fingarette (1972).

Some Themes of *Li* (Book:Section):

1. *Li* is used as a guide to govern or to rule (2:3, 3:19, 4:13, 13:6, 15:4, 15:17).

2. *Li* is a ritual vessel (utensil) (5:3, 15:1).

3. Those who are *jen* (good, noble, benevolent) are restrained by *li*; submission to *li* is needed to be *jen* (3:3, 6:25, 8:2, 9:10, 12:1).

4. *Li* is more than the behavior; it requires the right emotion and reverence (2:7-8, 3:4, 3:11, 3:12, 3:26, 9:3, 17:11).

5. *Li* establishes one as a human being and gives one firm footing (2:4, 8:8, 16:13, 20:3).

6. *Li* generates a power, establishes *te* ("moral"[12] power) (2:1, 3:11, 4:11, 12:19).

From the *Analects*, we are given that *li* (ritual), for the Chinese, was a very formal and important part of living a distinctively human life. In fact, *li* is described as the essence of living a life in dignified harmony with others. Most crucially, *li* is relational, in the sense that it provides patterns of conduct with others that are also essential to defining the person. For instance, one cannot be a mother without having a child; one cannot be a teacher without having students; one cannot be a friend without having a friend, and so on. *Li* defines the roles of those engaging in them, and from a Confucian point of view, since human beings are intrinsically social beings, *li* defines the person[13] him- or herself. In effect, *li* must be directed toward someone or something else— one's ancestors, the gods, one's parents or siblings, one's superiors, or one's friends. *Li* is also learned; it requires guidance from tradition and cannot exist without a foundation of proper social values.

With time and continual practice, however, *li* becomes *wu-wei* (action-less activity). In other words, with perseverance and dedication, ritual becomes effortless; we become masters at behaving in these ways that initially were not easy to perform. This is the case for performing any activity well—for one to become skilled, or for the activity to become "actionless," it first has to be learned and perfected. We may come to take for granted the language we use, our gestures for greeting others, for expressing emotion in certain contexts, or for properly sharing a meal. We can do this, though, only after we have sufficiently learned the gestures—that is, once they have become "socialized," as we might say. However, the magic that Confucius saw in what he considered the distinctively human ability to relate in a civilized, harmonious way could never be just a matter of habit. It involves a sincere and dedicated orientation toward the person or (more rarely) the thing being engaged.

So those who have the post to "govern" surely need *li*—the ability to act appropriately toward one's fellow human beings in a respectful and dignified way—if they are to govern well. But this is a basic principle "governing" all human relationships; we have simply come to take *li* for granted in so many instances because it has become "second nature" or because we no longer have to be painfully and self-consciously aware of what we are doing in so many social contexts.

To repeat, this is not to imply that we can take for granted the magical quality that Confucius saw to be the essence of *li*. If we did, ritual would no longer be proper ritual; it would merely be the rote behavior an automaton could perform if programmed to do so, not the personally significant, even sacred, gesture of one human being who stands in relation to another. In other words, the conventions of *li* must *mean* something. This requires something much more mysterious than behavior—something that cannot be measured as systematically: This is the proper spirit or conscious orientation with which the ritual act must be performed. This, in short, is *jen*.

Some Themes of *Jen* (Book:Section):

1. *Jen* is hard, a burden, difficult (6:20, 14:2, 8:7).
2. We have the strength to be *jen*; it is at our side if we want it (4:6, 7:29).
3. *Jen* requires that we care for it (9:30).
4. The good person speaks little of *jen*; it is difficult to capture in words (9:1, 12:3).
5. The person of *jen* rests content, is never unsettled or disquieted (9:2, 6:21, 9:28).
6. The person of *jen* is always *jen*; *jen* is a "trait of character" (9:28, 4:5).
7. Nothing should be done at the expense of *jen*; *jen* is central to one's life, essential, all pervasive (15:8).
8. *Jen* requires the ability to take one's feelings as a guide, or more literally, "to take the analogy from what is near" (6:28).

Jen is a benevolent orientation toward another that is reflected in how one lives his or her life. Now it is easier to understand why *jen* is more mysterious than li: because it is the *conscious aim* one adopts toward another; it is the "spirit" of openness and decency with which one interacts with others. We in the West would be inclined to say that one is *jen* if it is characteristic of that person to act toward others in a genuine, empathetic, and respectful way or in a way that demonstrates personal integrity. This is not too far off the mark as long as one's integrity is understood to be committedly *expressed through li*. *Jen* is a feature of the actions or rituals themselves; it is reflected in the ready and masterful way one who is truly cultivated in social grace can effectively relate to others. *Jen* is not, therefore, an intrasubjective, psychological state. In essence, *jen* is something we can rightly say is characteristic of someone only insofar as he or she consistently *acts benevolently*, nobly, or humanely. For this reason, *li* and *jen* are inseparable concepts.[14]

From all of the themes and passages referred to above, one can surmise that two central principles apply to *jen*. First, *jen* requires a formal dimension of acting according to *li*—directed toward various objects of reverence. Second, *jen* requires a conscious or imaginative dimension of "analogizing" with others— that is, of being empathetic and respectful toward them. These features of *jen* are described by Fingarette in a way that shows their essential relation. To state this relation briefly, *li* are forms of conduct done with the right spirit, and *jen* tells us what that spirit is: to approach others empathetically and to treat them with the dignity they deserve.[15] This requires a proper regard for their roles as persons as well as for their humanity. Fingarette puts the matter this way:

> Thus *Li* and *Jen* are two aspects of the same thing. Each points to an aspect of the action of man in his distinctively human role. *Li* directs our attention to the traditional social pattern of conduct and relationships; *jen* directs our attention to the person as the one who pursues that pattern of conduct and thus maintains those relationships. *Li* also refers to the particular act in its status as exemplification of invariant norm; *jen* refers to the act as expressive of an orientation of the person, as expressing his commitment to act as prescribed by *li*. *Li* refers to the act as overt and distinguishable pattern of sequential behavior; *jen* refers to the act as the single, indivisible gesture of an actor. (Fingarette 1972, 42)

According to Confucius, this is precisely how we are established as persons: as wives or husbands, subjects, professionals, parents, friends, lovers, and so forth. We must act appropriately toward others depending on their relation to us, and this requires acting with the proper spirit. This is also what Confucius saw to be the essence of a peaceful and civilized society, established by harmonious human interactions therein.[16] Now it is hopefully clear that this sort of interaction is described by Confucius in terms of the inseparable ideas of *li* and *jen*.

To understand these concepts, however, I must stress that *jen*—although mysterious—is *not* a subjective, intrapersonal concept. *Jen* is a personal and even spiritual concept, to be sure, but instead of being a private or inaccessible psychological state, *jen* is "outer-directed," established through one's conscious interactions with others. The same is also true for *yu*, a concept taken to be the opposite of *jen* and which is roughly translated as "unhappy," "anxious," "troubled" (see theme 5 of *jen*, above). For example, a passage from the *Analects* cites parents who are *yu* when their child becomes ill (2:6). Does *yu* refer here to the private pain felt by the parents, to a psychological or intrapersonal state of discomfort? No; it refers to a *troubled response* to a genuinely troubling situation.[17] Another quote from Fingarette explains how the concepts of *yu* and *jen*, or any other expressed by Confucius, are not intrapersonal, subjective, psychological notions:

I must emphasize that my point is not that Confucius's words are intended to exclude reference to the inner psyche. He could have done this if he had such a basic metaphor in mind, had seen its plausibility, but on reflection had decided to reject it. But this is not what I am arguing here. My thesis is that the entire notion never entered his head. The metaphor of an inner psychic life, in all its ramifications so familiar to us, simply isn't present in the *Analects*, not even as a rejected possibility. Hence when I say that in the above passages using *yu* there is no reference to the inner, subjective states, I do not mean that these passages clearly and explicitly exclude such elaboration, but that they make no use of it and do not require it for intelligibility or validity. (Fingarette 1972, 45)

Thus, the subjective/objective distinction did not cross Confucius's mind, nor did he need it in order to offer a profound and influential philosophy on living a good life, a life of *li* and *jen*. My guess is that this sort of inner/outer distinction did not find any use in China until a couple of hundred years after Confucius—when Mencius presented a new, more abstract interpretation of Confucianism. For Confucius, however, it was not the case that *jen* or *yu* or any other concept was intrapersonal or subjective. His philosophy was concerned with *how people acted or lived* in the course of everyday life. More particularly, Confucius was interested in "goodness," or what I have called "harmonious human interaction," which I maintain is a kind of intentional event in itself—a kind of spirit of civility or decency directed toward or *about* others.

We can now understand that *jen* minimally requires one to be cognizant of the humanity of another, which often entails a more specific awareness of the responsibilities and kind of relationship one should be embracing with regard to that person. *Jen* may also be "about" the significance of a sacred vessel, or the obligations one has toward her ancestors. And because action and spirit are viewed as inseparable for Confucius, we also know that *jen* must be manifest in rituals or formal conduct appropriate to the social context *(li)*. This is an interesting point of contrast, because, in the West, many intentional events (like beliefs and emotions) do not appear to involve such formal, socially established conduct. The fact remains that all intentional events dispose us to act in various, and sometimes even formal, ways, in the same way that human civility or decency disposes us to *act decently*.[18] How we consciously regard others simply cannot be divorced from how we treat them. This is why human goodness, for Confucius, must be established and expressed in *acting toward others* in a humane and dignified way.

To make this point in a more general way, intentional events are purposive acts of consciousness themselves: They are ways of being conscious that are no more separate from the things we are conscious about than they are from the actions we are prone to engage in toward these objects—*because* we are distinctively conscious of them. This is precisely why Confucius's teaching is so profound, as he did not even think to employ a metaphorical split between "objective" and "subjective" or, correlatively, between "outer" behavior and "inner" consciousness, to teach about living a decent, humane life.

III

So far, we have seen that the dichotomy between "subjective" and "objective" cannot accurately be applied to intentional events—namely, to judgments and emotions. We have also seen that the Confucian concepts of *li* and *jen* also evade the subjective/objective distinction in being expressed before that distinction was even born. In this section, I will give my own view of the emotions, and then, remembering Confucius, will reiterate that the subjective/objective distinction cannot truly apply to any intentional event.

To begin, Solomon (1984) was well on the right track about the emotions, for they are undoubtedly intentional events. I object to the claim, however, that emotions are nothing more than normative judgments. Emotions are *not* reducible to critical or approving beliefs. I will argue this, first by showing that emotion and normative judgment cannot be identified and then by discussing the sort of intentional event emotions really are. In the end, we will see that the way Confucius approached morality is also the way to approach the emotions.

Let's go back to Solomon's example of being angry that "John stole my car." Let's embellish this example somewhat by adding that John is my brother and has been caught for stealing my car. The following is a list of statements expressing the normative content of my anger, or the critical judgments relevant to the situation.

1. John stole my car (and stealing is wrong).
2. John stole *my* car (which, as a personal affront, is bad).
3. John stole a car from his own sister (it is condemnable that he has degenerated to this extent).
4. John has become a menace, morally and personally (which is an unfavorable state of affairs).
5. John cannot be trusted anymore (which may be as bad for him as it is for others).

The above normative statements, including a myriad of variations and refinements of them, can only express cognitive appraisal that is *disapproving*; they express a general judgment about a state of affairs that one views critically or unfavorably. So what is the problem with identifying "anger" with such critical appraisal? Or, more generally, what is wrong with equating emotion with normative judgment? The answer is, All of the normative judgments above are compatible with any number of *different* emotions; therefore, they are unable to identify or adequately distinguish between emotions. I can hold all of the beliefs above and feel angry at John or feel grief for him, and there will be nothing in these judgments that can distinguish my anger from my grief. In addition, I could feel indignant with John, betrayed by him, ashamed of him, or regretful for him, and the five judgments above also fail to account for any difference in these emotions, for they are *interchangeable* with each and every emotion just mentioned. My argument, then, is basically that normative judgments, in merely being critical or approving (by definition), are just too general to distinguish adequately between the various emotions one may feel.[19] That is, normative judgments cannot characterize the specifically *affective* state of consciousness one experiences when feeling one emotion as opposed to another that may be similar in every other way. For different emotions may entail the same normative content, and may even involve the same basic bodily disturbances if any are experienced,[20] but they are still *different* emotions.

What is more, further refinement or addition to these judgments cannot rectify this problem, because what makes them *normative* is precisely that they reflect general standards of right and wrong or express "pro or con attitudes"[21] that serve only to appraise things favorably or unfavorably, by definition. In summary, then, the distinctively affective dimension of emotion involves subtle and extensive differences that normative judgment simply cannot capture or define, since any number of different emotions may entail the same normative content (and the converse holds as well). In effect, one may be critical of something, or even strongly disapprove of something, and this is *not* the same as being outraged, annoyed, sad, angry, or distressed about that same thing.

My claim is that the concept of emotion entails a different kind of feeling—but one that cannot be equated with felt bodily occurrences (as James held). Unlike bodily feeling, "emotionally relevant feeling" (ERF) is inherently and irreducibly intentional *and* affective in nature. What I need to show, then, is that an emotion is a kind of intentional event which (like all others) forms an *irreducible unity* which is *affective* in itself.[22] This applies to both dispositional and occurrent emotions, since the concept of emotion entails both. Briefly, I view a "dispositional" emotion as the tendency to experience or feel an emotion, but focus on "occurrent" emotion—which I call "ERF,"—in order to bring out more clearly the difference between emotion and belief.

In any case, the concept of emotion entails affect or feeling that is an irreducible state of (intentional) consciousness. ERF is only *analogous* to the kind of intentional event beliefs comprise, but each forms an irreducible unity in virtue of being an intentional event. Thus, by way of analogy only, beliefs can be used to expose the unity also essential to emotion (or to any intentional event for that matter). It has already been established that a belief cannot be understood as a belief on the one hand and an object on the other. A belief is a belief only insofar as it *entails* an object. Analogously, ERFs—or the feelings essential to emotions—have objects of consciousness that are entailed in them. The object of an ERF is what that feeling is about, but is no more separate from the feeling than the object of a belief is separate from what it is a belief about. In other words, in the same way that a belief must be about something in order to be a belief, a feeling must be about something in order to be an *emotionally relevant feeling*.

The difference between beliefs and emotions, however, is that emotions entail distinctively *affective* ways of being conscious about things, as was argued above.[23] Therefore, even if one still wants to claim that emotions entail a normative dimension, this must be qualified by saying that emotions may entail normative judgment but are *not entailed by* normative judgment. To follow the example, my anger at John for stealing my car may entail that I critically believe that he stole my car, while the converse does not necessarily hold. In this way, the irreducibly *affective* unity of emotion is exposed, establishing it as a unique kind of intentional event in its own right.

This is also why we distinguish feelings of anger from those of annoyance, indignation, and the like: because emotions entail *distinct ways of feeling* or being *affectively conscious* of things in the world. The problem, stated briefly, is that we have been conditioned to think that all "feelings" are nonintentional, like felt bodily disturbances, and that the only intentional events are thoughts, beliefs, and judgments. Indeed, there are as many kinds of intentional events as there are ways of being conscious *about* things in the world,[24] but cognitivists, among others, have led us away from just this understanding. The truth is that the emotions we feel cannot be distinguished from what we are conscious about. Thus, a more accurate analysis of emotion cannot ignore their distinctively intentional *and* affective character. As such, emotions must be viewed as being a lot like actions—as being purposive and therefore amenable to rational evaluation and control *because* they are essentially directed at objects.

I have also tried to bring to light that the same kind of point was expressed by Confucius, well over two millennia ago, in describing the path one must take to become a good person—or to live a humane, civilized life. For *jen* (goodness) is *about* the sacredness and significance of others, and is no more separate from *li* (how one consciously acts) than our emotions are separate from their objects and how we are disposed to act toward those objects. In this way, emotions are like human goodness in being overtly established, evaluated, and expressed in how we live. But there is also a highly personal significance that intentional events like human decency and emotions have which inheres in the fact that each is a distinctive way of being conscious—a mysterious and almost magical orientation toward persons and things in our world which simply cannot be reduced to bodily feelings, to mere behavior, or to normative beliefs.

Not surprisingly, my conclusion is that the subjective/objective distinction, in all of its variant forms, has served more to pull us away from seeing the irreducible unity characteristic of intentional events, and has instead caused us to think incorrectly of intentional objects as separate from the myriad and often allusive acts of consciousness that entail them.

Notes

1. This sort of "subjective relativism"—which may be epistemological, moral, aesthetic, etc.—hinges largely on whether accurate communication and interpersonal understanding are possible.

2. This concept was initially introduced in the nineteenth century by Franz Brentano. Interestingly enough, even Brentano indicated that emotions are, at least in part, intentional ("mental") events.

3. This historical transition of the treatment of the emotions is discussed at length in Bockover (1990).

4. I say this because a central task of section 3 of this chapter is to *distinguish* emotions from normative judgments—while still granting that emotions are intentional events. To be more precise, what is called the "cognitive" or "rational" character of emotions follows directly from the fact that they are intentional. It does not follow from this, however, that emotions are normative judgments. The argument for this is fully elucidated in section 3.

5. Solomon (1984) briefly discusses the difficulty of accurately identifying the object of one's emotions.

6. Joel Marks pointed out to me that a conceptually appropriate object of emotion may be inappropriate in some other sense. For example, hating my enemy is conceptually appropriate but ethically inappropriate, from a devoutly Christian point of view, while hating evil would be perfectly appropriate.

7. I am aware that there are significant differences between actions and other kinds of intentional events like beliefs and emotions. Attending to this topic would require another paper. The claim is only that emotions and beliefs are "like" actions, which is meant to leave the issue unresolved. The point is only one of similarity: Emotions and beliefs are like actions insofar as they are about something, and, therefore, are amenable to rational evaluation and control.

8. See Bedford 1956-1957; Bockover 1990; Solomon 1984.

9. The subjective/objective distinction leads to a very slippery, often arbitrary, slope and *not* to any clearly relevant difference between the private and the

176

nonprivate, the inaccessible and the accessible, the unknowable and the knowable, as it was intended to do. Instead of offering any clear solutions, this distinction really serves only to beg rather badly the question of what, and how, and how much we can really know with any degree of certainty. The history of philosophy has seen this fundamentally epistemic question phrased in terms of related dichotomies: Consider those of the inner vs. outer (internal vs. external), the personal vs. nonpersonal, the conditioned vs. the absolute, the individual vs. the universal, and so on, each suggesting a genuine difference in each case and, thus, a genuine inability to understand one side of the dichotomy from the point of view of the other or to understand one side of the dichotomy (usually the latter, "objective" side) at all. In truth, though, this question is really far from solved, and is probably just poorly cast. This is suggested by the endless and various debates on relativism which rage on now and have persisted through the centuries.

10. There are other morally relevant concepts that could be discussed in connection with Confucian philosophy, such as *te*, or "moral" power, and *yi*, or appropriate conduct. For the purposes of this essay, however, *li* and *jen* are sufficient to show how Confucius viewed morality, especially with respect to his not employing the subjective/objective distinction.

11. This insight was initially offered by Fingarette (1972).

12. Strictly speaking, there is no term for "moral" in ancient Chinese, but this is not to say that the concept as we know it does not apply quite well. Indeed, this section should make apparent that it does.

13. This is a main difference between the Confucian view of what it means to be a person and a typically Western view. Namely, the West conceives of a "person" as being an independent, autonomous, and often isolated individual. This can be sharply contrasted with the Confucian concept of "person," which, again, refers to a fundamentally *social* being. For Confucius, a person is *intrinsically* defined by his or her roles, by his or her relationships with others.

14. This was probably why Confucius was so "chary" of speaking of those who are, or are not, *jen*—because *li* and *jen* are inseparable. Together they constitute a way of life, a path (*tao*) one must always follow in the proper spirit. This is not a quality that can be attributed to someone easily or lightly, nor is it something that comes easily to one. Such a "moral" way of life must be nurtured, developed, and practiced consistently and with dedication.

15. I am not trying to suggest that Confucius was espousing an egalitarian philosophy where all humans were considered worthy of respect. To the con-

trary, this would depend upon the person, that is, on how one carries out one's various roles and responsibilities. Regardless, the person who is *jen* can tell what conduct would be appropriate, taking such differences into account. And surely, people who are not worthy of respect will be treated differently from those who are, by a person who is *jen* and who can ascertain the difference.

16. I think that Confucian philosophy is also very applicable today. The concepts of *li* and *jen* can also help us to establish meaningful—and, one hopes, peaceful—relations with human beings who are "strange" or "alien" to us. For starters, we must learn about them, which means we must learn about the *li* which, although different from our own in form, is not necessarily that different in spirit. In any case, we will learn about the humanity of the other, which diffuses the sense of otherness we so often experience in the midst of people who are different.

17. This point is also discussed by Fingarette (1972) in Chapter 3, "The Locus of the Personal." Specifically, see pages 43-47 for his detailed examination of Confucius's use of the term *yu*.

18. For Confucius, acting *jen* versus the concern or desire to do so is discussed, but in a rather paradoxical way. I think the implication is that one must desire to be *jen* and then, with proper learning and practice, the rituals will become second nature. With beliefs and emotions, by way of contrast, we are disposed to act in certain ways but are not necessarily aiming to perfect standards of conduct in virtue of possessing such a disposition.

19. I have argued for a distinction between "occurrent" and "dispositional" emotion elsewhere (Bockover 1990), but such an analysis falls outside the scope of this paper. I need only to say that while emotions do not always have to be occurrently experienced or "felt," when they are, the feeling is not essentially defined by specific bodily disturbances. The actual nature of such an "emotionally relevant feeling" will be discussed shortly. This is not to treat dispositional emotions as trivial, for the tendency to experience emotions in particular ways is basic to defining personal character and the like. For instance, we can say that one is an "angry person" if he or she is often disposed to feel angry (and hence, to act angrily). It is the concept of dispositional emotion, then, that allows us to make meaningful predictions about a person's conduct.

20. Just to mention one of the many examples of this, consider that, in and of themselves, the bodily disturbances typically experienced with anger and pride are virtually interchangeable. The face becomes flushed (one becomes "red" with anger and "glows" with pride), the chest swells, and a slight muscular tension pervades the upper body.

21. Franz Brentano used this term to describe the general, evaluative nature of emotions. Pro or con attitudes may differ in strength or degree, but they are still simply pro or con, i.e., favorable or unfavorable.

22. I should acknowledge the contrasting tendency to analyze emotions as consisting of component parts; one could suggest, for instance, that an emotion consists of a normative judgment and something else—in this case, an affective component—to account for the intentional *and* affective nature of emotion. I have argued in detail (Bockover 1990) as to why such a "component" analysis of emotion always ends up producing a fortuitous connection between intention and affect. For the purpose of this article, however, I only need to provide an alternate view that sufficiently explains how emotions can be both intentional *and* affective without being reducible to component parts.

23. Let me reiterate that this would apply to both dispositional emotions and to ERFs (the occurrent experience of emotion), since a dispositional emotion conceptually entails the *tendency* to experience an ERF. That is to say, I am not equating emotion with ERF, but focus on the conscious experience or the feeling, because it is easier to distinguish emotion from belief in this way.

24. Consider that dreaming, speculating, doubting, imagining, and desiring are also intentional. Despite the fact that these are different forms of intentionality, each and every one requires that one is conscious about—and not just of—something. This is what distinguishes intentional from nonintentional consciousness. For instance, one can be nonintentionally aware of a pain in one's foot; that is, one is conscious of pain in the sense that he *perceives* it. This is to be distinguished, however, from intentional pain expressed by statements such as "I am pained that my brother betrayed me" or "I am pained about his betrayal." In this case, one must *conceive* that she was wronged by her brother. For this reason, it is accurate to say that an ERF—or any intentional event, for that matter—is a "cognitive" event. This is still somewhat misleading if one then assumes that the event reduces to a belief or judgment. Again, intentional events may entail, but are not entailed by, judgment. This is the basis for distinguishing judgment from emotion, or from any other kind of intentional event.

Bibliography

Bedford, Errol. 1956-1957. "The Emotions." *Proceedings of the Aristotelian Society* 57: 281-304.

Bockover, Mary. 1990. "Emotionally Relevant Feelings." Ph.D. diss., University of California at Santa Barbara.

Brentano, Franz. 1984. "Loving and Hating." [1889.] In *What Is an Emotion?*, ed. Cheshire Calhoun and Robert Solomon, 205-14. Oxford: Oxford University Press.

Fingarette, Herbert. 1972. *Confucius—The Secular as Sacred.* New York: Harper Torchbooks.

James, William, and Carl Georg Lange. 1967. *The Emotions.* [1922.] New York: Hafner.

Solomon, Robert. 1984. "Emotions and Choice." In *What Is an Emotion?*, ed. Cheshire Calhoun and Robert Solomon, 305-26. Oxford: Oxford University Press.

Waley, Arthur, trans. 1938. *The Analects of Confucius.* New York: Vintage Books.

Qing (Emotions) 情
in Pre-Buddhist Chinese Thought

Chad Hansen

Recent philosophy of mind has aggressively addressed problems with "folk psychology"[1]—the theory that human action is caused by beliefs and desires. I will not recite the difficulties of that familiar view here, but turn to some implications of those difficulties. Some philosophers conclude that we should jettison folk psychology and develop a new psychological theory. Others prefer to retain our familiar concepts and construe the problems as challenges to work out a valid understanding of still viable concepts. (Perhaps beliefs and desires are features of communities and real situations rather than minds.) One reason for preferring the latter strategy is that we may regard the conceptual structure of folk psychology as instinctive or as obvious common sense. The philosophical ancestors of the view (Aristotle), the Enlightenment exemplars of it (Locke), and contemporary champions of the mental (Fodor) present various versions of this assumption. The rival, more dismissive view suggests that folk psychology is at best a learned theory either transmitted by subtle childhood indoctrination or presupposed in learning our language—mastering and using intensional verbs like *believes* and *desires*.

Comparative philosophy might seem to offer a straightforward way to approach this part of the dispute. If we find a counterexample—a philosophical tradition of reasonable sophistication whose implicit psychology is radically different from Western folk psychology—that should confirm the view that folk psychology is neither innate nor rationally obvious. I have argued in some detail that classical Chinese philosophy is such a tradition.[2]

The counterexample strategy, however, is not all that straightforward. Most translators have absorbed and accepted folk psychology and the classical Western view of its "obviousness." They thus "charitably" credit Chinese philosophers with implicit acceptance of this commonsense theory. So that Chinese is a counterexample turns out to be a controversial claim. And the interpretive controversy turns on a similar issue.

Clearly, an adequate argument for any interpretive hypothesis should treat a writer as referring to a feature or entity only if that writer has a way of coming to know about it. If belief and desire are instinctive ways of understanding human behavior, then the interpreter is not merely relying on the "truth" of folk psychology. His assumption does yield an explanation of how ancient Chinese philosophers could access the concepts. He does not need to find explicit signs of such concepts; they are innate.

If, on the other hand, we argue that the concepts are learned as a widespread cultural theory or learned along with mastering the grammar of crucial terms of folk psychology, then ancient Chinese thinkers' use of such a theory would be serendipitous at best. If beliefs and desires are theoretical objects in an explanatory theory, then cognitive access to them would come by exposure to that theory. Absent some explicit statement of such a theory, we should not assume Chinese thinkers were referring to content-ful mental states characterized by propositional structure and "aboutness."

So the details of the Chinese case concern equally both sides in this debate. If folk psychology is theory laden, then we should find something quite different in the pre-Buddhist period. If folk psychology is hard wired, then we will want some explanation for the lack of explicit intentional grammar and of the need to supply so much of it as a background assumption. I proceed with my account on the assumption that it will provoke the defender of folk psychological concepts to specify in more detail the content of the hard-wiring. In *some* sense and to *some* degree, the psychological theory we argue for in China will resemble folk psychology. It will still be interesting to attend to the differences. Those, at least, we will not want to explain as hard-wiring or obvious common sense.

I shall concentrate on this interpretive question. The way to make a case for an interpretation is to present enough detail to show how it gives a comprehensive account of the texts. I propose in the present paper only to outline the non-belief-based account of Chinese thought and then concentrate on that part of the case most directly addressed in the present collection—the concept of emotion. I shall attempt not to prove a negative (that there is no such concept) but rather to develop a rival theory of the meaning of the ideograph usually used for translating emotion—qing^feeling 情.[3] Qing^feeling 情 is particularly apt for our purposes, because the assumption that it forms part of the Western commonsense psychological theory yields a puzzle. That interpretive theory ends having to assign two seemingly incongruous meanings to qing^feelings. A typical Chinese–English dictionary (e.g., Matthew's) has two entries under 情 qing^feeling: The first is "affections, the feelings, desires"; translations of character compounds under this meaning include *love, desire, emotion,* and *sentiment.* The second definition is "Circumstances; facts of a case"; examples of compounds under this meaning include *truth, situation, reason, origin, real facts.* On its face, this admixture is puzzling. If Chinese thinkers accept Western folk psychology, then emotions and feelings should be paradigms of subjective, inner phenomena—the exact opposite of the circumstances, facts, and truth that we regard as objective and external.

Standard interpretive theories usually accept both meanings as independent, and allege that the character simply "changes meaning" from time to time. A. C. Graham, however, identifies *passions* as the meaning appropriate after Neo-Confucianism of the Song (960+ A.D.) and argues that 情 $qing^{feeling}$ "never means 'passions'" in Pre-Han (500–200 B.C.)[4] literature (1990, 59). Still, most translators fall back on mainly English near-synonyms for *emotion—feeling, desire,* and *passion*—for Pre-Han uses of $qing^{feelings}$.

THESIS

I will discuss the role of *qing* in the surrounding system of classical Chinese theories of language and human action and argue for a "smooth-curve" analysis of the meaning of the term. I will modify Graham's analysis to explain how both translations might stem from a single, unified meaning. The key to that analysis is spelling out Chinese thinkers' alternative to Western folk psychology, one that elides the reality/appearance and the reason/emotion oppositions. Chinese views of language, mind, and action do not center on an inner subjectivity or a conception of a mental/intellectual world populated by mental/intellectual objects set off against an external world of physical objects or matter. Nor do they make the familiar Indo-European faculty and functional distinction between cognitive and affective states. A single faculty/organ, the $xin^{heart-mind}$, guides action rather than separate faculties of heart and mind.

In section 1, I outline what I take to be the structure of a Western account of how emotion and reason explain human action and human knowledge. That structure draws on ancient Greek theories and informs traditional Western explanatory roles on desires, feelings, and emotions. This Western scheme will be intuitively familiar to most readers. I will, accordingly, be brief—my outline is designed mainly to highlight features of folk psychology that differ from classical Chinese views. Section 2 will develop the alternative, pre-Buddhist Chinese explanation of human behavior, guidance, and knowledge. This more exotic Chinese conceptual neighborhood I will map in more detail.

In section 3, I will propose a theory of the specific philosophical role of $qing^{passions}$ in classical pre-Buddhist Chinese thought. At that point I will address some crucial passages that figure in standard interpretive theories of $qing^{feelings}$ and $yu^{desires}$. I implicitly accept the possibility that the introduction of Buddhism imported an Indo-European psychological theory and thus introduced new theoretical roles for $qing^{feelings}$ and $yu^{desires}$. Thus, I leave unchallenged Graham's view that "passions" is a suitable translation after the Song (960+ A.D.). I will not, however, discuss or try to support that development here. I intend to uncover in this paper only the philosophical background that would make $qing^{feelings}$ an apt candidate for such appropriation. $Qing^{feelings}$ could help render possible the importation of Indo-European folk psychology to China.

1. WESTERN REASON AND WESTERN EMOTION

Euclidean geometry leaps out at us as an obvious starting point in explaining the deep differences between Western and Chinese thought.[5] The mathematical subject matter is not important. What is crucial is the way Euclid combined the Greek invention of the notion of a proof with the study of geometry. The Euclidean *way* directs us toward a system of knowledge based on proof-structures. The subject matter of geometry was relevant primarily in that it allowed the confident assumption that constructing a successful axiomatic structure would reveal a geometrical picture of reality.[6]

Axioms and Definitions

That ancient Euclidean paradigm first appropriated, and then came to embody, the Greek concept of *reason*. It is from this model that we now elaborate this pivotal Western philosophical idea. It also generated many of the traditional views of closely related philosophical terms such as "truth" and "meaning." This model has guided the central (though sometimes controversial) Western conception of philosophical activity right up to modern times.

Reason starts with a few axioms; these, together with a rule of inference, give the logical content of the system. Then we add definitions. These allow us to apply the logic to some specific subject matter (lines, points, angles, etc.) and to convert terms into sentences. The sentences can then be slotted into valid arguments for theorems. Arguments are sequences of sentences beginning with axioms and definitions (premises) and ending in some new truth (the conclusion). The system is a structure of truths—The Truth.

Most Western theories of reasoning come from this conception. Truth is the property of sentences that conclusions inherit from the premises in proofs. The definitions (meanings) are part of the *a priori*, self-evident, necessary base. Reasoning is the mental proof process; reason is the faculty of engaging in that process and reasons are premises in proofs. In the prescientific rationalist versions of the theory, the body of provable knowledge was restricted only by the imperative to avoid contradiction. The rational was real and the real was rational.

That rationalist confidence in the reality of *logos* overflowed the boundaries of geometry. The assumption of a subject–predicate structure of sentential truths, together with the assumption that change must be explained by something permanent, buttressed the substance and property analysis of the structure of reality. That structure led, in turn, to a distinction between essence (definitional, unchangeable properties) and accident.

A definition, accordingly, was not merely an account of linguistic usage but an understanding of the real nature of the thing—its essence. The ancient notion of *logos* reflected this blending of the logical and the real. *Cause* and *reason* still overlap in common speech. The Scholastic view, that natural causal structure replicates the structure of God's reason in creation, may have contributed to the formation of science. It still dominates the popular conception of science and morality.

Aristotle elaborated this rationalist model in still familiar ways. He generalized proof to apply to all thought and emphasized syllogistic form. In a syllogism, the relations of terms in the structure of sentences determines whether the argument is valid or not. If the argument is valid, the conclusion can inherit truth from the premises—if they have it to bequeath. Aristotle's presentation of valid syllogistic form as relating terms emphasized again the role of definition and meaning. We normally take knowledge of the meaning of the common words to be obvious to native speakers. Thus anyone can "follow" meaning-based proofs.

Aristotle presented logic as laws of thought. Humans are rational animals. Their premises are beliefs. Putting beliefs together (as one might construct an argument on paper) leads us to conclusions which we then include among our beliefs. The ultimate axioms of any system of knowledge are self-evident to rational beings. Definitions embody our knowledge of the meanings of the terms we use. When empirical content enters the system, it does so in the form of other basic, immediately obvious beliefs—those induced by present experience. Thus we are led by *reason* to *true* beliefs about things in general.

Ethics: Definition and the Practical Syllogism

There were two keys to converting this rationalist, realist structure to human guidance—ethics and psychology. The first was definition. Socrates launched an early revolution in philosophy when he applied the proof model to "analyze life." Socrates and Plato thought that the way to study ethics was through finding the meaning or definition of ethical terms. When Socrates adapted the rationalists' structure to ethics, he did it by seeking the definitions of *justice*, *good*, and other ethical terms. Socratic method sought definitions of these terms guided again only by (1) the assumption that we implicitly know the meaning and (2) the imperative to avoid contradiction. Thus, he opened a debate about whether values or virtues were real—and Greek philosophy primarily took the realist position implicit in the scheme of reason itself.

Although the Greeks (particularly Socrates) had a healthy acceptance of the body and love, Plato's Socrates, as Nietzsche notes, welcomes death as a liberation from the bodily induced emotions—perturbations of reason. The notion of desire played little essential role in this early account of rational, ethical action. Their working assumption was simply that no person knowingly does evil. Knowing what virtue is, knowing the definitions, would guarantee that rational animals would be virtuous.

So the theory of reason came to define the Western notion of the mind. The outlines of that ancient and venerable Western view were complicated, however, by the second key to applying the Euclidean structure to ethics and action. This one is due to Aristotle. His rationalist account of our inner dialogue leads to an obvious problem. Sometimes we reason about descriptive beliefs, but more often we reason about what to do. We normally assume that our inner dialogues affect our actions. The story so far, however, is barren of explanation. It concerns only the relations of sentences or beliefs—Aristotle's beloved realm of pure thought. How can we explain voluntary action?

Aristotle modified the account of the faculty of human reason to allow the mind to control action. This involved adapting his theory of the syllogism and postulating the *practical syllogism*. A practical syllogism differs from a normal syllogism in that at least one of its premises is a desire. Its conclusion is an action. Aristotle thus launched the belief-desire explanation of action that stood virtually unchallenged in philosophy until this decade. He patterned his doctrine of how belief and desire cause action on his theory of how the mind passes from one belief to another.

The rationalists clung to the assumption that reason, through the practical syllogism, causes voluntary human action. Yet, as Hume notoriously argued, it entails that reason is inert without desires—only "a slave to the passions." We find here the interchangeable cluster of popularly linked dichotomies embodied in our Greek heritage: reason/emotion, belief/desire, intellect/passion, and mind/body. Western folk theory still reverberates with pronouncements that language can express or define ideas but not feelings. Feelings are attached to words in different, less controlled or determinate ways. This informs the popular dichotomy between denotation and connotation, and the model has led to some notorious problems in Western philosophy.[7] I shall, however, leave this cursory summary at this familiar point for a look at the contrasting Chinese view.

2. CHINESE PHILOSOPHY'S *DAO*

The cluster of concepts at the center of the origins of Chinese philosophy are interestingly different. Carus is most famous for hypothesizing a connection between *logos* and *dao*. The parallel is apt in identifying central organizing conceptions of the two philosophical traditions. But the two concepts play radically different central roles, and different companion concepts surround *dao*^way in traditional Chinese theory.

The Chinese conception of a *dao* 道 reflects none of the apparatus of axiomatic deductive systems. The core notion was of a pattern of ritual behavior transmitted in literature and social conventions from semidivine sage-kings—the inventors of culture. So *dao*^way 道 is like *logos* in being quasi linguistic. The paradigm of a *dao*^way is the transmitted instructions of the sage-kings in the form of a code book—a book of *li* ^ritual 禮.⁸ A plausible precursor could be the oracle bones of the Shang. We usually interpret these as guiding oracles and notice that they were valued and stored as a repository of valuable guidance. The notion of a transmitted *dao*^guiding discourse 道 in literature was as central to Chinese thought as the notion of a proof-structured *logos* was to the Greek.

An obvious difference is that *dao*'s practical application is immediate, not an added complexity. *Daos* inherently guide action. Still, like the earliest Greek theory,⁹ *dao*^guiding discourse 道 originally operated without overtly appealing to desires as motivations. The assumption was that any person who had learned a *dao* would follow that *dao*. Another fundamental difference is this: Socrates' system has a natural contrast between reason and tradition. Consequently, ethics proper, in the West, contains an inherent contrast with positive morality—traditional rules of behavior. The early Confucian view was of essentially a positive morality.

No Sententials

The Chinese guiding *logos* differs further in that Chinese thinkers did not segment their *dao* into the building blocks of proofs—sentences, judgments, opinions, or beliefs. A *dao*'s internal structure is simply a string of *ming* ^names 名 (characters). The order of characters matters. In the Confucian *dao*, that order was that in the traditional literature. In the rival Mohist *dao*, the order was that dictated by utility considerations. Along with the absence of sentences and a proof structure, we also note the absence of any epistemological contrast of propositional belief and knowledge, of any mental picture of inner belief processing, the marginality of the Hellenic conception of truth, and apparent lack of the associated semantic concepts of meaning and its companion "definition" (Hansen, 1985, 1992).

Rectifying Names and the Performance *Dao*

A fascinating Chinese alternative to the last two concepts—meaning and definitions—emerged. Confucius's *Analects* introduces the notion of *zheng*^rectifying *ming*^names 正名. "Suppose you were about to engage in 正 *zheng*^government, what would be your first measure?" "Certainly—*zheng*^rectify *ming*^names 正名" (*Analects* 13:3). The passage presents their strategy as part of Confucius's social political *dao*. The process was not that of giving formulae that reveal analytic truths or inference relations of terms. Chinese thinkers were not searching for propositions about meaning out of which to construct proofs.¹⁰ Their problem was how correctly to apply instructions to particular situations.

For a set of instructions to guide us, we need skill at applying words in different situations. Confucius probably noticed that we acquire this skill when we emulate social superiors—parents, older siblings, teachers. We mimic their ways of pronouncing or writing names; we try to act in similar ways toward similar objects; and we copy these patterns of behavior in response to the instructions containing names of things and actions. Thus we learn to interpret a *dao* into action. Confucius used this basic social process as the model of practical interpretation of a 道 *dao*—正名 $zheng^{\text{rectifying}}$ $ming^{\text{names}}$. Rectifying names was thus the key to successful use of a *dao* in a social setting—to making a *dao* 行 $xing^{\text{walk}}$. Lacking this, he said, li^{ritual} 禮 would not work and people would lack that by which they move hand and foot (13:3).

This notion of guiding literature, together with the ability at practical interpretation, fills the space that reasoning and definitions occupy in the Socratic theory of human action. Rectifying names so a *dao* guides behavior in the real world makes our use of guiding discourse possible. We rectify names when we *pick out* the correct object in applying a rule of action—a maiden aunt or a ritual goblet or a silk cap. If the wrong object were picked, the guidance would go awry. The simple psychological assumption is that we do guide behavior using the words in instructions.

The Implicit Psychology: Names,
Practical Interpretation, and Virtuosity

This view of *dao* and 正名 $zheng\text{-}ming^{\text{rectifying names}}$ presupposes a level of prelinguistic, presocial dispositions. We must be disposed to mimic, disposed to notice and distinguish siblings, disposed to identify certain objects, and so forth. Early Confucians, however, did not focus on those psycholinguistic abilities, nor did they make desires central in their account of human guidance. The main problem for them was posed by intraschool controversies about the correct way to perform 禮 li^{ritual}—to execute the sage's instructions. Appealing to a model leaves two questions open: How does the model know? And how do we interpret or extrapolate from a concrete case of a model performing in one situation to the next, slightly different case?

Confucius suggested a unified answer to both questions. An ability to rectify names comes from a notoriously mysterious moral quality we share with the sages, ren^{humanity} 仁. Ren^{humanity} 仁 enables us to select the morally correct action-interpretation of a code. It mysteriously warrants that we will act as the sage intended us to act. Some Confucian schools thought only an educated, cultivated elite could achieve *ren*; others suggested it was innate. Mohists had a different theory of ren^{humanity} corresponding to their different *dao*. For Mohists, *ren* consists in a presocial inclination or moral instinct favoring general utility (li^{benefit}) 利 in interpretation. That is, a ren^{humane} 仁 person would interpret a *dao* 道 in the way that created the greatest li^{utility} 利 for all concerned.

Ren^{humanity} is a particular case of 德 $de^{\text{virtuosity}}$. Tradition describes ren^{humanity}

as a general moral virtue. Tradition also explains *de* 德 as "the internalization of *dao* 道." On the assumption that Chinese views on human nature are nondualistic,[11] we best understand *de*[virtuosity] 德 as the actual psychophysical change that takes place when we learn to behave according to a *dao*. *De* is the dispositional-state form of a *dao*. A person's *de* thus governs how she will perform the *dao* she has learned.

I have suggested (Hansen 1992, Introduction) that we think of the relation of *dao* and *de* on the model of the relation between a computer program and the internal electrical state of a computer which has been programmed. The translation of the program into machine language and the computer's physical architecture determine just how the computer will execute the program. We engage in debugging to adjust the internal translation of *dao* into patterns of action. Parents and teachers, who not only recite the *dao* into us but also judge our execution as *shi*[right] 是 or *fei*[wrong] 非, fine-tune the *translation* into our actual physical character.

Distinctions and Dispositions

Mozi challenged the Confucian *dao* by raising the point of departure for ethics: Being traditional does not mean being moral. Contrary traditions cannot all be correct. Still, Mozi represented the conflict between divergent *daos* as different ways of *making the distinction* between *yi*[moral] 義 and its opposite. Ethical disagreement was rooted in the different ways we use and rectify names. He still understood rectifying names as socially guiding how we all 辯 *bian*[make distinctions].

Mozi used *bian*[distinction making] 辯 even to explain how the content of the social *dao*—the order of terms in the guiding-literature content—might be different. A *dao* should include the string *you-shen*[have spirits] and lack the string *you-ming*[have fate]. Knowing whether to *you*[there exist] *shen*[spirits] 有神 or to *wu*[not exist] *shen*[spirits] 無神 was knowing how to 辯 *bian*[distinguish] 有無 *you-wu*[exist-not exist]. To use these words correctly is to use them next to some terms and not others. Thus, there can be *shi*[right] *dao*[guiding discourse] 是道 (with terms in the right places) or *fei*[wrong] *dao* 非道. This analysis led to an assumption that all disagreement was about distinctions and where to draw them. It then generated an ambiguous Chinese debate about the ultimate *fa*[standards] 法 that guide the use of language and *bian*[distinctions] 辯. The standards are both standards of application of terms in a *dao* and standards for the choice of the *dao*[guiding discourse] 道 itself.

The attention to standards also produced a characteristic philosophical problem. The standards themselves were a bit of language. Adopting any standard involved making a linguistic distinction one way rather than another. Clearly a standard—such as Mozi's *li-hai*[benefit-harm] 利害 standard—needed a further standard to guide its application. It began to seem that the question of which *dao*[way] was correct led to an infinite regress.

The problem of standards for rectification of names masks an ambiguity in the notion of a *dao*. On the one hand, a *dao* is the actual linguistic instruction set that is transmitted from A to B. On the other hand, it is the performance that would result from theoretically correct interpretation of that *dao* into real-time behavior. I call these "discourse *dao*" and "performance *dao*."

Mozi's position, in effect, was that we use a utilitarian standard applied to the performance *dao* to identify the correct discourse *dao*. Confucius's position was that the discourse *dao* was set by traditional literature and any problems had to be solved by using moral intuition to translate that into the morally correct performance *dao*.

Yu[desire]'s 欲 role in the discussion so far was peripheral. All pre-Daoist thinkers assumed that humans have a natural disposition to behave according to a learned conception of *dao*. Mozi also suggested that there was a universal attitude (*tian*[natural] *zhi*[will] 天志) favoring benefit over harm. Mozi used the concept of *yu*[desire] 欲 more often to describe the desired behavioral disposition, while Confucius used it more to describe dispositions that conflict with his favored *dao*. Confucius also used the term in his famous "negative golden rule."

Mozi's chief Confucian rival, Mencius, brought desires more directly into his theory. Mencius tried to finesse the standards problem by treating all Confucian moral distinctions as prelinguistic—as coming from *tian*[nature, heaven]. Like Mozi, he postulated culturally universal, unchanging, preconventional dispositions to interpretative distinctions and action. Mozi may be taken to represent the position that the natural disposition was to let the benefit–harm distinction guide us. That disposition gives specific and unambiguous (measurable) content both to the notion of a correct form of guiding discourse and to a correct implementation of it in public policy and private behavior (Mozi 45/17/63–74; 48/18/69–74.[12]

Mencius's theory was much more ambitious. He noticed, as all moral conservatives do, that the utility standard does not warrant what we traditionally regard as correct behavior. In response, he adopted the theory that the *entire* traditionally accepted form of behavior was intended by 天 *tian*[nature, heaven]. Conventional rituals, such as burial rituals (obviously wasteful), would not have come about unless they had been outcomes of human moral impulse (Mencius 3A:5). So he theorized that 天 *tian*[nature, heaven] instilled the traditional Confucian *dao* in humans. Instinctively natural behavior and the correct practical interpretation of the traditional Confucian *dao* should coincide. The instinctive pattern of 是非 *shi-fei*[this-not this] in people fixed what was right for those people to do.

Both ancient Chinese rivals were, therefore, moral realists. Both thought there was a uniquely correct performance *dao* and that 天 *tian*[nature, heaven] was its source. Given his account of the natural dispositions to practical interpretation, Mozi's position also entailed that we should promote or *make constant* whatever discourse would best bring about the results approved (是-ed) by our natural, benefit-guided sense of 是非 *shi-fei*[right-wrong] (Mozi 82/47/16–19). He differed from Mencius in that his position required both one natural motivational distinction and a system of motivational distinctions instilled by social programming.

Mencius objected to the simultaneous appeal to natural dispositions and the essential reliance on a discourse *dao* to guide behavior.[13] The dispositions themselves should generate the naturally fixed performance *dao*. He called his theory of four innate virtues the "four 心 *xin*hearts" and also occasionally used both the language of 欲 *yu*desires and 情 *qing*feeling in expressing it. Both Mencius and Mozi thus postulated a psychological, motivational reality underlying and justifying their rival theories of the fixed, natural, or constant *dao*.

In this dispute, the implicit goal, prior to Laozi, had been merely to identify the correct *dao*. Mozi and Mencius both understood this to be the *tian*natural, heavenly *dao*. Mozi theorized that society should *chang*make constant that ideal *dao*. The notion of *chang*constancy implicitly embraced a number of desiderata mined from the above cluster of issues. A constant *dao* should differ from a conventional one in that it does not change or need to change over time or for different circumstances. It would not be different for different traditions and social groupings. A constant *dao* should not need rectification of names. It should be *interpretively* natural and unchanging. Given people's natural or constant inclinations to practical interpretation, that *dao* should have whatever content would generally lead to the correct interpretation. Laozi's 道德經 *Daode Jing* skeptically addressed this goal of a constant 道 *dao*—a natural and reliable guiding discourse—and declared there is none.[14]

The Problem of Desires—Laozi

Although 欲 *yu*desires was a common term in early Chinese thought, no one prior to Laozi had focused on the need to postulate an affective state to accompany the distinctions so they can motivate action.[15] *Yu*desire 欲 had not played the familiar Western role of turning a rational process into an action-guiding one. The *dao* process was inherently a guiding process, and it proceeded by means of names and cultivated abilities to make distinctions. The concept of a distinction was shaped by the pair 是非 *shi*this, right *fei*not this, wrong. That pair was both descriptive and affective—it suggested a pro and con attitude, assent or dissent. For any term X and any object or action or situation O, the recipient of the instruction set involving X in the context of O needs to assign 是非 *shi*this, right or *fei*not this, wrong to O. Chinese philosophers, as we noted above, understood all controversies and disagreements to be grounded in different ways of making distinctions.

Laozi's more systematic attention to the concept of desire in this philosophical tradition is, thus, particularly interesting. It accompanies his systematic doubt that there can be any constant *dao*. Laozi's system (which is expressed in poetry, not argument) suggests that the implicit goal of a system of guidance based on names and distinctions is unachievable. The performance *dao* is inherently indeterminate. Even a fixed set of distinctions can be combined with a reversed pattern of desires—the reversal of opposites.

No *dao* can be *chang*^{constant}, Laozi argues, because no names/distinctions can be *chang*^{constant}.[16] No rule can fix the line of distinction between what is and what is not to be called by a name. The key to mastering a *dao* is learning its names and being able to apply them. Learning a name consists in learning to make a socially appropriate distinction with that name and having the socially appropriate pattern of desires.

Laozi focuses particularly on evaluative guiding terms. We learn evaluative distinctions (good/bad, beautiful/ugly) together, and where we draw the line between them is a matter of learning the practices of one school or group rather than another. When we learn those guiding conventions, Laozi observes, we inevitably also learn along with them that group's pattern of desire—for the beautiful and aversion to the ugly.[17] Like the distinctions, these desires are socially conditioned. Each tradition trains us in the socially appropriate responses to things after we have named them.

The naming thus inherently carries with it a "fitting" pattern of pro or con attitudes. (This is also signaled by the dual translation of 是 *shi*^{this: right} and 非 *fei*^{not this: wrong} as demonstratives and thin evaluative terms.) Since names are conventional, there are no constant names. Conventional distinctions could be drawn in different, equally serviceable ways. Different distinctions would be guided by different goals. Drilling the conventions into us instills desires for those goals. Different traditions instill different patterns of desires. We are, that is, conditioned to have the tastes of our parents, older siblings, teachers, and peers.

That all of these could be otherwise Laozi illustrates using the "reversal of opposites." Reversal of opposites exploits the multiplicity of conventions in popular culture. Laozi cites assorted bits of conventional wisdom that reverse the normal desire pattern associated with any name or distinction, such as dominance/submission or active/passive. This does not show that the name has no constant *descriptive* application but that it has no constant *guiding* implication. The implicit function of the distinction that creates the two names is guidance. If the guidance is not constant, the pragmatic justification for the distinction is not constant.

So *yu*^{desires} are not linked to a mind–body distinction but to a natural–social distinction. Most typical desires are linguistically charged, but they are correlates of names, not of beliefs. We get those desires by learning language and names. The *Daode Jing* reminds us of an assumption behind Mencius's innatist theory: Action should be guided only by natural desires. Thus, although *yu*^{desire} anchors the attack on the possibility of any constant *dao*, it also anchors the alternative possibility of a natural, nonconventional, constant *dao*. Presocial desires could constitute a protonatural *dao*. These desires guide how we would act if no one had ever instilled relative social distinctions in us. These natural desires might well be universally shared desires, but, in Laozi's view (in contrast to Mencius's), they are not desires for some universal good. The operation of natural desires would yield no impulse for human contact outside the local village.[18]

Despite this positive possibility, the dominant tone of Laozi's analysis, like that of Western rationalists, is antidesire. His reason, however, is not desire's effect on calm reason but its social, linguistic origin and effect. The socially induced desires dominate his treatment because, in his view, they are the problem. Socially induced desires both enslave our natural drives and lead to destructive competition and strife. Natural desires, he optimistically assumes, would lead to human harmony.

The Antilanguage Dao

Mencius's and Laozi's antilanguage theories yield a notion of a performance 道 *dao* without any guiding discourse 道 *dao*. Each invites us to consider the course of history (the world's performance *dao*) that would result from avoiding language altogether, avoiding all teaching, all transmission, all accumulation of guiding knowledge (know-how or cleverness). Laozi supposed that such a world history would be free from competitive desires. Mencius supposed it would result in perfect Confucian behavior. Both positions require the notion that there are some presocial, unprogrammed desires.

The psychological key to this anticonvention, antilanguage theory is that there must be a presocial, preconventional, dispositional structure on which social, conventional systems build. There must be a hard-wired program in the computer before it can accept any software programming. Thus, that hard-wired program must include some natural desires as well as some natural distinctions. Any linguistic *dao* and its associated *de* presuppose a prior, nonlinguistic *de*.

That natural *dao* in the form of a natural *de* is the antilanguage theorists' candidate for the constant *dao*. Any social *dao*, any *dao* that can be put into language, could have a different content and could operate other than it does. Declaring any particular social *dao* to be right presupposes a pattern of 是非 *shi*[right] *fei*[wrong] assignments both in applying that *dao* and in approving of its outcome. These simply beg the question against rival social 道 *daos*.[19] Every 道 *dao* judges itself as 是 *shi*[right] and its rivals as 非 *fei*[wrong].

Any standard for selecting which *dao* is correct, or for judging which interpretation of any given *dao* is correct, itself requires use of a 名 *ming*[name]. It therefore presupposes some distinction, creates an opposite, and comes accompanied by a 欲 *yu*[desire]. Utility, for example, comes with its opposite, and the choice of 利害 *li–hai*[benefit–harm] as the ur-standard (as opposed to some Confucian standard, egoism, naturalness, etc.) is disputable. Further, the identification of *li*[benefit] in a particular situation requires interpretation as much as other terms do in the proposed linguistic *dao*.

We could translate the famous Humean form, "You cannot get an *ought* from an *is*," as "There is no natural *dao*" (probably because all *daos* are equally natural rather than because there are no *daos* in nature). Zhuangzi, who makes this point most clearly in Classical thought, does not use our familiar language of proof, premise, presupposition to make it. He says that getting a 是非 *shi-fei*[right-wrong] out of an unbiased 心 *xin*[heart] is like going to Yue today and arriving yesterday (Zhuangzi 4/2/22).

3. THE PROBLEM OF *QING*

With that outline of the surrounding philosophical context and key concepts, we can now turn to the concept of 情 *qing*[feelings]. My analysis, as I noted above, follows up a hypothesis of A.C. Graham, who treated the 'reality' sense of 情 *qing*[feeling] as the original and basic sense.

> Although the word [*qing*[feeling]] is very common in pre-Han literature I should like to risk the generalization that it never means 'passions' . . . . As a noun it means 'the facts', . . . as an adjective 'genuine', . . . as an adverb . . . 'genuinely'. (Graham, 1990, 59)

Graham's account also related 情 *qing* to naming. "The (*qing*[feeling]) of X is 'what is genuinely X in it', 'what X essentially is'." *Qing*, Graham says, is "what X cannot lack if it is to be called X" (1990, 63).

Graham's analysis recalls the familiar Euclidean interest in definition, relations of terms, and substance-property analysis.[20] It identifies, defines, and relates types by clusters of essential properties. Any substance that has the chosen set of properties has the essence. To have the essence is to be able to fit in the scheme of deductive knowledge of the particular external subject matter. It suggests a Greek metaphysical interest in names more than a Chinese pragmatic approach to naming. Chinese theories of naming would not require theories of a thing's essential character. Humans need to have a way to make the distinction—that is all.

The *dao* context, however, reminds us that the interest of the Chinese is in using language to guide action more than in using language to describe or represent things. They showed scant interest in the abstract relations of terms[21] and none in any substance-property analysis of how objects belong to natural kinds. Their interest seems focused on the kind of issue that *undermined* the Greek definition paradigm: How do you break out of the circle of terms to the real world? They worried about practical interpretation of 道 *daos*. How do we apply the names in the *dao* to the world? In that project, the definition model looks circular. The 正名 *zheng-ming*[rectify names] emulation answer has problems, but it is not blatantly circular.[22]

In dealing with their version of the practical interpretation question, Chinese philosophers concentrated on the relation of terms in two ways:

1. The relation of a term and its opposite: If we can apply term X to the real world, then the same discrimination ability guides our application of non-X to the world. One ability to 是非 *shi-fei*[this-not this] gives us two opposite names.

2. The relation of standards: A standard for practical interpretation of the entire cluster of names used in a 道 *dao*[guiding discourse] presupposes a prior ability to apply the set of names used in the standard. Some ur-distinction or dichotomy guides 是非 *shi-fei*[this-not this] judgments as applied to every other term pair in the language.

Graham expresses his own reservations about his *essence* analysis of 情 *qing*[reality]. He says he rejects *essence* as a translation[23] in favor of "what is essential." Absent more explanation, this seems an empty, verbal difference. The essence is what is essential and vice versa. Graham's explanation that 情 *qing*[facts, feelings] somehow goes from meaning "reality" (cum "essence") to meaning "passions" is also unsettling. It still requires that the term shifted from referring to something metaphysical and objective (reality, essence, or the facts) to referring to something subjective and psychological (passions).[24] This anomaly prompted our original skepticism that the term functions against the background of anything like Western folk psychology. Postulating such a radical meaning change also violates the principle of humanity's call for explanation on analogy to us. Our words would hardly be intelligible if they arbitrarily changed meaning so radically while no one seemed to notice.

Graham's baseline insight about 情 *qing*[reality] is sound, however. *Qing* is connected with reality, and it does have to do with naming. This is especially clear for the Later Mohists, but can be discerned, as Graham notes, in usage from Early Mohism to Mencius, Zhuangzi, Xunzi, and a host of early texts (1990, 60–65). The challenge for any Graham-like account is to produce a modified theory that links this reality core with affective states. It should do so without presupposing a background of Western proof processes, subject–predicate grammatical analysis, and abstract metaphysical focus. Our unified-meaning theory should coherently account for the whole range of pre-Buddhist uses and avoid unexplained shifts in meaning.

We can modify Graham's account first by noting that Chinese thinkers explicated naming in a pragmatic rather than the Greek semantic way. Naming is tied to publicly accessible criteria of application, not to an abstract substance–property metaphysical analysis. The 情 *qing*[reality responses] *are* criteria of naming, but they entail no theory of properties, still less of a distinction between accidental and essential properties. *Qing* 情 ties naming pragmatically to the human ability to 是非 *shi-fei*[this-not this] with a term in real situations. It responds to the concern with standards used to guide saying 是 *shi*[assenting to] or 非 *fei*[dissenting from] of a term–object pair. The 情 *qing*[reality responses] are the *inputs from* reality on the basis of which humans do this. We must have such inputs in order to apply conventional naming standards to those realities.

When we are executing an internalized program, we come to the word *X*. At that point we need to determine if an X is before us. The *qing* are extralinguistic feedback from X. The *qing* of a thing are the reality-related, accessible criteria that practically guide use of its name. Theoretically, they should come to us in the same way no matter which *dao* we are executing. On the basis of different *daos* and different standards of interpretation, and the actually received *qing*, we act in one way or the other toward X.

Now we can identify immediately the source of the *passive* connection that allows association with passions. *Qing* are received. They are our *connection* to reality, the facts, circumstances of action, and so on. *Qing* supplements convention, however, not reason. Thus, as Graham notes, Chinese writers frequently contrast *qing* with 名 *ming*[name], 文 *wen*[fame], 聲 *sheng*[sound], and 爲 *wei*[artificial, false].[25]

Qing 情 sometimes approximates general sensory input. It plays a different theoretical role, however. Some *qing* 情 are inputs that trigger basic sensible distinctions. This input from the world is the distinguishable. It has not the logical form of a picture but of a field for discrimination. It is not data, information, or facts, nor is it a map of external reality. *Qing* 情 has no sentential form and does not input into a system that needs or appeals to basic premises and gives content to a deductive system.

In Western tradition, the sense of sight, sense *data*, and pictures of facts dominate its conception of experience. For Chinese theory, a better model would be taste and discrimination.[26] Their comments almost rule out that *qing* can be in sentential or picture form. Thus, again as Graham notes, 情 *qing*[reality input] contrasts with 貌 *mao*[description, guise, demeanor] and, more surprisingly, with 形 *xing*[shape].[27] Description is obviously akin to naming—hence conventional and linguistic. Shape is less obviously linguistic—until we remember that we are dealing with a Chinese view of language where shapes are more intimately associated with language. *Qing* are prior to the shape-recognition training that accompanies language.

Qing 情, in sum, are all reality-induced discrimination or distinction-making reactions in *dao* executors. They guide the application of terms in a *dao* in real time in real (and inevitably unique) situations. Thus, the fundamental sensory distinctions (dark–light, left–right, sweet–sour–salty–bitter, high–low pitch) are 情 *qing*. But so also is the reality feedback we get from executing a 道 *dao*[guiding discourse]. Feedback in this form—pleasure, anger, sadness, fear, love, hate, desire—gives us Mozi's pragmatic test of a 道 *dao* and of its practical interpretation.

The Role of 情 *Qing*$^{\text{reality inputs}}$ in Classical Disputes

We find the earliest confirmation of this role of *qing*$^{\text{reality input}}$ in the synoptic Mozi. Mohist texts use both a 心 *xin*^{heart} radical 情 *qing* and a 言 *yan*^{language} radical 情 *qing* in connection with names and language.[28] His three standards of 言 *yan*^{language} include the 情 *qing*$^{\text{reality input}}$ of the eyes and ears—a phrase he uses frequently.[29] Mozi treats the desire for general utility as something that "情將欲 *qing*^{feeling} *jiang*$^{\text{lead us to}}$ *yu*^{desire} (feeling leads us to desire)."[30] Mozi uses the heart-radical 情 *qing*$^{\text{reality input}}$ especially when discussing the natural impulses (e.g., to family partiality) which he thinks the right 道 *dao* should correct. He describes several natural distinctions (boy–girl to bird–beast to *yin–yang*) as 情 *qing*$^{\text{reality input}}$.[31]

The names/reality issue that grips early and later Mohists is how we can apply names consistently. When we learn a public name from our parents, we must apply it to the thing in virtue of distinctions we can already make. Thus Mozi urges that the standards of naming must be accessible to "the eyes and ears of the people" (58/36/5, 57/35/9). When we name things, we name them according to those features that strike us, the features they present to us.

When the Later Mohists talk about 情 *qing* and 名 *ming*^{names}, we need not conclude they are interested in definitional essences. They are more likely to be interested in a practical substitute for definition—the publicly or sensibly accessible criteria guiding the use of a name.[32] These enable all the members of a linguistic community to use the name in reasonably consistent ways. It requires that we receive the same 情 *qing*$^{\text{reality inputs}}$.[33] The 情 *qing* are the apprehensible, reality-based criteria for shared, objective naming.

Here is the strength of Graham's analysis. *Qing* are a kind of *authentic* standard. They are authentic, however, in relation to the Ancient Chinese dichotomy between the natural and the social. They do not underwrite a contrast between reality and appearance. Conventions can be changed, and *qing* represent the background feedback we must use in applying any convention or any proposed changes. *Qing* are connected to naming and to reality, but do not incorporate a Hellenic notion of a *meaning, idea, essence,* or *property*.

Yi Wu (1986, 88) identifies the *Zhuangzi* as a text where the *reality* meaning of *qing*^{feeling} is most prominent. In a famous passage (which Graham also cites), Zhuangzi speaks of a 眞君 *zhen*^{authentic} *jun*$^{\text{ruler, lord}}$ (an ultimate warrant or authority for linguistic distinctions) which has 形 *xing*^{shape} but no 情 *qing*$^{\text{reality input}}$. Zhuangzi skeptically observes that our getting (or not getting) input from it does not determine whether it is 眞 *zhen*^{authentic} or not.[34]

The "true ruler" passage is intelligible if we treat *qing* as reality inputs that allow a discrimination guiding our use of names—reactions to reality rather than reality itself. In talking about the 眞君 *zhen-jun*[real ruler] having "no 情 *qing*," Zhuangzi is denying that we have any reality-based indication of its existence. It does not, that is, generate any sensible discriminations. "It seems that there must be one, and yet, uniquely, there is no trace. Its having no 情 *qing* neither adds nor detracts from its 眞 *zhen*[authenticity]." Wu Yi translates 眞 *zhen*[authenticity] as "reality," and is thus required to claim that the 眞君 *zhen*[authentic] *jun*[ruler, lord]'s having reality or not has nothing to do with its reality. That is hard to motivate. All skeptics, however, note that our failing to be able to *detect* something does not show that it does not exist. (Of course, contrary to the established, dogmatic interpretations of the passage, it does not prove the opposite, either. The context signals a classic statement by a skeptic more than it does some mystical assertion that something is real because it is unreal or unprovable.)

Now let us look at the exchange between Zhuangzi and Hui Shi that forms the heart of Graham's case. Yi Wu points to the same Zhuangzi passage and treats it as an exception—a case where, he says, 情 *qing* clearly means "desire."[35] Zhuangzi speaks of "having human 形 *xing*[shape] but without human 情 *qing*[reality responses]." "So," he says, "是非 *shi-fei*[this-not this] is not obtained by his 身 *shen*[body]." Hui Shi wonders if humans can really lack 情 *qing*[reality input]. Zhuangzi explains that it is 是非 *shi-fei*[this-not this] which he calls 情 "*qing*[reality responses]. What he means by having no *qing*, he goes on, is not allowing likes and dislikes to wound his 身 *shen*[body].

Graham supposes that Zhuangzi (an antirationalist) must be deliberately contradicting himself in talking of humans with no 情 *qing*—in other words, humans who are not human. In Graham's analysis, Hui Shi, whom Graham reckons a logician, is the only one concerned with consistency. Graham translates Hui Shi as calling Zhuangzi on the point. "May a man really be without his essence?" Graham's strategy here requires the translator to add the "his" to the passage. Hui Shi merely asks, "can *ren*[humans] *gu*[really, inherently] *wu*[lack] *qing*[reality responses] (humans really/inherently lack reality responses) 人故無情乎?" Graham needs the surreptitious shift from 情 *qing*[reality inputs] in general to the essence of being human—hence feelings. Graham covers this shift by noting that "distinguishing right from wrong is hardly passion." We can view this passage as a crucial step in the development of the theory of 情 *qing*[reality inputs]. Zhuangzi here could be making this point: Making a 是非 *shi-fei* distinction involves having a pro or con attitude that is guided by language. This would continue the Daoist link between name-criteria and affective attitudes that we earlier saw in Laozi.

This famous exchange with Hui Shi now makes straightforward sense.[36] Zhuangzi's point is that the form that the input takes is always a 是非 *shi-fei*[pro-con: right wrong] response. All feedback is therefore infected with an interpretive and attitudinal bias. That issuing 是非 *shi-fei*[right-wrong] responses is a natural, presocial reaction comes close to Mencius in one sense. Zhuangzi, contrary to Graham's analysis, can allow, with Mencius, that *issuing* such judgments is natural. That merely entails that humans are naturally social and judgmental animals. All the existing ways of shaping that natural judgmental inclination are equally natural. All human qing^(reality input) takes the form of a shi-fei^(right-wrong) judgment—infected with a learned, linguistic content. So the most we can hope for is not letting those interpretive, attitudinal judgments harm us. Supposedly, we do that by remembering that they are conventional. All might be otherwise—they are not constant.

The passage thus makes clear sense on the analysis that 情 qing are discrimination responses which arise from reality to guide our application of names. Zhuangzi, we have assumed, is making Laozi's further point that any such reaction to reality is inherently action guiding. In learning names we are acquiring likes and dislikes. Thus, we can see a theoretical relation between "qing" and "desires" without treating the terms as synonyms.

Finally, we turn to Xunzi's views on 情 qing^(reality input) and 性 xing^(human nature). Xunzi defines 性 xing^(human nature) two times: once as inborn and once as what naturally eventuates from what is inborn in its interaction with things. Thus, the 情 qing are natural—in the second sense. Xunzi says, "Nature's liking, disliking, pleasure, anger, sadness and joy—call these qing^(reality responses)."[37] Xunzi later elaborates: "性 xing^(human nature) is what flows from 天 tian^(nature, heaven). Qing^(reality inputs) 情 are the basic stuff of the 性 xing^(human nature). Yu^(desires) 欲 are the ying^(reactions) 應 to 情 qing^(reality inputs)."[38]

A particularly interesting feature of Xunzi's discussion of 情 qing^(reality responses) comes in his stern denunciation of Song Xing's phrase, "情欲寡 qing^(reality response) yu^(desires) are gua^(few)."[39] Prior to Graham, most writers probably would have followed Yi Wu in treating "情欲 qing^(reality inputs) yu^(desires)" as a synonym compound—and the passage as merely saying "emotions and desires are few." Graham's explanation treated the compound as referring to a subclass of desires. Graham thought the relevant subclass was the essential (i.e., human-defining) desires. These, in Graham's interpretation, are what Song Xing argues are few.

Again I agree with Graham's grammatical analysis—情欲 qing-yu^(reality input desires) is a modification structure. But Graham's explanation of qing^(reality input) as essence again creates a problem for his explanation of Xunzi's position. Why would a Confucian argue against a Daoist that the desires that *define* human nature are all presocial? Confucians, the Xunzi wing especially, usually treat humans as inherently social, as convention-following animals. When Xunzi directly discusses the place of the human in the natural "chain of being," he says the distinctive human faculty is 義 yi^(morality). That, in turn, he says, comes from making distinctions.[40]

Against the background of theories we have sketched, however, we can now appreciate a Daoist flavor in Song Xing's theory. His position also resembles that of Laozi—only a few desires are nonlearned reality responses. The bulk of the disruptive and competitive plethora of human desires is in-

duced by conventional distinctions, by language—in short, by learning a traditional *dao*. Song Xing's position is inherently anti-conventional. That also coherently explains Xunzi's rather cantankerous reaction to the slogan.

Xunzi's own argument for the importance of traditional 禮 *li*ritual relies on
the opposite assumption. The natural, uncultivated, and civilized desires are
many. They are shared with the animals and lead inevitably to disorder and
strife. Instead of the Daoist position that conventions multiply desires, he argues that they merely determine what is the proper object of desire.[41] The Confucian traditional rituals, he says, tame and control a myriad of natural desires.

Thus, Xunzi treats the natural, presocial human responses to the world as
bad things. For him, the paradigmatic bad things are avaricious desires—the
natural responses to reality input. The Daoists, however, argue that such desires are induced by social practices such as valuing rare or old objects, cultivating elegant or expensive tastes, and so forth. If we were not socialized to
have such desires, our instinctual desires would enable us to live quite comfort-
ably in small, uncomplicated villages.

Understanding the source of these desires, Song Xing must have argued,
can help us reduce and control those competitive urges. Xunzi's political position is precisely the opposite. Where the Daoists want to reduce learning, Xunzi
wants to increase and more rigidly regulate it. He cannot, therefore, accept the
Daoist theory of the source of those desires; he favors conventions. He wants to
reduce competitiveness by *more* conventions—more rigid, more regular, and
more controlling. Conventions should so reliably govern the objects of desire
that each social class desires only the things economically available to it. Thus,
the "little people" will not want rare and valuable art, and aristocracy will have
no competition for them. The aristocracy will not hoard sackcloth, so the little
people will have their now favorite clothing material.

Xunzi, thus, cannot tolerate a Daoist position on what constitute the 情欲
*qing-yu*reality input desires. Given his analysis of the problems in human society as the
product of desires, the whole range of desires must create a problem serious
enough to warrant his more authoritarian political theory. His analysis in the
chapter "Human Nature Is Evil" confirms his view that the natural inclination
of humans is to have many disorderly desires. Like Hobbes, Xunzi needs that
pessimistic assumption to justify his authoritarian and slavish devotion to the
Sages. If the disruptive desires turn out, themselves, to be a product of misrule,
then it will be hard to defend, as Xunzi does, rulers using amputation and other
mutilating punishments.

This political dispute and its resolution, however, are not the central concern here. What is conceptually interesting here is that by a very different route,
some Classical Chinese thinkers seem to have come to a position that resonates
with the modern Western analysis of desires. Most desires are not a matter of
pure bodily or natural reaction, but are a product of conceptualization, conven-

tion, society, and language. *Qing-yu*[reality input desires], on the other hand, specify only those few desires which are not.

Xunzi's attitude to 情 *qing*[reality input] does make it *seem* closer to passions. Graham thus agrees with traditionalists like Yi Wu in identifying the *Xunzi* as initiating the *usage* onto which a "passions" meaning could be grafted, but still fails to explain the change smoothly. Graham struggles with his consequent account of Xunzi. He denies that the meaning had actually changed in Xunzi's use. This is correct. Yet, he describes the difference between Xunzi and Zhuangzi, for example, semantically—that is, in terms of narrowing reference from essence in general to the feelings which are the essence of being human. This is still an arbitrary and unexplained change—and it is a change in meaning.

Graham says, "In [Xunzi's] texts, but nowhere else in pre-Han literature, the word [情 *qing*[reality]] refers only to the genuine in man which it is polite to disguise, and therefore to his feelings" (1990, 64). So, for Zhuangzi the character meant "essence," which for Xunzi it means "the essence of humanity only." Although both contain the word *essence*, they are wholly distinct meanings. To get Graham's explanation, we must add to this shift in meaning an unexplained and heretofore unnoticed postulate that the essence of humanity is passion.

That inconsistency in Graham's analysis of meaning, coupled with the worry that it requires us to import a dubiously motivated notion of the essence of humanity, motivates rethinking Graham's analysis. He requires us suddenly to attribute to Chinese thinkers the Western Romantic's view that *feelings* are what are definitionally essential to humans. This makes it hard to accept the details of Graham's analysis. He offers no coherent explanatory account of why Xunzi would argue that 'the genuine' (except now interpreted as "desires") *should* be disguised. His superficial translation consistency still leaves us with an unwieldy and incoherent interpretive stance.

That meaning-change result can be avoided. Xunzi's usage is straightforwardly consistent with the "reality input" interpretation. The difference between Xunzi and Zhuangzi is not in the meaning of the term 情 '*qing*[reality response]' but in their contrasting prescriptive theories and attitude toward the presocial natural responses that are prior to names.

Zhuangzi, as Graham notes, is normally positive about 情 *qing*[reality responses]. Xunzi is notoriously negative. Zhuangzi is negative about Confucian traditions and conventions. Xunzi is positive toward them. Since the present account contrasts reality responses and conventional systems of naming, we can easily understand this theoretical and attitudinal disagreement against a background of a shared meaning. Xunzi assumes that nearly all (especially selfish) desires are among the reality inputs. He objects to the Daoist claim that such disruptive desires arise from optional socialization.

Graham also cites Han Feizi's commentary on the Laozi saying "禮 *li*[ritual] is to 貌 *mao*[disguise] the 情 *qing*[reality responses]." This passage, too, on its face, signals

Xunzi's influence on his student and confirms the present natural versus conventional analysis better than it does an essence versus accident analysis. Conventions are added to and intended to control the preconventional, attitudinal reactions to the world.

We can further support the smooth-curve analysis of the meaning by looking at a later *Li-ji* passage to which Graham appeals. It contains a traditional list of paradigmatic 人情 *renqing*[human feelings] (pleasure, anger, sadness, fear, love, hate, desire). Graham cites the passage and translates the continuation, "These seven *we are capable of without having learned them*" (1990, 64 [italics in original]).[42] This is a helpful formula, but it does not identify the property of being *essential*. It identifies the property of being preconventional or prelearned.

The *Li-ji* passage recalls a similar passage in the *Zhuangzi*. Zhuangzi says, "Pleasure, anger, sadness, happiness, concern, regret, love, hate, fascination, nonchalance, expressions, attitudes—like music from holes, mushrooms from moisture, day and night they replace each other before us and no one knows where they come from. Enough! Enough! Day and night they are before us. Who cares where they come from?"[43] Although Zhuangzi does not here identify these as 情 *qing*[reality inputs], he clearly intends to deal with the items in the list as inputs from "who knows where."

Conclusion: Borrowing *Qing* for Buddhist Folk Psychology

Qing[reality responses] 情, I have argued, were theoretically distinguished from 欲 *yu*[desires] by being presocial bases for the application of terms, while *yu*[desires] 欲 may be natural or socially induced attitudes toward the things as named. The key to the gradual narrowing between the two is the receptive character of *qing* along with Zhuangzi's argument that *qing*[reality inputs], coming as they do in the form of 是非 *shi-fei*[this-not this], are both linguistically shaped and attitudinal—they involve pro and con attitudes. This parallels the *Laozi*'s argument about 欲 *yu*[desires]. That, together with the fact that the inputs went from being mainly Mozi's 情 *qing*[reality inputs] of the eyes and ears to those that guide acceptance and interpretation of whole 道 *dao*[guiding discourses], underpinned Zhuangzi's identification of states of satisfaction, anger, pleasure, and the like as 情 *qing*[reality inputs]. These then make their way into paradigm lists like those found in the *Xunzi*, the *Zhuangzi*, and the *Li-ji*. The range of *qing*, I have argued, is broader than those emotive states, and includes all reality inputs. Unless we avoid the assumption that *qing*[reality inputs] are subjective, content states, we will be forced to an improbably mixed account of the meaning of the character when we deal with the Later Mohists and Zhuangzi. We cannot, that is, assume that Chinese philosophers make the usual assumptions of Western folk psychology and still give a smooth explanation of the use of this character in the key texts and disputes.

We have, however, seen that theoretical development informs a growing skepticism about *qing*[reality inputs]. The skepticism does not arise from any claim about their subjective, mental, or inner character. It arises from doubt that any input is free from conventional, linguistic distortion. Zhuangzi expresses doubt that any *qing*$^{\text{reality inputs}}$ are free from linguistic content since they are *shi-fei*$^{\text{this-not this}}$ responses relative to a term. He further hints that, like desires, the *shi-fei qing*$^{\text{reality responses}}$ are attitudinal and influence our actions. Xunzi further effectively closes the gap in his vigorous objection to Song Xing's trying to mark a distinction between 情欲 *qing*$^{\text{reality inputs}}$ *yu*^{desires} and the 欲 *yu*^{desires} that are socially conditioned. For Xunzi, *qing* and *yu* are alike in that they disrupt ritual, conventional order.

Xunzi's authoritarian Confucianism further promotes the Buddhist appropriation in sharing with Indo-European systems the negative attitude toward *qing*$^{\text{reality inputs}}$. The domination of authoritarian Confucianism (and its offspring, Legalism) when Buddhism first reaches China gives us the outline of an explanation why Buddhist translators would have adapted 情 *qing* to refer to our familiar Western *feeling*-concepts. *Qing* threaten the order of ritual for Xunzi as passions or emotions disturb reason for Buddhists and Greeks. So, given the dominant theory of *qing*$^{\text{reality inputs}}$ at the time and the lists that concentrate on attitudinal states, when an Indo-European psychology is introduced into China, 情 *qing*$^{\text{reality inputs}}$ is an apt term to adapt to the new theoretical role.

Notes

1. I believe this term comes from Steven Stich's (1983) title *From Folk Psychology to Cognitive Science*. My thanks to Joel Marks and Roger Ames for helpful comments on an earlier draft of this paper and to my collegues in the Philosophy Department, University of Hong Kong, for helpful comments on an oral presentation.

2. Mainly in Hansen 1992.

3. I combine the pinyin spelling for the Mandarin pronunciation with an English tag in most context as a convenient way to incorporate Chinese characters into my metalanguage. Readers should note that I am discussing neither the sound (utterly distinct characters may have the same sounds, and each character has a different pronunciation in the different languages of Chinese) nor the English concept used in the tag. I intend the superscript tag to individuate characters and to aid readers in following the argument about the character. The tag should not be regarded as a definition or an equivalent concept. When I am discussing rival interpretive theories, I may use a tag that gives their reading. Chinese characters are not inflected for number, tense, case, gender, or part of speech. I normally adjust the tag to fit the grammar of the English sentence and the context. Chinese characers can be used in many different syntactical roles. I will sometimes simply use characters as they would be used in Chinese. The most jarring for an English reader is when nouns or adjectives are used as two-place verbs. This structure is particularly interesting for the point of this essay since it replaces belief contexts; for example, "X believes S is P" would be expressed in Chinese as "X P-s S."

4. This is the classical period of Chinese philosophy—the so-called Hundred Schools Period. Accounts of Chinese thought use a cluster of terms—ancient, classical, Pre-Qin (Pre-Ch'in), Pre-Han , and Pre-Buddhist—to describe this period. The latter three are significant. The Qin (221 B.C.) literally brought philosophical activity to a close by burning books, burying scholars alive, and suppressing all philosophical expression. The Han (206 B.C. to A.D. 220) made Confucianism a state orthodoxy. Philosophy was barely visible behind a morass of superstitious cosmology. Buddhism began to spread toward the end of the Han, and introduced new philosophical excitement but also introduced the radically different assumptions of our familiar Indo-European conceptual

scheme: mind–body dualism, reason; belief, ideas in contrast to emotions, feelings, desires; mental substance and an inner world populated with ideas which are images of objects in physical substance; sentential focus, truths, principles, laws, duties, syllogistic logic, and belief-desire explanations of action. How much of this "took" in China is controversial. I shall not address that issue.

5. Needham (1954) argues that the Chinese interest in mathematics, and especially algebra defuses any explanatory significance that the absence of geometry might have. But that defense, I think, misjudges the nature of the explanation. It is not the content of geometry but the axiomatic form that is significant. An axiomatic mathematics could have played the role I have in mind here.

6. In an intuitively obvious way it addresses reality more than numbers do. We find the Pythagorean assumption that numbers are real objects obscure unless we visualize them as points. Shape *seems to be* a feature of the real world in a way in which number is not. This appeal to subject matter, however, does not make geometry logically different from mathematics. The difference comes mainly from attibuting reality to individual objects rather than to collections of objects. The ancient Western thinkers regarded numbers as being fully as real as geometical shapes. Moderns see geometry as being fully as conventional as are different axiom systems for logic and mathematics.

7. The additional, *desire* element is supposed to move the body. Desires are perturbations introduced into the reasoning process by the body which, in turn, result in bodily action. Grammatically, desires regularly take things as their objects, but the theory requires that the content of desires, like beliefs, must actually be sententials. We must treat desires as propositional attitudes. The *logical* form of a desire for X, this theory entails, is the desire that I have X. Thus, we discover, by analysis of this model of human functioning, that desires must be cognitive and have linguistic content.

8. There are several extant versions of different books of *li*[ritual]; all are relatively later than Confucius. We traditionally assume that Confucius used some early text of a similar nature.

9. I.e., that theory expressed in the slogan "No person knowingly does evil." It presents cognition as self-contained motivation to action.

10. In this series of claims, I am challenging Graham's analysis of the Later Mohist Canon. For more detailed arguments on this issue, see Hansen 1983, 1985, 1991, 1992.

11. That is, they are not mind–body dualist. There is an implicit dualism in the view, namely, that between nature and convention. Thanks to Roger Ames for pointing out this possible confusion to non-philosophers.

12. Mozi and Zhuangzi citations follow the Harvard–Yenching Concordance.

13. *Mencius* 3A:5. I am here following Nivison's analysis (e.g., Nivison 1979.)

14. *Daode Jing* ch. 1, l. 1. The typical interpretation is that Daoists allege there is a constant *dao* but it cannot be spoken. The text does not warrant that conclusion, which comes from the common translator's error that "No X is Y" entails "Exactly one X is non-Y." For a more detailed discussion see Hansen 1992, 196–219.

15. *Yu*[desires] 欲 clearly do motivate behavior. Confucius spoke of 欲 *yu*[desires] sometimes as impulses that a follower of 道 *dao*[guiding discourse] can and will ignore. Other times he talks about 欲 *yu*[desires] for moral things. Mozi used 欲 *yu*[desire] primarily for the natural and universal desire for 利 *li*[benefit]. He notes that people's 欲 *yu*[desires] can be conditioned when superiors exhibit the right ones themselves. Confucius had made a similar appeal to the rulers—if you desire *shan*[good] 善 the people will be 善 *shan*[good]. Some of the noticeable differences between *yu*[desires] and desire include that Chinese thinkers speak of the 欲 *yu*[desires] of separate bodily parts. The grammar of 欲 *yu*[desires] is otherwise closer to that of Western folk psychology than are most other candidate psychological terms. There is no term for sentential belief, and 知 *zhi*[know] usually takes a noun phrase as an object. *Yu*[desire] 欲 can take sentential, and verb-phrase as well as noun-phrase, contexts.

16. *Daode Jing* ch. 1, line 2.

17. Ibid., ch. 2.

18. Ibid., ch. 80.

19. The exception is self-defeating *daos*—see Hansen 1992, ch. 4.

20. Graham, I believe, first broached his approach while working on the Later Mohist Canon. Graham thought it was a deductive system of interlocking definitions organized on a Euclidean model of the proof. For a critique see Hansen 1992.

21. For example, things like "All A are B, but not all B are A."

22. I say "blatantly" because the same problem arises in copying a performance in new circumstanstances that arises in using a term in new circumstances.

23. Graham's ambivalence flows out of his denial that Chinese has, properly speaking, a concept of 'being' or 'reality' in the Greek sense. The essence, the predicative *is*, must also be absent. Yet he thinks Chinese analysis of names is concerned with definitions. Thus, he is both drawn and repelled by the theory that Chinese talked about a thing's essence. He sees 情 *qing*[essence] as what is captured in definitions (1989, 412–14). I agree with the claim Graham is ambivalent about and reject the one he is sure of. *You*[exists] 有 is a perfectly adequate concept of 'being'. The absence of a concept of 'essence' is only very remotely tied to the early Greek philosophical confusion of the existential and predicative functions of *to be*.

24. Graham's account relies on his theory of the relation of 情 *qing* to naming and goes as follows: That without which 人 *ren*[humans] could not be called 人 *ren*[human] is passions. Therefore, the 情 *qing*[essence] of human nature is passion. Therefore, 情 *qing*[feeling] comes to *mean passions*. Graham traces a number of different examples and postulates that the meaning changes occur gradually. He suggests that in the *Xunzi*, 情 *qing*[feeling] refers to the passions but does not yet mean *passions*. The trouble, of course, is that if Graham is right, Xunzi would have no way to express the internal conclusion. All he could say is that the 情 *qing*[essence] of human nature is 情 *qing*[essence]. This requires that the meaning of 情 *qing*[essence] be suddenly and inexplicably relativized to humans. So Graham's explanation still presupposes an unexplained change in meaning.

25. Graham 1990, 59.

26. A particularly clear example occurs in the *Xunzi* 83/22/16–20.

27. Graham 1990, 60.

28. A great many Chinese characters combine elements which suggest an intended meaning —we call these "radicals." Philosophers especially seemed to coin new distinctions by changing or adding radicals to existing characters. The character constructed by this means was, we assume, pronounced the same, but this need not always have been the case. See Hansen (1992, 35–39) for a more complete discussion. The 言 *yan*[language] radical 請 *qing*[please] is normally used as a request. One tempting hypothesis is that Mohists regarded requests as another form of external input that guides program execution. Xunzi typically uses 請 *qing*[please] of requests from below—inputs to rulers.

29. *Mozi* 58/36/6 (heart-radical 情 *qing*), 16/12/7, 10 (language-radical 請 *qing*).

30. *Mozi* 33/19/62. I take this to mean that there is a presocial, reality-input desire for utility. Reality delivers this desire in contrast to the desires generated by language *daos*.

31. *Mozi* 7/6/35.

32. We might be tempted to say the Chinese philosophers were interested in the *nominal* as opposed to the *real* essence—what competent speakers all believe about the referent of a term versus what is really true about that reference. Still, that traditional formula defining the nominal essence would mislead us. The Chinese are interested in what *actual input* guides the application of the term. The traditional formula is parasitic on a prior interest in the real essence.

33. Xunzi makes this requirement explicit in the passage cited above—83/22/16–20.

34. The usual interpretation of the passage is to treat Zhuangzi as asserting the existence of the mystical true-ruler. I rest with the more natural skeptical reading that it *seems* as if there must be one but we can find no evidence. Hence, we cannot know if there is one or not.

35. Graham (1990, 61–63) is concerned to argue against those who, like Yi Wu, regard this as a passage where 情 *qing* means *passion*. Yi Wu says there is another passage where *qing* means *desire*, but the second actually lists 情 *qing* and 欲 *yu*[desires] as two distinct things a sage wants to decrease. This shows that they are theory related, but is not a good argument that they are synonyms. Yi Wu's entry then suggests, quite plausibly in my view, that the main impetus for identifying *qing* with *emotion* in the Indo-European sense comes from Buddhism.

36. Graham's analysis, as we noted above, required that Zhuangzi deliberately contradict himself—some human lacks the defining essence of being human. Hui Shi was supposed to play the role of rationalist and naively object to such a blatant contradiction. Graham's excuse for this puzzling approach was a repeated assertion that Hui Shi somehow "involuntarily demonstrate[s] the futility of all logic" (1990, 62). Graham never explained how Hui Shi's pointing out a contradiction demonstrates the futility of logic.

37. *Xunzi* 83/22/3 (translation from Graham 1990, 65).

38. *Xunzi* 85/22/63.

39. Ibid., 70/18/114.

40. Ibid., 28/9/69–72. This conflicts, notoriously, with the slogan "Human nature is evil." See Hansen 1992 ch. 9, 334–38.

41. This is surely a dodge. If desires are not individuated by their objects, then it is hard to see how there could be many of them. Xunzi offers little more than a verbal shuffling of Laozi's and Zhuangzi's analysis.

42. Graham does not observe that this phrase, by itself, undermines his analysis. It confirms that *qing*[reality input] is still quite general and these are specifically human inputs. So *qing* by itself has not come to mean "what is essential to humanhood."

43. Zhuangzi 4/2/13–14.

Selected Bibliography

Carus, Paul. 1913 *The Canon of Reason and Its Virtue*. Chicago: Open Court.

Chan, Wing-tsit. 1963 *A Source Book in Chinese Philosophy*. Princeton: Princeton University Press.

Graham, Angus. 1978. *Later Mohist Logic, Ethics, and Science*. Hong Kong: Chinese University Press.

——. 1981. *Chuang-tzu: The Inner Chapters*. London: George Allen & Unwin.

——. 1989. *Disputers of the Tao: Philosophical Argument in Ancient China*. LaSalle, IL: Open Court.

——. 1990. *Studies in Chinese Philosophy and Philosophical Literature*. Albany: State University of New York Press.

Hansen, Chad. 1983. *Language and Logic in Ancient China.* Ann Arbor: University of Michigan Press.

——. 1985. "Chinese Language, Chinese Philosophy, and 'Truth.'" *Journal of Asian Studies* 44 (33):491–519.

——. 1991. "Should the Ancient Masters Value Reason?" In *Chinese Texts and Philosophical Contexts: Essays Dedicated to A. C. Graham*, ed. Henry Rosemont Jr. La Sale, IL: Open Court.

——. 1992. *A Daoist Theory of Chinese Thought*. New York: Oxford University Press.

Mathews, R. H. 1960. *A Chinese–English Dictionary*. Taipei: Southeast Asia Book Co.

Mencius. *A Concordance to Meng Tzu*. Harvard-Yenching Institute Sinological Index Series, supplement no. 17. Cambridge: Harvard University Press.

Mozi. *A Concordance to Mo Tzu*. Harvard-Yenching Institute Sinological Index Series, supplement no. 21. Cambridge: Harvard University Press.

Needham, Joseph. 1954. *Science and Civilization in China*, vol. 2. Cambridge: Cambridge University Press.

Nivison, David. 1979. "Mencius and Motivation." *Journal of the American Academy of Religion* 47:417–32.

Stich, Stephen. 1983. *From Folk Psychology to Cognitive Science: The Case against Belief.* Cambridge: MIT Press.

Wu, Yi. 1986. *Chinese Philosophical Terms*. Lanham, MD: University Press of America.

Xunzi. *A Concordance to Hsün Tzu*. Harvard-Yenching Institute Sinological Index Series, supplement no. 22. Cambridge: Harvard University Press.

Zhuangzi. *A Concordance to Chuang Tzu*. Harvard-Yenching Institute Sinological Index Series, supplement no. 20. Cambridge: Harvard University Press.

Nietzsche and Zen Master Hakuin on the Roles of Emotion and Passion

Graham Parkes

> Only fools think that dead sitting and silent illumination suffice and
> that Zen consists in the source of the mind's being in tranquility.

This typically outspoken statement by the Zen Master Hakuin Ekaku, shocking
to his contemporaries in eighteenth-century Japan, would no doubt surprise
many readers in the West today, where the Sōtō school of Zen continues to be
better known than the Rinzai tradition.[1] A distinctive feature of the latter is
the role it accords the emotions in the process of realizing one's "true nature"
and the part they play in subsequent, enlightened human existence. This feature
becomes powerfully salient in the ideas of Hakuin, who may be taken as
emblematic of the mature Rinzai school in this respect. It is generally not
appreciated that strikingly similar views of emotion were entertained in nineteenth-century Europe by Friedrich Nietzsche. A comparison between the two
recommends itself on the grounds that both Rinzai Zen and Nietzsche have
been subject to misunderstanding concerning their stance vis-à-vis the emotions. The stereotypical view—which sees, on the one hand, the Nietzschean
Übermensch overflowing with unbridled Dionysiac passion and, on the other,
the serene Zen master sitting in dispassionate contemplation, unperturbed by a
single affect—stands in need of correction. An examination of the distinctive
ways in which each side is responding to received views of the nature of emotion in its respective tradition will enhance our appreciation of the subtleties of
both.

   The role and function of the emotions and passions in the overall economy
of the psyche have been largely neglected, or else simply denigrated, in the
Western philosophical tradition. The general disparagement of the affective
side of life with which Nietzsche is faced has its roots in the ascetic aspects of
the Platonic tradition, proponents of which are perturbed by the way emotion
tends to work counter to the proper exercise of reason. In his rejection of Pla-

tonic and Christian metaphysics, Nietzsche gives the emotions and passions an unprecedentedly important role, seeing them as providing ways to a more fulfilling existence as well as to various truths concerning the human condition. Instead of pitting the intellect against the emotions, he encourages the cultivation of a passion for knowledge and understanding (*eine Leidenschaft der Erkenntnis*).[2]

While the East Asian philosophical tradition has not been informed by a comparable exaltation of the rational as the paramount principle, it nevertheless displays a strong strain toward detachment from the affective sides of psychical life. And while Zen warns against the distracting power of the emotions, it also distinguishes itself from most Western philosophies in disparaging purely rational or calculative thinking. Much of the revolutionary force of Rinzai Zen comes from its reaction against the quietistic tendencies of some of the schools of Buddhism that preceded it. Thus, in order to appreciate Hakuin's ideas about the emotions, it will help to look at how they were viewed by the Ch'an Buddhist tradition before him, especially as embodied in *The Platform Sutra* attributed to Hui-neng (Jpn., *E'nō*) and in the sayings of Rinzai.[3]

Zen and Nietzsche share the premise that our ordinary way of being in the world is permeated by delusion and that more fulfilling modes are possible. Zen speaks of "seeing into one's true nature" or of realizing oneself as the "true human of no rank," while Nietzsche is concerned with a transformation that issues in the condition, or attitude, of the *Übermensch*. With respect to the emotions, we may distinguish three moments in the process of self-transformation: the way each side views the function of the emotions in everyday, ego-centered awareness, the role of the emotions in attaining liberation, and their place in the constitution of the figures proposed as models by each side, the *Übermensch* and the "true human of no rank" (*mui shinnin*).

I

Nietzsche would concur with many thinkers in the Buddhist tradition concerning the drawbacks of the ego-centered emotions: they tend to blind us by drastically narrowing our perspectives and obscuring our view of things, to carry us away in sometimes dangerous ways, so that we risk inflicting damage on ourselves or others; and, in general, they can move us to inappropriate behavior, making us later regret what we have said or done. One of the Four Great Vows in Buddhism is "to cut off all emotions and passions,"[4] since only by eliminating "grasping," or desire, can the false sense of the self as something substantial be dissolved. But although there is in *The Platform Sutra* a line of verse that reads, "Crush the passions and destroy them" (*PS* 36), and though Rinzai, too, warns against the "binding power" of the emotions,[5] there is more to it than this. And while Hakuin speaks of the hindrances to enlightenment in terms of such traditional classifications as the "five desires," the "five coverings," the "seven misfortunes," the "eight winds" that fan the passions, and the "ten bonds"[6]—with anger, envy, joy, grief, pain, and pleasure figuring repeatedly among them—we shall see that detachment from, or circumvention of, hindrances does not entail the extirpation of emotion.

The affective aspects of human experience are discussed by Nietzsche throughout his works, and with ever greater frequency toward the end of his career. His basic position on the "passions" (*Leidenschaften*) and the more episodic "affects" (*Affekte*—closer to what we refer to as the "emotions") is that it is impossible to fulfill the task of "becoming what one is" if the passive-affective sides of our nature are simply given free rein and allowed to dominate. Nevertheless, Nietzsche is highly critical of the previous prescriptions that have issued from his predecessors on this problem. Whereas the ascetic in Plato condemned any situation in which emotions or passions are allowed to tyrannize the rational part of the soul, the corresponding strain in the Christian tradition concentrated on the proscription of "negative" emotions—and recommended *extirpation* as the way to deal with them. Nietzsche brands both the Platonic and the Christian prescriptions for human well-being as symptoms of *décadence*, as a desperate response on the part of natures too weak to bring their emotions under control.

> There is a stage during which all passions are simply damaging, when they drag their victim down with the sheer weight of their stupidity—while at a later, much later stage they are wedded with the spirit, and are "spiritualized." . . . To *annihilate* the passions and desires simply because of their stupidity and the unpleasant consequences of yielding to their stupidity appears to us now today as itself an acute form of stupidity. . . . The Church combats passion with excision in every sense: its practice, its "cure" is *castration*. They never ask: "how does one spiritualize, beautify, deify a desire?" . . . To attack the passions at their roots means to attack life at its roots: the practice of the Church is *hostile to life*. (*TI* 5:1)

This may appear to set Nietzsche against the Buddhist as well as the Christian position on this issue—especially since, in another work from the same year, he claims that Buddhism and Christianity "belong together as nihilistic religions, as *décadence* religions" (*AC* 20). But he goes on to distinguish Buddhism from Christianity as having "[put] the self-deception of moral concepts behind it" and as thereby standing "*beyond* good and evil"—which suggests that there may be some important common ground between Nietzsche and Buddhism.

There is, at any rate, agreement between the two sides concerning the deleterious effects of the emotions in ordinary, everyday existence: If simply given free rein, they give rise to delusion and stupidity. For our present purposes, the pertinent question concerns the extent to which the Buddhist prescriptions concerning emotion entail a hostility toward life.

II

While some forms of Buddhism may be life denying in their stance toward the emotions, this is by no means true of Zen, thanks (at least in part) to the Sinicization undergone by Buddhism in its transplantation to China in the early centuries of the Common Era. There the soil was already rich in Daoist ideas, and thinkers like Zhuang Zi (*Chuang-tzu*) would later exert a particular fascination on Hui-neng and Rinzai. Of the texts of classical Daoism, the *Zhuang Zi* is richest in emotion—and the emotions celebrated there are perceptive ways of being open to the world rather than coarsely instinctual reactions to it. In the well-known story of Zhuang Zi's being discovered after the death of his wife drumming on a pot and singing (ch. 18), his explanation is not that he was so detached as to be unaffected by the bereavement. Rather, he prefaces the account of his realization that his wife had "gone over to be companion with spring and autumn, summer and winter, in the procession of the four seasons" by asking: "When she first died, do you really suppose that I was not able to feel the loss?" The implication is that he was—so deeply, indeed, that it was now issuing from him in song and rhythms of the body.

An explicit formulation of the Daoist attitude toward the emotions is to be found in a passage by the famous commentator Wang Bi:

> That in which the sage is superior to ordinary people is the spirit. But what the sage has in common with ordinary people is the emotions. The sage has a superior spirit, and is therefore able to be in harmony with the universe . . . but he has ordinary emotions, and therefore cannot respond to things without joy or sorrow. He responds to things, yet is not ensnared by them.[7]

For the Daoists, to be ruled or ensnared by the emotions is to fail to realize one's true humanity—and yet to become devoid of emotion altogether is not to be fully human either. The idea of a responsiveness to the world that is free of attachment is one that runs through the entire Rinzai Zen tradition, although a development in the attitude toward emotion is discernible as one moves from Hui-neng to Rinzai and then to Hakuin.

The name of Hui-neng is associated with the establishment of the Southern school of Ch'an Buddhism which advocates "sudden enlightenment" as opposed to the "gradual enlightenment" favored by the Northern school.[8] Both schools share the premise that, at bottom, human beings are essentially enlightened—that the "original self-nature" of sentient beings is fundamentally identical with "Buddha-nature"—and that the task of Zen practice is to *realize* (in the double sense of "making real" and "becoming aware of") this original nature. The difference between the schools lies in the methods they prescribe, and is well expressed by two contrasting images from *The Platform Sutra*. The Northern school is said there to liken the heart-mind[9] to a clear mirror and the deluded state of ignorance to a condition where the mirror is encrusted with dust and dirt. In order to realize one's true nature, one must polish the mirror assiduously (practice meditation) to let it reflect clearly, and keep polishing it so that no more dirt or dust may accumulate (*PS* 6).

Two images used by Nietzsche come to mind here that would seem to correspond to this idea. In *Thus Spoke Zarathustra* the protagonist speaks of the image that "sleeps in the stone" of every human being, and that can be awakened or brought to life if one hammers away the surrounding stone so as to reveal "the beauty of the *Übermensch*" that is potentially in everyone (Z II.2). And in *Beyond Good and Evil*, Nietzsche writes of the "strange and wonderful task" of "translating the human being back into nature," which would involve working on "the eternal basic text of *homo natura*" that, like a palimpsest, has been "scrawled on and painted over" with numerous "vain and enthusiastic interpretations and connotations" in the course of history (*BGE* 230). Both images signify a working to remove what surrounds or covers up some kind of original human nature, though the first also carries the implication—contrasting with the Zen image of constant polishing of the mirror—that once the accretions are removed, the original form would stand forth revealed and in need of no further work. The idea of *homo natura* as text, however, implies that further misinterpretations of it would continually be forthcoming and would have to be removed.[10]

In contrast to the Northern school's exhortation to polish the mirror, Hui-neng proposes a number of more natural images. Whereas the figure of constant polishing implies a causal relation between meditation practice and enlightenment, the Southern school denies this causality—while still asserting the necessity of practice as an expression of our original nature. One does not practice *in order to* attain enlightenment, nor does enlightenment occur as a consequence of practice: One simply practices, and, when the time is right, enlightenment will come. The spontaneous nature of the process is expressed in meteorological images, with deluded ideas or delusive emotions being represented as clouds and mists.

> The sun and moon are always bright, yet if they are covered by clouds, although above they are bright, below they are darkened, and the sun, moon, stars, and planets cannot be seen clearly. But if suddenly the wind of wisdom should blow and roll away the clouds and mists, all forms in the universe appear at once. The purity of the nature of man in this world is like the blue sky; wisdom is like the sun, knowledge like the moon. Although knowledge and wisdom are always clear, if you cling to external environments, the floating clouds of false thoughts will create a cover, and your own natures cannot become clear. (*PS* 20)

There are remarkable parallels between this passage and meteorological images used by Zarathustra in a similar context. As a lover of wisdom, Zarathustra's kinship with the sun is established from the very beginning of the prologue to that work (§ 1) and is reaffirmed throughout the text.[11] The precursor of the image of the clear sky in Zen is the Daoist notion of *tian* (heaven), which figures in the exhortation to full awareness in terms of "seeing things in the light of *tian*."[12] Comparable is the open sky to which Zarathustra offers praise in the chapter entitled "Before Sunrise," which begins: "O heaven above me, you pure one! you deep one! you abyss of light!" (*Z* III.4). Zarathustra goes on to inveigh against the clouds (which he later associates with ideas of good and evil—sources of emotional reactions) that soil the purity of the open sky:

> "And whom should I hate more than drifting clouds and all else that stains you? And I even hated my own hatred since it itself stained you!
>
> . . . [t]he drifting clouds . . . steal from you and me what is common to us—the vast and unbounded Yes- and Amen-saying." (ibid.)

Zarathustra's Yes-saying would correspond to the Zen affirmation of all things in their "suchness." Less patient than the Zen master, however, Zarathustra is not content with waiting for the wind of wisdom to blow away the clouds of delusion—though he does urge his disciples to emulate the storm-wind that clears the air of gloom (IV.13, § 20). He imagines getting rid of the clouds by pinning them together with jagged wires of golden lightning so that he can, like thunder, play the drums on their kettle-bellies. The Zen master would surely appreciate this wonderfully strange image, with its implications for a symphony of karmic accretions.

A commonality between sky and soul is intimated in *The Platform Sutra*, in the context of a discussion of the original vastness of the heart-mind, whose capacity is said to be "broad and huge, like the vast sky" (*PS* 24).

> The ten thousand things are all in self-nature. Although you see all men and non-men, evil and good, evil things and good things, you must not throw them aside, nor must you cling to them, but you must regard them as being just like the empty sky. . . . The wise man practices with his mind. There are deluded men who make their minds empty and do not think . . . [t]his, too, is wrong. The capacity of the mind is vast and wide, but when there is no practice it is small. (*PS* 25)

What is recommended here is an acknowledgement of evil and good things (again as potential stimulators of emotional responses): not a rejection of them, but an acknowledgement without attachment. The attitude of openness without attachment allows one to see things "in the full light of heaven" and to realize that the openness of the heavens is coextensive with the vastness of the heart-mind itself.

The realization of the vastness of the soul is a major theme in *Zarathustra*. In the prologue, Zarathustra confesses his love for "him whose soul is overfull, so that he forgets himself, and all things are in him: thus all things become his going under" (§ 4). He speaks later of the highest soul as "the most comprehensive soul, that can run and wander and roam farthest within itself . . . the one that loves itself most, in which all things have their flow and counterflow, their ebb and flood" (III.12, § 18). Insofar as raw emotion is generally a response to something attractive or repulsive "out there," the realization that everything is also "in here" conduces to detachment from such emotional responses.

The Dionysian overflowing that pervades *Zarathustra* ends up dissolving the bounds of the soul in such a way that "all things" may be in it. This overflowing is imagined as an outpouring of love in the form of rivers flowing to the ocean:

> "My impatient love overflows in rivers, downward, toward rising and setting. . . .
>
> And may my river of love plunge into pathless places! How should a river not finally find its way to the sea!
>
> Indeed, a lake is in me, solitary and self-sufficient; but my river of love tears it away, downward—to the sea!" (II.1)

In line with a tradition of imagery in Western thought that has its source in Plato's likening *erōs* to a stream or river, Nietzsche often imagines the passions and emotions as flows of water.[13] Fully aware of their potential for damage if they are allowed to run out of control, Nietzsche emphasizes repeatedly that an indispensable first step on the way to "becoming who one is" is mastery over the passions and emotions. But such control is a means rather than an end in itself, and must be clearly distinguished from suppressing emotion and passion altogether. A note from 1888, in which he criticizes "the insanity of religious moralists" in wanting to extirpate the passions, sums up Nietzsche's attitude well:

> This most shortsighted and pernicious way of thinking wants to make the great sources of energy, those wild torrents of the soul that often stream forth so dangerously and overwhelmingly, *dry up* altogether, instead of taking their power into service and *economizing* it. (*WP* 383)

The verb *ökonomisieren* not only suggests that the energy of the passions needs to be retained and channeled within the "grand economy of the soul," but, with its roots in the word *oikos* (household), it also connotes the domesticating of their wildness. But ultimately the economy of the soul will merge with that of the universe as a whole—as expressed in the image of the lake flowing through rivers into the ocean. The task would then be to channel the currents of passion and emotion in such a way that they become one with the larger currents of the energies that comprise the cosmos.

We find imagery corresponding to this idea in *The Platform Sutra*, in another passage containing the image of clouds obscuring the sun. It is claimed that even "people of shallow capacity" may attain enlightenment on hearing the Sudden Doctrine if they attend to their own original natures rather than to externals:

> Even these sentient beings, filled with passions and troubles, will at once gain awakening. It is like the great sea which gathers all the flowing streams and merges together the large waters and the small waters into one. (*PS* 29)

The flow of the passions may therefore carry one to "the great sea . . . of the original natures of sentient beings" (*PS* 28)—or, in Nietzsche's terms, to the vast ocean of will to power.[14]

Again, in Zen, the crux is detachment, planting a foot on "the other shore" so that one may negotiate the sea of life without being overwhelmed by it.

> When you are attached to environment, birth and destruction arise. Take waves arising on the water—they are something that occurs on "this" shore. Being apart from environment and putting an end to birth and destruction is like going along with the flow of the water. . . . If you practice [this wisdom] for one instant of thought, your own body will be the same as the Buddha's. Good friends, the very passions themselves are enlightenment [*bodhi*]. (*PS* 26)

The idea of "going along with the flow" echoes the Daoist ideal of *wu wei* (nonobstructive action), which—far from implying quietism—might better be thought of as *flowing* with rather than simply "going" with the flow. There is a parallel here with Nietzsche's praise of *Strömen* (streaming), which suggests a powerful flowing. In contrast to the real philosopher, the passionate thinker, the mere scholar is, for Nietzsche, a pathetic creature: He is

> like one who lets himself simply go along rather than *flow*; and precisely before the person of great streaming he stands with all the more cool reserve— his eye is like a smooth and reluctant lake in which there is no ripple of sympathy or delight. (*BGE* 206)

Such a person, afraid to let emotion move him into the stream of life, unaware that the passions may themselves enlighten, will not be party to any great revelation from existence—and would correspond to what *The Platform Sutra* calls "the deluded person" or the "person of shallow capacity."

III

The major figure in Chinese Zen between Hui-neng and the founding of the Rinzai School by Linji was Ma-zu Dao-i (709-788), who developed the idea of "straightforward mind" in *The Platform Sutra* (secs. 14 and 34) into an explicit equation between Buddha-nature and "ordinary mind." Ma-zu is renowned for having injected a considerable physical dynamism into the Zen of the Patriarchs, and this emphasis on the somatic aspects of practice brought with it a greater concern for the emotions, which move between the spheres of the psychical and the physical. In opposition to the quietistic tendencies of the Northern school, Ma-zu introduced shouting (Jpn., *katsu*) and physical violence (tweaking of noses, hitting with fists, blows from the master's staff) into Zen practice. Just as we talk of being "struck" by a feeling or a bright idea, so for the Zen practitioner to be struck by the master's staff could shock him into the realization of his "true nature." A century later, Rinzai would assign such physical activity—and the thundering shout especially—an important role in the practice on which his school was founded.

Rinzai's way of presenting the central idea of Mahāyāna Buddhism was shocking in its directness: The "true human" is not to be sought in the Buddhas and Patriarchs of the tradition, nor in some ideal to be attained in the future, but rather in the very persons of the individuals listening to his speeches. "Do you want to know the Patriarch-Buddha?" he asks; "He is none other than you who stand before me listening to my discourse" (*RL* 10). When Rinzai says of the "true human of the Way" that "merely according with circumstances as they are, he makes use of his past karma," one can assume that such a person has "seen through" the delusive emotions in a way that allows things to present themselves as they are, while at the same time his "according" is informed by appropriate affect. He responds to things (to paraphrase Wang Bi) with joy and sorrow, but without ensnarement.

Rinzai was an admirer of Zhuang Zi, and many of his discourses contain strong Daoist elements. (He often addresses his students as "learners of the *dao*.") Two complementary mentions of the ocean—the emulation of water is a prime virtue for the Daoists—convey a good sense of the way the Zen path employs emotion after undoing its binding power. Rinzai quotes a verse from a fifth-century source:

> If you love the sacred and hate the secular
> You'll float and sink in the birth-and-death sea.
> The passions exist dependent on mind:
> Have no-mind, and how can they bind you? (*RL* 18)

Elsewhere he says: "Even though you bear the remaining influences of past delusions or the karma from [having committed] the five heinous crimes, these of themselves become the ocean of emancipation" (*RL* 12). In the context of the traditional Mahāyāna idea that nirvana is not different from samsara, Rinzai employs the image of the ocean to emphasize that the obstructions and ensnarements of the samsaric world can conduce to the process of liberation.

Rinzai's tactic of constantly focusing his listeners' attention on their own immediate experience implies that the goal of Zen practice is not a condition of *apatheia* but rather one as vibrant with affective force as our liveliest everyday awareness.

> The human being who is right now listening to my discourse . . . is without
> form, without characteristics, without root, without source, and without any
> dwelling place, yet is brisk and lively [*kappatsu patsuji*]. As for all his mani-
> fold responsive activities, the place where they are carried on is, in fact, no-
> place. (*RL* 14)

The term "brisk and lively" (used again in *RL* 18) comes from Chinese Buddhism and connotes the spontaneity of a leaping fish as well as a sense of
being sharply focused. The "manifold responsive activities" of the true human
will not exclude the appropriate emotional reactions. That they take place in
"no-place," however, means that the emotional responses have ceased—to
speak in Nietzschean terms—to restrict or tie us down to any particular perspective. Being carried on nowhere, they free us to move anywhere.

A striking feature of Rinzai Zen is the vehemence with which its founder
inveighs against what he regards as the stultifying dogmatism and rigidity of the
conventional Buddhists of his time. His language is often reminiscent—in tone
as well as content—of Nietzsche's Zarathustra's diatribes against advocates of
"the world beyond":

> There are a bunch of blind shave-pates who, having stuffed themselves with
> food, sit down to meditate and practice contemplation: arresting the flow of
> thought they don't let it rise; they hate noise and seek stillness. This is the
> method of the heretics. (*RL* 17)

Hakuin was faced with a corresponding degeneration of the Rinzai teachings,
and his critique of the "Hinayanists of old" is similarly trenchant—though
leavened with a little irony:

> It was only because the direction of their practice was bad, because they liked
> only places of solitude and quiet, knew nothing of the dignity of the bod-
> hisattva . . . that the Tathāgata compared them to pus-oozing wild foxes and
> that Vimilakirti heaped scorn on them as men who would scorch buds and
> cause seeds to rot. (*ZMH* 35)

It will be clear by now that the practice advocated by the Rinzai school, far
from suppressing the emotional life, is concerned to transform and enhance
it.

IV

Like Rinzai, Hakuin emphasizes that practice undertaken in peaceful seclu-
sion, which he refers to contemptuously as "dead sitting," is useless in comparison with what he calls "practice in the midst of activity" (*ZMH* 30-34).
Followers of the latter way are contrasted with "those fools who starve to death
on mountains, thinking that dead sitting and silent illumination suffice and
that Zen consists in the source of the mind being in tranquility." Such people, he

says, "fail to see into their own natures" (*ZMH* 57). They fail to understand that life is itself a manifestation of Buddha-nature, and that this can be realized through an appropriate transformation of perspective. Just as *The Platform Sutra* maintains that "the very passions themselves are enlightenment," so Hakuin writes that "the five desires themselves will be the One Vehicle [that leads to a realization of one's self-nature]" (*ZMH* 36). But whereas the earlier Zen writings have little to say about the nature of the transformation that is required, the later ones provide a few pointers.

Hakuin makes it perfectly clear that quietism is not the way: "A person who fanatically avoids the objects of the senses and dreads the eight winds that stimulate the passions unconsciously falls into the pit of the Hinayana and never will be able to achieve the Buddha Way." But before delusions and karma can be realized as "the ocean of emancipation," the barriers of the ego-centered self have to be broken down; and one reason "the eight winds" are not to be shunned or stilled is that the energy from the emotions, as the most powerful motive forces in the psyche, may help to effect the breakthrough—and this in two rather different ways.

The student of Nietzsche who contemplates what has been aptly called the "psychodynamics" of Zen practice according to Hakuin[15] will find strikingly familiar two contrasting yet complementary features there, both of which have significant emotional correlates. One concerns the importance of *sickness*—suffering, incapacitation, lack of power—as a facilitating factor in the process;[16] the other concerns the necessity of cultivating what Nietzsche calls "the *warrior spirit*," which infuses one with a feeling of power, with the courage to see things through.

Of the forces that move our souls, the emotions are among the somatically most significant, with the closest ties to the body.[17] They also have a special connection with pathology, being capable themselves of engendering illness as well as participating in its cure. The comparable estimations of the importance of sickness on the part of Hakuin and Nietzsche may derive from a similarity of physical and psychical constitution: Like Nietzsche, Hakuin placed such intense demands on his body and mind in the relentless pursuit of his task that he suffered a series of breakdowns which brought him to the verge of complete despair and physical collapse. What is important is not the similarity of the psychosomatic disturbances but the fact that both sufferers came to regard their incapacitations as instructive and beneficial for their respective tasks. Just as Nietzsche frequently expressed his profound gratitude to the illnesses that plagued him for the insights they afforded into life, so Hakuin in his "Letter to a Sick Monk" quotes the words of another sick monk: "This severe illness of mine has been an honored good teacher.'"[18] Here is an excerpt from one of Hakuin's firsthand accounts of the sufferings that supervened upon his resolve to "stake his life" on assiduous practice.

My heart began to make me dizzy, my legs felt as cold as if they were immersed in ice and snow. . . . My liver felt weak and in my behavior I experienced many fears. My spirit was distressed and weary. . . . My armpits were perpetually bathed in sweat and my eyes were constantly filled with tears.[19]

This account could easily pass for one of the numerous passages in Nietzsche's letters to his friends concerning the physiological tribulations occasioned by his resolve to keep on writing books. For Nietzsche, such afflictions correspond in part to the psychological effects of abandoning the security of traditional ways of thinking and embarking upon the "vast ocean of becoming." In Zarathustra's words: "Now finally there comes the great terror, the great sickness, the great nausea, the great sea-sickness" (Z III.12, § 28).

Indeed, what Hakuin calls "Zen sickness" may be seen as a physiological correlate to the "Great Doubt" (*daigi*) and the "Great Death" (*daishi*), stages that he insists must be passed through on the way to enlightenment. In another letter, he offers the following, nicely understated remarks on the process:

When you call forth this great doubt before you in its pure and uninvolved form you may undergo an unpleasant and strange reaction. However, you must accept the fact that the realization of so felicitous a thing as the Great Matter . . . must involve a certain amount of suffering. (*ZMH* 145)

In order to drive through the Great Doubt to the Great Death and beyond, it is necessary to "cut off the root of life." If this sounds like a case of what Nietzsche denigrates as "attacking life at its roots," we must remember that such cutting off is merely a means and not an end. Hakuin explains his exhortation as follows:

Sometimes it is called illusory thoughts, sometimes the root of birth and death, sometimes the passions, sometimes a demon. It is one thing with many names, but if you examine it closely you will find that what it comes down to is one concept: that the self is real. (*ZMH* 134)

With the idea that the self is unreal, we come upon another crucial point of similarity between Zen and Nietzsche, who emphasizes throughout his works that the "I," or ego, is a mere fiction. Hakuin stresses the difficulty of attaining this realization of the illusory nature of the ego-self:

If you are not a hero who has truly seen into his own nature, don't think that [non-ego] is something that can be known so easily. . . . [y]ou must be prepared to let go your hold when hanging from a sheer precipice, to die and return again to life. (*ZMH* 135)

Nietzsche's *Zarathustra* is—at least on one level—an account of the process in which one dies to the ego-self, or "goes under" into the abyss, in order to cross over to the condition of the *Übermensch* (Prologue, § 4). Hakuin continues, using some remarkably Zarathustrian imagery:

> Supposing a man should find himself in some desolate area where no one
> has ever walked before. Below him are the perpendicular walls of a bottom-
> less chasm. His feet rest precariously on a patch of slippery moss, and there is
> no spot of earth on which he can steady himself. He can neither advance nor
> retreat; he faces only death. . . . His life hangs as if from a dangling thread. . . .
> Then when suddenly you return to life, there is the great joy of one who
> drinks the water and knows for himself whether it is hot or cold. . . . This is
> known as seeing into one's own nature. (*ZMH* 135)

One is reminded here of the crucial role that *courage* (*Mut*)—as well as the
concomitant affects of melancholic depression (*Schwermut*) and exuberance
(*Übermut*)—plays in *Thus Spoke Zarathustra*, in the protagonist's final engagement with the thought of eternal recurrence.[20] It is only through courage that
Zarathustra is able to overcome his archenemy, the "spirit of gravity," whose
weight would drag him down into the depths of the abyss:

> There is something in me I call courage . . . Courage that attacks: for in every
> attack there is ringing play. . . . Courage even slays dizziness at the edge of
> abysses: and where would human beings not be standing at the edge of
> abysses! Is seeing not itself—seeing abysses? (Z III.2)

The mood of the warrior (albeit complemented by certain "feminine" traits[21])
was initially encouraged by Zarathustra's realization that "[his] enemies too are
part of [his] bliss":

> And when I want to mount my wildest steed, it is always my spear that helps
> me up the best . . . My spear, which I hurl against my enemies! How grateful
> I am to my enemies that I may finally hurl it! (Z II.1)

There is a suggestion that Zarathustra's "enemies" refers not only to those of his
listeners who have distorted his teachings, but also to the general human lean-
ings toward self-deception and the comforts of illusion. The range of Hakuin's
attack is perhaps even greater, and he mounts it in imagery that is, again, reso-
nant with Zarathustra's and serves to banish any misconceptions of the mood of
Zen practice as apathetic.

> How does one obtain true enlightenment? In the busy round of mundane
> affairs, in the confusion of worldly problems . . . behave as a valiant man
> would when surrounded by a host of enemies. Mount your steed, raise your
> lance, and, with a good showing of your courageous spirit, make up your
> mind to attack, destroy and annihilate the enemy. . . . At all times in your
> study of Zen, fight against delusions and worldly thoughts, battle the black
> demon of sleep, attack concepts of the active and the passive, order and dis-
> order, right and wrong, hate and love, and join battle with the things of the
> mundane world. (*ZMH* 65)

These passages from Hakuin's writings make clear that enlightenment
comes about in the medium of the energies associated with the affective pas-

sivity of sickness and impotence as well as of those that drive the martial activities of the Zen warrior. For a detailed understanding of how these energies are channeled and configured, one would have to consider Hakuin's understanding of *kōan* practice, which is central to the Rinzai tradition; but that is a topic too complex to go into here.[22]

v

When Hakuin advocates detachment from the passions in terms of "cutting off the root of life," he is employing a horticultural metaphor that echoes images found in *The Platform Sutra*. Since Nietzsche also uses vegetal imagery to convey what he sees as the most fruitful way to deal with the forces of emotion and passion, it will be best to remain in this field in order to round out our comparison.

A section near the end of *The Platform Sutra* relates how, just before his death, Hui-neng recited to his disciples a series of four-line verses composed by the Six Patriarchs of Zen (*PS* 49). Referring to the transmission of Buddhism to China, and predicting the advent of five more patriarchs, Bodhidharma wrote: "One flower opens five petals, / And the fruit ripens of itself." The remaining five verses all center on imagery of seeds in the ground of the mind which eventually grow and blossom into flowers. Hui-neng's own verse ends, "The fruit of enlightenment matures of itself"—echoing the spontaneity with which the wind of wisdom blows away the clouds of delusion.

A similar image appears in one of Nietzsche's earliest writings, at the end of a fragment entitled "New Year's Eve Dream" from 1864, where a disembodied voice says to the narrator: "When you are ripe, the fruit will fall, and not before!" The motif of ripening fruit runs throughout Nietzsche's works, and is especially prominent in *Zarathustra*; but it is overshadowed by a more active strain of horticultural imagery. The art and science of horticulture depends on the maintenance of a dynamic balance between work and observation, doing and not-doing, between intervening and letting be. In spite of Zen's emphasis on the spontaneity of enlightenment, there is a counterpart to horticultural work in the emphasis on practice itself.

Corresponding to the Buddhist idea of "cutting off the emotions" is what Nietzsche calls "overcoming the passions," which is the title of an aphorism from 1880.

> The human being who has overcome the passions has come into possession of the most fruitful soil. . . . *To sow* the seed of good spiritual works on the ground of the subdued passions is then the urgent next task. The overcoming is itself only a *means* and not an end; if it is not so viewed, all kinds of weeds and devilish stuff will quickly grow in this cleared, rich soil, and soon there will be more rank confusion there than ever before. (*HA* II.2, 53)

Just as Hakuin's "cutting off the root of life" is a preliminary to "returning to life," so overcoming the passions is, for Nietzsche, a preparatory stage to planting and then cultivating the same forces of life in a different way. The possibility of such transformation is developed in an aphorism from *Dawn of Morning* (1881), in which Nietzsche speaks of the various ways of practicing a horticulture of the drives: "One can deal with one's drives as a gardener and . . . cultivate the seeds of anger, pity, curiosity, vanity as fruitfully and productively as a beautiful fruit-tree on a trellis" (aph. 560).

An unpublished note from 1886 is a good statement of Nietzsche's later stance vis-à-vis the emotions (*die Affekte*)—and prompts an important question from the Zen perspective:

> *Overcoming the affects?*—No, not if that means their weakening and annihilation. *But to take them into service*: which involves tyrannizing them for a long time. . . . Eventually one gives them back their freedom with confidence: they love us like good servants and ultimately go where our best interest inclines. (*WP* 384)

The important question, put in a Zen-like form that Nietzsche is himself fond of employing, is this: "*Who* is it that overcomes the passions and does the new planting?" or "*Who* is to tyrannize the affects and then take them into service?"[23] Nietzsche's answer, as expressed in another note from the same year, would be "the will": "The greater the will's power of mastery, the more freedom may be given to the passions" (*WP* 933). However, this would be the will not in the sense of the willing ego but, rather, in the sense of will to power—the matrix of forces that animate all sentient beings.

The most succinct presentation of Nietzsche's attitude toward the emotions is to be found in one of the last works he prepared for publication, *Twilight of the Idols* (1888). The theme is not prominently presented, and, indeed, one of the advantages of pursuing the parallel with Zen is that it draws our attention to Nietzsche's final position on this issue. It is a matter of a quasi dialectical progression, the initial state of which is "the inability to resist a stimulus—one *must* react, one follows every impulse" (*TI* 8, 6). The next phase is characterized by "*not* reacting immediately to a stimulus, but taking control of the inhibiting instincts that are able to cut off [reactions]." This corresponds to "overcoming" the passions or "cutting off" the emotions. By the end of this stage one will have attained the "Dionysian state" in which "the entire affect-system is energized and enhanced"—a state that is characterized, interestingly, by "the inability *not* to react" (*TI* 9, 10). But after the protracted tyranny of the second stage, these reactions will be spontaneously appropriate to the situation, rather than the immediate, uninformed reactions of the initial state. One will have effected the "return to life" that Hakuin talks about, and one's actions will be (in Rinzai's phrase) "brisk and lively."

Nietzsche offers a paradigm of the Dionysian human being, a man of the most powerful drives who has "disciplined himself into a totality, [and] *created* himself," in the person of Goethe (*TI* 9, 49). Goethe's greatness lies in his ability to "dare to grant himself the full range and richness of naturalness." He can dare to do this because he has practiced sufficient self-discipline to be confident that, on being "granted their freedom," his emotions will go "where his best interest inclines."[24]

What the perspectives of Hakuin and Nietzsche have in common, then, is an appreciation of the vital power of the emotions and a refusal to let that power be lost through the reduction or extirpation of affect. There is a shared sense that the emotions are dynamic forces that can be channeled to effect a breakthrough in our normal ways of being in the world. It is difficult to find a precise counterpart in Zen to the many descriptions of tyrannizing the emotions one finds in Nietzsche, and it could be argued that Zen is more relaxed in this area, inclining toward Daoist spontaneity rather than Teutonic discipline. The appropriate place to look would be in the area of *kōan* practice, a major component of which is the dissolution of barriers between the various psychical functions and the opening up of a dynamic continuum ranging from conceptual reflection to emotional response.

The similarities between Hakuin and Nietzsche that have been outlined above are all the more remarkable in view of the striking difference in their *modi operandi*. While the practice of Zen involves close interaction between master and student or master and master, Nietzsche was, for most of his productive life, more solitary and divorced from human intercourse than any Zen master of the order of Rinzai or Hakuin. Indeed, the Rinzai tradition was born out of an intensification of the relationship between two practitioners, and it was from the physical vitality of the engagements between master and pupil that the school's "warrior spirit" emerged. The major episodes surrounding Rinzai's enlightenment, for example, are characterized by frequent and sudden loud shouts, as well as by violent exchanges between Rinzai and his teacher Ōbaku and another master, Daigu, involving violent striking and jabbing with heavy sticks (*RL* 50-56). In Nietzsche's case—and this was surely a factor behind his eventual collapse—the enormous affective energies stemming from his work had to be confined within the circuits of his own psyche.

In any case, the point of this comparison has been not to show that Hakuin and Nietzsche are "saying the same thing" about the emotions but to show that each is saying something different from what he has usually been taken to be saying. To the extent that their respective positions on the roles of emotion and passion are now somewhat clearer, the comparison will have served its purpose.

Notes

An earlier version of this essay, shorter and with a different emphasis, appeared under the title "The Transmutation of Emotion in Rinzai Zen and Nietzsche" (*Eastern Buddhist* 23[1]), and thanks are due to the editors for their permission to reproduce some of that material here. I am grateful also to Peter Hershok for helpful comments on the earlier version.

1. "Rinzai Gigen" (approx. 810-866) is the Japanese name of Linji I-xuan, the Chinese founder of a school of Ch'an (Zen) Buddhism that arose in the late T'ang dynasty. Many of his sayings are recorded in the *Lin ji lu* (Jpn., *Rinzai-roku*), which has been translated into English by Ruth F. Sasaki under the title *The Record of Lin-chi* (Kyoto, 1975) and by Irmgard Schloegl, *The Zen Teaching of Rinzai* (Berkeley, 1976). Hakuin Ekaku (1685-1768) is the leading figure of the later Rinzai School and is responsible for its revitalization in the eighteenth century.

2. Friedrich Nietzsche, *The Gay Science*, aph. 374; see also *Beyond Good and Evil*, aph. 210. Nietzsche's works will be referred to by abbreviations of their titles and the number of the aphorism (preceded, where applicable, by the chapter or section number).

3. The ideas of Hui-neng (638-713), who is believed to have been illiterate (a rare distinction among Zen masters), are set down in *The Platform Sutra of the Sixth Patriarch* (hereafter abbreviated "*PS*," followed by the section number).

4. The term corresponding to "emotions and passions" in the Chinese formulations of this Vow is *fan nao*, which connotes the vexations and distress that the emotions—whether positive or negative—inflict upon one's being.

5. *The Record of Lin-chi* (hereafter abbreviated "*RL*," followed by the number of the discourse), 18.

6. *The Zen Master Hakuin* (hereafter "*ZMH*"), 34, 35, 44.

7. *Sanguozhi*, ch. 28, Commentary; cited in Fung Yu-lan 1948, 238.

8. The best history of Zen in English is the two-volume work by Heinrich Dumoulin (1988-1990).

9. Inelegant though this compound may be, it is hard to find a better translation for the Chinese *xin*, which connotes the affective-emotional as much as the mental-intellectual aspects of psychical life. As used in Zen texts, the term might well correspond to "soul" (*Seele*) in Nietzsche's *Thus Spoke Zarathustra*.

10. Both *Zarathustra* and *Beyond Good and Evil* contain passages that enhance or develop these images. In a psychological-alchemical mode, Zarathustra advocates the use of fire to rid the self of detrimental accretions: "You must want to burn yourself up in your own flame: how could you wish to become new unless you had first become ashes!" (Z I.17). Nietzsche also writes of the way the "material, fragments, superfluousness, clay, dirt, nonsense, and chaos" within the human being have to be "formed, broken, forged, torn, burned, made red-hot, and purified" (*BGE* 225).

11. See, especially, *Zarathustra* I.22. For a detailed treatment of the force of the solar (and other meteorological) imagery in *Zarathustra*, see Parkes 1994, ch. 4. Zarathustra's wisdom is also frequently imagined as lightning—a fine image for "sudden illumination" (IV.13, § 7; II.1; III.12, § 30; III.16, § 1). Two more lines from *The Platform Sutra* with a strikingly Nietzschean tone— "Within the dark home of the passions, / The sun of wisdom must at all times shine" (*PS* 36)—remind one of Nietzsche's claim that in every passion is a "quantum of reason" (*WP* 387).

12. *Zhuang Zi*, chapter 2; also ch. 17.

13. There is a significant correspondence between Nietzsche's idea of will to power and Platonic *erōs*: see Parkes 1994, ch. 6.

14. The ocean is used as an image of the totality of will to power in a number of Nietzsche's works, and especially in *Zarathustra*; see Parkes 1994, ch. 4.

15. See Kasulis 1981, ch. 8. This offers an excellent account of Hakuin's aims and methods.

16. In the third of his *Untimely Meditations*, Nietzsche quotes a pertinent line from Meister Eckhart, who is regarded by many Japanese scholars as the Western thinker who comes closest to Zen: "The beast that bears you fastest to perfection is suffering."

17. One might compare Hakuin's emphasis on "nourishing the body" and "the art of nurturing life" (*ZMH* 42-44) with Nietzsche's emphasis on the body,

and especially with his idea that the true Self behind the ego is precisely the *Leib*, the lived body (Z I.4).

18. *ZMH* 77. See also the section entitled "Zen Sickness" in Dumoulin (1988-1990, 2:376-79). The *locus classicus* for the expression of Nietzsche's philosophical debt to his illnesses is the Preface to *The Gay Science*.

19. Hakuin, *Yasen kanna jōkan*; cited in Dumoulin (1988-1990, 2:376).

20. There is something corresponding to this triad of courage, depression, and exuberance in the emotional swings undergone by Hakuin in the progress of his practice. At one point he reports on a breakthrough as follows: "I felt that I had achieved the status [of the former Masters]. . . . My pride soared up like a majestic mountain, my arrogance surged forward like the tide" (*ZMH* 118). He then presents himself to his Master to have his "enlightenment" authenticated—upon which the Master laughs, tweaks his nose, and dismisses him with the exhortation to keep practicing. His subsequent practice involves a succession of further breakthroughs, each flanked by experiences of total despair and boundless joy.

21. Zarathustra's quasi-heroic characteristics are complemented throughout by some less conventionally heroic traits, including a matrix of feminine images having especially to do with pregnancy and labor—which are again related to sickness and suffering.

22. See the numerous discussions of *kōan* in *The Zen Master Hakuin*; see also Miura and Sasaki 1966.

23. This is a crucial question to keep asking in the context of Zen practice, in view of the Protean tenaciousness of the ego, which persists in re-presenting itself in various guises and disguises. The Rinzai Zen answer to the "who" question would be "the true human without rank" who depends on nothing (*mu*).

24. For an extended treatment of the dialectic between self-discipline and spontaneous freedom in Nietzsche, see Parkes 1994, ch. 8.

Bibliography

Dumoulin, Heinrich. 1988-1990. *Zen Buddhism: A History*. 2 vols. Trans. James W. Heisig and Paul Knitter. New York: Macmillan.

Fung Yu-lan. 1948. *A Short History of Chinese Philosophy*. New York: Macmillan.

Kasulis, T. P. 1981. *Zen Action/Zen Person*. Honolulu: University of Hawaii Press.

Miura Isshū and Ruth Fuller Sasaki. 1966. *Zen Dust: The History of the Kōan and Kōan Study in Rinzai Zen*. New York: Harcourt Brace and World.

Nietzsche, Friedrich. 1980. *Sämtliche Werke: Kritische Studienausgabe*. Munich: de Gruyter.

Parkes, Graham. 1994. *Composing the Soul: Reaches of Nietzsche's Psychology*. Chicago: University of Chicago Press.

The Platform Sutra of the Sixth Patriarch. 1967. Trans. Philip B. Yampolsky. New York: Columbia University Press.

The Record of Lin-chi. 1975. Trans. Ruth F. Sasaki. Kyoto: Institute for Zen Studies.

The Zen Master Hakuin: Selected Writings. 1971. Trans. Philip Yampolsky. New York: Columbia University Press.

The Zen Teaching of Rinzai. 1976. Trans. Irmgard Schloegl. Berkeley: Shambala.

Abbreviations

Need, Nurturance, and the Emotions on a Pacific Atoll

Catherine Lutz

This chapter describes the cultural contexts for use of a particular emotion term on Ifaluk atoll in the Pacific. My attempt is to show the rich cultural meanings circulating through the term and to suggest some of the connections between the ethnopsychological ideas about emotion evident in everyday conversations and the configurations of power and social relations on the island. In addition, the anthropological approach used here and elsewhere (e.g., Rosaldo 1980; Abu-Lughod 1986; Scheper-Hughes 1985) questions assumptions about the connections between emotions, interiority, irrationality, and the natural that have tended to dominate in many Western thought systems.

At the time of my fieldwork in the late 1970s, the 430 people of Ifaluk atoll in Micronesia were a subsistence horticultural and fishing society (for details, see Lutz 1988). Talk about emotions is quite frequent and is a central means by which many aspects of social life are promulgated. One concept in common use is that of *fago* (compassion, love, sadness). In their use of that word, people on Ifaluk communicate a central part of their view of human relationships; they impart their sense of the place of suffering in their lives, of the naturalness of interpersonal kindness in the face of that pain, and of their feeling that maturity consists, above all, in the ability to nurture others. *Fago* speaks of the sense that life is fragile, that connections to others are both precious and liable to severance through death and travel, that love may equal loss. *Fago* is uttered in recognition of the suffering that is everywhere and in the spirit of a vigorous optimism that human effort, most especially in the form of caring for others, can control its ravages.

My sense of what people were saying when they used the term *fago* emerged only slowly over the course of my stay on the island, requiring an effort to disentangle my own native emotional understandings from theirs. From the perspective of the implicit notions entailed in the American English terms—including "compassion," "love," and "sadness"—that together best translate *fago*, the concept involves some basic internal contradictions. Among other things, "love" is positive and activating, "sadness," negative and enervating; the loving person is strong, the sad person, weak. The ethnotheoretical notions surrounding the emotions with which I had come to Ifaluk created the structure of bafflement that I felt at seeing the diverse contexts within which the term was used.

The following accounts of several events I either observed or participated in exemplify the problems encountered in translating *fago*.

Ilefagochang,[1] a woman in her late twenties, walked with me past the church one early evening as the sounds drifted out of a group of women singing at daily vespers. Ilefagochang recognized the voice of her younger friend, Lauchepou, in the chorus, and said in the sentimental tone that people typically use to express affection, "*Mawesh* Lauchepou" (Sweetheart Lauchepou).

Ilefagomar asked me one day if I had ever seen a person who had no toes. I replied by describing the somewhat more horrible condition of a man whom I had seen in New York City some years before. This man, I explained, had no legs, but propelled himself along the city streets on a low board outfitted with wheels. To this, another woman who was listening exclaimed, with much intensity in her voice, "I would *fago* him if I saw him." She then immediately asked me where his family was and why they were not taking care of (*gamwela*) him.

As we sat listening to a love song on the radio that was tuned to a Guam station that played American music, Ilefagochang indicated that she had "goose bumps," and added that they are caused by, among other things, our "*fago* for the person who is singing."

A young married man, Gachipemar, became very ill. His relatives attributed the illness to his excessive drinking. When his stomach swelled out grossly, the standard, elaborate scenario for caring for the sick (to be described in a moment) began. Several weeks later, the interisland ship took Gachipemar, in the care of Pakesowel, his older brother, to the hospital on Yap. They returned when his condition improved, but Pakesowel told his relatives on his arrival that Gachipemar had begun drinking again, against his brother's advice. Pakesowel reported that he had rebuked Gachipemar for this behavior on Yap, saying to him, "You do not *fago* my thoughts." He reminded Gachipemar, he went on, that he (Pakesowel) had taken him to Yap's hospital even though it meant leaving his young son, for whom his "*fago* is strong" and on account of whom he was homesick on Yap. By way of final reprimand, he told Gachipemar, "You do not *fago* your own breath [life]."

On another occasion, I was sipping coffee early one morning with Ilefagomar, when she told me she had heard her younger brother singing as he fished in the lagoon the previous evening. As she heard him, she said, she "had a bit of *fago* for him."

The field ship was making a day-long stopover at Ifaluk. It had gotten dark and the time was nearing for the boat's departure. I was sitting near the shore with Getachimang, an older man, when his 25-year-old (nonbiological) son, who was to leave on the ship, came to bid him a formal goodbye. The two men spoke in particularly serious and quiet voices, calling each other "father" and "son," terms that are rarely used in addressing (rather than simply in referring to) one's kin. They held hands for some time, as Getachimang said to his son several times, "Be careful." The younger man reciprocated by speaking of his *fago* for the father.

These episodes indicate that the translation of the concept of *fago* requires an understanding of the way in which the Ifaluk conceptualize the nature of positive relationships with others. *Fago* is used to alert others to the strength of particular relationships, to talk about the pain involved in the severance of those relations by death and travel, and to signal a readiness to care for the other. To explore in more detail the daily events that set the stage for *fago* is to examine the relationships that matter to people on Ifaluk, *how* precisely they matter, and the kinds of action—including primarily nurturance—that the relationships with others draw from the self.

THE FORMS OF NEED AND NURTURANCE

The primary contexts in which *fago* occurs are those in which the person confronts another who is somehow *in need*. The link between *fago* and "neediness" (*gafago*) is indexed grammatically in the latter term; the causative prefix *ga-* is added to the emotion term *fago* to produce the term, which can be translated as "needy" or "poor." Thus, the person who is needy literally "causes compassion" in others. The idea that neediness *necessarily* produces nurturant feelings and actions in mature others not only is seen linguistically, but is a deep and consistent theme running through Ifaluk culture more generally. This assumption—that a durable and automatic link exists between the suffering of one person and the nurturing of others—lies at the heart of Ifaluk emotional and moral life.

The *gafago* (needy, poor) are those individuals who are lacking one or more of the qualities necessary for a good life. To understand those qualities is to understand the proper use of *fago*. In exploring them, I will describe aspects of the emotional meaning of illness, death, hunger, children, social hierarchy, and good citizenship.

Illness

The use of emotion words in everyday life can be said to "mark," or acknowledge, the existence of particular kinds of relationships. One of the most common kinds of relationships that *fago* points to is that which exists between the sick and the healthy. What makes the concept of *fago* an appropriate marker of this is the expectation that the sick person is suffering and in need not only of recovery but of elaborate and constant care by others. In addition, the concept of *fago* is often used in these situations to indicate one's concern that the sick person will die, or, in other words, one's sense that ultimate separation and loss are imminent. Ifaluk's experience with sudden epidemics and the inadequacy of the cosmopolitan health care system that exists on the island partially engender the intense expectation that illness will lead to death.

The scene that occurs at the bedside of a sick person on Ifaluk is a dramatic one from the perspective of someone such as myself, whose previous experience was restricted to some middle-class American patterns of treatment of the sick. If the illness is considered a serious one, people begin to take measures such as those taken for the young man in his twenties, Gachipemar, whose stomach suddenly swelled, leaving him prone and in great pain. The patient's sisters and father went to visit him at least twice daily for the first few days of his illness. Divination was carried out by one of the few older men who has the skill, and several family members who knew the medicinal recipes for Gachipemar's condition went out into the bush to collect the necessary ingredients, and each brought and administered their mixture to him.

When Gachipemar's condition did not improve, his large extended family began to move their sleeping mats and mosquito netting over to his wife's household. Such moves by the seriously ill person's family are common and allow for the extensive twenty-four-hour patient care that is required, prevent absence at the moment of the death that is often anticipated, and allow people to communicate to others the extent and degree of their *fago* for the patient, involving, as the move does, no small amount of effort and inconvenience.

Several weeks passed with continued provision of medicines and daily massage treatments. Each day would find Gachipemar lying on his mat with at least two or three individuals in attendance to his needs. Between household members and those who had come from elsewhere to be with the patient, more than fifty individuals could be found in and around the house during any one day. As is standard practice, one, two, or even, on some occasions, ten people sat immediately next to him fanning away the heat and flies. If Gachipemar wished it, his head and shoulders would be propped up on the lap of someone who sat behind him. He would be gently carried down to the lagoon several times a day for elimination and bathing. Fresh flower wreaths were constructed for his head, and he was anointed with coconut oil. The early morning hours would find several people at his side who had remained awake caring for him throughout the night.

The treatment accorded Gachipemar, who eventually recovered after his evacuation to a regional hospital, was seen on numerous other occasions when people became ill. When the death of the patient becomes a certainty, the expression of *fago* intensifies beyond this example. As one elderly man slowly died of tuberculosis, he was dressed in a bright new blue loincloth, anointed with imported perfume, and bedecked daily with multiple freshly woven flower wreaths. Several villages sent collective gifts of drinking coconuts to his household, and nearly everyone on the island made a visit to him at one time or another during the last few weeks of his life.

Death

The sick, or rather the dying person, is the prototypical object of *fago*. When I asked people about recent experiences with *fago*, many spoke of death. One woman, whose elder relative had recently died, said,

> The last time I [experienced] *fago* was when our "mother" died two days ago. We really felt bad inside. It was like our insides were being torn. We beat our chests and scratched our faces because our *fago* was so strong, because there is no other time that we will see her.

A man whose brother had recently died in a fall from a tree said,

> At the time, I felt like I was going to cry all the time, every time I remember what we did together, like drinking and fishing together, and then I feel like I will cry.

The *fago* that begins in illness is intensified as death occurs and the experience is described as that of a "ripping stomach" (*ye tewasi segai*).

The scenario of response to death that the woman above makes reference to was, like the scene that accompanies illness, a dramatic and even shocking one for me, given that I, like most young Americans, had neither observed death nor encountered anything but the subdued ritual of one funeral. My first view of the emotional response to death on Ifaluk occurred when Tomas, a five-year-old boy, contracted a sudden high fever (most probably as the result of meningitis) and was comatose within twenty-four hours. People began to gather at the house of his biological parents, where he had been brought by his adoptive parents when he first became sick. The usual routine of washing down a child's feverish body was followed by several women through the morning until it became clear that such pragmatic expressions of *fago* were futile. Expecting death and anticipating its timing, the close male relatives took turns holding his semirigid and rail-shaken body. Tomas's two fathers, his biological father's brothers, and his several adult half-brothers wept as they cradled him. His biological mother, in a dazed state, lowered from the rafters the bundle of lava-lavas and grave goods that each household keeps prepared for the deaths of close relatives.

At the moment of death, a great wailing went up. The dead boy's biological mother, seated on the floor mats near him, rose to her knees as if she had been stabbed, and pounded her fist against her chest. The adoptive mother, a woman of about sixty (and the boy's father's sister), began to scream and throw herself about on the ground. Others rushed forward to restrain both of them from hurting themselves, and the biological mother was soon sitting in stiff shock. The house was filled with crying, which varied from low moaning to loud, wrenching, and mucus-filled screaming to wailingly sung poem-laments and continued without pause through the night. Both men and women seemed to cry in equal measure. It is customary that people take turns coming forward (or rather being invited forward by the closest relatives) to cry in the immediate circle around the body. A careful choreography of grief generally requires that those who are "crying big" (or loudly and deeply) do so closer rather than further from the body, and that those who are not crying move back from it.

The next morning, the body was placed in a coffin that had been built by the men of the village. Objects from the bag of grave goods were placed in the box alongside items given by other relatives and neighbors as visible signs of their *fago* for the deceased. Lava-lavas were also brought for the family of the child. As a final gesture, close family members cut their hair (in some cases to within an inch of the head) into the coffin. The box was then carried to the graveyard and lowered into the ground; an uninscribed wooden cross was added to mark the site.

Traditionally, the Ifaluk buried their dead at sea (Burrows and Spiro 1953, 311). Land burial was encouraged by the Catholic missionaries who prosely-tized on the island in the 1950s, and the last ocean burial was in 1963. Some people complained, however, of their unhappiness with the use of the graveyard as it serves as a constant reminder of the death of loved ones. Sea burial, they maintain, made it easier to do the necessary forgetting of the deceased. The graveyard stands in contradiction to the several cultural practices that are designed to aid in this forgetting (such as taboos on speaking the name of the dead person). Although Tomas's family would return to weave flower gar-lands for the grave for the next four mornings and evenings, and although his mother's brother would cry big on the gravesite on his return from another island, in general this and other graves are avoided.

For the next four days, Tomas's family would do no work. They cried big again the morning after the funeral and spent much of their time lying down, as is customary. Relatives and neighbors came to visit frequently over the next days and months in an explicit effort to help them "forget about" the dead child. "Kindly" talk was in much more frequent use than usual in talking to those who were grieving.

A two-sided approach to dealing with the loss of death is promoted on Ifaluk. On the one hand, people are advised by others to cry big, particularly at the funeral, with the proviso that those who do not will likely become sick afterwards. On the other hand, the grieving person is told to think of the living and in essence to refocus their *fago* on those who are in need of nurturance, such as their children. In talking to me several months later about the death of her son, Tomas's biological mother, Lemalesep, said,

> I didn't think he was very sick at first, that it was just the flu. But then he didn't speak. When he couldn't open his mouth, then I got *rus* [panicked, afraid, surprised]. I just laid down here; I didn't know what the people around me were doing. My head hurt, probably because my thoughts and feelings [*nunuwan*] came up from my insides to my head. I couldn't walk because my legs hurt. But they talked to me to think about my other children and to take care of the baby and I thought, maybe it's true [that I ought to do that].

At the funeral and in the weeks following it, several people repeatedly advised the principal mourners (the four parents) to try to forget about the dead child.

The shadow of the relationship that existed with the person who has died continues to be described for some time afterwards with the concept of *fago*. One woman described the *fago* that lingers after death by talking about a hypothetical person who has lost a daughter.

> They will see the taro patch planting of their dead child and cry and leave. Or they will see the flower wreath worn by their dead child and they cry and wrap it up carefully in a new cloth to keep. Or they will see their child's friends and be reminded. They are not hungry.

The person who dies is said to "die away from" the living. This turn of phrase reflects the fact that death is seen not so much as the end of an individual life as the end of a set of relationships. In some cases, it is also a "dying toward" the spirit world; certain deaths are said to be caused by the spirit of a predeceased relative who had strong *fago* and *pak* (homesickness, missing) for the dead person. The emotion of *fago* marks the existence of a relationship, including a relationship that is threatened by death.

To Be without Kin

Perhaps the worst fate that most Ifaluk can imagine is to be without kin—due to demographic chance, death, or travel from the island. In the two latter circumstances, the concept of *fago* is used to communicate the importance of those missing relatives. In daily conversation, people speak of their *fago* for those relatively rare individuals whose kinship networks are small or are missing crucial members. By use of the concept, the islanders also announce and renew their kin ties to the increasing number of people who leave the atoll for schooling, health care, wage labor, or marriage.

One's kin represent both companionship as well as social and economic support and survival, as they do in most preindustrial societies, and on Ifaluk, the companionship and support are spoken of in the idiom of nurturance and, particularly, of food. People without kin on Ifaluk are said to have no one "to take care of them" (*gamwelar*); they are, above all, people without food. The man who has no sisters can be in the precarious position of being without access to taro gardens and their fruits; the old woman without sons is said to be pitiable, as she has no one to bring her fish. The tragedy of being without relatives is also due to the fact that one then eats alone; and for the solitary diner, "food does not taste sweet." Each meal is a reminder that one is denied the opportunity to share food with the relatives who are either permanently or temporarily missing.

Most of Ifaluk's people have been born, live, and will die within the boundaries of the atoll's one-half square mile. The ties to other people that result from this embeddedness are multiple, strong, and enduring. While travel from the atoll has always occurred, as men have sailed to distant atolls for trade or marriage, it has dramatically increased in the more recent colonial past as young men have left for schooling or, in some cases, waged and unwaged labor. The primary vehicle by which travel now occurs is not the canoe but the interisland steamer that arrives approximately every six weeks. An emotional cycle runs in parallel to the ship schedule as people are taken away to visit sick relatives on other atolls, to high school on Ulithi, and to work or hospital on Yap.

After the ship has left with its Ifaluk passengers, people remark again and again about the missing. Sitting around at work or rest, someone will spontaneously remark, in reference to the person who is gone, "That sweetheart" (*"Maweshe iy"*). For those closest to the traveler, the experience of *fago* is as painful as it was for one woman whose two brothers left on the ship:

> When [my brothers] went away to high school, I *fago*. Maybe because I was used to them always coming here to eat. When they left, my *fago* made me unable [to function]. That night, the ship stayed for a while and I could hear the engine and I couldn't get to sleep. I was incapacitated with my *fago*. I sat up, opened the doors, and smoked outside. I just cried and cried. My back hurt so I lay down. . . . In the morning, I didn't want to see the house where they slept. Now it [the *fago*] has calmed down a bit because it's been a long time.

While travel creates one kind of kinlessness, demographic variation creates another. Couples may be childless, a man may have no sisters, a household may have no men. To understand the *fago* that people express for the barren woman, the only child, or the man without sisters, as well as the *fago* felt for one's existing kin, is to understand how the Ifaluk kinship system is experienced by individuals. *For whom* people feel *fago* is an index of which kin relations are seen as most necessary to the quality of life. *Why* the emotion is felt for each type of relative indicates the kinds of duties and benefits attached to that relationship. Ifaluk ideas about what people need and about how relatives serve to fill those needs are evident in the concept's use.

Several relationship types can be explored by examining the way in which *fago* is used to articulate their meaning.

The parent-child relationship is, along with that between sisters and brothers, the one most frequently understood with the concept of *fago*. The child is the quintessential needy person—vulnerable to illness and death and without the wherewithal to get his or her own food—the ultimate subordinate, and the ultimate object of *fago*. In needing the parents' care, the child needs the parents' *fago*. Children are often named in accordance with this emphasis on their vulnerability and the nature of their relationship with the adult world. There are, for example, women on Ifaluk named Lefagochang and Lefagoyag and men called Fagolimul and Fagoitil, names which may be translated, respectively, as "love and desire," "love binding," "love and generosity," and "love quickening."

When Ifaluk parents talk about their *fago* for their children, it is frequently when the child is sick; their use of *fago* to describe the situation is an attempt to communicate their sense that the child is helpless and may die; fevers in particular are cause for both alarm (*rus*) and *fago*. Again and again, people would recount their children's illnesses, and, in so doing, would describe the thoughts and behavior indicative of *fago*: "I didn't sleep all night"; "I bathed my baby in cool water)"; "I thought she was going to die." Healthy children are also recipients of *fago*, which is seen when a parent fans away the heat, gently captures mosquitoes as they alight on her sleeping child, or carries a four-year-old on his back.

On the other hand, the parent also needs the child, both for its eventual contribution to the household labor pool and to the parent's care in old age, as well as for the enjoyment and fullness he or she brings to the home. To be without children, then, makes the adult an object of *fago*. To give a child in adoption to such a person is a commendable act of *fago*. Although virtually every household on Ifaluk has adopted children, the rate of adoption is much higher among barren couples, with several having adopted four or five children. A woman who loses a child to death is sometimes given another child in adoption soon afterwards, people say, "because we *fago* her." As parents reach infirm old age, the emphasis shifts from their *fago* of the child to the child's *fago* for his or her mother and father. When conflicts arise over the extent to which the child is fulfilling obligations to an aging parent, however, the failure may be discussed by the elder as an emotional failure.

The complementarity and central importance of the relationship that exists between brothers and sisters on Ifaluk is reflected in the *fago* which is expressed between them and the pity that is bestowed on those who have no cross-siblings, particularly men in such a position. Women often speak of their *fago* for their brothers, as did Ilefagomar after hearing her brother fishing in the lagoon. Ilefagomar's statement draws on the notion that women need brothers (and men more generally) to fish for them.

In talking about adoption, a woman will commonly say that she has taken in her brother's children "because I *fago* my brother, and therefore take care of his children." In feeding these children, she, in effect, gives her brother access to the produce of her gardens. In addition, a man's sister will often send him cooked taro or breadfruit as an explicit sign of her *fago* for him. Implied here is that the man is needy in having no gardens of his own; although he eats from his wife's gardens, it is, in a sense, only at the latter's pleasure that he does so. A man has tenuous ties to taro land, and so is pitiable; his most solid ties are through his sister, however, and so she feels her obligation, expressed as *fago*, to send him food and to feed his children. One man in his fifties was frequently spoken of as an object of *fago* for the reason that he had no biological sisters. This man was an only child, and, although it is pitiable to have no brothers, people much more commonly remarked on his lack of sisters. The gifts of food that were frequently sent to him by his clan sisters and those sisters' children were signs of their *fago*. The recognized complementarity of men and women (both brothers and sisters as well as husbands and wives) is revealed in the attempt that people make to put together a household, through birth and adoption, of both genders. One woman whose marriage had been barren remarked that she had followed the common wisdom in adopting both boys and girls; the boys, she said, "will take care of the girls, getting them fish and hashi and climbing for coconut and breadfruit," while the girls will get taro.

The relationship between two sisters is also a very close one on Ifaluk. Frequently, sisters will spend their entire lives together under the same roof, eating from the same pot, weaving at adjacent looms, and tending each other's children. Although the relationship is at least as central to their everyday lives as any other, the concept of *fago* is not used by women as often to talk about their sisters. This seeming paradox might be explained by the fact that relations between sisters do not share two of the important characteristics of the other relationships which are marked by declarations of *fago*, that is, clear differences in rank and a cultural and objective sense of the vulnerability of the relationship. In contrast with the cross-sibling and the parent-child relationship, sisters are relatively equal in status, and social structural arrangements place them solidly in alliance and proximity. The concept of *fago* is used to mark relationships whose inequality highlights the need for nurturance and whose vulnerability to loss is more likely due to death or social arrangements, conditions which do not normally exist for sisters.

The solitary anthropologist in the field must represent, virtually everywhere, a somewhat anomalous type of human being, insofar as he or she lives without kin. Despite the anomaly, the whole complex of Ifaluk ideas about the relationship between *fago* and kinlessness was activated to understand my position in the community. People frequently remarked that they had *fago* for me because I was so far from my family and because I must be terribly homesick. My adoption by an Ifaluk family and their feeding of me was understood as an expression of *fago*—as the normal and necessary response to my vulnerable situation.

Although I was, in fact, homesick throughout the research period, my use of the concept of *pak* (homesickness) to understand the situation came more slowly to me than it would have to an Ifaluk person in a similar situation. This contrast corresponds to that which exists between Ifaluk's political economy and our own; the survival value of strong and enduring ties between people on Ifaluk has made the paired concepts of *fago* and *pak* central to their emotional understandings of the meaning of separation from kin. The necessity for a physically and emotionally mobile labor force under industrial capitalism, on the other hand, has been one factor in the minimal cultural elaboration around the emotions of (at least temporary) separation in the United States. Discussions of the field experience in the anthropological literature reflect this by failing to mention it as a possible, much less a central, element in the fieldworker's response.

When the Ifaluk say that they *fago* the person who is without kin, they say that people need, above all, to be embedded in a network of people who "take care of" them. No person can survive alone, either physically or emotionally; no person ought to be denied the opportunity to be dependent on the judgment and caretaking of others. Perhaps paradoxically to the Western observer, the idea of being taken care of connotes a strong rather than a weak position. The incredulity expressed over the story of the legless man on a New York City street was not due to the repulsiveness or the anomaly of his physical state. What astonished the women who heard about him was that a man in such need was not being taken care of by his relations. While the Ifaluk value their relatives as bulwarks against loneliness and as routes to the wealth of larger numbers of taro gardens and fishing expeditions, these advantages are surmounted by or subsumed within the notion that kin, through their *fago*, alleviate suffering and need.

The Good or Gentle Person

While most of the contexts in which the word *fago* is used represent major or minor disasters for those involved, the emotion is also importantly linked to encounters with exemplary people. As one person told me, "You *fago* someone because they do not misbehave. You *fago* them because they are calm and socially intelligent." This use of *fago* was exemplified in the following case. When the interisland ship arrived late one afternoon, it carried a young Trukese man who came ashore to visit Tamalekar. Although they had not met previously, their shared clan affiliation made the visit an appropriate one. They and the rest of Tamalekar's family spent the evening in quiet talk, with the Trukese speaking with respect and politeness. The visitor also distinguished himself by bringing a gift of a carton of cigarettes. The evening wore on past the point at which the family usually retired, and when the young man stepped out for a moment to relieve himself, Tamalekar said to his family, "We *fago* this one because he's calm [*maluwelu*]. Even though we're sleepy, we'll stay up and talk with him [until he's ready to go back to the ship]." Later, when the man was about to leave, Tamalekar gave him something from the locked cubicle where he kept his most valued objects.

Time and again, people would link the emotion of *fago* and the highly valued trait of *maluwelu* (calmness, gentleness) in their speech. Two kinds of connection were made. In the first, people who have *fago* for others will be calm and gentle as a result. Stated another way, "calm" people demonstrate, through their behavior, their compassion for others. What is compassionate about "calmness" is that the calm person does not frighten others. The word *maluwelu* itself combines the negative prefix *ma-* with the reduplicated form of a word meaning fright (*lu*); the calm person is literally not frightening. He or she speaks quietly and politely and behaves gently, actions that the Ifaluk see as necessary for putting people at ease and relieving the fear that might otherwise result from being around others.

A second ethnotheoretical link between the two concepts is that the calm person creates the emotion of *fago* in others. In other words, everyone loves those who are *maluwelu*. Lesepemang relied on my making these inferences when she told me, in the midst of a conflict with her mother's mother's sister, "I am 'justifiably angry' with Laufelichou because she talks sharply and abruptly to me. She doesn't talk *maluwelu* like [our adoptive mother] who we therefore *fago* and obey." It is important to add, however, that Lesepemang's praise of her adoptive mother was strategic, being used to dramatize her condemnation of Laufelichou. When she was, on other occasions, displeased with her adoptive mother, Lesepemang complained to anyone who would listen that her mother was "hot-tempered" (*sigsig*), a trait diametrically opposed to both calmness and to *fago*.

FAGO AS MATURITY, NURTURANCE AS POWER

The ability to experience *fago* is seen as one of the central characteristics of the mature person, perhaps even the ultimate quality defining the good person and the competent adult. God, chiefs, parents, and elders all maintain the position and respect they command through their exercise of this emotion. The relative equality of status that women enjoy in many domains on Ifaluk is due in part to the fact that they are seen as able to feel and act on this emotion at least as much as men and thus can be defined as equally mature.

Ethnopsychological ideas about the development of *fago* over the life cycle support the association between this emotion and maturity. The ability to *fago* is dependent on the acquisition of mature language skills and, more generally, of social intelligence (*repiy*). It is said that children first feel the emotion only after the age of about seven, which is the age by which they are also said to first become socially intelligent. As one woman told me, "When children understand the meaning of talk, then they know how to *fago*." Conversely, a deaf ten-year-old boy was said not to *fago* people because he could not hear or understand speech. Individual differences are recognized in the extent to which children learn to *fago*—differences that result from variation in their levels of social intelligence. The child who is socially intelligent will *fago*, but, in Ilefagochang's words, "others don't 'think/feel' [*nunuwan*] and so *fago* only a little bit." A child must be thought-full if he or she is to be able to *fago*. This emotion is, in effect, treated as a form of intelligence, and is valued by the Ifaluk more than virtually any other kind of emotion.

Given its association with maturity, the concept of *fago* is commonly used to praise those whose behavior is exemplary in certain kinds of ways. Individuals will be praised by saying of them, "She (or he) is good. She [has] *fago* for people." While any individual can receive acclaim for their especially nurturing or compassionate behavior, the chiefs, benevolent spirits, and the Catholic priest who sometimes visits the island are frequently spoken of as ones who *fago* in great measure. These chiefs, spirits, and priests are distinguished by the fact that their intelligence (*repiy*) is expressed in the form of *fago* or caring for others. The chiefs, who are said to "take care of" the people of the island, do this by protecting them through regulation of such things as potentially aggressive outsiders, the law breakers among them, and overfishing of the lagoon. The good spirits of individual ancestors are also said to *fago* people, particularly their descendants. The *fago* of the spirit of a dead mother for her sick adult child often results in the spirit sending a recipe for the necessary medicinal cure. In contrast to the *fago* of humans, however, the spirits' *fago* may result in some harm to the object of that emotion. This sometimes occurs when the spirit, out of *fago* and longing for the living relative, causes death so that they may be reunited in the spirit realm. The priest is also seen as a person of much *fago*. He is said to be concerned particularly for the emotional well-being of his parishioners. People often mention that the priest helps them to recover from negative emotions of all kinds, advising them to calm down from their anger and comforting them when relatives die. In this the priest acts in a parallel fashion to God (*got*), who is also said to *fago* all people. The prayers of both priest and parishioners, however, are also said to be used to calm God and make him *fago* the people. This belief (as well, perhaps, as its weakness) was illustrated by one woman's complaint, after news of a nearby typhoon reached Ifaluk, that no one was praying to God to *fago* them and make the typhoon swerve away from the atoll.

The chiefs, spirits, priest, and God, as well as other individuals, *fago because* they are mature or intelligent. One index of that *fago* is their nurturance of those who are in need of their care. A secondary index of *fago* is their calm, well-behaved, or *maluwelu*, demeanor. As already noted, the calm person can be said to exhibit *fago* because his or her gentleness protects others from the fright and discomfort caused by aggression or other social disruptiveness.

In a sense, it is not only maturity but also *power* which is defined on Ifaluk as the ability to nurture others. Power resides particularly in those who have the mental, social, and physical resources to help others. Thus, the higher one's position in the social hierarchy on Ifaluk, the more frequent and compelling are the contexts in which one is called on to *fago* and to "take care of" others.

The hierarchy of power that exists in the islands between Yap and Truk is also phrased in terms of the ability and duty of the higher-ranked islands to "take care of" the lower-ranked. At one point in 1978, news reached the island that the education bureaucracy in Yap was planning to build a junior high school on Woleai for the outer islanders. On hearing this, an elderly man, Gatachimang, said that he was afraid (*metagu*) that the Woleaians would hit the students, if given the responsibility for such a school, "because they are not used to taking care of others." Gatachimang's listeners would probably share his conclusion that Woleaians (who otherwise have no reputation for violence) might be capable of such behavior based on their knowledge that the atoll of Woleai is ranked lower than Ulithi, which currently hosts the high school for outer islanders. Although island ethnotheory does not hold that low rank, in and of itself, induces one to violence, rank does bring experience in nurturing, and in the Ifaluk view, inexperience might lead to the roughness which would strike against the essence of what it means to "take care of" others.

A similarly instructive story reached Ifaluk from Woleai in 1978. Plans had also been announced for an airstrip to be built on Woleai. Although the chiefs had given their approval to the project, many people on Woleai were apparently concerned that they could not afford to lose such a relatively substantial portion of their 1.7 square mile atoll, particularly as the projected strip would cut through a large section of taro gardens. After this announcement, Woleai's high school students took it upon themselves to write a letter to the Trust Territory's High Commissioner saying that they did not want the airport on Woleai. Their rationale was phrased in terms of the equation between nurturance, maturity, and power. Their island, the students informed the Commissioner, is the biggest atoll in the area, and so plays an important role in sending food to the other atolls when a typhoon has hit and damaged their food supply. If the airport cut into Woleai's taro patch, they would not be able "to send their [the other islanders'] food."

Although the motivation for nurturing is portrayed by the Ifaluk as both mature and altruistic, it can also be seen that the ability to *fago* and care for the needy allows for and legitimates control over the needy person. People who are without kin are not only pitiable because they are lonely or because they have fewer land and labor resources; such people are also to be pitied or even scorned because they do not "take care of" others. In being denied the opportunity to care for others, they are unable to control others, and in being unable to do so, they cannot command respect, which has both socioemotional and more tangible rewards.

This was illustrated by a conflict that erupted in one household where Yasechaul, an extremely unpopular older man with a reputation for having a hot temper, burst into shouting at his niece and nephew. The cause for his fit of pique was, according to others, his "bad-heartedness," or jealousy, over the fact that his younger relatives were not giving him cigarettes. If he had been another person, Yasechaul would have been within his rights to expect others in his household to share such a scarce resource with him; sister's children, in particular, will be generous with their mother's brothers out of respect for them. Yasechaul was unusual, however, in both his hyper-irritability and in his chosen pattern of postmarital residence; while this household was that of his biological mother, his wife was a woman of Woleai, and he ought to have had his primary residence there.

In later discussions of the conflict, people remarked on Yasechaul's "hot temper" (*sigsig*), selfishness (*farog*), and bad-heartedness (*lalongau*). But most remarkable for those who recounted the story was the statement he was reported to have made during his tirade: "I am," he told his niece and nephew, "the chief of this household." Ilefagochang expressed her astonishment to her sister at a neighboring household, "He is not the head of [that household]. He doesn't get food for them. He doesn't climb for breadfruit or coconut." She went on to describe the role of several of the other adult men of that household in collecting those foods and concluded that "Yasechaul cannot take care of the people of [that household]." The vehemence with which this man was denounced reflects both the value attached to the "calm" characteristics that he lacked and the centrality of nurturance to the Ifaluk definition of power. It is these two components of maturity—gentleness and nurturance—that contribute to the configuration and the importance of the concept of *fago* to everyday life on the atoll.

It is perhaps only in a society in which autonomous action to ensure individual survival is neither socially encouraged nor ecologically or economically feasible that nurturance will become central to the definition of power. For it may only be in that context that caring for others creates the greatest dependency in the recipient and control in the caregiver.

The relatively powerful position of women on Ifaluk is generated through their ownership of garden lands and control of their products and through their position as the heads of matrilocal households. But the strength of women is also reinforced by the cultural ideology surrounding the concept of *fago*—an ideology which defines their food provision and their care of children as indices of both their maturity and their superordinate social position. Western ethnotheory tends, by contrast, to emphasize the "softness," or even the "weakness," of the person who nurtures; the nurturant person may be seen as morally noteworthy, but caring for others is an activity that tends to place one further down, rather than up, in sociopolitical ranking. Mothers, women more generally, and those who are engaged in personal service occupations—each category of which is culturally defined as nurturant—have lower status than their opposite counterparts. The explicit idiom for power is force rather than compassion.

CONCLUSION: EMOTIONAL MEANING AND
MATERIAL CONDITIONS ON A CORAL ATOLL

Although experience "does not in itself dictate the terms by which the world is understood" (Gergen 1985, 266), language and, more generally, consciousness is formed in at least partial service to the task of organizing social responses to the problems presented by particular environments. The structure of the language of emotion can be viewed in this same light. While emotion concepts are more typically portrayed as emerging from an internal world of sensations and thoughts, they can be seen, instead, as having been constructed in the same environmental crucible as the language of such things as ritual, land tenure, or ethnicity. More specifically, emotion concepts are constructed in part by reference to the culturally influenced observation of the "objective conditions" of life in a particular place—of the frequency of death, of the nature and suddenness of dangers and losses, of the number and kind of exchanges between individuals. Each emotion concept also exists in dialectical relationship with a set of cultural practices, both shaping and being shaped by them.

Fago, like other emotion concepts, reflects the objective material and social relational conditions of the society in which it is produced and used. A host of cultural practices, and the social structures formed through them, articulate with both the ideas and the behaviors embedded in *fago*.[2] Both those practices and the emotion concept can be related to Ifaluk's precarious and bounded atoll environment. Its people make emotional sense of the conditions of life on a coral atoll and are motivated to thrive within them in part through the concept of *fago*. Food sharing, adoption, the treatment of visitors, relations between brothers and sisters, forms of and attitudes toward authority, and the system of health care are all examples of central features of everyday life that take their importance and character in part from the ideological charter provided by the notion of *fago*. *Fago* is central to the way people understand their relationship to others—to their sense that the suffering of others is of vital concern, that attachment to others entails active nurturance more than self-contained feelings, that love is explicitly an emotion of power, and that love is heavily tinged with pathos because love's object is weak and because love often equals loss.

Notes

1. All names used to describe individuals are pseudonyms.

2. Ifaluk is certainly not unique in either general environmental and social conditions or in its construction of an emotion concept like *fago*. *Fago* shows important similarities with related emotion words in other Pacific languages—with the Samoan *alofa* (Gerber 1975), the Hawaiian *aloha*, the Marquesan *ka'oha* (Kirkpatrick 1983), and the Tahitian *arofa* (Levy 1973) .

Bibliography

Abu-Lughod, Lila. 1986. *Veiled Sentiments: Honor and Poetry in a Bedouin Society*. Berkeley: University of California Press.

Burrows, Edwin G., and Melford Spiro. 1953. *An Atoll Culture: Ethnography of Ifaluk in the Central Carolines*. New Haven: Human Relations Area Files.

Gerber, Eleanor. 1975. "The Cultural Patterning of Emotions in Samoa." Ph.D. diss. University of California at San Diego.

Gergen, Kenneth J. 1985. "The Social Constructionist Movement in Modern Psychology." *American Psychologist* 40: 266-75.

Kirkpatrick, John T. 1983. *The Marquesan Notion of the Person*. Ann Arbor: UMI Research Press.

Levy, Robert. 1973. *Tahitians: Mind and Experience in the Society Islands*. Chicago: University of Chicago Press.

Lutz, Catherine. 1988. *Unnatural Emotions: Everyday Sentiments on a Micronesian Atoll and Their Challenge to Western Theory*. Chicago: University of Chicago Press.

Rosaldo, Michelle Z. 1980. *Knowledge and Passion: Ilongot Notions of Self and Social Life*. Cambridge: Cambridge University Press.

Scheper-Hughes, Nancy. 1985. "Culture, Scarcity, and Maternal Thinking." *Ethos* 13: 291-317.

The Cross-Cultural Comparison of Emotion

Robert C. Solomon

INTRODUCTION

Philosophers have often contrasted reason and the passions, typically championing the former against the latter and defending philosophy itself as the love of reason. So, too, casual comparativists contrast the East and the West, caricaturing the former as a vast continent of mysticism, meditation, and odd Zen one-liners, as opposed to the latter, which is founded on a solid foundation of science, reason, and argumentation. But on at least one point the two would seem to agree, and that is in their shared contempt for the passions. The ideal that emerges for philosophers both East and West too often tends to be a kind of contemplative detachment, dispassion, if not full-fledged *apatheia* or nirvana.

The truth, of course, is that the distinction between reason and the passions is as suspect and ultimately as misleading as the dichotomy between East and West. To begin with the latter, the cultures and philosophies of India are as different from one another as they are from the cultures and philosophies of Northern Europe, while on the other hand there are multiple influences, crisscrossing, and similarities between South Asia and Europe as far as the Thames. China has little in common with Iran, Japan displays at least superficial similarities with other "advanced" industrial nations, and what we call the three great "Western" religions all originate in what was formerly called "the Orient." Conquest and colonialism have forged many mergers and compromises, and, indeed, the East-West opposition has been played out *within* the East and the West—in East Asia, for example, when the infiltration of Indo-Aryan ideas transformed the culture of China in the first millennium and in the case of Germany from the Middle Ages to modern times.[1] As for the crude philosophical identification of logic with the West and mysticism with the East, one finds mysticism in nineteenth-century Germany, even in Kant's backyard, so to speak, and there are traditions in hard-headed logic in India that go back more

253

than a thousand years.[2] But with reference to the emotions, which is what concerns us here, no simple statement about philosophers' attitudes toward emotion will suffice, either East or West. Graham Parkes shows in his essay in this volume that there are Zen Buddhists who ridicule "dead sitting" and the dispassionate life, and June McDaniel similarly displays the importance of emotion in Bengali life. Leroy Rouner defends the importance of ecstasy in every culture as an emotional form of transcendence, and other contributors defend the importance of both compassion and dispassion whether East or West. In Europe, that passionate movement that, in the early nineteenth century, received the name "romanticism" has its counterparts throughout the Western philosophical tradition, in Heraclitus and, even before him, in the various cults of Dionysus. David Hume (1975), in the middle of the Enlightenment, uttered the shocking pronouncement that "reason is, and ought only to be the slave of the passions." G. W. F. Hegel (1953) famously insisted that "nothing great is ever accomplished without passion" (as did Kant before him), and Nietzsche (1967b), a philosopher who in many ways belies the dichotomy between East and West, also attacks the distinction between reason and the passions: "as if every passion did not contain its own quantum of reason," he argues in his notes in *The Will to Power*.

The essays in this volume represent a dozen or so different attempts to go beyond both the false geographical divisions that separate us from other cultures (all but two of the authors are white North Americans) and the false antagonism between reason and the passions. Purushottama Bilimoria opens the question with one of the classic tales of the *Mahabharata*, already twisting the distinction between reason and passion, duty and feeling. Mary Bockover uses China as an example of a culture in which the subjectivity-objectivity distinction, and therefore the reason-passion dichotomy, play little or no philosophical or practical role. Chad Hansen joins veteran Sinologist A. C. Graham here in teasing out the language of feelings in ancient China, replaying some of the classic disputes between Confucianism and Taoism on the nature of desire. Joel Kupperman also turns to China and Confucianism in this volume, but with an eye on a special notion of "altruism," which he compares and contrasts with seemingly similar notions in Western ethics. Once again, the reason-passion dichotomy turns out to be much less important than the structural similarities of very different philosophies, in this case having to do with various and competing versions of "compassion" and "indifference." The question is, How similar are these apparent structural similarities? What are the conceptions of a person and his or her relation to other people that provide the ethical framework for these emotional structures? Catherine Lutz takes us to a very different kind of culture, neither East nor West, the Ifaluk of the South Pacific islands. She discusses in this volume a seeming equivalent of compassion, the emotion known as *fago*. But as she has shown elsewhere (Lutz 1988), the Ifaluk emo-

tional world is constructed quite differently from our own, and the translation of
this one emotion word (and the understanding of the emotion) carries us deep
into the problem of cross-cultural comparison and understanding and social
construction theory of emotions. Emotions, according to this view, are locally,
culturally, and contextually constituted, and there is no reason—certainly no *a
priori* reason—to suppose that emotions are the same the world over. Leroy
Rouner, on the other hand, stresses here what he takes to be a universal (and
uniquely) human emotion, ecstasy, or being "beside oneself," a form of self-
transcendence. Finally, Joel Marks bravely defends an old philosophical ideal,
the ideal of *dispassion*. This is an interesting, not to say ironic, climax to a
book on the passions. But as a defender of the passionate life, I shall eventually
have to take on Marks as my mark. In what follows, however, I will try to
build on—as well as challenge—what he and Roger Ames have put together
before me.

In place of the false antagonism between reason and the passions, other distinctions emerge from these papers which are more learned, more promising,
and more tantalizing. Some concern internal cultural divisions, such as the difference between northern and southern and pre-Han and post-Han China;
between Taoism, Confucianism, and Buddhism; between different areas and
philosophies of India and different schools of Zen Buddhism in Japan. Some
concern truly cross-cultural comparisons—for instance, Graham Parkes's comparison of Nietzsche and Hakuin, Bilimoria's discussion of Jeffery Masson's
application of psychoanalysis to Vedanta, Kupperman's comparisons of moral
sentiment theory, Buddhist "indifference," and utilitarianism along with Hume,
Kant, and Confucius. Other distinctions and discussions concern the nature
and status of the emotions themselves, between different though seemingly
related passions—anger, faith, love, compassion, and ecstasy in various societies. In every society, some emotions are prized and honored, while others are
feared, condemned, or held in contempt. Some emotions are considered violent,
dangerous, and disruptive, while others are considered essential social virtues.
Indeed, in place of the general dispute between reason and emotions and the
kind of questions typically asked of the emotions, the strategy that seems to
emerge from this book is rather to ask, Which emotions, when and where?—for
there is no reason to think that emotions are all the same or can be treated *sui
generis* under a single, universal philosophical or psychological category.

Before we can begin to talk about the cross-cultural comparison of emotions, we first have to be clear about what we mean by "emotion," what family
or family resemblance is intended or referred to, and what is to be included and
what is not. It would seem that any question about emotion must initially come
to terms with the fact that emotions are, first of all, in some sense to be defined,
"subjective" phenomena, "in the mind" of the subject, though, to be sure, this
language of "mind" and "subject" is itself culture specific and, even within

that culture, often viewed with suspicion.[3] What this means, in one common formulation, is that while we can observe the emotional behavior of others and listen to their verbal expressions and reports of their emotions, we cannot observe the emotion itself. That we can do, in some equally odd and hard-to-analyze sense, only for ourselves, in one's own case. With regard to our friends, family, and neighbors, this inaccessibility of others' emotions, contrasted with the immediate accessibility we have to our own, presents something of a philosophical puzzle. In fact, of course, it sometimes seems that we recognize other people's emotions better than they do, and they, ours; this, in itself, points to a serious problem in the common equation of subjectivity and accessibility (Bockover). With people from a very different culture, however, the inaccessibility of emotion presents us with a genuine dilemma. How do we interpret their behavior, their expressions, and their reports without simply assuming (in the absence of evidence) that their feelings are the same as ours? How do we extrapolate from what we see and hear to what they feel, to the emotion itself? How would we recognize or understand differences? Anthropologists, long faced with this problem, have adopted a number of not always satisfactory solutions. Some have employed a "method" of empathy, getting to know the language and living in the culture.[4] Others, of a more positivist bent of mind, restrict themselves to reporting what they can observe, abstaining, as much as possible, from interpretation and extrapolation.[5] In practice, probably all anthropologists—and all of the rest of us, too—employ a mix of both methods, translating, observing, interpreting and extrapolating from our own experience, and forming one tentative hypothesis after another, drawing analogies to our own experience and trying to imagine experiences very different from our own. Of course, translation itself represents a deep problem in such matters, although perhaps not so inscrutable or "indeterminate" as the noted philosopher (and accomplished practical linguist) W. V. O. Quine (1960) once argued. What one people mean by a word that we (or they) learn to translate (into English) as "anger" or "love" or "ecstasy" may nevertheless be quite a different phenomenon. Is Tahitian *riri* really a fair translation of *anger*, and is *angst* adequately translated by *anguish*, *anxiety*, or *angoisse*? (It is worth noting that both American and French existentialists prefer to leave it in the German.) What we have to translate, in effect, is not a word but a whole culture, to see how an emotion—and the name for that emotion—fits into the systematic worldview, language, and way of life of the society. I am reminded of what the late J. L. Austin (1956-7) said of philosophical analysis in general: that it was essentially a form of "linguistic phenomenology" (which, he objected, "is quite a mouthful"). I have at hand no more digestible phrase, except perhaps the newly popular and somewhat New Age term "holism," but it is this global, systematic view of emotions, cultures, and language that I want to endorse and develop here.

In the context of a cross-cultural comparison, "emotion" is not an ultimately defensible category, or what Aristotle called a "natural kind." The word
emotion shifts its meaning from age to age, culture to culture—even where
the language remains ostensibly the same. The word *emotion* itself has been in
common use (as opposed to the older word, *passion*) for only a few hundred
years, and what counts as an emotion (and what does not) also changes. To be
sure, some emotions—anger and fear, for example—seem to be more or less
regulars. But others—especially various desires and sentiments and many of the
virtues and vices such as generosity, kindness, lust, and greed—wander in and
out of the category, depending not on the whim of philosophers, psychologists, or dictionary makers but on larger social and ethical issues. Sufficiently
important passions—for example, love, faith, and hope, in traditional Christian
theology—have been deemed too important to be counted as mere emotions.
(Indeed, the argument that even ordinary secular love is not an emotion but
something much more is a thesis that remains popular among philosophers
and social theorists.⁶) Indeed, the great rationalist Kant faced something of a
problem along these lines himself, for having dismissed all sentiments and
other "inclinations" from serious consideration in the estimation of moral
worth, he then found himself somewhat at a loss as to how to understand
"respect" and even "the sense of duty."⁷ Insofar as the passions have not been
demeaned, they have been given an auxiliary or oppositional role in ethics.
Thus, Aristotle and Confucius counted "appropriate" and "modest" emotion as
virtue, while Hume made the "moral sentiments" the core of his ethical theory.
It is said that Buddhism rejects the emotions—along with desire—in all forms,
but, as several of the essays in this volume take pains to point out, Buddhism
rejects only certain kinds of emotions, particularly those we would be prone to
call "passions" or "cravings." Again, it is not the nature of emotion that matters
so much as the nature and place of particular (kinds of) emotions in a particular worldview.

The reason for the shifting of meaning and status of various particular
emotions (and non-emotions) has much to do with the all-important relationship
between emotions and ethics.⁸ Emotions are not just disruptions of our otherwise calm and reasonable experience; they are at the very heart of that experience, determining our focus, influencing our interests, defining the dimensions
of our world. "The depressed man lives in a depressed world," wrote Wittgenstein (who evidently knew that world rather well). So, too, all emotions define
a world, or worlds, whether frightful, joyful, or infuriating. Emotions are not
just phenomena to be analyzed and understood; they lie at the very heart of
ethics, determining our values, focusing our vision, influencing our every judgment, giving meaning to our lives.⁹

In what follows, I want to address the general problem of understanding
emotions in a cross-cultural context, paying particular attention to the authors,

essays, and cultures in this volume. To be sure, an adequate commentary would require a book in itself, but it is not my intention—for the most part, anyway—to engage in direct debate with Joel Marks and his contributors, except, of course, where the bait is irresistible. I have tried to use what I learned from them at every opportunity. Their familiarity and knowledge of other cultures is exactly what I need, old stay-at-home that I am, to address the various problems of mutual emotional understanding. But first, let's explore the possibility that the cross-cultural dilemma described above is not a dilemma at all—namely, the possibility that emotions (or at least the most "basic" emotions) are, after all, universal human phenomena, invariant from culture to culture, and that the various names for emotions in different cultures are therefore not prone to any extraordinary translation or mutual-understanding problems.

1. THE UNIVERSALITY OF EMOTION

Suppose that it were true that "deep down," as they say, all people are essentially alike. The metaphor "deep down" is itself tantalizing, as are a great many metaphors concerning the emotions, but we understand here clearly enough what is being asserted. Stripping away the various layers of language and culture, different terms, different modes of expression, different idioms, different concepts and contexts, different religious beliefs and practices, different rules about property and propriety, different conceptions of right and wrong, different social "temperaments" that are cultivated through breeding and upbringing, we are left with a being that is, in some sense, perfectly "natural," who has only the wiring and the wisdom that God or nature provided, and whatever emotions remain have no longer been determined by the particularities of this or that culture or society. This very Rousseauian picture of "natural" human existence is, of course, itself the subject of one of the great philosophical debates of all times. It begins before Socrates and continues with the Stoics. It commands center stage in Hobbes, in Locke, in Mandeville, in Hume, and in Rousseau. It continues in Sartre, Levi-Strauss, and the postmodernists. Are our "natural" emotions, as Hobbes contended, essentially selfish and inconsiderate, or are they as benign and sympathetic as Rousseau and the sentimental capitalist guru Adam Smith suggested? But, however we answer this question, it is hard to get rid of the presumption that there is *some* natural repertoire of emotions that constitutes "human nature," some set of "basic" emotions which, like the raw materials of an artist or a chef's ingredients, can then be combined and cultivated to provide the rich variety of cultures and temperaments in the world. But though we may need to analyze these final products in terms of a particular culture, we do not need to engage in any particularly difficult linguistic or anthropological maneuvers to understand and "empathize" with the basic emotions, those that we all share, according to this "universalist" view. It is easy enough to find persuasive examples: children running through the streets in terror away from an armed invader, a friend or family member betrayed and furious, two friends or a family united after a long and painful separation. But it is by no means obvious, first of all, how much of our emotional lives can be so explained, nor is it obvious that these emotional scenarios are, indeed, the same, so summarily described. Why should we not assume that there are subtle—and not so subtle—differences between the emotions of one culture and those of another, even in such scenarios; and why should we deny that, on further examination, such examples may, in fact, present the most striking challenges to our understanding?

The arguments for this universalist thesis, however, do not always turn on such examples but rather tend to be *a priori*, that is, simply presumed from the outset rather than put to the test, subjected to exploration, experiment, and analysis, opened to question, to scrutiny, to skepticism and self-criticism. (It should be noted that the contrary thesis, that emotions necessarily vary from culture to culture, has also been taken as an *a priori* presumption, particularly among anthropologists and those philosophers who sometimes call themselves "relativists.") I have often made a plea for empiricism in these matters, that is, simply to say, for an open mind.[10] Whether or not there is anything that deserves to be called "human emotion" (and not just in the trivial sense, that some humans have them) is something to be found out, something to be investigated, whether or not a final theory of "human nature" will ever be available. The question will always be open: Do we in fact understand? It happens to most of us, from time to time, that we momentarily realize how little we understand even those closest to us. That is a heuristic (not to mention therapeutic) experience, and we should certainly keep it in mind whenever we are tempted to assert, with unquestioning confidence, what people in other cultures do or must feel.

The *a priori* assumption that people are "deep down" all the same is typically grounded in one or another quite reasonable thesis about human nature, although, to be sure, the assumption itself does not always or even usually seek such grounding. The first is the discovery (now so well established by science that it does deserve to be taken as a well-grounded assumption) that all psychological phenomena, the emotions and emotional behavior included, depend on the activity of the central nervous system and, more generally, human physiology. We sometimes forget how long-coming and difficult this discovery has been, and how far we still have to go before we understand the details of this systematic dependency. But even if our knowledge of the details and the mechanisms of neuropsychology is still in its infancy, the fact of the relationship (or many relationships) between the emotions and the body is undeniable. And since human brains and bodies are, from a biological point of view, all pretty much the same, one might conclude that human emotions are the same as well, the world over.[11]

Contra Freud, however, biology is not destiny. Culture counts, too. As Rousseau (1983) pointed out in his own attempt to discern the nature of "natural man," insignificant biological differences may nevertheless constitute very significant social and cultural differences. And if there are significant and seemingly inborn differences in abilities and temperaments as well, even between members of the same family, why should we not suppose—indeed, how can we possibly deny—that there may well be systematic and significant emotional differences between families, groups, tribes, and whole societies? Neither nature nor nurture need be in question here, for emotional temperament may well be (and no doubt is) the result of both genetics and upbringing. A culture may amplify (or it may suppress) one or another aspect of its emotional temperament. It may, for example, encourage displays of anger or grief or affection, or it may discourage not only the displays but the emotions themselves. In neurological terms, there seems to be little doubt that although the "reptilian" and other "lower" parts of the brain may be essential to emotional excitation, the cerebral hemispheres are also involved in any emotion or passion worthy of the name. Concepts and learning, not just simple "arousal," are part and parcel of every emotion.[12]

To make matters even more complicated, the brain itself develops with age and experience, and it seems to be premature, if not splitting neurons (as well as abusing the now-prevalent computer metaphor), to debate whether these organic changes involve the "hardware" or "software" of the brain. But this is, in effect, to say that it is by no means clear what is meant by "the brain." The brain is not just a network of neurons but an organic, dynamic, functional part of a larger system misleadingly called "the body" which cannot, without severe paradox and confusion, be readily distinguished from the person, the living, feeling human being. Thus, in traditional Cartesian terms, it is by no means clear what is intended as "the body." It is not a dead but a living body, the body of a person. It is not just the subject of physiology but of psychology, sociology, and philosophy, too. Does it make any sense to talk of "pure physiology" where the emotions are concerned? I would argue that it does not, and as we interpret and embellish (but do not ignore) the findings of the psychoneurologists, what must be added to the workings of the central nervous system are not only such basic terms of psychology as "stimulus" and "reinforcement" but the exigencies of the context, the terms of the culture and even the concepts of philosophy and religion. Buddhists refer to "the subtle body," an ideal body that is constructed through meditation and philosophy, and recent attention to alternative medical practices has made it quite evident that there are "maps" of the body—in terms of *chakras*, *chi*, and energy flows—that are quite at odds with the black-and-white drawings of *Gray's Anatomy*. Thus, there are alternative understandings of the body and biology, and with these alternatives our understanding of the emotions may vary as well. But the important point is that biology does not entail the universality of emotions. If anything, biology would seem to establish the possibility of in-born temperamental differences between races, societies, in-breeding groups, families, and individuals. It could be true that all human beings except Clint Eastwood are hard-wired to panic under certain terrifying circumstances, but very little of cross-cultural interest follows from this. We want to know, What circumstances? How much panic, and how does this differ from fear? To what extent can this in-born tendency be overcome, through education, training, practice, or experience? Is panic acceptable in that society and those circumstances, or is the panic accompanied by shame or humiliation? Is the panic understood as a "natural" reaction or as a weakness? Is it experienced as an involuntary seizure or as a voluntary albeit spontaneous act?

Second, and quite apart from the more scientifically exciting questions of neuropsychology, there are the undeniable similarities of what has been called "the human condition." It is a simple fact about all of us that we are born into families; that we are initially helpless and extremely vulnerable; that we are prone to pain, injury, illness; that we need food, water, sleep, air to breath, and protection from the harsher elements of nature. Moving quickly into the realm of philosophy, we are all going to die, and we know that we are going to die. We all have a need, like Harlow's monkeys, to be held, to be touched; and, as it happens, the continuity of the family and the species depends on reproduction, which is prompted by its own often mysterious (and sometimes dangerous) biological urges to engage in that potentially delightful and much-embellished activity we summarize as "sex." Although courtship rituals, sexual mores, marriage, and the nature of the family vary dramatically from culture to culture, there are certain basic and possibly immutable structures that are essential to all cultures, even in the face of *in vitro* and surrogate pregnancy, "alternative" family structures, and various sexual revolutions and counterrevolutions. But what these structures might be, and how "immutable" they are, is a matter of considerable political as well as biological debate, and it has been persuasively argued that, in the midst of such controversies, there can be no neutral or "objective" research or arguments. More generally, all human beings seem to be more or less endowed with the ability to think, imagine, and abstract; and, on the basis of these biologically remarkable facilities, cultural plasticity has become the essential mark of the human, furthered and articulated by the various religions and philosophies. But there again, the interesting and by no means easy question is the extent to which these all have some common core, albeit nothing more than the nature of thinking, imagination, and abstraction as such, and there is always the temptation to elevate one form of thinking, imagining, and abstracting as the highest, truest, or only acceptable form. This, of course, is at the very heart of much of the discussion and debate that has taken place in this book and in comparative philosophy in general. But the idea that there is some core of conditions, however minimal, that is both universally and distinctively human seems beyond reproach.

That acknowledged, however, we once again face potential and frequent abuses and faulty inferences from this basic knowledge. It is too quickly concluded that because some of these features of the human condition are universal, many or all are universal. From the fact that one-on-one male-female copulation is (for the time being) more or less essential to human reproduction, and from the fact that human infants are extremely helpless and must be raised by adults, it is too quickly concluded that what is oddly known as the "nuclear family" is, as such, one of the essential features of human nature. From the fact that all human beings are capable of abstraction and imagination it is too quickly concluded that human existence has a built-in or readily cultivated sense of "transcendence," and that "spirituality"—almost always defined in some restricted and sectarian way—is essential to human nature. Even on a more minimal level, the need to eat, for example, allows of only limited universalization. Not only do dietary preferences and prohibitions vary enormously from culture to culture (termites are a delicacy in East Africa; pork is prohibited in Palestine), but nutritional requirements seem to vary enormously, too. The meaning of food and of certain foods also varies, prompting emotional reactions from delight to disgust. True, all human beings need to eat, and our basic biological apparatus is such that the food has to go in one end and waste has to emerge from the other, but around that minimal universality the emotional range of particular practices is remarkable indeed.

In addition to these two theses concerning the biological and basic universality of the human condition, one could elaborate a series of other theories about the alleged universality of (certain) emotions, from evolution and natural selection to the philosophically pretentious notion that one can ascertain the rules and limits of "the human mind" through the investigation of one's own experience, a method now known as "phenomenology."[13] An adequate critique of these views would, again, both require and deserve a book, but I intend to pass over them here. So, too, I will pass over in polite silence the sentimental idea that love is universal and the Hollywood premise that "getting even" is essential to human nature. My point here has simply been to cast some doubt on the idea that the universality of emotions is a thesis so obvious that it can simply be taken for granted, without for a moment suggesting that the opposite thesis, that different cultures *necessarily* have different emotions, is any more plausible.

2. THE SOCIAL CONSTRUCTION OF EMOTIONS

One alternative to *a priori* universalism, which has come into prominence in recent years, goes by the name of "the social construction of emotions" (Harré,

1986).[14] It has been of particular interest, naturally enough, to anthropologists, but it has proved to have appeal to any number of theorists in philosophy and the social sciences as well. It is the theory, as the name implies, that emotions are not "natural," that there is no "essentially human," that emotions are "constructed" within and by a society. As such, of course, this leaves out a great deal. It does not follow, for example, that societies therefore construct emotions differently. Nor does it follow that there are not some emotions, at least, which might nevertheless be the same the world over. Emotions are constructed *out of* something, from raw material that is, first of all, to be found in human experience, in the human body, and in the human condition. Whatever else they may be, emotions are experiences, experiences of circumstances, some of which we share, some of which are distinctively bodily experiences. William James asks us, rhetorically, whether we can imagine anger without shaking and tension, without the "impulse to vigorous action." So, too, we might ask to what extent we can imagine anger in a creature without a body (though, to be sure, we can imagine an infuriated ghost with a merely ghostly body). The question, of course, depends on an answer to our prior question, namely, What is an emotion? If an emotion were essentially a physiological disturbance, the social construction theory would be, at most, a theory about the various ways in which we affect and interpret our bodies, but it could not properly claim to be a social construction theory *of emotion*. If an emotion were nothing else but a socially determined bit of behavior, a specific ritual for specific circumstances, social construction theory would, indeed, tell the whole story, but virtually everything that has been touted under the banner "the subjectivity of emotion" would have to be abandoned. But mere behavior is not what is at issue here. What the social construction theory sees quite clearly (and what too many physiological theories ignore) is the extent to which *concepts* play an essential role in our emotions and our emotional life. Concepts, however crude, are in evidence in even the most primitive emotional reactions. These concepts may be the product of social learning and sophisticated religious or philosophical teaching, but they may also be a basic component of the human condition—the concept of food, the concept of exhaustion, the concept of kin, the concept of death. If the physiological theory tends to go wrong in putting too much emphasis on biology and not enough on psychology and sociology, social construction theory may too easily be tempted to overemphasize socially learned concepts and to ignore or neglect the possibility of universal concepts based on the contingencies of the human condition as such.

In a later section, I will argue that an emotion consists, at least in part, of ways of consciously being in the world, which I call (for reasons I will detail) "judgments." Judgments require concepts, and the question, then, is, What concepts are required for emotions, or, rather, what concepts are required for which particular emotions? Philosophically sophisticated emotions such as angst and anguish, passionate faith, moral indignation, and outrage against injustice seem to require quite complex philosophical concepts (of nothing-ness, transcendence, morality, and justice, respectively). Other emotions, notably those which one can readily imagine expressed in the eager, disap-pointed, or anxious face of one's dog, obviously require much less sophisticated concepts. Which of these more common concepts are socially constructed, socially learned, socially based? Certainly not all of them. It is an old philo-sophical prejudice, happily now on the wane, that insists that only human beings—that is, only beings with a language—have concepts. This confusion is, I believe, part and parcel of the confusion of consciousness with self-con-sciousness and of selfhood with self-reference and self-reflection. But in any case, it seems obvious, both to me and to Professor Rouner's students, that dogs, for example, make distinctions, recognize people and objects, and have some sense of themselves, which is to say, they employ concepts, even self-ref-erential concepts (Leroy Rouner, this volume). But, of course, not all concepts precede language. The concepts of mathematics (as opposed to the recognition of certain patterns, which dogs can demonstrably do) require language, a lan-guage acquired by human beings only over a sizable stretch of time and con-siderable ingenuity. Certain (but by no means all) self-references and concepts of self require a language, and much of what we call self-consciousness requires a very sophisticated language with various syntactic and metalinguistic prop-erties. Not every human language has these properties, or, in any case, they vary considerably. Most philosophical concepts, from death to divinity, require lan-guage—and what a language! As Nietzsche (1954) once wrote, "I am afraid we are not rid of God because we still have faith in grammar." And just as moral indignation requires the concepts of morality, romantic love, I would suggest, requires not only the language but the narrative of romance. My dogs may adore me, but they do not, cannot, alas, love me. No loss to them. Only to me, for only I, not they, know the language and the concept of love.

What concepts are required for which emotions? And what concepts require culture as their prior condition? There are both conceptual and content issues here. Many emotions—indeed, I would argue, most human emotions—presuppose participation in society, established relationships, and open possi-bilities for relationships that can then be fulfilled, promised, violated, or betrayed. Shame is an obvious example, but there are hundreds, if not thou-sands, more. One cannot feel shame or be ashamed outside of the context of society (although one can, of course, feel or be ashamed when no one else is around. So, too, for embarrassment). One cannot feel any of those emotions of love, loss, or nurturing (cf. Ifaluk *fago*, illustrated so well in Catherine Lutz's paper) unless there are others upon whom to bestow that love, others to lose, others to nurture. But there are also questions about how one might *learn* this or that concept, possibly apart from the tutelage of a culture. Could one master an emotion by mastering the language and concepts of a society from an anthropology book and a language-learning tape? Could there be an anthropological Robinson Crusoe who makes up a language and even learns to identify and reflect upon his own emotions? What emotions would he come to have, "naturally," as it were? Fear, to be sure, frustration, and therefore possibly anger. Would he feel for his island that special form of nostalgia (a wholly inadequate translation) acknowledged by the Japanese, for his "home"? Could he conceivably be embarrassed or humiliated? Would he suffer from a lack of love? The question is, what is needed to learn what one must learn (if one must learn it) in order to have certain emotions? Does a person learn to be angry? Does one learn to feel affection? Infants deprived of hugging will not easily learn to hug later on. Birds deprived of other birds will not learn to sing, and chimpanzees deprived of other chimpanzees will not learn how to mate. How much of our emotional life proceeds by imitation, by emulation, through the internalization of concepts which can be taught only by the culture of which they are a part? "Assertiveness training" programs teach people how to get angry (or do they just "give them permission" to do so?). Romantic love is learned from books, movies, and television, but what could be learned without them? The questions here are as subtle as they are difficult, and the idea of socially constructed emotions, like the idea of natural emotions, is not a fit subject for dogmatic pronouncements.

It is not as if, deprived of a culture, we can simply assume that a person would be deprived of all experience and all emotion. Clifford Geertz (1977), one of the most illustrious anthropological defenders of social construction theory, has notoriously proclaimed that "a human being, deprived of culture, would be a helpless, pathetic creature." But what would such an experience be like, without cultural categories, without learned concepts, without names? What would such purely "natural" emotions be like? Fear, we can be confident, would still be part of the repertoire of emotions. Once attacked by a bear or a jaguar, we can be pretty sure that most of us would feel fear at the approach (or the thought) of another such incident. Desire, at least desire based on the appetites, would be there, too. But would there be anything like what we call "sexual desire," or even the possibility of jealousy?[15] Could there be anger (as opposed to mere frustration) without the concepts of blame and responsibility, seemingly social (if not also cultural) concepts? Moral indignation, in the absence of moral principles, would seem to be out of the question. Could there be shame or guilt or pride? Would there be virtues or vice? Again, these are questions that are difficult (though much fun) to answer, but the minimal point I want to make is that, just as there is little justification for simply assuming that emotions are indeed natural and universal as well, there is equally little justification for assuming that emotions are *nothing but* the product of society.

It is hard to believe that there would be no emotions that are shared by every society, despite the cultural embellishments and interpretations, perhaps, and expressed in different ways and subject to different belief systems. We have already suggested several candidates for such emotions. Fear is an obvious candidate, as are some sort of affection or other "attachment" and kinship emotions, although even here we have to appreciate just how deeply cultural symbols and interpretations cut into whatever sort of affection we take to be shared. What is meant by "family" varies considerably from culture to culture, and "romantic" love is a quite specifically culturally defined and cultivated emotion. It has recently been argued that even motherly love is a cultural artifact, created and not merely "natural," and some sociobiologists and many cynics have long made the same point about fatherhood. Compassion, or some sort of distanced concern for others, seems to be the presupposition of every society, and it is built into virtually every philosophy. (Thus the near universality of the so-called Golden Rule.) Joel Kupperman's arguments here would seem to point in this direction, and so, too, the assorted discussions of related emotions in other essays, notably Lutz's discussion of Ifaluk *fago* and de Silva's and Marks's discussions of compassion in Buddhism. Ecstasy is also a possibility, as Leroy Rouner suggests, but here we meet a rather interesting complication of the social constructionist thesis. Ecstasy would seem to be an emotion whose nature is precisely to cut through or leap beyond the ordinary social-emotional constructions, and its universal nature—if such can be defended—might therefore consist in its transcendence of each and every social scheme. Even so, however, the nature of that transcendence would itself have to be expressed in terms of the standards of the culture, so that ecstasy in Buddhism would be very different from ecstasy in Christianity or from the ecstasy involved in a great scientific discovery or winning the Olympic 400-meter run. The ecstasy of orgasm, which is obviously not universal (or for that matter singular) even in its crudest description, shifts both its significance and its essential nature depending on the cultural mores, myths, and prohibitions surrounding its execution.

Insofar as an emotion is constructed within and by a society, what is it that is constructed? An emotion, I suggested (and it is generally accepted, except by particularly rabid behaviorists), is first and foremost a mode of experience. This does not mean that it has to be acknowledged, named, or reported. This does not mean that the subject knows better than anyone else what he or she is feeling. This does not mean that the subject of the emotion even knows "what is going on." What it does mean is that the subject must be conscious, that is, must be experiencing something, and that something must be defined, in part, in terms of the emotion.[16] But how does the social construction view capture the experience of emotion? It is not that it cannot explain the nature of emotional experience, and I will argue (as I have argued) that the social construction view provides many of the tools we need in order to understand how we come to have the emotions that we do have. But the social construction view as such too easily tends to be agnostic on the question of consciousness and, accordingly, to ignore the experience (the "phenomenology") of emotions.

What worries me in particular is the tendency of some social constructionist views to lean sympathetically toward behaviorism, as if what is learned is merely a pattern of social behavior, not a mode of personal experience. To be sure, the two are intricately intertwined, as William James so clearly recognized. Unfortunately, James confused and conflated his insights concerning the intimate interrelation between emotions and expressive behavior with a very different physiologically based view of emotions.[17] The question—which was not a question for James—was whether the emotion is also, indeed essentially, an *experience*. For James (and for me), the answer is an obvious Yes. One cannot be content with a theory that explains only the learning of emotional behavior (and the conditions and contexts in which it is appropriate to display that behavior) but does not account for the experiential content of emotion.

All of which brings us back to the question of cross-cultural comparisons of emotion. What the social construction theory does very well for us is to remind us to let go of *a priori* prejudices about the universality of emotions and to look carefully at the different contexts and causes, the different conditions, the different expressions of emotion, the different emotions that are "appropriate" in different societies. But once one subtracts all of those differences, what is left? One is tempted, at least, to say the emotion—the emotional experience—itself. But the social construction theory provides us with an excellent way of approaching the problem of mutual understanding without falling into the pitfalls and *a priori* presuppositions of "empathy." It is not enough to empathize with people from a very different culture. One has to know the rules, the conditions, the mores, the local myths and popular expectations. One has to understand the society and not merely the emotion.

3. CONTEXTUAL BEHAVIORISM

The reaction against the seemingly commonsense view that emotions are feelings (supplemented with one or another physiological theory) came to define much of the twentieth century. In the name of "science," the polemical view commonly known as "behaviorism" rejected all references to unmeasurable "ghostly" entities, and insisted, with some warrant, that our knowledge of emotions could be understood only as the knowledge of public, observable phenomena. At its extremes, behaviorists denied the existence of anything like private mental events and ignored the "black box" of the brain, which was then (and is still) largely unknown, at least so far as the details of behavior are concerned. Emotions—insofar as they survived at all—were said to be nothing but patterns of behavior. Some behaviorists postulated innate, universal emotions (e.g., Watson), but others did not, leaving the question open. But, as scientists, the behaviorists imposed a heavy demand on their colleagues in the field, notably the anthropologists, who were hence instructed to take careful notes on the overt behavior of their subjects but abstain entirely from "meaningless" speculation about what went on "inside the heads" of those they studied. The cross-cultural comparison of emotions gained a great deal in return for this loss. The cross-cultural comparison of emotions becomes the cross-cultural comparison of behavior. "Empathy" is not required. Indeed, sensitivity is optional. What is required is careful observation and detailed reporting. "Data!" What seems to get lost, we woolly-headed humanists continue to insist, is the experience of emotion and, with it, the meaning of emotion. Whether it is a social construction (i.e., a pattern of behavior taught and reinforced by a particular society) or a universal natural pattern of behavior (hard-wired, perhaps instinctual, and reinforced by the contingencies of the environment), an emotion becomes *nothing but* a pattern of behavior, which is more or less useful or functional within a larger pattern of collective social behavior.

Philosophers, most of them anyway, were not quite so adamant about being "scientific."[18] While they, too, insisted that we all but ignore the Cartesian "inner workings" of the mind (what Gilbert Ryle sarcastically called "the ghost in the machine"), they did not wholly deny the existence of the obvious, namely, mental events. Thus Ryle offers us his famous list of mental ingredients: "thrills, twinges, pangs, throbs, wrenches, itches, pricklings, chills, glows, loads, qualms, hankerings, curdlings, sinkings, tensions, gnawings and shocks" (1949, 83-84). He then summarizes the emotions as "agitations" (Ryle 1949, 104). But although the "contents" of the mind and experience remain, they have lost all significance, all meaning. A throb or an itch is not an emotion. It need not even be an aspect of an emotion. If there is any significant phenomenon worthy of the name "emotion," it cannot be on a par with this pitiful list of twitches and the like. An emotion is, rather, a significant pattern of behavior. Thus, Ryle introduces the notion of a "multitrack disposition," an indefinitely complex cause-and-effect hypothesis that links the ascription of a mental state to predictions ("inference tickets") of various behaviors. In fact, Ryle rarely talks about the emotions, perhaps because they so obviously present a problem for his analysis, but it is clear that, were he to do so, he would say that the ascription of an emotion (the application of an emotion name) is, in every case, a prediction that the subject will behave in certain ways: "If he is so angry, he will surely write to the Chancellor," and so on. In philosophy, as in the social sciences, emotions (and "the mind" in general) tended to lose their "ghostly" character. What had to be ignored on this account, however, is the ascription of emotions to oneself and the experience of emotion, "in one's own case."

The leader of this powerful move in philosophy was the emotionally tortured genius, Ludwig Wittgenstein. One might resist the temptation to speculate about the differences in analysis proposed by a distinguished Oxford don (Ryle), on the one hand, who all but denied the significance (if not also the existence) of emotions, and those proposed by a famously neurotic Viennese Romantic, on the other, who clearly had enormous respect for the emotions. Wittgenstein refused to render them incomprehensible, however, which he saw as the inevitable result of conceiving of them as private and strictly "inner" events, and he insisted on viewing them as part of social life, as socially constituted, if not socially constructed. The pattern of behavior that is an emotion is significant only because of its role in a culture, a "form of life," according to Wittgenstein, and whether or not the pattern is inborn or learned, peculiar to some societies or common to all of them (and Wittgenstein says little to indicate whether he believes or cares one way or the other on either question), the *significance* of such behavior depends on the culture. One need not deny experience or the "inner" or "subjective" dimension of emotion to insist, as a matter of logic, that the emotion itself must be a public event and identified according to criteria that may or may not be accessible to the subject who has the emotion.[19]

We might call the perspective that develops from this starting point "contextual behaviorism." It is not committed to any particular ontology of emotions. It need not be committed to any particular view on the innateness or cultivated character, the particularity or universality of emotion (or particular emotions). It need not be so restricted, as in conscientiously "scientific" behaviorism, to merely recording the data and abstaining from interpretation. What is required is knowledge of (or sensitivity to) the context and, in particular, the cultural context. One has to know the rules, the roles, the folkways, including the knowledge of when to be (or not to be) solicitous or offended or defensive or affectionate or prideful. In one's own immediate society, such knowledge is (for the most part) simply shared. But as cultural differences accumulate (your neighbor has a different religion, different national origins, different politics, different sexual orientation, different educational background), room for misunderstanding increases considerably. Much of what is usually called "empathy" might better be called "learning to participate" in an alternative personal, cultural, historical, or philosophical framework.

Catherine Lutz, in her description of her own embafflement, trying to understand the emotional behavior and vocabulary of a very different society, describes for us the tools she needed to achieve that understanding, namely, a piecemeal, very day-to-day accounting of the variety of situations and perspectives in which the emotion in question got expressed, referred to, talked about. With such careful detail, the temptation to simply find "the closest equivalent" in English and our own experience is thwarted at every turn. So, too, in a very different way, Bilimoria's quotation and slow dissection of a particularly significant crisis in classic Hindu literature maps out the dimensions of an emotional confrontation whose nature could not possibly be familiar to most Western readers. To understand your Jamaican neighbor's panic about losing a tooth and not being able to find it, perhaps you need to learn something about certain common Jamaican superstitions, and whether or not you come to believe them, at least you will be able to understand why he should be so upset about something which seems (to you) without significance, the mere inconvenience and expense of having to go back to the dentist. If you do not understand why your Japanese visitor is so visibly shaken by your asking him whether or not he is hungry, perhaps you should learn something about Japanese etiquette and the utter inappropriateness of such questions. To understand the suicidal behavior of the Chinese student who failed your course, perhaps you should learn something about the pressure he feels from the family, that sense of disgrace which, perhaps unfortunately, is virtually unknown to most other American students. If you don't understand why your African-American co-worker gets so indignant when you continue to use the word *Negro*, perhaps you should learn something about the psychological legacy of slavery in this country and the importance of group autonomy—minimally, the right of a people to name and identify themselves. According to the contextual behaviorist, it is neither the pattern of behavior nor the facts of the matter that are in themselves significant. It is the pattern of behavior and the facts of the matter *in context* and *as understood by the participants*. This is, perhaps, considerably weaker than the full-blown social constructionist view but also much richer than the standard behaviorist view. It is, however, the key to a workable theory of the cross-cultural comparison of emotions, precisely because it puts the cultural context and culturally defined experiences in first place, displacing the usual role given to "feelings" and physiology or to mere patterns of behavior, pure and uninterpreted.

It is in this context, I believe, that we might best appreciate the force of Mary Bockover's argument that the Chinese sense of ritual (*li*) wreaks havoc and ultimately undermines the familiar Western distinction between the subjective and the objective. It is a kind of argument that has been made in other ways and other contexts as well,[20] and it does indeed point to the inadequacy—as well as the treacherous ambiguity—of such distinctions in philosophy. In ritual, but not only in ritual, it is the behavior that counts, though not just the behavior. Confucian doctrine—like the Aristotelian doctrine of the virtues in ancient Greece—is rich in admonitions concerning the proper state of mind and appropriate emotions in such behavior. In such behavior, the distinction between what is "in" the mind and what is intended, meant or "ex-pressed" in the behavior is clearly beside the point. What the Confucian insists upon is what the contextual behaviorist hypothesizes, that the total meaning of the performance is to be found in the performance itself, in its proper context, performed in the appropriate manner. There is nothing "left over," no ghostly performance behind the performance, like a dance coach behind the curtain going through the motions with her pupils. But neither could a ritual, or, for that matter, any expressive behavior, be carried out by a robot, "mindlessly." (This common translation of "effortlessness" in ritual and habitual action leads to a great deal of misunderstanding.)

According to the contextual behaviorist point of view, cross-cultural variation in emotion is only to he expected, but on a "deep" level, that of interpretation and significance, not on the "superficial" level of behavior as such. Thus, we can accept and admire Paul Ekman's painstaking research on the apparent universality of facial expressions of emotions without accepting the universalist and reductionist theory such research is sometimes employed to advance. An emotion is not merely its physiological, perhaps hard-wired behavioral expression, and even if its bodily behavioral expression were demonstrably universal, that does not imply that the emotion as such is universal, for the emotion *is* its significance, not just its expression. And once we move away from the minimal expressions of emotion in winces, frowns, smiles, and raised eyebrows—just as we moved from the minimalist sensation aspects of emotion of "thrills, twinges, pangs, throbs, wrenches, itches, pricklings," and so forth—there is by no means any assurance that emotions will be the same the world over and every reason to think that they will not be. In different climates and in the context of different customs and expectations, in political hierarchies, dictatorships, and egalitarian societies, in the light of different religions and philosophies, "the same" acts have very different meanings. A French kiss is an offense in England, and munching a muffin (or anything else) with your left hand in Yemen is considered disgusting. As that great jail-cell anthropologist the Marquis de Sade (1965) pointed out, not without self-justification, in the years just before the Revolution, "How can I still retain any feeling of guilt for having committed . . . a crime in France which is nothing but a virtue in China? Or should I make myself miserable or be prodigiously troubled about practicing actions in France which would have me burned in Siam? . . . Moral science," he concludes, "is simply geography misconstrued."

In every culture, there will be certain situations that will provoke certain emotions. There is no reason whatever to suppose that the same emotions will be provoked by the same circumstances or that every or even any emotion will be provoked in some circumstances in every society. Insofar as an emotion is intricately tied to its interpretative context, there is every reason to suppose that emotions, even seemingly similar emotions, will differ from culture to culture, if only subtly, in ways that are not evident through casual observation or crude or merely thin description. This so-called relativist position needs to be defended against an obvious objection, and it needs to be qualified. The objection is that if emotions differ according to context, and all contexts differ (minimally, they occur in different places, or at different times), then how can anyone ever understand anyone else's emotion, much less the emotion of someone in a very different culture and in wholly unfamiliar circumstances? The proper answer, in fact, will require all of this essay and then some, but the direction of the reply is that while what the cross-cultural comparison of emotions is all about is the recognition of differences, the cross-cultural understanding of emotions is all about commonalities, sometimes gained with great effort (for example, by an anthropologist in the field, a foreign-born Sinologist or Sanskrit scholar). There are always such commonalities, and they provide the "Archimedean point" from which mutual understanding is possible. But this is not necessarily to say, as Richard Rorty has recently argued—for example, in his dialogue with Anindita Balslev (Balslev 1991)—that it is in rather high-level, more or less academic discussions that these commonalities are discovered (see MacIntyre 1992), nor is it to raise the specter of what Quine (1960) has called "radical indeterminacy/untranslatability." No, two perspectives may never match exactly, but, yes, we can and occasionally do understand one another. Contextual relativism is not a form of skepticism, and it is not an excuse for willful ignorance. But it is down in the nitty-gritty of everyday life, not only in the carefully distilled airs of academia, that such mutuality is to be meaningfully sought and found.

What is wrong with the social construction theory of emotions and contextual behaviorism as well is the fact that, for all of their virtues, they tend to leave out subjectivity, "experience." Sometimes, this is just an oversight, a shift in emphasis. Meanings, social construction and contextual behaviorist theorists will rightly argue, are public and not private affairs. More often, the problem is a certain familiar timidity, an unwillingness to talk about one's own experience (for who else's experience would one talk about?), or a hesitancy to discuss something which too readily seems undiscussable, "ineffable." If we can discuss in detail the context, the behavior, and its meanings, then why should we have to talk about anything else, namely, the way it seems (or "feels") to the subject? At the extreme, of course, social construction theory and contextual behaviorism are simply a reintroduction, under a more respectable name, of the old behaviorist prejudice, that not only is there nothing to say about "inner" experiences, but there are no such experiences, and any self-respecting scientist or philosopher would not be caught untenured talking about them. But this is a mistake, for whatever else the emotions may be, however caused, however learned, however cultivated and contextualized, they are, first of all, experiences. And it is to the nature of those experiences that I now want to turn.

4. EMOTIONS AS JUDGMENTS: THE SUBJECTIVITY OF EMOTIONS DEFENDED

What tends to get lost in social construction theory is subjectivity, experience, the irreducibly personal aspect of emotion. A retreat to "feelings" does not answer this objection, for the appeal to feelings then sacrifices not only the sociocultural aspect of emotions but, in an important sense, their personal aspect as well. Insofar as the "feeling" involved in emotion is some set of sensations, notoriously the "Jamesian" affects of physiological disturbances emphasized in the James-Lange theory of the turn of the century, there is nothing particularly "personal" about them, despite their much-celebrated Cartesian properties of immediacy and privacy (although emotions are clearly not, as some Cartesians suggest, either indubitable or unmistakable). What makes an emotion personal is the fact that it is a particular person's outlook on the world, embodying his or her peculiar perspective, background, hopes, fears, and concerns. Love is personal not because one suffers from those sometimes insufferable physical symptoms but because the lover has a very special and personal perspective on the beloved. Anger is personal not because of the sensations of rage but because of the fact that one has been personally offended or frustrated.

To simply repeat what is by now well-charted ground and has been well enough presented by Bilimoria in this volume, emotions are by their very nature *intentional*—they have intentional objects in the world and are not merely "inner" occurrences—and they consist of (among other things) *evaluations*. These evaluations are not just "Yea!" or "Nay!"—as the popular positivist A. J. Ayer once suggested—but they cover a wide variety of judgments, from very personal embarrassment, for example, to the objective ethical judgments involved, notably, in moral indignation. An emotion, in other words, is not a feeling—if by that we mean something concrete and readily specified, as James intended, something which is merely an "affect," a sensation caused by visceral commotion, an "epiphenomenon."[21] But if we mean something more by "feeling" than what is loosely suggested in the colloquial equation "emotions are feelings," then we had better be able to specify what that is.

It is here that I find myself most sharply disagreeing with Mary Bockover, with whose analysis of emotions and rejection of the "subjective/objective" dichotomy I am elsewhere in agreement. It is an old objection, answered many times, that a purely "cognitive" theory seems to leave out the "distinctively affective dimension" of emotions, and, to be sure, there is much to say on this topic. But the one response that serves no purpose other than to hide the issue is to proclaim the necessity of some sort of "emotionally relevant feeling," "affectivity," or "affective tone," for this does no more than repeat the fact to be explained, that it is emotion that interests us and not simply belief. But to understand what a proper response should be, we should go back to the much-demeaned notion of "subjectivity" and ask, with some care, exactly what is meant by the claim that emotions are subjective. In particular, I would like to examine the claim that "emotions are judgments" and explain how such an analysis can clarify the notion of subjectivity and contribute to the cross-cultural and contextual comparison of emotions.

Emotions, I claim, are a species of judgment. There are a number of immediate qualifications, which I have elaborated on elsewhere (Solomon 1988) but will only outline here. First and foremost, judgment is not the same as belief, and the fact that critics typically exchange the one term for the other is responsible for a number of confusions. Second, judgment need not be overly intellectualistic. It need not be conscious, reflective, or articulate. We make kinesthetic judgments all the time, for example, usually without being aware of the fact that we are making them, much less articulating them (to ourselves or to others) as we go. Third, emotional judgments (like kinesthetic judgments) are always evoked *from a perspective*, defined in part (as in kinesthetic judgments) by one's physical embodiment but, more generally, by one's place in the world, one's cultural context, status and role(s) in that cultural context, one's personal situation. In this they are distinctively opposed to mere beliefs, which, in the attenuated if central role they now occupy in cognitive science and philosophy of mind, are distinctively not perspectival nor, properly articulated, indexically located. (Thus, such a routine judgment as "It looks like rain" is reconstructed in terms of "a belief in the probability of rain given evidence e at time t at place p.") Furthermore, judgments are not necessarily (and perhaps not even usually) *propositional*, as beliefs always are.[22] Fearing Satan or being angry at John is not necessarily translatable into any set of propositions of the sort "fearing *that* Satan will . . ." or "angry *that* John. . . ." What importance this may have for cognitive science is beyond the scope of this paper, but the significance for the analysis of emotion can he simply stated. The sorts of judgments that are essentially involved in emotions, as opposed to beliefs and propositions, which they may entail or suggest, are personal, perspectival, and, as such, not particularly vulnerable to the charge that they are merely cognitive and devoid of affect. What do we mean by "affect," assuming that we are not simply retreating to repeating that it is emotion and not belief that concerns us and without treating affect (as Freud sometimes did) as nothing more than the various bodily sensations and other physical feelings that sometimes (but by no means always) accompany emotion? What we mean is that the "feeling" in question is irreducibly personal—that it is not anger that is in question here but *my* anger, that it can be understood only from *my* perspective (or one sufficiently like it), that it involves a matter of considerable concern to me and is not a matter of abstract indifference or mere curiosity. Perhaps I should quickly say that these first-person pronouns are by no means necessarily first-person singular, and it is not unintelligible—and in some societies it is essential—that the first-person role is fulfilled by a "we," an actual or potential group who either could be or are together in the emotional situation specified.

Now we can broach the question of "subjectivity." Bockover is surely right to question the consistency and utility of its role in Western thought, where it has indeed caused much mischief. And she is on an interesting and promising track when she suggests that Confucian philosophy, with its emphasis on *li*, or ritual, easily dispenses with any such concept and its contrast, "objectivity." But I believe that she sells short the notion of subjectivity from the beginning when she not only defines it as "dependent on time, place, context, frame of mind, etc." (reasonable enough though obviously incomplete) but further insists that to know something subjectively means "in a way that presumably cannot be adequately defined or justified for another person for the very reason that it is a product of one's own unique experience." Subjective truths, she tells us, are justified for one person but not for another, whereas something is known objectively if it is known to exist regardless of one's unique individual experience or conception of it. This is overkill, and one might properly object that the contrast Bockover rejects is one of her own creation.

I think she is right on the mark, however, when she complains (against James and the many Jamesians) that "drawing the line between internal and external bodily feelings is actually somewhat arbitrary" and when she brings up the notion of intentionality to further confuse the "inside-outside" dichotomy. But this provides insufficient ammunition against any clever Cartesian, for whom the intentional objects of emotion (and experience in general) are nevertheless *within* the realm of experience (a position rendered far more sophisticated by Kant, Husserl, and the phenomenologists, who seem to be ignored in her account of their subject). The problem is not that subjectivity necessarily entails the rather absurd consequences she cites but that it has proved to be a remarkably fluid concept, not necessarily tied to vulgar Cartesianism and not necessarily dualistic in the rather rigid sense she suggests. "Subjectivity," in the most minimal sense, simply refers to the first person standpoint, "pertaining to the subject and his or her particular perspective, feelings, beliefs, and desires," as she otherwise defines it. It does not follow, however, that a subjective judgment is *about* the subject—that is, that the subject is the object of his or her own emotional judgment—or that it is therefore opposed to objectivity.

With respect to the emotions, Ronald de Sousa (1987) has helpfully outlined four different meanings of subjectivity: There is the response to the phenomenological question, "What is it like?" from the rather ordinary adolescent query "What is it like to be in love?" to the exotic perplexity initiated by Tom Nagel (1974) in his intriguing and now classic essay, "What Is It like to Be a Bat?" Second, there is the tendency to project one's own attitudes upon the world and take these as properties of the world. Here, of course, we enter into some delicate philosophical issues, particularly with the sorts of properties involved in emotions (offensive, threatening, attractive, repulsive, crushing, humiliating, etc.). Is beauty, for instance, only in the eye of the beholder, or must we say by way of contrast that beauty is an objective property of beautiful things, quite apart from any possible perceiver? Both positions are obviously inadequate. Third, there is the notion of relativity, that is, the fact that some properties require a relationship between a subject and the world. Thus, it is an essential property of a great many objects of emotions (qua objects of emotions) that they stand in some significant relation to the subject. Thus, love is subjective in the rather banal sense that the beloved is, in fact, beloved just by virtue of the fact that he or she is loved. Again, there is an enormous philosophical literature here, but it should be obvious that the complexity of such quasi-ontological (phenomenological) issues cannot be simply dismissed by the inadequacy of certain vulgar "inside-outside" distinctions. Fourth, there is the importance of perspective, the fact that all emotions imply a point of view. Jealousy presupposes a certain role for the subject, namely, as involved, as vulnerable, perhaps as having some sort of claim on the coveted object or person (or a person's affections) in question. These four notions of subjectivity are obviously related but clearly quite different, so that some may be in effect when others are not. They can conflict. They can also apply together, as is the case in most instances of emotion. Can we "escape" our subjectivity? Can we avoid the notion of subjectivity? Perhaps. (Heidegger tried to formulate a philosophical language without any such terms or concepts.) But we should be very wary; what will we gain? More important, what might we lose?

To say that emotions are judgments is to say that they are modes of construal, ways of viewing and engaging in the world, including, sometimes, ways of construing the self. Like most judgments (leaving aside that rather problematic set of Kantian *a priori* judgments), they are culturally taught, cognitively framed, but implemented by the individual. They are not opposed to but intrinsic to experience. (Here, a lesson from Kant.) They are not just descriptive but constitutive of the world, *our* world, as fearsome, offensive, appealing, hopeful, painful, devastating, or devastated. They are not (usually) deliberative, and they are often spontaneous, habitual, unthinking, "natural." Several of the authors in this book, in both Buddhist and Confucian traditions, have elaborated on the importance of effortless, "nonaction" behavior, and they have coupled this, in several instances, with a clarification of the proper role of emotions (and desires) in these traditions. Without going into the details of their analyses, it might be helpful to note that emotions, in the view that I have briefly discussed here, are usually the same sort of effortless, spontaneous activity. This means, on the one hand, that they are not full-blooded intentional[23] actions, but, more importantly, they do not just happen to us either. They are an essential part of our repertoire of responses to the world, "subjective," perhaps, in the sense that they are distinctively personal and perspectival in the senses discussed above, but deeply significant nonetheless.

In conclusion, let us return once again to the concept of *li* and its implications for the nature of emotion and subjectivity. As we argued earlier, the concept of *li* does indeed destroy the usual idea that emotions are internally self-contained and only "ex-pressed" in behavior. In ritual, and in many forms of ordinary emotional behavior, the emotion is not simply "expressed," but it can and must be located in the behavior, which is not to say, of course, that it is merely a bodily function without any relation to experience. I have often meditated on the nature of emotion in my dogs, for example, who, when "overjoyed" (ecstatic?) at the modest prospect of a walk in the park or a ride in the car, literally leap in loops and otherwise display (rather than express) their considerable emotion. There the distinction between inner and outer is surely inappropriate, and this is not merely cynical (from *kynikos*, literally "like a dog" in Greek). In any action where we do not ourselves force the separation between the inner and the outer—that is, in our emotional perspective on the world and our behavior in it—that distinction is blown as well. If this is what Bockover has in mind, I believe that she is exactly right.

5. EMOTIONS AND METAPHORS: TAXONOMIES AND THEORIES

I began by denying, rather perfunctorily, that "emotion" names a single coherent category and refers to what Aristotle recognized as a "natural kind." As Amélie Rorty (1982) has argued rather convincingly, concepts of the mind have changed considerably over the ages and, in particular, conceptions of emotion have changed. "Instead of being reactions to invasions from something external to the self, passions became the very activities of the mind, its own motions.... During this period [roughly, from Descartes to Rousseau], emotions also cease to be merely turbulent commotions: among them appear sentiments, ways of feeling pleasures and pains as evaluations, and so as proper guides to action" (Rorty 1982, 159). But if we find such dramatic shifts in the meaning of emotion within our own recent intellectual history, how much more dramatic might the differences be between another culture's categories and our own. And as the conception of emotions in general changes, Rorty reminds us, the prime examples of the passions change, too. Thus we should expect—and we are not disappointed—to find that the primary emotions, those of the greatest concern, vary considerably from culture to culture. And even when those emotions remain superficially the same, they may have very different status and play very different roles in social interactions. Anger, one of our favorite emotions, is virtually nonexistent and, when it appears, is considered childish in some Eskimo cultures.[24] In the United States, anger quickly becomes moral indignation, and we sue. Fear is a vice in a warrior society, but in all too many unfortunate cultures in the modern (and not-so-modern) world, it is the normal condition of life. Family affections, which would seem so essential to virtually every society, are very different depending on the conception of family, the conception of family roles, and so forth. And these conceptions, needless to say, undergo change, both gradual and violent, as in the several social revolutions of the past few decades.

The comparison of categories of emotions is a somewhat neglected subject, in part because of the temptation to rely on one's own language and emotional repertoire as the basis for analysis, in part because of the enormous difficulty involved in mastering a significant number of languages (and forms of life) in order to carry out such comparisons, but, more philosophically, in part because of the mistaken impression that an emotion is some kind of distinctive mental entity. So, too, the various particular emotions are thought to be discrete phenomena. That which may be called "anger" in one society is called "*riri*" in another, but in every case remains the same even if called by different names. According to this common theory (if it deserves to be called a "theory"), "emotion" (or its equivalent in other languages) is the name of a family or genus, and the particular emotions (anger, fear, love, jealousy, pride, envy, resentment, etc.) are various species of emotion. This leads to a quest, classically formulated by William James (1984) in his titular question, "What Is an Emotion?"— namely, how are we to identify that general class of phenomena which includes the particular emotions? But, as the history of the subject so clearly shows, there is no definitive answer to that question. There are, rather, several perspectives, each one convinced of its own "obviousness," depending on the context in which certain paradigm emotions are considered. For example, sometimes emotions are considered in terms of arousal, in which case such emotions as anger and fear are given prominence, but sadness, depression, and quiet affection are conveniently ignored. On the other hand, insofar as the attention is on what have been called "the moral sentiments," sympathy and compassion are well noted, but fury, jealousy, and envy, for instance, are treated as mentally defective distant relatives. In the history of Western ethics, especially that dynamic period that included Kant, Hume, and Adam Smith (the two latter being "moral sentiment theorists"), the contrast between such "inclinations" and "duty"—defined by reason—was central to the debate about the respective roles of reason and the passions in ethics.[25] When emotions are taken to center around attachment, love and affection take center stage, while when desire is emphasized, lust eclipses love, and vengeance tends to replace simple anger as paradigm. Not surprisingly, Buddhist accounts of emotion often take such a perspective, insofar as attachment and desire are of central importance to them. When status becomes the central concern, such "ranking" emotions as contempt and resentment become particularly important (e.g., in the philosophy of Nietzsche). One can variously distinguish between the "calm" and the "violent" emotions (Hume) or the "positive" and the "negative" emotions (Spinoza) and cut the category in any number of ways, but, even within the rather narrowly delimited Western tradition of philosophy, one finds no single adequate criterion or set of criteria to sort out the emotions from the non-emotions. For certain purposes, joy, ecstasy, and depression count; for others they do not. For certain purposes, faith and love are unquestionably emotions; for others they are not. For certain purposes, only the violent upheaval of romantic desperation may count as love, but for others, quiet affection and fidelity may serve far better. For certain purposes, hate and anger may count as paradigms of a "negative" emotion, but in other contexts, they may be quite "positive" and well worth prescribing.[26]

It is in this context that I read with some fascination about the ongoing debate in Sinology about the historical changes in the meaning of *qing*, pursued here by Chad Hansen. I am led to understand that, while "*qing*" has never meant "emotion" or referred to any such category, its meaning nevertheless requires some subtle association with certain emotions. The problem, among others, is that we take the category of emotions to be something settled, and then wonder whether or to what extent the Chinese category corresponds to our own. But, of course, it does not, not only because we do not have any such settled category ourselves but because there is no reason whatever to think that the Chinese concept—which seems to have more to do with what we might call "authenticity" than with a particular realm of "the mind"—bears any interesting relationship to the kind of classificatory category that "emotion" is supposed to be in English.

So, too, I read with fascination the complex comparative taxonomies of emotions and emotion language in Sanskrit and Bengali, in Bilimoria and McDaniel, respectively, and I realize that the seeming complexity has to do not only with my own ignorance of the language but also with my unfamiliarity with the ways in which the emotional world—to make it sound more singular than I should—is carved up and distributed. I recognize the distinction between the rather grand and merely commonplace emotions, but I find much more exotic the three-part distinction in the *Mahabharata* between *sattva* (lightness), *rajas* (movement), and *tamas* (heaviness) as the key attributes of various mental modes. ("Positive" and "negative" are obviously inadequate to represent *sattva* and *tamas*, and our excessive sense of emotions as "inner" tends to block our understanding of *rajas*, which, again, destroys that too-easy dichotomy.) Looking over the specifications and examples of *sattva* (lightness: cheerfulness, joy, equanimity, bliss, dispassion, nobility), *rajas* (movement: egoism, mendacity, lust, anger, desire, vanity, pride, hatred, agony, grief, greed, intolerance), and *tamas* (heaviness: delusion, paranoia, indolence, oversight, nondiscrimination, languor), we realize that the emotional experience of ancient India is being carved up in a way that is not at all familiar to us. Many of the above examples are not even candidates for emotion, according to our more familiar taxonomies, and many of our favorite emotions don't seem to make the list. According to Bilimoria, the ancient psychologist Caraka employs something of a Jamesian model, using pleasure and pain, the harmony and disharmony of bodily humours (flatulence, bile, and phlegm) to characterize and categorize emotions. But though Western physiopsychologists, too, have accounted for the emotions in terms of various "humours" (bile, gall, choler, and spleen, for instance) it should be evident to us that something very different is confronting us here, and it is not simply a different choice of fluids any more than it is a simple problem of translation. The notion of "flatulence" as not only an occasional cause but as the basis of emotion will strike the Western reader as odd, to say the least, and the inclusion as emotions of languor, confusion, deceit, hypocrisy, and doubt and the very idea of lightness and heaviness as major categories of emotion obviously point to a conception of the emotions and their role in human life that is very different from our own.

Such differences in conceptions, categories, images, and life might too easily lead us into the lazy theory of "incommensurability" or sophomoric subjectivism—that is, the impossibility of understanding (and therefore the futility of trying to understand) another culture's emotional life and language. Thus, one might argue that in order to understand Indian emotions, one must first understand and to some extent live as an Indian and practice Indian philosophy. There is something to this—to understand another culture's emotional life, one must, to some extent, steep oneself in that life—but, again, the dangerous implication is that understanding emotions is an all-or-nothing affair: Either one shares an emotional world or one does not. But degrees of understanding are essential to the emotions. If you are grief-stricken because you have lost your pet tarantula, I can understand *how* you feel but not *why* you feel that way (I think about how I would feel if I lost one of my dogs). If a stranger is obviously grief-stricken but I have no knowledge whatsoever why, I nevertheless feel compassion, which presupposes a kind of understanding. We might note, however, that compassion does not require true understanding, that is, actual comprehension of the situation or the ability to empathize with the stranger's suffering. The feeling with which I empathize is my imagined, projected feeling, and not necessarily his feeling at all. Nevertheless, it may be genuine compassion, even if it should be misplaced. So, to say that one would really understand an Indian's feeling only if one understood and, to some extent, lived as an Indian and practiced Indian philosophy is to make an important point but to drastically overstate the case. Furthermore, Bilimoria's list of emotions (mirth, pleasure, sorrow, fear, disgust, sexual attraction) and passions (anger, pride, deceit, greed), McDaniel's list of the five *klesas* (ignorance, desire, hatred, fear, pride), and de Silva's numerous Buddhist enumerations surely remind us of some of our own "lists" (e.g., "the seven deadly sins"); and the advantage of seeing such taxonomies spelled out (as opposed to confronting one emotion at a time or trying to consider the whole noncategory, "emotion") is that we start to get a sense of the configurations and sensibilities that define a people's emotional life. For example, the Jain idea that noninjury is the only positive affect strikes us as extreme, but such a simple formula allows us to get at least a glimpse of what such an emotional life might be like.

The point of this discussion, of course, is neither to bemoan our own ignorance and ethnocentricity nor to make mysterious and rather impossible the very subject of the cross-cultural category of emotions. It is to create a sense of progress, of possibility, from glimmers and glimpses of other emotional worlds to deep insights transported from one culture back to another. But, nevertheless, comparing emotions in a cross-cultural context is not merely a matter of matching emotions and their contexts and explaining (or explaining away) their differences. Sometimes, it is rather an extremely complex and difficult matter of examining two more or less holistic systems.[27] To begin with a rather grand example, compare the ancient Greek vision of the *logos* with the ancient Chinese conception of the *Tao*, and it is obvious that we should expect that the geography of human nature as well as the taxonomy of emotions will be radically different in light of these two very different philosophies. How emotions fit into and relate to the *logos* has been one of the perennial debates of the Western tradition, but one of the features of the debate that has been most noticeable has been the tendency of emotions to appear as disturbances, distractions, and disruptions. In Chinese philosophy, however, it is not clear that anything like this opposition has ever been established, and so the question has focused much more subtly on the cultivation of particular emotions. But consider a seemingly very specific instance of emotion, one that provides a common theme for several of the essays in this book: the emotion (or, perhaps, a set of very different emotions) which is often translated and summarized as "compassion" (for example, *hsin* and *jen* in Chinese and *karuna* in Sanskrit, none of which is strictly conceived as "emotion").[28] I want to consider this "one" emotion in some detail in the section to follow, but first it is necessary to broaden once again the dimensions of our discussion to include not only the emotions (and the cultures and philosophies that cultivate and provoke them) but the concepts and theories within which emotions are articulated, described, and explained.

We do not just have emotions. We also recognize that we have them. We think about them, talk about them, speculate about them, theorize about them. And this is not the activity of social scientists and philosophers alone. We all do it, and our modes of recognition, thought, talk, and theory are then played back into both the language of emotion and, just as importantly, the emotions themselves. Discussion of emotion in general, however, is, for the most part, an academic pursuit, parasitic on the very general noncategory of "emotion" and largely confined to the Western tradition.[29] Most discussions of emotion, in academia as well as in the "real world," tend to focus on particular emotions, and from the discussions in this book it should be clear that these discussions tend to be very different. In our society, conversations often tend to focus on outrage, envy, resentment, and, in a very different mood, romantic love. We talk very little about grief, very little about gratitude, although these two emotions form the foundation of a great many extended conversations in a great many other cultures. Among the Kaluli of Papua New Guinea, for example, grief and gratitude form two of the central themes of the entire culture, while American males, to be very specific, seem to feel very uncomfortable with both of them.[30] What is particularly interesting, however, is that the amount of talk about an emotion may have very little to do with its actual frequency of occurrence. In Tahiti, people seem to be obsessed with the topic of anger even though it is extremely rare to see anyone get angry (Levy 1973). In America, I would suggest with some hesitation, talk about love tends to be much more pervasive than the actual emotion. Robert Levy (1973) has suggested that we recognize the differences and the connections between such emotion talk and the emotions themselves with the concept of *hyper-* and *hypocognized* emotions. Anger is hypercognized in Tahiti and gratitude is hypocognized in America. But these differences between talk and emotion are not irrelevant to the emotion, as the chatter of a press box kibitzer is irrelevant to the action below. Anger is so demonized in Tahitian society that people are too terrified to get angry (and when someone does, it tends to fall into the extremely pathological category of "running amok"). Gratitude presupposes so many judgments about debt and dependency that it is easy to see why supposedly self-reliant American males would feel queasy about even discussing it. Part of the emotional portrait of any culture, accordingly, is an account of how much, how often, and how they talk about the different emotions. And, again, although we might write as if there is or could be a single overarching conception of emotion (or particular emotions), the varieties of emotion-chat make this, too, rather dubious.

Perhaps the most striking thing to note, in ourselves as well as in other cultures, is the prevalence of metaphor in our theories. This is not necessarily a weakness in a theory (the theory of particles in physics is, first of all, a series of metaphors), but it is worth noting the extent to which even our supposedly most scientific theories are founded on metaphors. The most prevalent, for reasons that are themselves worth considerable speculation, is what I have called "the hydraulic metaphor" (Solomon 1993). It is the treatment of emotions as fluid quantities, capable of filling, overflowing, and being channeled in the psyche. Freud, of course, accepted this metaphor quite literally, calling the affects variously Q and *psychic energy* flowing through the tubing (aka "neurons") of the "psychic apparatus." The classic notions of cathexis, catharsis, and sublimation are part and parcel of this metaphor, and the new, hip language of "flow" is just another version. What is particularly fascinating, however, is to find similar metaphors in other cultures, but with significant differences. Freud, a creature of romanticism, took the passions to be explosive and dangerous, and, in one of his most famous diagrams, portrayed the psychic apparatus as a rather unstable boiler system.

In Buddhism, the fluid metaphor is rather that of the ocean (*citta*) (a metaphor also adopted by Freud), suggesting calm and boundlessness. In the usual hydraulic metaphor, emotions keep us in a constant state of tension. In the ocean metaphor, however, emotions represent a transient disruption, a "fluctuation" or "agitation" in an otherwise peaceful sea. The differences here are significant. Thus, in the Western tradition, a great poet like Goethe could write, "With most of us the requisite intensity of passion is not forthcoming without an element of resentment, and common sense and careful observation will confirm the opinion that few people who amount to anything are without a good capacity for hostile feeling upon which they draw freely when they need it."[31] Compare that to the "joy of quietness" in the *Dhammapada*, and then compare both to the fire and water metaphors in Bengali discussions of emotion (McDaniel, in this volume). Are these differences in theory? Differing poetic images? Or are these not, rather, differences between cultures, ways of life, and no mere metaphors, no mere theories?

Many of the most important metaphors having to do with emotions are those that concern the body. Compare the traditional European discussion of emotion in terms of the bodily humours (and the updated versions in terms of neurology and computer analogies) with the Tantric notion that the emotions are located in the chakras, in the "subtle" noncorporeal body, or the Yogic suggestion that even the grandest emotions are but intellectual disorders, fluctuations, afflictions (*klesas*), psychic "sedimentations." Consider, again, the Chinese conception of *chi*, power or energy, and consider what different meanings the body and the emotions take on with such a conception. The hydraulic model is, of course, a bodily metaphor, but so are other, more aesthetic, expressive conceptions of the body, including a number of challenging feminist conceptions which are just now beginning to work their way into the literature. It is taken for granted, in virtually every culture, that the body has something to do with emotions, that emotions are, in some way, embodied, but these different conceptions of body are by no means the same.

What I have been suggesting about the category of emotions in general also applies—but with more concreteness and, consequently, more useful possibilities for real cross-cultural comparison and contrast—to the particular emotions, such as anger, grief, affection, and jealousy. One can appreciate how this works even without leaving the Western tradition, but the discussion becomes so much richer as soon as we take other cultures into account. Hatred, for example, is an emotion often cast as negative, negative not only because it constitutes the Other as hateful but because it corrodes and corrupts the character of the person who hates. But it is of no small importance, in a culture that believes in Evil, that one hates the right things, and hatred becomes less hateful just insofar as it is justified. But in a culture that rejects the notion of Evil or otherwise teaches that nothing is hateful, the emotion of hatred takes on a very different meaning. So, too, resentment is an emotion that has often been condemned as petty and pathetic, notably by Nietzsche. But the difference between resentment and a justified sense of oppression is not always obvious, and the latter, as an aspect of a passion for justice, has a very different value than the former.

The question of cross-cultural comparison is not, I want to emphasize, merely a matter of how different emotions are viewed in different ethical, religious, or cultural systems. It is a difference in the very nature of these emotions and how the people who have them construe the world and their place and significance in it.

6. COMPASSION: A UNIVERSAL SENTIMENT?

Two hundred fifty years ago, David Hume and then Adam Smith suggested that human nature was composed, in part, of a natural disposition toward sympathy, a sense of "fellow-feeling" with other human beings. Their discussion was marred by a certain inconsistency in their use of the term *sympathy*, which sometimes referred to our supposedly inborn ability to understand, to "put ourselves in the place of," even to feel the emotions of another—what we now call "empathy"—but elsewhere referred to a rather specific emotion or sentiment, namely, feeling "sorry for" another person who was in worse straits than oneself. In Hume, there was an actual switch of meanings, between his early *Treatise of Human Nature* and his later *Enquiry Concerning the Principles of Morals*, from the capacity to share another's emotion to a general sense of benevolence.[32] There was some disagreement between Smith and Hume about the "natural origins" of such emotions, and the tension between empathy (a vivid idea of another's emotion which evokes a similar emotion in ourselves) and the rather specific emotion of sympathy is not reconciled. One may well wonder in what sense one can actually "share" the pain of a friend who is suffering from a compound fracture, no matter how much sympathy one may have for him, and one can readily distinguish all of this from a sense of injustice one may feel on another's behalf (Smith) or a benevolent urge to improve his or her situation (Hume). I am rehearsing this familiar philosophical drama here at the outset just to remind us that even within the narrow confines of our own language and tradition the meaning of *sympathy* is by no means settled. Articles attempting to distinguish, once again, *sympathy* from *empathy* still fill the social psychology journals, and the very intelligibility of "feeling with" and "sharing feelings" is still being challenged.[33]

With such confusion in a small domain, we had best brace ourselves for genuine perplexity once we expand our attention to the global context. Both Hume and Smith assumed that sympathy, in at least one of its versions, was inborn and "natural," an essential and universal feature of human motivation. Compassion, also literally (from the Latin rather than the Greek) "feeling with," would seem to be sufficiently broad and nonspecific to be a universal emotion if anything is, and this suggestion is readily reinforced by any number of quotations easily found in Mencius (1970), a Confucian ("No man is devoid of a heart sensitive to the sufferings of others. . . . Whoever is devoid of the heart of compassion is not human"), and in any number of Buddhist texts, which include the recommendation of a "boundless good will toward the entire world."[34] It is by no means obvious, however, that this indiscriminate Buddhist good will is the same as Judeo-Christian "compassion," nor should either of them be confused with the (more or less) rational principle that one *ought* to aim for "the greatest good for the greatest number," the centerpiece and bumper sticker of utilitarianism.

Kupperman rightly points out the rather odd notion of altruism that lies at the root of both Buddhism and utilitarianism, meaning "giving equal weight to the well-being of all sentient beings, including oneself as counting for one." This "indifference," a matter of rational principle for the utilitarian and a virtue of character for the Buddhist, is quite at odds with our more usual sense of altruism, which means "selflessness" or, more modestly, being motivated to do good for another without evident advantage to oneself. These more usual senses—which also form some of the more provocative hypotheses of recent biology and radical economic theory—are anything but "indifferent."[35] I confess that I am somewhat perplexed by Kupperman's admittedly ingenious comparison of Buddhism and utilitarianism, but mainly because I find both halves of the comparison quite different from any adequate notion of sympathy or compassion. The problem is, as Kupperman recognizes, that the usual notions are quite particular—sympathy for a particular individual, compassion for a (possibly very large) number of nevertheless particular people who are suffering. The idea of sympathy or compassion for all of humanity is a rare, if barely intelligible, conception, appropriate for saints, perhaps (which is just another way of saying that we find it unintelligible), or a misdescription of a general sympathy which in fact is an indiscriminate openness to particulars. There is then the problem, faced squarely by Hume (with some rather disturbing—and perhaps tongue-in-cheek—replies): namely, that compassion inevitably tends to diminish with distance and with extended scope. In this model, the choice seems to be to care truly for *every* sentient creature, which would inevitably result in "psychic overload, benevolence burnout." Indeed, simply watching a single episode of *National Geographic* would produce possibly lethal consequences. Or one could distribute one's compassion equally, an infinitesimal bit for everyone and every creature and an utterly insignificant and inadequate amount in any given case. (Kupperman quite explicitly recognizes the "hydraulic" quality of this metaphor.) Of course, one might directly encounter only a relatively small number of human beings, and so the question of universal concern is rarely tested as such. Fleeting feelings of universal sympathy, lasting just long enough to get out one's checkbook, do not seem to be a serious psychological problem. But living in cities of two to ten million, with television bringing the suffering of millions of others into our living rooms, this matter-of-fact limitation—which may have been valid in Edinburgh in 1750 and in the Chinese country-side in the fourth century B.C.E.—no longer seems effective. How do we, how could we, care, not just for ourselves and "our own" but for everyone (and every living being) equally?

The usual model of altruism, of course, is not particularly concerned with this problem. Biologists naturally conclude that altruism consists of intense concern regarding one's offspring and nearest kin with quickly diminishing concern as genetic kinship becomes smaller in proportion. Hume and Smith, while taking note of universal benevolence, simply assume that people will be far more concerned about those closest to them and far less about those at a distance and whom they have never met. The point, after all, was not to argue for universal care or boundless benevolence but to defend the already contro-versial anti-Hobbesian and anti-Mandevillian thesis that people are not wholly selfish. Peter Singer (1981), a contemporary utilitarian briefly mentioned by Kupperman, argues from a sociobiological point of view that kinship relations account for the existence of altruism (that is, unselfish concern for others), but beyond a certain limited arena of concern, reason must take over, and the util-itarian principle then supplies the arguments—not the feelings—for further concern. To recognize a rational obligation to be concerned for the interests of others, in other words, is very different from feeling sympathy, which is not the conclusion of an argument but—if Hume, Smith, and Mencius are correct—an inborn sentiment that extends just so far. And neither of these seems to be the same as Buddhist "indifference," the "refusal to make preferences."

To complicate matters much further, I want to add two more ingredients to this supposedly simple and allegedly universal moral sentiment. First of all, I want to add the apparently related if not almost identical emotion of pity to the pot. Pity would seem to be a lot like compassion—concern for and a slight "suffering with" someone else in more dire straits than oneself. But pity has an unmistakable hint of condescension. People seek sympathy, but they resent pity. Callahan, a quadraplegic cartoonist of the contemporary "sick" school of American humor, has said that he would much prefer being considered "maimed" rather than pitied according to the pathetic euphemisms of "politi-cally correct," sensitive speech. Nietzsche, of course, had a great many harsh things to say about pity, and he suggested that the emotion itself was a symptom of resentment and bad character. But, now, is pity "the same" as compassion, given the rather considerable difference in connotations—not only of the words *pity* and *compassion* but of the emotion(s) to which they refer? Once again, a larger cultural consideration complicates what seemed to be a reasonably concrete description of an emotion. How we think of "feeling with" others, the content and structure of the emotion itself, depends on the moral stage on which it is supposed to play its role.

The second complication involves an importation from a very different culture, the emotional concept of fago from Ifaluk society, as reported and analyzed by Catherine Lutz. Lutz roughly characterizes *fago* as "compassion/love/sadness," making it quite clear from the outset that she has nothing in mind like Kupperman's Buddhist "indifference" or, for that matter, Buddhist *karuna*. Compassion, insofar as such an emotion can be recognized in Ifaluk society, is indistinguishable and inseparable from love, affection, attachment. Compassion is not an emotion held in reserve for distant suffering strangers but part and parcel of one's most important relationships, and, in case such an obvious contrast is even worth stating, the Buddhist ideal of freedom from attachment would seem to the Ifaluk like a death sentence.[36] One could also make the contrast between the Western notion of romantic love, which has often been characterized as desire, even as an adventure, with this more modest notion of love as attachment, a recognition of precious, fragile connections.

The most fascinating part of Lutz's analysis and her many examples, however, is the connection with sadness. "Life is fragile," she reminds us, and "connections are precious." But the combination of love and sadness seems to us (and, initially, to her) a kind of internal contradiction. Love is positive and activating, she says, an emotion that makes us strong. Sadness is negative, enervating, weakening. But in the cultural complex and context that constitutes Ifaluk society, the combination—which for them is no combination but a singular sentiment—is natural and comprehensible. "It is perhaps only in a society in which autonomous action to ensure individual survival is neither socially encouraged nor ecologically or economically feasible that nurturance will become central to the definition of power," she writes; and, indeed, it would be difficult for an American, raised to be autonomous and independent, to understand the web of concepts and consequently the emotions that constitute such a society. What we mean by "compassion" may bear some dim resemblance to the fellow-feeling *fago* that provides the glue of Ifaluk society, but it is by no means obvious that there is any single emotion or emotion component that could be promoted as universal. So, too, with those kindred Chinese sentiments, *hsin* and *jen* and the Buddhist *karuna*. It is also worth noting that *fago*, like *jen*, equals maturity and intelligence, and thus quite explicitly avoids the intellect/emotion dichotomy that has led to the rather rigid (Kantian) distinction between practical reason and the inclinations, including the moral sentiments, in our own tradition. Can we understand our notion of compassion without the implicit contrast to more rationally prescribed principles and forms of behavior? I think not, and if that is so, then our global aspirations for peace and understanding may need to seek some firmer foundation than the often appealed to "universal goodwill" that is said to be at the heart (*hsin*, not *cardium*) of every human being."[37]

7. DISPASSION AND THE MEANING OF THE PASSIONS

Finally, I would like to tackle what, for many readers, lies at the heart of the appeal of multicultural emotion studies, namely, the dim but distracting suggestion that we (alienated students of the West) are doing it all wrong, while somewhere else, high in the Himalayas or on some dusty desert steppes, there are folks who are doing it right. Why are we so unhappy, so unsettled and dissatisfied? Because life is suffering. So spoke Jesus and the Buddha, millennia ago. So said Hamlet and M. Scott Peck, in his perpetual best seller among the self-help set. It is an appealing message. Why? And what is the response? We will get rid of suffering by getting rid of our passions, by becoming dispassionate. But what would this mean? And is it in practice desirable? Without exaggerating its importance, I take this to be one of those profound philosophical confrontations in which (in the words of Joel Kupperman) forms of life can change and develop, according to which we learn to orient our lives. But what is truly at stake here? Let me take on my host, Joel Marks, and betray my own rather Nietzschean romantic attitude toward life.

Consider two contrasting views of life, which can be traced back in philosophy at least as far as Heraclitus and Parmenides, which climax in the internecine, almost Oedipal disagreement between Nietzsche and his one-time mentor Arthur Schopenhauer. According to one vision, there is the ideal of the passionate life, life defined in energetic and dynamic terms, in which enthusiasm and passionate engagement are the marks of a life well lived (Heraclitus and Nietzsche). According to the other vision, there is the ideal of calm, peace, and detachment from the whirlwind that sometimes seems to surround and affect our lives, a place of escape, whether through reason and some noetic sense of a world without change (Parmenides) or through aesthetic contemplation and a denial of the Will (Schopenhauer). I call the first "romantic." The second, in order not to prejudice the issue, might be called the "classic," although I will describe it as "dispassionate" in what follows. These are extreme versions of both visions, of course, and one can specify many more modest conceptions of the good life—by way of the Aristotelian virtue of moderation, for example. But, as so often in philosophy, they do point to two very different pulls in life, two very different temperaments. Whole cultures, and not just individuals, find themselves so pulled, and one of the functions of philosophy is to express such sentiments. The romantic vision, however, sometimes seems to be better expressed through music and dancing—and that is certainly the sense often conveyed by Nietzsche—while the classic vision is that which seems to have taken over most of philosophy—East and West, the search for permanence, the appeal of the "otherworldly," the demand for "transcendence," the ideals of *apatheia*, enlightenment, dispassion.

In an earlier piece of writing (as in his introduction here), Marks has rightly lamented the "neglect of the East" in emotion studies as well as the fact that philosophers both East and West have "not always been, shall we say, partial to emotion." He insists upon "the heuristic value of paying attention to cultural influences," and encourages "empirical studies of an ethnographic character." He views the study of emotion as, first and foremost, part of the study of ethics in the grand sense of "How shall one live?" and he links the question "What is an emotion?" with the often neglected question "*Why* emotion?" and raises the question of "the desirability of emotion *tout court*." So far, so good, but the question of the desirability of emotion *tout court* can be a dangerous one, as Marks clearly recognizes. Here, as always, we both want to raise the question "*Which* emotions?" Nevertheless, I take it that the dispute here is nothing less than a confrontation between two very different images of the good life: one that thrives on passion, another that prefers dispassionate peace and a "modest happiness."

The confrontation can easily get side-tracked, however, by a misunderstanding of the two sets of terms, "passion," on the one hand, and "dispassion(ate)" on the other. I take "passion" to be a term with two rather distinctive meanings in its current usage. First, it is a more or less global term to cover a wide variety of emotions, moods, desires, strong sentiments, and other "affects." Second, it is a rather specific term that refers to a rather small number of particularly intense, even obsessive, emotions, interests, and desires. Romantic love, in its dramatic manifestations, is clearly an example of the second type, but so-called conjugal love, by which many authors seem to mean no more than harmonious comfort, is not.[38] Intense hatred would be such a passion, but impotent resentment, no matter how fuming, would not. One might have a passion for sailing or stamp collecting, but mere interest is certainly not enough.

A passion need not have a particular object; for example, one can have a passion for justice, but no mood, no matter how intense, counts as a passion. (A person who displays general [and genuine] enthusiasm may be said to *be* passionate, but it does not follow that his various enthusiasms are themselves passions.) I would like to say that a passion, in this second sense, is marked off from ordinary emotions, desires, and interests by a kind of grandeur, but this is to already start loading the issue toward romanticism. Suffice it to say that passions are not, to avoid the opposite bias, necessarily harmful or "addictive" (Marks, in this volume) although they may be, and they are not as such "victimizing" (as the word itself would suggest). Passions occupy that ill-defined and largely unexplored middle ground in the philosophy of mind in between actions and mere events, ambiguous between the voluntary and the involuntary, the purposive and the merely functional (or dysfunctional). In this second sense, however, they are certainly what Marks calls "strong feelings," although their relationship to strong desires may not be so obvious. (This would certainly be true where strong desires are themselves the passions in question, but where the passion is an interest or an enthusiasm or an ongoing emotion such as love or passionate faith, it is not clear to me that it is the "desire component" that is definitive here.)

To think of "passion" in the global sense renders the defense of dispassion virtually insupportable, for that would imply a life without interests, without even the most functional and perfunctory desires, without attachment or affection, without compassion or caring or emotion virtually of any kind. It is this misunderstanding that Marks rightly warns us against in his essay. But if we think of "passion" in the particular sense, as an especially strong emotion, desire, or interest, we must also be careful not to load the issue with certain psychological assumptions which are already part of the argument, assumptions of the "half-full or half-empty" variety, such as the idea that desires, by their very nature, tend to be frustrated or that strong passions are always based to a certain extent on illusion or self-deception. Whether these claims are true or even plausible, whether or not they could be settled by any amount of argument and observation, they are already part of the defense and intrinsic to the viewpoint of the dispassionate life and not a fair statement of the problem itself.

The passionate life, in other words, must be understood in terms of the desirability of strong passions in a rather particular sense, a sense that may well include romantic love, religious ecstasy, strong aversions, even hatred and the desire for vengeance and a highly charged sense of the drama of life. The dispassionate life, on the other hand, is one that does not find such passions desirable but, nevertheless, may be full of (modest) emotions and desires. Nietzsche's antagonist does not have to be a zombie, or the pathetic creature he presents in *Zarathustra* as "the last man." Our romantic hero, however, does not have to be a maniac, a drunken Dionysus crazed with passion. Nevertheless, it should be obvious that we have two very different ideals here: a Buddhist bodhisattva on the one hand and perhaps Lord Byron on the other. (Nietzsche's own life was, apart from his writings, anything but an inspiration.[39])

Part of Marks's argument consists of an analysis of emotion, a theme which has occupied him before as well. He rightly rejects the "feeling" view of emotion and tentatively accepts cognitivism, "the dominant ideology among emotions theorists today." But Marks, like many theorists, distinguishes between the strictly "cognitive" belief component of emotion and an equally necessary desire component, and he sometimes even distinguishes between two distinct theories, cognitivism and conativism, respectively. This allows him to focus in on the "strong desire component" of emotion, to defend the (Buddhist) ideal of the dispassionate life, and to "deny neither the value of feelings nor the cognitive content of the emotions, in order to defend dispassion as a virtue." I think that this move is illegitimate. The view of emotion I have tried to defend above (and elsewhere) is conscientiously holistic, and although it is certainly possible (and usually easy) to specify which desires go with which emotions, it does not follow that emotions have a "desire component." I agree with Marks that not every instance of "entertaining a belief and a desire about something [is] an emotion," but the implication that concerns him is the one that goes the other way. Granted that belief-desire combinations do not entail emotion (even where the combination is of the right sort for the emotion in question), the question is whether emotions can be analyzed in terms of beliefs and desires. I claim that the answer is No, and my argument affects several of the other essays in this volume (and elsewhere) as well.[40]

My reason for defending the theory of emotions as judgments is, in part, because judgments, unlike beliefs, do not imply or suggest impersonality, value neutrality, or, to get right to the point, lack of desire. One would be hard put to state most of the judgments that constitute emotion without clearly involving such desires. Grief, for example, involves a judgment of severe loss. One might suggest that this reduces to a belief, *that* someone has died, for example, and a desire (or rather a counterfactual wish), namely, that they would not have died. But is such an analysis necessary, and does it clarify or, rather, confuse the nature of the emotion? I would argue (but this is not the place) that such belief-desire analyses, which have become the unquestioned paradigm for much of cognitive science and "folk psychology," are misleading and often quite beside the point. First of all, these terms are not employed in their ordinary meaning but expanded far beyond recognition and often rendered utterly trivial.[41] Second, the terms employ a false dichotomy. Desires entail beliefs (although not vice versa). Third, as I have suggested above, although emotions may yield beliefs and desires (in some sense), the argument is not symmetrical and therefore not a proper understanding of emotion. You can analyze water into its elemental ingredients, hydrogen and oxygen, but you have not thereby understood the concept of "water." Fourth and finally, it is from the utter inadequacy of such analyses that one can readily appreciate the claims of several authors that emotions are unique and neither beliefs nor desires nor any combination thereof.[42] I think that the question of what is "unique" requires a far more fine-grained analysis, given that I do not think that, in any case, "emotion" names a natural kind, a single category. But I certainly understand the resistance to the analysis of all "mental" states and events in terms of beliefs and desires, and I think Marks's argument takes advantage of the inadequacies of that analysis.

The key argument in Marks's defense of dispassion is, somewhat predictably, the Buddhist syllogism:

> Suffering is bad.
> The singular cause of suffering is strong desire (passion, emotion).
> Therefore, strong desire (passion, emotion) is bad.

Marks claims that "the common denominator of all suffering is desire." This seems to me to be plainly false, but Marks has a ready answer to the most obvious counterexamples. In normal discourse, a person in normal health (who is also free from hypochondria and relatively immune to television advertising) would not be described as having a desire for health (or a desire not to get sick). A sick person may well have a desire for health, and a person who clearly sees the possibility of getting sick (having just shared a cup with a highly contagious friend) may well have a desire not to get sick. But sickness is surely suffering (again, allowing for some obvious exceptions, such as the hypochondriac who can say, "You see, I really was getting sick," and the schoolboy who now has an excuse to stay home), and it is not necessarily the frustration of any particular desire. But Marks counters, "What matters for suffering is not illness per se, but our state of desire [not to be sick]. Illness is not the cause but only the occasion of suffering." Although I disagree with him about the propriety of speaking of desire here, I do think he is making an important point. It has recently been argued that pain, for instance, is composed of two ingredients, sensation and suffering, and while one may have the relevant sensation, whether or not that sensation is indeed pain depends on a number of other factors, including a variety of beliefs and desires, which, coupled with the sensation, constitute suffering. Dropping the inappropriate desire talk, one could therefore agree with Marks that suffering depends on our larger state of mind, and altering that state of mind might well alleviate or eliminate suffering.[43] I leave such fascinating questions aside, however, because they do not address the central claim about the desirability of passion, that is, of strong desire. So let us restrict our view to just those forms of suffering that are, in fact, the result of frustration, disappointment, and loss, that is, which would not exist unless a prior strong desire had somehow been thwarted.

I suggest that Marks has in mind here just one kind of desire. Let me call it a "goal-defined" desire or, after Gilbert Ryle and John Atkinson, an "achievement-oriented desire." Such desires clearly allow for and sometimes invite disappointment. The desire that one should win the heart and hand of X is clearly a desire that can be thwarted, and, if it is a very strong desire, one might well be crushed by the rejection. Some of my Reaganite students' desire to be millionaires by the age of thirty (a desire that is no longer in fashion, I am happy to say) surely invites disappointment and defeat. But not all strong desires are goal defined or achievement oriented, and that is one reason why I pushed at the very beginning to include "strong interests" as an example of a passion in the relevant sense. To be sure, a passion for sailing or stamp collecting allows for disappointment, and a passion for justice invites failure and frustration, but no one, I believe, has the right to say that such passions are, as such, "the singular cause of suffering," much less to call them "addictive," as Marks does. Romantic love and a long-lived vendetta, now to expand the example, may also be neither goal defined nor achievement oriented. Indeed, one of the virtues of romantic love, wrote Stendhal in the midst of one of his many raptures, is the fact that it deflects all disappointments and frustrations. It is the joy of loving as such, the grand passion, that makes life worth living. So, too, millions of people give their otherwise empty lives meaning with a sustained hatred, one that may well be occasionally punctuated with acts of violence or vengeance; but these acts, if successful, are not the fulfillment of the passion in question.

Marks considers the objection that only frustrated desires are the cause of suffering while satisfied desires are the source of joy. His answer is telling: We are more likely to suffer than to experience joy. This reply is particularly reminiscent of Schopenhauer, who shares Marks's preference for the dispassionate and also his admiration of Buddhism. It is here that we find the clearest confrontation between the two views of life: Schopenhauer, like Marks, sees willfulness in terms of suffering. His erstwhile disciple Nietzsche talks about will in terms of joy and "cheerfulness." "Better to have loved and lost," insists the romantic rationalizer. Nietzsche talks about "living dangerously." "Moderate happiness is enough," insists Marks, but for whom? "Joy is systematically elusive," he tells us, but where are we trying to find it? Is joy the intended result of the satisfaction of our desires? (Most people over thirty know better than that.) Or is it the passion itself that makes life worthwhile, not the satisfaction that may or may not accompany it? Writing a book or an essay, for example, need not and usually does not carry with it the expectation of a final sense of joy, nor even a feeling of satisfaction (as opposed to being satisfied with the work) nor even a sense of relief. Typically, the end is marked by a state of collapse, or the immediate beginning of another work. "Anticipation is often more joyful than achievement," Marks reminds us, but doesn't this argument belong on our side of the ledger?

I do not want to make it look as if there is a "right answer" to this dispute, for the whole point of this essay has been to argue that emotions and attitudes toward emotion define (in part) the life of a culture and lives within a culture as well. The desirability of passion is one of those rather philosophical positions that gets played out, in fact, every day. Marks assures us that "moderate happiness" is an alternative to the passionate life, but whether it is a preferable happiness is a matter of temperament rather than correctness. One person's addiction is another's joy, once we remove the misleading paradigm of drug addiction from the analogy. Hegel said, "Nothing great without passion," and with that in mind we should look with care at Marks's argument for "moderate desires." Do we want to encourage only a casual fight against injustice, one that avoids passion in order to avoid disappointment? ("Strong desire directed toward moral ends is at least as likely to generate suffering as is strong desire directed toward personal ends.") Marks suggests that our strongest desires tend to be egoistic ones. I think a brief glance at the daily newspaper or local TV news will disabuse him of that psychological hypothesis. The passion resides with the flag burners and their outraged audience, with the gay bashers, the anti-abortionists, as well as the oppressed who are indignant not (just) about their own experience but about the system of oppression that affects their neighbors as well. Marks leaves us with a wise prescription for compassion, which he says need not strengthen our concern for others but, rather, should work on a reduction of egoism instead. Amen. But while we are counting to ten, as he advises, we might also reflect on the justification and validity of the sometimes violent passions that we seek to subdue. Sometimes our answer may be the Yes of enthusiastic acceptance rather than the No of "indifference," no matter what the consequences.

Notes

My special thanks to Joel Marks and Roger Ames for their encouragement, Bill Eastman for his cooperation, and the Rockefeller Center in Villa Serbelloni in Bellagio, Italy, for their gracious hospitality. Parts of this essay were presented at the East-West conferences in Mount Abu, Rahjistan, in 1990 and in Brisbane, Queensland, in 1992.

1. In Europe, the term "the East" once referred to Germany and the other more backward cultures of Europe. Once Germany had proved its cultural, political, and military prowess, "East" moved eastward to Poland and Russia, and then was used by the Russians to refer to Siberia.

2. Johann Georg Hamann, for example, attacked the Enlightenment and reason itself in defense of the obscure and ineffable. He lived in Konigsberg and befriended Immanuel Kant, always insisting that he would not let his friendships get in the way of his convictions.

3. William James wrote one of his more provocative essays under the title "Does Consciousness Exist?," and his answer, essentially, was No. Heidegger attempted to develop his philosophical language of *"Dasein"* precisely in order to bypass the Cartesian terminology of "the mind" and "the subject." The whole of behaviorism, both in philosophy and in the social sciences, is similarly based on a deep distrust (or outright rejection) of all talk about the mysterious "mind."

4. For example, see Mead 1971; Briggs 1970; Lutz 1988 and in this volume.

5. Marvin Harris (1968), for example, criticizes Mead's method in particular.

6. I am thinking, for example, of O. H. Green's (1972) argument to the effect that love isn't an emotion because it is rather a long-term, complex disposition; of Jim Averill's (1986) argument that love is a "commitment"; and, on the popular front, of M. Scott Peck's argument that "mature love" (as opposed to the "infantile regression" of "falling in love") should not be construed as any kind of mere "feeling."

7. In his *Grounding of the Metaphysics of Morals*, Kant makes the dubious claim that "love as an inclination cannot be commanded; but beneficence from duty, when no inclination impels us, . . . is practical, and not pathological, love. Such love resides in the will and not in the propensities of feeling, in principles of action and not in tender sympathy" (Kant 1981, 12). Cf. *Metaphysics of Morals* (Kant 1983, 60).

8. Amélie Rorty (1982, 1988) has traced some of these shifts and relationships. An excellent, very specific study of such changes and relationships is historian Peter Stearns's and psychologist Carol Stearns's (1986) account of anger.

9. I have argued this thesis at length in my book, *The Passions* (1993).

10. For example, Solomon 1984.

11. Cf. Spiro 1984, 323. Of course, it should not be supposed that these universal similarities exist only on a "deep" level, that is, on the level of the central nervous system. They may also be quite superficial, in the skin and musculature. Paul Ekman (1980), notably, has done ground-breaking and definitive research on the universality of facial expressions of emotion and certain emotional gestures.

12. A putative counterexample to this claim, in fact, suggests a fascinating area of understudied complexity. Rage is sometimes cited by neurologists as an emotion that can be neurologically induced without any particular context or conceptual content whatever. But on closer scrutiny, even such seemingly neurological phenomena must involve some minimal cognitive content, distinct modes of perception and response, as well as the characteristic physical manifestations so readily visible, for instance, when cats are used as the experimental subject. And it is important to distinguish rage from anger, where the latter is, by its very nature, "intelligent" (no matter how inappropriate or wrong-headed). A similar argument can be made for panic (cf. fear) and, perhaps, certain sorts of affective need or longing (cf. love).

13. On the evolutionary psychology of emotion, see Plutchik (1962) and, more recently, Gibbard's (1990) more philosophical account. For two classic works on the phenomenology of emotion, see Scheler (1970) and Sartre (1948).

14. Also see Averill 1980. For the best immediate source, see Catherine Lutz, in this volume.

15. Rousseau (1983), in his rhapsodic reconstruction of the "state of nature" in his second *Discourse*, imagines that sex would be perfectly "nat-

ural," no attachments, no jealousy, and "each would go his or her own way." It is a distinctively male view, of course, one since defended (but no less self-indulgent) in the name of both sociobiology and gender studies of the emotions.

16. I am ignoring here the very difficult matter of defining "consciousness," except to point out, again, that consciousness should not be confused with self-consciousness, as it has been through most of modern philosophy and, consequently, through much of cognitive psychology, too. See, for a good recent discussion, Daniel Dennett (1992). Also see Ross Buck (1993).

17. I have argued that James has at least three different and sometimes radically opposed theories of emotion. In his 1884 essay, "What is an Emotion?," he argues both for a physiological and for a behavioral conception of emotions, both of these conflated with the experiential "sensations" that accompany bodily disturbances and movements. But a visceral disturbance or a flushed face is very different from a gesture or a full-blown action, although certain muscular tensions may seem to fall in between. James also proposes a very different view of emotions in his religious writings, notably in *The Varieties of Religious Experience*, such that emotions clearly emerge as a species of spiritual phenomena and are hardly physical or physiological at all.

18. At Oxford, where much of the Anglo-American philosophy of the postwar era was centered, there was a belligerent opposition to science, one of the consequences of what C. P. Snow famously called the "two cultures" of the time.

19. Here is the locus of Wittgenstein's (1953) famous "private language argument," which purports to show that there could be no such private reference and that emotion names, if they are to have any meaning at all, must be ascribed on the basis of behavior, not "feelings."

20. David Wong (1991), with a response by Craig Ihara. The focus in that debate is rather the primacy of "reasons" in *Jen* or benevolence, and the conclusion, similar to Bockover's, is that there is no distinction between reason and emotion in Mencius.

21. "It is not the least virtue of a theory that it can be refuted," wrote Nietzsche, and the virtue of James's theory was precisely that it was sufficiently precise so that it could be refuted, as it soon was, by W. B. Cannon (1984) in the early part of this century and, more recently, by Schachter and Singer (1962).

22. An excellent argument to this effect is Annette Baier's (1978) response to Donald Davidson's (1977) essay, "Hume's Cognitive Theory of Pride."

23. The word *intentional* must be carefully distinguished from the notion of "intentionality" that we discussed earlier in this section. Here, it refers to purposive action, often deliberative and self-conscious. The relation between these two homonymic words (and the technical monstrosity, *intensionality*) is not a suitable subject here.

24. Specifically, the Utkuhikhalingmiut ("Utku") Eskimos of the Canadian Northwest Territories. See Briggs 1977.

25. Cf. Kupperman, in this volume.

26. The distinction between "positive" and "negative" emotions, which is found in many cultures and philosophies, is itself worth a detailed investigation. The late Shula Sommers, who was in the middle of such a study before her untimely death, used to capture the confusion inherent in the subject by asking rhetorically, "Is there anything negative about hating evil?"

27. I say "more or less." because there are always internal and external dynamics, mutual exchanges and influences, more or less conscientious borrowings, imitations and mockings, not to mention mutual misunderstandings and their consequences. Thus, any attempt to understand the emotions of the Tao, for example, requires a study of not only Taoism but its disputations and exchanges with its rivals, such as Hansen relates to us in his account of Mozi and Mencius. Their argument, about prelinguistic moral distinctions and "natural" cultural universals, throws light not only on an important set of ethical disagreements but on the conceptions of desire and emotion that are presupposed by them. If natural desires are believed to lead to harmony, they will be conceived and treated very differently than if they are believed to lead to chaos.

28. In Buddhism in particular, *karuna* is not counted among the emotions or, more carefully, the *klesas*. The Yogi Dharmakirti writes, for example, that *karuna*, unlike emotions and desires, cannot be rejected, for such interconnectedness is an essential part of the Void. In Mahayana Buddhism, the *bodhisattva*, who has rejected the various "afflictions," nevertheless holds tenaciously to *karuna*. I owe what understanding I have of these matters to conversations with my colleague Stephen Phillips.

29. I belong to the International Society for Research on the Emotions (ISRE), one of whose perennial concerns has been the preponderance of Amer-

ican and European psychologists and the comparative paucity of scholars from other fields and, even more so, the almost total absence of researchers from other parts of the world. But the problem is not difficult to diagnose. The very category in question has no equivalent or much significance in other parts of the world. Indian scholars, who tend to be well versed in both traditions, have a certain advantage, but still their numbers are small. Chinese and Japanese scholars tend to focus on the physiological aspects of emotion, thus bypassing awkward questions about culture dependency and translatability.

30. Steven Feld (1982) talks extensively about the Kaluli and their practices. Shula Sommers (1984) has done an extensive analysis of attitudes toward gratitude, in particular in American (and other) societies. On American attitudes toward grief, see Colin Parkes (1972) and B. Schoenberg (1975).

31. Goethe is quoted in Francis Richardson and in W. Gaylin (1984, 79). Moving from the Classical Romantic to the current and cynical, we might quote a similar line from a popular American children's cartoon show, *Ren and Stimpy*: "I love getting angry. It makes me feel great!"

32. This shift in Hume is mentioned, in somewhat different terms, by Joel Kupperman (this volume), who gives credit to Ernest Albeer (1957). I have come to believe that Hume's shift is even more complex and possibly confused, in part after reading Alasdair MacIntyre's (1988) *Whose Justice? Which Rationality?* on Hume and the other Scottish "moral sentiment theorists." For my own discussion of these matters, see (Solomon 1990).

33. For example, Wispe 1986; Harris 1968, esp. 410ff.

34. Mencius, quoted by Kupperman (in this volume) from Conze (1959, 186).

35. In sociobiology, the classic texts on altruism include Trivers 1971 and Wilson 1975. In economic theory, see Frank 1988.

36. Describing a somewhat similar society, the Kaluli of Papua New Guinea, anthropologist Steven Feld tells me that the people in his village "felt sorry for" the singers they heard on the jazz tapes he brought with him from America. They were sad for them because they were singing for no one in particular, they were without attachments. They were lost human beings, though the beauty of their music nevertheless allowed the Kaluli to feel close to them. By way of contrast, I couldn't help but think of Sartre's (1964) rather perverse early (anti-)hero, Roquentin, in *Nausea*. At the end of the book, Roquentin

listens with awe and envy to the sounds of jazz singers on an old recording, envying their eternal detachment and abstract existence.

37. The centrality of the heart as the seat of the soul, and thus of the most essential feelings, in several different traditions is a metaphor to be pondered, and not only because the organ, in its dumb, repetitive way, represents (and is the physiological precondition of) continuing life. It is worth noting that some cultures prefer the stomach and the bowels, or a more holistic or a hierarchical distribution, for example, along the chakras. Can we understand the meaning of compassion (*hsin, karuna, fago*) without also accounting for these metaphors?

38. The classic text here is Denis de Rougemont's (1940) much-celebrated but truly perverse *Love in the Western World*, although de Rougemont, like many moralists before him (notably Kierkegaard in *Either/Or*) tends to slip in the notion of "bliss" by way of compensation for the lack of passion. I am not denying the possibility of happiness in marriage, of course, but there is a long history of cheating the passions by rendering passionate *eros*, for example, as a kind of obsession or sickness while overpurifying supposedly more modest (but in fact much more pretentious) sentiments such as *agape, caritas*, and conjugal love.

39. See, for example, Nehamas 1985.

40. I have in mind, for example, John Searle's (1983) analysis in *Intentionality* and O. H. Green's (1972) analysis of emotions and belief.

41. An excellent discussion of this is in Annette Baier (1986). On the other hand, in recent French philosophy—particularly the work of Jacques Lacan—the term "desire" has become so bloated, so dramatized, so dripping with lust, that it, too, is all but unrecognizable. But in a philosophical conversation in which "violence" has become appropriate to refer to the use of metaphor or merely taking a term out of context, the utility of any such term should now be viewed with suspicion.

42. De Sousa 1988; Bockover, this volume.

43. And yet Marks insists that suffering is "intrinsically aversive," which weakens his argument considerably. True, one does not need a further desire (the desire not to suffer), but it is the *distance* between suffering and circumstances that allows the Buddhist (or the Stoic) to exercise dispassion.

Bibliography

Albee, Ernest. 1957. *History of English Utilitarianism.* [1901.] London: Allen & Unwin.

Aristotle. 1985. *Nichomachean Ethics.* In *The Works of Aristotle.* Trans. T. Irwin. Indianapolis: Hackett.

————. 1992. *Rhetoric.* Indianapolis: Hackett.

Austin, J. L. 1956-7. "A Plea for Excuses." *Proceedings of the Aristotelian Society* 47: 1-29.

Averill, James. 1980. "The Social Construction of Emotions." In *Emotion: Theory, Research, and Experience*, ed. R. Plutchik and H. Kellerman.

Baier, Annette. 1978. "Hume's Analysis of Pride." *Journal of Philosophy* 75: 27-40.

————. 1991. *A Progress of Sentiments: Reflections on Hume's "Treatise."* Cambridge: Cambridge University Press.

Balslev, Anindita. 1991a. *Cultural Otherness: Correspondence with Richard Rorty.* Shimla: India Institute of Advanced Study.

————. 1991b. "The Notion of *Klesa*, and Its Bearing on the Yoga Analysis of Mind." *Philosophy East and West* 41(1): 77-88.

Blum, Lawrence A. 1980. "Compassion." In *Explaining Emotions*, ed. A. Rorty, 507-17. Berkeley: University of California Press.

Briggs, Jean L. 1970. *Never in Anger.* Cambridge: Harvard University Press.

Buck, Ross. 1993. "What Is This Thing Called Subjective Experience? Reflections on the Neurophysiology of Qualia." In *Neuropsychology* 7: 490-99.

Calhoun, Cheshire, and R. Solomon, eds. 1984. *What Is an Emotion?* New York: Oxford University Press.

Camus, Albert. 1946. *The Stranger.* Trans. S. Gilbert. New York: Vintage.

Cannon, Walter B. 1984. "A Critical Examination of the James-Lange Theory of Emotions." In *What Is an Emotion?*, ed. C. Calhoun and R. Solomon, 143-51. New York: Oxford University Press.

Conze, Edward. 1959. *Buddhist Scriptures.* Harmondsworth, UK: Penguin.

Deigh, John. 1983. "Shame and Self-esteem: A Critique." *Ethics* 93: 225-45.

Dennett, Daniel. 1992. *Consciousness Explained.* Cambridge: MIT Press.

Descartes, Rene. 1989. *Passions of the Soul.* Trans. S. Voss. Indianapolis: Hackett.

de Sousa, Ronald. 1987. *The Rationality of Emotion.* Cambridge: MIT Press.

Deutsch, Eliot, ed. 1992. *Culture and Modernity.* Honolulu: University of Hawaii Press.

Ekman, Paul. 1980. "Biological and Cultural Contributions to Body and Facial Movement in the Expression of Emotions." In *Explaining Emotions*, ed. A. Rorty, 72-101. Berkeley: University of California Press.

Feld, Steven. 1982. *Sound and Sentiment.* Philadelphia: University of Pennsylvania.

Frank, Robert H. 1988. *Passions within Reason: The Strategic Role of the Emotions.* New York: Norton.

Freud, Sigmund. 1935. "The Unconscious." In *Essays in Metapsychology.* London: Liveright.

Gaylin, Willard. 1984. *The Rage Within.* New York: Viking.

Geertz, Clifford. 1977. *The Interpretation of Cultures.* New York: Basic Books.

Gibbard, Allan. 1990. *Wise Choices, Apt Feelings*. Cambridge: Harvard University Press.

Gordon, Robert M. 1987. *The Structure of Emotion*. Cambridge: Cambridge University Press.

Green, O. H. 1972. "Emotions and Belief." *American Philosophical Quarterly* 6: 24-40.

Greenspan, Patricia. 1988. *Emotions and Reasons*. New York: Routledge.

Harré, Rom, ed. 1986. *The Social Construction of Emotions*. Oxford: Blackwell.

Harris, Marvin. 1968. *The Rise of Anthropological Theory*. New York: Crowell.

Hegel, G. W. F. 1953. *Reason in History*. Trans. R. S. Hartman. Indianapolis: Bobbs-Merrill.

―――. 1977. *The Phenomenology of Spirit*. Trans. A. V. Miller. Oxford: Oxford University Press.

Heidegger, Martin. 1962. *Being and Time*. New York: Harper & Row.

Hobbes, Thomas. 1985. *Leviathan*. New York: Hafner.

Hume, David. 1957. *Enquiry Concerning the Principles of Morals*. Indianapolis: Bobbs-Merrill.

―――. 1975. *A Treatise of Human Nature*. Ed. L. A. Selby-Bigge. Oxford: Oxford University Press.

James, William. 1902. *The Varieties of Religious Experience: A Study in Human Nature*. Many editions.

―――. 1984. "What Is an Emotion?" [1884.] In *What Is an Emotion?*, ed. C. Calhoun and R. Solomon, 127-41. New York: Oxford University Press.

―――. 1990. *What Is an Emotion?* New York: Dover.

Kant, Immanuel. 1981. *Grounding of the Metaphysics of Morals*. Trans. J. Ellington. Indianapolis: Hackett.

——. 1983. *Metaphysics of Morals*. Trans. J. Ellington. In *Ethical Philosophy*. Indianapolis: Hackett.

Levy, Robert. 1973. *The Tahitians*. Chicago: University of Chicago Press.

Lutz, Catherine A. 1988. *Unnatural Emotions*. Chicago: University of Chicago.

MacIntyre, Alasdair. 1981. *After Virtue*. Notre Dame: University of Notre Dame Press.

——. 1988. *Whose Justice? Which Rationality?* Notre Dame: University of Notre Dame Press.

——. 1992. Review of *On Cultural Otherness* by Anindita Balslev. *Philosophy East and West* 42(4): 682-84.

Marks, Joel. 1982. "A Theory of Emotion." *Philosophical Studies* 42 (September): 227-42.

——. 1983. "The Rationality of Dispassion." In *Emotions*, ed. K. D. Irani and G. E. Myers, 57-71. New York: Haven.

——. 1991. "Emotion East and West: Introduction to a Comparative Philosophy." *Philosophy East and West* 41(1): 1-30.

Marks, Joel, ed. 1986. *The Ways of Desire*. Chicago: Precedent.

Markus, H. A., and S. Kitayama. 1991. "Culture and the Self: Implications for Cognition, Emotion, and Motivation." *Psychological Review* 98(2): 224-53.

Mead, Margaret. 1971. *The Coming of Age in Samoa*. New York: Morrow.

Mencius. 1970. *The Mind of Mencius*. Trans. D. C. Lau. New York: Penguin.

Murphy, Jeffery, and Jean Hampton. 1988. *Mercy and Forgiveness*. Cambridge: Cambridge University Press.

Nagel, Thomas. 1974. "What Is It Like to Be a Bat?" *Philosophical Review* 83: 435-50.

————. 1986. *The View from Nowhere*. New York: Oxford University Press.

Natsoulas, T. 1988. "Sympathy, Empathy, and the Stream of Consciousness." *Journal of the Theory of Social Behavior* 18(2): 169-95.

Nehamas, Alexander. 1985. *Nietzsche: Life as Literature*. Cambridge: Harvard University Press.

Neu, Jerome. 1977. *Emotion, Thought, and Therapy*. Berkeley: University of California Press.

————. 1987. "A Tear Is an Intellectual Thing." *Representations* 19: 35-61.

Nietzsche, Friedrich. 1954a. *Thus Spoke Zarathustra*. In *The Viking Portable Nietzsche*, trans. and ed. W. Kaufmann. New York: Viking.

————. 1954b. *Twilight of the Idols*. In *The Viking Portable Nietzsche*, trans. and ed. W. Kaufmann. New York: Viking.

————. 1967a. *On the Genealogy of Morals*. Trans. W. Kaufmann. New York: Random House.

————. 1967b. *Will to Power*. Trans. W. Kaufmann. New York: Random House.

Noddings, Nell. 1984. *Caring*. Berkeley: University of California Press.

Panksepp, J. 1982. "Toward a General Psychobiological Theory of Emotions." *Behavioral and Brain Sciences* 5: 407-76.

Parkes, Colin. 1972. *Bereavement: Its Psychosocial Aspects*. New York: International Universities Press.

Plato. 1990. *Symposium*. Trans. A. Nehamas and P. Woodruff. Indianapolis: Hackett.

Plutchik, Robert. 1962. *Emotions*. New York: Random House.

Quine, W. V. O. 1960. *Word and Object*. Cambridge: MIT Press.

Rawls, John. 1971. *A Theory of Justice*. Cambridge: Harvard University Press.

Richardson, Francis. 1918. *The Psychology of Pedagogy and Anger*. Baltimore: Warwick & York.

Rorty, Amélie. 1982. "From Passions to Emotions and Sentiments." *Philosophy* 57: 159-72.

———. 1988. *Mind in Action*. Boston: Beacon.

Rorty, Amélie, ed. 1980. *Explaining Emotions*. Berkeley: University of California Press.

Rosenthal, David. 1983. "Emotions and the Self." In *Emotions*, ed. K. D. Irani and G. E. Myers, 164-91. New York: Haven.

Rougemont, Denis de. 1940. *Love in the Western World*. New York: Random House.

Rousseau, Jean-Jacques. 1983. *Discourse on the Origins of Inequality*. Trans. D. Cress. Indianapolis: Hackett.

Ruddick, Sara. 1988. *Maternal Thinking*. Boston: Beacon.

Ryle, Gilbert. 1949. *The Concept of Mind*. New York: Barnes & Noble.

Sade, Marquis de. 1965. *Justine*. Trans. R. Seaver and A. Wainhouse. New York: Grove.

Sartre, Jean-Paul. 1949. *The Emotions: Sketch of a Theory*. Trans. B. Frechtman. New York: Philosophical Library.

———. 1956. *Being and Nothingness*. Trans. Hazel Barnes. New York: Philosophical Library.

———. 1964. *Nausea*. Trans. L. Alexander. New York: New Directions.

Schachter, S., and J. Singer. 1962. "Cognitive, Social, and Physiological Determinants of Emotional State." *Psychological Review* 69: 379-99.

Scheler, Max. 1970. *The Nature of Sympathy*. New York: Archon.

Schoenberg, B., ed. 1975. *Bereavement*. New York: Columbia University Press.

Schopenhauer, Arthur. 1961. *The World as Will and Idea*. Trans. E. S. Haldane and J. Kemp. New York: Doubleday.

Scruton, Roger. 1980. "Emotion, Practical Knowledge, and Common Culture." In *Explaining Emotion*, ed. A. Rorty, 519-36. Berkeley: University of California Press.

Searle, John. 1983. *Intentionality: An Essay in the Philosophy of Mind*. Cambridge: Cambridge University Press.

Singer, Peter. 1981. *The Expanding Circle*. New York: Farrar, Straus & Giroux.

Smith, Adam. 1880. *The Theory of Moral Sentiments*. London: George Bell.

Solomon, Robert C. 1978. "Emotions and Anthropology." *Inquiry* 21: 181-99.

————. 1980. "Nothing to be Proud Of (Emotions and Intentionality)." In *Understanding Human Emotions*, ed. F. Miller, 18-35. Bowling Green, OH: Philosophy Documentation Center.

————. 1984. "Getting Angry: The Jamesian Theory of Emotion in Anthropology." In *Culture Theory*, ed. R. Levine and R. Schweder, 238-54. Cambridge: Cambridge University Press.

————. 1988. "On Emotions as Judgments." *American Philosophical Quarterly* 25: 183-91.

————. 1990. *A Passion for Justice*. Reading, MA: Addison-Wesley.

————. 1993. *The Passions: Emotions and the Meaning of Life*. [1976.] Indianapolis: Hackett.

Solomon, Robert C., and Kathleen Higgins. 1993. *From Africa to Zen: An Invitation to World Philosophy*. Lanham, MD: Rowman & Littlefield.

Sommers, Shula. 1984. "Adults Evaluating their Emotions." In *Emotion in Adult Development*, ed. C. Malatesta and C. Izard. Beverly Hills: Sage.

Spiro, Melford E. 1984. "Some Reflections on Cultural Determinism and Relativism with Special Reference to Emotion and Reason." In *Culture Theory*, ed. R. Levine and R. Schweder. Cambridge: Cambridge University Press.

Stearns, Peter, and Carol Stearns. 1986. *Anger: The Struggle for Emotional Control in America's History*. Chicago: University of Chicago Press.

Tavris, Carol. 1989. *Anger: The Misunderstood Emotion*. 2d ed. New York: Simon & Schuster.

Thomas, Lawrence. 1983. "Morals, the Self, and Our Natural Sentiments." In *Emotions*, ed. K. D. Irani and G. E. Myers, 144-63. New York: Haven.

Trivers, Robert. 1971. "The Evolution of Reciprocal Altruism." *Quarterly Review of Biology* 46: 35-57.

Weiner, Annette. 1980. *Women of Value, Men of Renown*. Austin: University of Texas Press.

Wilson, Edward O. 1975. *Sociobiology*. Cambridge: Harvard University Press.

Wispe, L. 1986. "The Distinction between Sympathy and Empathy." *Journal of Personality and Social Psychology* 50: 314-21.

Wittgenstein, Ludwig. 1953. *Philosophical Investigations*. London: Routledge.

Wong, David. 1991. "Is There a Distinction between Reason and Emotion in Mencius?" *Philosophy East and West* 41(1): 31-44.

Notes on Contributors

ROGER T. AMES is Professor of Philosophy and Director of the Center for Chinese Studies at the University of Hawaii. He has published widely in Asian and comparative philosophy. His books include *The Art of Rulership* (1983); *Thinking through Confucius*, with David L. Hall (1987); *Nature in Asian Traditions of Thought*, ed. with J. Baird Callicott (1990); *Interpreting Culture through Translation*, ed. with S. W. Chan and M. S. Ng (1991); *Self as Body in Asian Theory and Practice*, ed. with T. Kasulis and W. Dissanayake (1993); and *Sun-tzu: The Art of Warfare* (1993).

PURUSHOTTAMA BILIMORIA was educated in New Zealand, Australia, and India, and has held fellowships at Oxford, the State University of New York at Stony Brook, and Harvard. He has published widely in the areas of Indian philosophy, Hinduism and cross-cultural critiques in bioethics, education, social thought, and diaspora studies. He edits the journal *Sophia* in the philosophy of religion and theology, and is currently managing editor for two monograph series: *Indian Thought*, with E. J. Brill, and *Studies in Indian Traditions*. He is Associate Professor at Deakin University in Australia, where he teaches East-West Philosophy, Sanskrit, and Philosophy of Religion. He is a co-editor for the Mīmāṃsa project within the *Encyclopedia of Indian Philosophies*.

MARY I. BOCKOVER took her Ph.D. in Philosophy in 1990 from the University of California at Santa Barbara. She taught there as a graduate student, and also was a visiting lecturer at her undergraduate alma mater, St. Mary's College of Maryland. She is now an Assistant Professor in the Department of Philosophy at Humboldt State University. Her work has been published in various journals including *Philosophy East & West, Journal of Asian Studies, Journal of the American Academy of Religion,* and their annual supplement, *Critical Review of Books in Religion.* She has also edited a book called *Rules, Rituals, and Responsibility: Essays Dedicated to Herbert Fingarette.*

PADMASIRI DE SILVA has been a Senior Teaching Fellow in the Philosophy Department at the National University of Singapore and the Director of Research for the Program on Environment, Ethics, and Education at the Information and Research Center in Singapore. He was formerly Professor and Head of the Philosophy and Psychology Department at the University of Peradeniya in Sri Lanka and is currently a Research Fellow in the Department of

Philosophy at Monash University in Clayton, Australia. He is author of *An Introduction to Buddhist Psychology, Buddhist and Freudian Psychology, Tangles and Webs, Value Orientations and Nation Building,* and *Twin Peaks,* and editor of *Suicide in Sri Lanka* and *Environmental Ethics in Buddhism.*

CHAD HANSEN is Reader in Philosophy at the University of Hong Kong. He is the author of *Language and Logic in Ancient China* and *A Daoist Theory of Chinese Thought,* along with over forty articles and reviews dealing with Classical Chinese thought. He specializes in Chinese metaphysics, theory of language, philosophy of mind, and Daoism. He has taught at the University of Michigan, University of Pittsburgh, University of Hawaii, UCLA, University of Vermont, and Stanford in addition to his present appointment in Hong Kong. In 1991 he was selected as University Scholar at the University of Vermont. He is presently working on a translation of the *Daode Jing* and a reader in comparative ethics.

JOEL J. KUPPERMAN is Professor of Philosophy at the University of Connecticut, and has been a visiting fellow at Corpus Christi College, Oxford, Clare Hall, Cambridge, and the Rockefeller Foundation's Study Center at Bellagio, Italy. He is author of *Ethical Knowledge* (1970), *Foundations of Morality* (1983), and *Character* (1991).

CATHERINE LUTZ (Ph.D. 1980, Harvard University) is a sociocultural anthropologist with interests in the cultural construction of emotion and self, critical theory, gender, and U.S. mass media representations of cultural difference. Her books include *Reading National Geographic,* with J. Collins (1993); *The Social Life of Psyche: Perspectives in Psychological Anthropology,* ed. with T. Schwartz and G. White (1992); *Language and the Politics of Emotion,* ed. with L. Abu-Lughod (1990); *Unnatural Emotions: Everyday Sentiments on a Micronesian Atoll and their Challenge to Western Theory* (1988); and *Micronesia as Strategic Colony: The Impact of U.S. Policy on Micronesian Health and Culture* (1984). She is currently Associate Professor of Anthropology at the University of North Carolina at Chapel Hill.

JOEL MARKS is Professor of Philosophy at the University of New Haven. He received his B.A. in Psychology from Cornell University and his Ph.D. in Philosophy from the University of Connecticut. His areas of special interest are emotion theory, comparative philosophy, and ethics, including professional ethics. In addition to writing numerous published articles in these and other areas, he has edited two volumes besides the present one: *The Ways of Desire: New Essays in Philosophical Psychology on the Concept of Wanting* (1986) and, with David E. E. Sloane, *The Hoffnung Festschrift,* a scholarly celebration of the British cartoonist-musician-humorist-impresario Gerard Hoffnung, 1925-1959 (*Essays in Arts and Sciences,* vol. 21, October 1992).

JUNE McDANIEL is Assistant Professor of Religious Studies at the College of Charleston. Her Ph.D. is from the University of Chicago in History of Religions, specializing in South Asian devotional religions; her M.T.S. is from Candler School of Theology at Emory University, and focused on Psychology of Religion. She has done fieldwork in India, some of which is described in her book *The Madness of the Saints: Ecstatic Religion in Bengal* (1989). Her current research is on religious emotion and ecstatic states, and her publications include work on Indian religion, religious ritual, holy women, and mysticism.

GRAHAM PARKES is Professor of Philosophy at the University of Hawaii. He is the editor of and a major contributor to the anthologies *Heidegger and Asian Thought* (1987) and *Nietzsche and Asian Thought* (1991), and, with Setsuko Aihara, the translator of *The Self-Overcoming of Nihilism* by Nishitani Keiji (1990) and co-author of *Strategies for Reading Japanese: A Rational Approach to the Japanese Sentence* (1992). His latest book is *Composing the Soul: Reaches of Nietzsche's Psychology* (1994).

LEROY S. ROUNER is Professor of Philosophy, Religion, and Philosophical Theology, and Director of the Institute for Philosophy and Religion at Boston University. From 1961 to 1966, he was Assistant Professor of Philosophy and Theology at the United Theological College, Bangalore, South India. He has taught at Boston University since 1970. He planned and edited the *Festschrift* for William Ernest Hocking, *Philosophy, Religion and the Coming World Civilization* (1966); co-edited *The Wisdom of Ernest Hocking* with John Howie (1978); and wrote *Within Human Experience: The Philosophy of William Ernest Hocking* (1969). He is the author of some sixty papers on the philosophy of religion East and West, and has recently published two books, *The Long Way Home* (1989) and *To Be at Home: Christianity, Civil Religion, and World Community* (1991). He is currently writing a book on the philosophy of education and beginning a study of "Civil Religion and the American Dream."

ROBERT C. SOLOMON is Quincy Lee Centennial Professor at the University of Texas at Austin. He received his Ph.D. from the University of Michigan and has taught at Princeton University, the University of Pittsburgh, and the University of California. He is the author of *From Rationalism to Existentialism* (1972), *The Passions* (1976), *In the Spirit of Hegel* (1983), *About Love* (1988), and *From Hegel to Existentialism* (1988). He is also the editor, with Kathleen Higgins, of *From Africa to Zen: An Invitation to World Philosophy*.

Name Index

Adams, Robert M., 15
Adigal, Prince Ilango, 57
Albee, Ernest, 123
Alt, Wayne, 156
Ames, Roger T., 105, 131
Analects, 167, 187
Ānandamayī Mā, 45, 52
Arieti, Silvano, 58
Aristotle, 8, 84, 96, 100, 181, 185, 186, 257
Armon-Jones, Claire, 3, 10
Armstrong, D. M., 11
Arnold, Magda B., 14
Auden, W. H., 99f
Aurobindo, Sri, 101
Austin, J. L., 256
Averill, James, 295, 296
Ayer, A. J., 273

Baier, Annette C., 12, 13, 128, 139, 298, 300
Balslev, Anindita, 272
Barnes, Hazel, 15
Beckett, Samuel, 14
Bedford, Errol, 176
Belfiore, Elizabeth, 15
Benson, Herbert, 157
Bentham, Jeremy, 135
Bhagavadgītā, 66
Bharata, 46, 58
Bhaṭṭa, Kumārila, 69
Bhavabhūti, 70, 83
Bhūpāla, Śiṅga, 47
Bi, Wang, 216
Bilimoria, Purushottama, 84, 254, 270, 273, 279, 280
Black, Perry, 14
Blum, Lawrence A., 8, 11, 156
Bockover, 176, 178, 179, 254, 256, 270, 273, 275, 297, 300

Boruah, Bi joy H., 15
Bowes, Pratima, 71
Brandt, Richard B., 10, 157
Braun, B. G., 60
Brentano, Franz, 176, 179
Briggs, Jean L., 295
Broad, C. D., 10, 149
Buck, Ross, 15, 297
Budd, Malcolm, 11, 15
Buddha, 65
Burke, B. David, 14
Butler, Joseph, 156
Buytendijk, F. J. J., 15
Byron, Lord, 290

Calhoun, Cheshire, 3, 8, 12, 13, 114
Cannon, W. B., 297
Caraka, 41, 67, 280
Carroll, Noel, 15
Chisholm, Roderick M., 15
Chrysippus the Stoic, 9
Ci, Jiwei, 135
Clarke, Stanley G., 10
Collins, John, 11
Confucius, 167ff, 187ff, 257
Conrad, Joseph, 11f, 140
Cooper, John M., 8

Daniels, Charles B., 15
Danto, Arthur C., 155
Daode Jing, 191ff
Dasgupta, Sri Birendramohan, 50
Davidson, Donald, 298
Davies, Stephen, 15
Davis, Wayne A., 3, 11
De, S. K., 47
deBary, Theodore, 105
Dennett, Daniel, 297
de Silva, Padmasiri, xi, 82, 266, 280
De Smet, Richard, S. J., 84

313

Subject Index

Printed in the United States
97402LV00003B/100-108/A